Human Resource Management in the Public Sector

NEW HORIZONS IN MANAGEMENT

Series Editor: Cary L. Cooper, CBE, *Distinguished Professor of Organizational Psychology and Health, Lancaster University, UK*

This important series makes a significant contribution to the development of management thought. This field has expanded dramatically in recent years and the series provides an invaluable forum for the publication of high quality work in management science, human resource management, organizational behaviour, marketing, management information systems, operations management, business ethics, strategic management and international management.

The main emphasis of the series is on the development and application of new original ideas. International in its approach, it will include some of the best theoretical and empirical work from both well-established researchers and the new generation of scholars.

Titles in the series include:

Human Resource Management in the Public Sector

Edited by

Ronald J. Burke

Emeritus Professor of Organizational Studies, Schulich School of Business, York University, Canada

Andrew J. Noblet

Professor, Deakin University, Australia

Cary L. Cooper CBE

Distinguished Professor of Organizational Psychology and Health, Lancaster University, UK

NEW HORIZONS IN MANAGEMENT

Edward Elgar
Cheltenham, UK • Northampton, MA, USA

Published by
Edward Elgar Publishing Limited
The Lypiatts
15 Lansdown Road
Cheltenham
Glos GL50 2JA
UK

Edward Elgar Publishing, Inc.
William Pratt House
9 Dewey Court
Northampton
Massachusetts 01060
USA

A catalogue record for this book
is available from the British Library

Library of Congress Control Number: 2012948158

This book is available electronically in the ElgarOnline.com
Business Subject Collection, E-ISBN 978 0 85793 732 2

ISBN 978 0 85793 731 5

Typeset by Servis Filmsetting Ltd, Stockport, Cheshire
Printed and bound by MPG Books Group, UK

Contents

Figures

Tables

Contributors

Agnes Akkerman, Radboud University, The Netherlands

Amanda F. Allisey, Deakin University, Australia

Michela Arnaboldi, Polytechnic of Milan, Italy

Giovanni Azzone, Polytechnic of Milan, Italy

Tessa S. Bailey, University of South Australia, Australia

Arnold B. Bakker, Erasmus University, The Netherlands

Mark Bradbury, Appalachian State University, USA

Ronald J. Burke, York University, Canada

Cary L. Cooper, Lancaster University, UK

Maureen F. Dollard, University of South Australia, Australia

Mary E. Guy, University of Colorado (Denver), USA

Jari J. Hakanen, Finnish Institute for Occupational Health, Finland

J. Edward Kellough, University of Georgia, USA

Tony LaMontagne, University of Melbourne, Australia

Jared J. Llorens, Louisiana State University, USA

Miguel Martínez Lucio, Manchester Business School, UK

Karen Manning, Victoria University, Australia

Sarven S. McLinton, University of South Australia, Australia

Patrick McGurk, University of Greenwich, UK

Kenneth J. Meier, Texas A & M University, USA

Meredith A. Newman, Florida International University, USA

Andrew J. Noblet, Deakin University, Australia

Laurence J. O'Toole (Jr), University of Georgia, USA

Kathryn Page, University of Melbourne, Australia

Christopher J. Rees, University of Manchester, UK

Parbudyal Singh, York University, Canada

Jessica E. Sowa, University of Colorado, Denver, USA

Pauline Stanton, Victoria University, Australia

René Torenvlied, Leiden University, The Netherlands

Catherine Truss, University of Kent, UK

Wouter Vandenabeele, Utrecht University, The Netherlands

Acknowledgements

We have worked for several years in order to understand ways in which work experiences affect individual and organizational health, and have closely examined policies and practices that can support the effectiveness of employees and the organizations in which they work. In this collection, we turn our attention to human resource management in the public sector. We previously examined human resource management in the private, nonprofit and small business sectors. During the two years in which this collection has been realized, the public sector has come under increased attention and scrutiny. The global economic recession has impacted heavily on the revenue available to governments and, as a result, severe cost-reduction measures such as service cuts, job shedding and departmental amalgamations have been implemented in most countries. Yet, at a time when public sector austerity measures have reached record highs, the community's need for welfare protection, safety services, health care and other state-funded programs has also escalated. 'Doing more with less' is now the mantra of governments at every level – local, state and federal – irrespective of their political allegiances. In this context, it is hard to imagine an organization's human resources being of greater importance than they are today. We hope this collection is of value in these trying times.

Many people have made valuable contributions to this collection. First and foremost, we are indebted to our contributors for all their hard work in researching and writing their respective chapters. We have been fortunate enough to attract some of the most productive and well-credentialed researchers in the management and behavioural sciences and we have thoroughly enjoyed working with them in planning and shaping their contributions. The staff at Edward Elgar have also played a pivotal role in developing this publication, and we have greatly appreciated their encouragement and guidance. Of course, our efforts were well supported by our respective university's – York University, Toronto, Canada (Ronald Burke); Deakin University, Melbourne, Australia (Andrew Noblet); and Lancaster University, Lancaster, UK (Cary Cooper). Lastly, we would like to pay a special tribute to our family and friends; their support can never be underestimated when undertaking a project like this.

To Susan – having a professor, researcher and writer as a partner is never easy

Ronald J. Burke

To Belinda, Isabella, Dominique and Alex – I promise to 'smell the roses' more next time

Andrew J. Noblet

To the Cooper Family, big and small – Rachel, Scott, Beth, Laura, Sarah and Devi; and to the latest arrivals Jai and Isabella

Cary L. Cooper

1. The importance of human resource management in the public sector, future challenges and the relevance of the current collection

Ronald J. Burke, Amanda F. Allisey and Andrew J. Noblet

This volume presents current thinking and research evidence on the role of human resource management (HRM) policies and practices in increasing service quality, efficiency and organizational effectiveness in the public sector. Collectively, the contributions address a pressing worldwide need for public sector organizations to enhance the effectiveness of their products and services while at the same time accommodating tighter budgets and greater scrutiny from governments, media and community groups. State funded organizations such as public hospitals, ambulance services, law enforcement agencies, schools, social welfare programs, utility providers, business development units and other publicly funded services are all critical to the wellbeing and functioning of societies and it is in everybody's interests that these organizations provide timely, high quality services. In turn, the effectiveness of these services rests heavily on the knowledge, skill, and drive of their employees. Policies and practices involving workforce recruitment and retention, training and development, career progression, performance appraisal, employee relations and other key HRM responsibilities can all impact on the attitudes and behaviours of employees and have the potential to undermine or enhance the effectiveness of employees. Strategies for managing human resources (HR) therefore have a vital role to play in ensuring that public sector agencies have the capacity to address the needs of the communities they serve and to consistently achieve high standards of service.

The remainder of this introduction sets the stage for the chapters that follow. We begin by recognizing the importance of focusing on HRM in the public sector and highlight the reasons why greater attention needs to be directed to how HR are managed in State-funded agencies.

Internationally, public sector organizations face a range of social, political and economic challenges, many of which will have serious and on-going implications for public sector employees and the people they serve. An important aim of this introduction is to summarize some of the key challenges confronting public sector agencies and to highlight the impact that they will have on public sector HR. The final section of this introduction will provide a chapter-by-chapter summary of the current collection.

WHY FOCUS ON HRM IN THE PUBLIC SECTOR?

There are four main reasons for focusing on HRM in the public sector. These include: (1) the lack of attention given to the public sector context in the HRM literature; (2) the importance of public sector services and the role of human resources in delivering these services; (3) the level of public investment in civil services and the need for agencies to maximize this investment, and; (4) the scale of the workforce-related challenges confronting public sector agencies. The following is a more detailed discussion of these reasons.

(1) A Lack of Attention Given to the Public Sector Context in the HRM literature

Scholarly research and contemporary HRM texts often overlook or only give cursory recognition to the unique characteristics of public sector organizations (Brown, 2004). Yet, as discussed in more detail in the first section of this collection (see Chapter 2 by Truss and Chapter 3 by Rees), the public sector is distinct from the private sector on a number of important grounds. One of the defining features of the public sector (relative to private sector firms) is the extent to which State-funded services are influenced by government and its associated authorities, regulatory bodies and elected ownership. This degree of external influence, coupled with strong public-sector values and relatively idiosyncratic internal environments, has important implications for how HRM is practiced in the public sector (Farnham and Horton, 1996). A key purpose for bringing together the current collection is to focus more attention on the specific needs and circumstances of publicly funded agencies and to examine issues such as job stress, employee motivation, leadership, organizational change and management education within this context. Our hope is that the heightened relevance to public sector environments will provide practitioners, researchers and students interested in public sector HRM with a more informed basis for examining and addressing these issues.

(2) The Importance of Public Sector Services and the Role of Human Resources in Delivering these Services

The second reason for concentrating on HRM in the public sector relates the importance of the goods and services provided by State-funded agencies and the impact these have on public safety, social cohesion and national prosperity. These services range from those involving high levels of face-to-face interactions with clients and communities such as healthcare, education, policing, and family support services, to the public infrastructure operations involved in roads maintenance, public transport, water and sewage and other public utilities. There are also the more centrally administered services that involve, for example, distributing welfare payments and health benefits, identifying labour market opportunities, issuing passports, scrutinizing tax returns and deciding on migration issues. In each of these cases, the decisions made by public servants and the actions they take have the potential to significantly influence the safety, wellbeing and living standards of the citizens concerned. In view of the importance of the work performed by public sector employees and employers, there are compelling 'public interest' reasons for ensuring we have a strong public sector that has the capacity to consistently execute these roles and responsibilities to a high level. The manner in which an agency's HR are managed can hinder or enhance this capacity and it is therefore critical that, first, more research is directed to the specific HR needs of public sector agencies and, second, that key stakeholders (including practitioners and researchers) continually assess the influence of HR policies and practices in this sector.

(3) Levels of Public Investment in Civil Services and the Need for Governments and Agencies to Maximize this Investment

There are also major financial reasons for focusing on HRM in the public sector. As a measure of the scope and reach of public sector services, general government expenditures in 2009 represented nearly half of GDP on average across OECD member countries (OECD, 2011). Furthermore, government organizations employ almost a quarter of the total workforce in OECD countries (OECD, 2011) and, as a result, a significant proportion of government expenditure is dedicated to wages and salaries. In the UK, for example, the annual public sector pay bill in 2010 was 158 billion pounds and this amount accounts for more than 1 in every 4 pounds the Government spends (CIPD, 2010). Likewise, in the US 29.8 per cent of all direct expenditure by the states was allocated to wages and salaries during the 2001–2002 financial year (Befort, 2012). Considering the enormity of these costs, and the considerable budgetary pressures they create for governments and tax-payers, there is a strong need for civil services to show that these funds are being used as efficiently as possible and that the money invested in HR has a maximum benefit for clients and communities. This issue again highlights the need for HR research to focus on the specific contexts in which public sector organizations operate and to consider how matters such as employee wellbeing, job engagement, labour turnover, leadership and organizational changes can be best managed in this environment.

(4) The Scale of the Workforce-related Challenges Confronting Public Sector Agencies

The fourth and final reason for concentrating on HRM in the public sector is that, internationally, public sector organizations face unprec-edented challenges in the foreseeable future. These challenges have signifi-cant implications for the size and profile of the public sector workforce, the conditions in which employees work and the manner in which HR are managed in this sector.

Severe cost cutting strategies such as employee lay-offs and wage freezes
One of the most pressing concerns currently facing public sector organiza-tions is the large reductions in government spending. The global economic downturn has impacted on government revenue at all levels – local, state and federal – and with policy makers under pressure to reduce large budget deficits, the responses have invariably involved significant job losses. In the US for example, 627 000 public sector jobs were shed between June 2009 and July 2012, while Great Britain's 'Comprehensive Spending Review' will reportedly result in the loss of 490 000 public sector positions between 2010–2014 (Goldfarb, 2010; Shierholz, 2012). These and other austerity measures (for example, wage freezes, pension restrictions) pose major chal-lenges for HR, not only in terms of recruitment, compensation and service provision, but also in relation to job security and workforce morale.

Ongoing reforms aimed at enhancing organizational effectiveness, reducing inefficiencies and increasing accountability to governments and user groups
The recent cuts to public sector budgets come on top of a long series of reforms that have sought to achieve higher levels of efficiency and effectiveness in public sector organizations. Collectively referred to as new public management (NPM), these strategies have often involved high-levels of organizational re-structuring (for example, departmental mergers, privatization), stricter performance management and accounta-bility mechanisms, and the creation of a more market-oriented culture that

places greater emphasis on the needs of consumers rather than service providers (Osborne and McLaughlin, 2002; Williams, Rayner and Allinson, 2012). NPM-style reforms have been popular in both developed and developing countries over the past 2–3 decades and, although they have had some success, there are also indications that they have taken their toll on the health and satisfaction of employees (Ibsen et al., 2011; Korunka et al., 2003; Noblet and Rodwell, 2009). A key challenge facing many public sector organizations is how they can plan and implement NPM-oriented change programs in a way that enhances organizational effectiveness but at the same time protects the health and wellbeing of employees.

Large increases in the volume and complexity of services required to address community needs

At a time when governments are attempting to slim-down and rationalize public sector programs, the demand for State-funded services has been steadily increasing. A large proportion of this increased demand is due to broader population trends (for example, an ageing population requiring greater health and aged care services, see the next section), however there has also been an increase in the need for customization and personalization of services (APS, 2010). So another significant issue confronting many public sector agencies is how they can effectively address heightened community demands while at the same time reducing personnel costs. This challenge will be particularly acute in the human services (healthcare, law enforcement, education, social welfare) where the community's needs are particularly complex and the failure to respond to these needs can have immediate and often severe consequences.

Important demographic shifts such as an ageing population and a shrinking workforce

The portion of the population aged 65 and over is expected to increase from 13.7 per cent in 2010 to 19.1 per cent in 2021 (SSA, 2011). Yet, public health research indicates that around half to two-thirds of this increase in life expectancy will entail a period of severe handicap (Duckett, 2005). The number of elderly people requiring more complex, labour intensive public services (especially healthcare) is therefore expected to rise concomitantly over the next 1–2 decades. In the short-term, the budgetary restrictions and staff freezes will clearly hamper an agency's ability to meet these rising demands, however a longer-term problem is the shrinking workforce. In the Australian State of Victoria, for example, the portion of the population of working age (15–64 years) will reduce from 67 per cent of the State's population to 65 per cent in 2021 (SSA, 2011). The resultant skills shortages and competition for appropriately qualified personnel (particularly from the private sector) will make it increasingly difficult for public sector services to recruit and retain sufficient numbers of qualified staff.

Already high levels of stress, dissatisfaction and other indicators of job strain within public sector agencies

Doubts regarding the ability of public sector services to meet the current and future needs of their communities are fuelled further by studies indicating that the public sector is already experiencing high levels of job strain. In the UK, for example, research undertaken by the Health and Safety Executive (HSE, 2005) found that the symptoms of work-related stress were significantly more prevalent in the public sector than in the private sector and that a higher proportion of public sector employees report working while ill. Tellingly, this study also found that the symptoms of work-related stress were heightened in occupations involving greater face-to-face contact with the public (healthcare, education, law enforcement). The disproportionate level of stress in the public sector is in parallel with similar reports from other countries including Australia (see Chapter 4 by Bailey, McLinton and Dollard), the US, Denmark, Norway and Sweden and suggest that protecting and promoting the health of public sector employees is an international concern (Dolcos and Daley, 2009; Ibsen et al., 2011). How agencies respond to this concern will not only impact on public sector employees themselves, but given the links between job stress and client-related outcomes (for example, patient satisfaction, error rates, employee performance), will also influence the quality of services available to communities (for example, Aiken et al., 2001; Dugan et al., 1996).

Overall, the above challenges have serious implications for the volume and complexity of demands facing public sector organizations and the extent to which public sector services can meet these demands. Both the providers and the recipients of public sector services are impacted by these issues, and hence both parties stand to benefit from research focusing on how public sector organizations can best address these changes. An important goal of the current collection is therefore to draw greater attention to these and other challenges and using a combination of empirical research, literature reviews and case studies, provide practitioners with insights into how they can be managed.

SUMMARY OF CONTENTS

The current collection has been divided into four overlapping parts: (I) Approaches to human resource management in the public sector; (II) Assessing and addressing the health and well-being of public sector employees; (III) Human resource challenges in the public sector; and (IV) Human resource management practices and public sector performance. The final section of this introduction provides a summary of each of these parts and the chapters therein.

Part I – Approaches to Human Resource Management in the Public Sector

Part I provides an appropriate starting point for this collection by examining what is unique and different about how HR are managed in the public sector, particularly when compared to the private sector. Importantly, this section takes into account the HRM approaches adopted in both developed and developing countries.

Catherine Truss (Chapter 2) reports that while there are considerable differences in the types of HRM policies and practices that exist within the public sector, there are several characteristics that appear to be more unique to the sector, particularly when compared to the private sector. These characteristics include an employment relationship that is more closely controlled by the State, and where there is less discretion available to individual organizations; higher levels of unionization and union influence in matters such as wage determination and pension entitlements; a greater emphasis on values concerned with fairness, openness and equality, and a generally older and more stable workforce. NPM-style reforms have had a major impact on how HRM is practiced in the public sector and Chapter 2 also considers the influence of these reforms.

While the vast majority of the international HRM literature focuses on Western industrialized societies, Chris Rees (Chapter 3) discusses the role of public HRM in developing nations. Core HRM functions are similar across organizations in both developed and developing countries, although contextual factors are vastly different reflecting significant political, social, economic, environmental and health-related barriers to effective service delivery. Public HRM in developing nations is seen as essential to social and economic progress – in particular HRM policies related to the decentralization of power and programs of nationalization, which can help to reinforce local cultural norms. Despite recent interest in the developing world, further research on the contextual demands and specific environmental concerns of non-Western communities is warranted.

Part II – Assessing and Addressing the Health and Well-being of Public Sector Employees

As mentioned earlier in this introduction, the heightened need to develop more responsive and efficient civil services has placed significant pressure on public sector organizations to constantly assess how they manage their internal environments. Part II of this collection focuses specifically on one of the critical outcomes associated with a more dynamic and resource conscious working environment; the health and wellbeing of public sector employees.

The results presented in Chapter 4 support the view that public sector workplaces have become more stressful. Here, Maureen Dollard, Tessa Bailey and Sarven McLinton assess compensation claims for mental stress among Australian public sector employees and find that these are significantly higher than in the private sector. Looking to antecedents of compensation claims, the public sector appears to be a more demanding workplace than the private sector, particularly with respect to emotional and psychological demands. These findings are consistent with research from the US where public sector employees reported significantly more demands compared to private sector workers. There are also indications that poor communication regarding psychosocial risks and not heeding the views of workers in the development of psychological health policies may explain the higher stress claims in the public sector.

Andrew Noblet, Kathryn Page and Tony LaMontagne then examine the types of strategies that public sector organizations could employ to combat the stress associated with more demanding working environments (Chapter 5). Specifically, the authors report on the results of an employee health needs assessment that was designed to identify strategies (policies, systems, practices) that could enhance the psychosocial working conditions experienced by employees working in an Australian-based community heath service. Data was collected using an organizational-wide survey and a series of post-survey focus groups. The findings indicate that implementing strategies to improve employee control (for example, increasing decision-making influence) and support (for example, developing a more inclusive culture) present valuable opportunities for creating healthier and more motivating work environments for employees working in this sector.

Further acknowledgement of the stressful nature of state-funded health services is provided by Arnold Bakker and Jari Hakanen (Chapter 6). The working conditions of Finnish public dentists are examined with special attention given to the impact that healthcare reforms have had within the public sector. Utilizing the job demands-resources (JD-R) model the authors demonstrate that dentists operating in the public sector are exposed to greater demands (for example, negative contacts with patients) and fewer resources (for example, decision authority), and as a result report lower levels of work engagement than their private sector counterparts. Interventions based on the development of greater resources are recommended with the authors providing access to an online tool to assist with the application of the JD-R model in an organizational setting, a useful resource for practitioners within all areas of the public sector.

Mary Guy and Meredith Newman also address the psychological and emotional wellbeing of employees (Chapter 7). Their discussion centres on the emotional labour involved in performing human service roles in the public sector. Despite the rewarding nature of the work, human services often involve a high level of emotionally-intense work that can lead to employee burnout. The authors offer a strategic insight into the opportunities for HRM to reduce the negative impact of emotional labour. Providing a supportive environment that acknowledges and actively attempts to combat the demanding nature of the work performed by public services employees is important. Developing more appropriate screening tools, improving training and recognizing those employees with relevant skills relies on flexible and proactive HR policies that are integrated into the organizational framework.

Part III – Human Resource Management Challenges in the Public Sector

One of the keys to developing healthy and effective organizations, irrespective of the sector, is to recognize the challenges impacting on organizational functioning. Although the beginning of this introduction recognized some of the important external challenges faced by public sector organizations, Part III of this collection focuses on the more prominent internal challenges including leadership development, employee motivation, labour turnover, managing HR during economic downturn and the role of unions in organizational change.

Managing public sector resources more efficiently and effectively is a major goal of current public policy and, given that managers play a key role in how agency resources are used, strategies designed to improve the knowledge, skills and capacities of public sector managers are integral to achieving this goal. In Chapter 8, Patrick McGurk considers how management and leadership development interventions can be used to improve the quality and efficiency of public sector services, while also improving employee satisfaction and wellbeing outcomes. A distinction is made between management development (for instance, more prescriptive training designed to enhance task performance in management roles), leader development (for instance, individually-oriented development methods aimed at improving the managers' ability to influence their teams more effectively), and leadership development (for instance, collective learning and relationship building between managers that is concerned with enhancing social capital). Further, three case studies are presented to illustrate the outcomes associated with these approaches and to highlight the factors that can hinder or enhance the effectiveness of management and leadership development in public sector agencies.

In Chapter 9, Mark Bradbury, Jessica Sowa and J. Edward Kellough examine rates of employee turnover in the public sector with an emphasis on problematic voluntary separations. The anticipated retirement of the baby boomer generation places enormous pressure on public sector organizations to retain valuable talent and attract suitably qualified replacements. Voluntary turnover, a case in which the employee terminates the employment relationship when the organization arguably would prefer it to continue, represents a significant challenge for public sector organizations. Environmental (for example, employment legislation), organizational (for example, proportion of temporary workers) and personal (for example, age, work-family conflict) factors all contribute to voluntary turnover. The challenge for HRM in the public sector is identified as the development of upstream preventative strategies that can intercept the quit process and minimize the loss of valuable talent.

The management of public sector organizations during periods of economic downturn presents a further challenge for HRM, especially in the current climate when severe austerity measures have been introduced in many countries throughout Europe, North America, Latin America and Asia. Parbudyal Singh and Ronald Burke (Chapter 10) discuss the forces contributing to an altered public sector environment and the difficulties faced by public HRM in tough economic times. Public organizations that are facing economic crises most often respond by downsizing and attempts to reduce labour costs with a focus on the immediate threat to organizational survival. However, the negative short and long-term effects of downsizing are far-reaching and a proactive, flexible approach to HRM in economic uncertainty can create a more sustainable organization, which maintains a high-value approach to service delivery to the public.

Consistent with the perspectives presented earlier in this introductory chapter, Wouter Vandenabeele portrays the public sector as a constantly changing and increasingly output-oriented environment that presents unique challenges for HRM (Chapter 11). The attitudes and behaviours of employees have always been critical to the performance of public sector agencies, however in an environment characterized by heightened demands and declining resources, the question of how to best motivate, attract and retain becomes a critical question. 'Public service motivation' forms a distinct construct within the motivational literature where the intrinsic needs associated with contributing to the wellbeing of society, civic virtue, public interest and compassion for others are more likely to be fulfilled through public sector work. A key aim of this chapter is to translate knowledge gained from the motivational literature (including generic and public service motivational theories) and to consider the specific strategies public sector organizations could use to enhance the levels of motivation, satisfaction and retention among employees.

In Chapter 12, Miguel Lucio describes the trade union as a traditional stakeholder in public sector human relations, and a key voice in the regulation of public sector conditions. Issues of work intensification, gender equality and performance management are more recent concerns for the public sector and represent changes to managerial practices as well as changes to the social fabric of societies in which public sector organizations operate. Rather than representing a stagnant historical remnant of the bureaucratic public sector, trade unions exhibit a reciprocal relationship with modern HRM where unions respond to, and also influence, changing management practices in the public sector. In this way, trade unions maintain relevance in the current public sector framework, proving to be flexible and capable of strategic influence of HRM and management practices.

Part IV – Human Resource Management Practices and Public Sector Performance

The final section of this publication provides a more detailed discussion of issues involving work intensification and increased performance-management of the public sector. The shift towards NPM ultimately aims to improve organizational performance through the introduction of more flexible HRM methods and increased employee input. However, the extent to which these reforms have achieved their intended outcomes is still a matter for debate, especially when considering the potentially damaging effects on the satisfaction and commitment of employees.

In Chapter 13, Pauline Stanton and Karen Manning begin Part IV by discussing the role of employee participation and performance management in high performance work systems (HPWS). Although HPWS's have been typically associated with a range of positive attitudinal (for example, job satisfaction) and behavioural (for example, employee performance) outcomes, there are indications that the introduction of these systems in public sector settings that have undergone (or are undergoing) NPM-style reforms can lead to negative outcomes. In contexts heavily oriented to gaining greater efficiencies and increasing the accountability of employees, efforts to devolve decision making influence have been associated with increased responsibility and greater intensification of work. In these contexts, performance management systems are more likely to be seen as mechanisms for monitoring and controlling employees rather than avenues for improved learning and development. In all, the literature reviewed in this chapter suggests that for HPWS's to have their desired effect, there needs to be close alignment and support between the 'high performing' systems and the broader strategies adopted by the organization.

Laurence O'Toole, Agnes Akkerman, Kenneth Meier and René Torenvlied undertook an empirical investigation focusing on the relationship between public sector HRM and organizational performance within the Netherlands education sector (Chapter 14). The utilization of participatory HRM practices, particularly those that seek the input of employees in decision making and provide individualized reward systems, were directly associated with overall organizational performance (as measured by the schools' educational outcomes). However, some HR-related 'red tape' negatively influenced organizational performance.

Giovanni Azzone and Michela Arnaboldi (Chapter 15) further examine performance within the public sector and evaluate the HRM activities of peak performing public organizations. Arnaboldi and Azzone suggest that the disparities between high and low performing public sector organizations may, to a certain extent, be attributed to the adoption and execution of key HRM practices developing from the NPM framework. Internal drivers of peak performance revolve around a pervasive organization-wide commitment to performance, the ability to identify and address gaps in competences, a high degree of flexibility and ability to rapidly respond to external influences, and a consolidation of successful processes into the fabric of the organization. Ultimately, the ability of public sector organizations to recognize and respond to external opportunities through innovative HRM policies is a key determinant of organizational performance.

The final chapter of this publication (Chapter 16) takes us from the work environment to the classroom. Jared Llorens examines how recent changes to HRM practice have informed the education of public sector managers and HR professionals. In the future, public sector HRM leaders will be required to utilize more flexible approaches to managing employees, reflecting the changing nature of the sector. The use of more flexible employment contracts and compensation strategies, recruitment methods geared towards a younger and more transient workforce, as well as a greater reliance on technology are now important components of education for public HR practitioners.

REFERENCES

Aiken, L.H., S.P. Clarke, D.M. Sloane, J.A. Sochalski, R. Busse, H. Clarke, P. Giovannetti, J. Hunt, A.M. Rafferty and J. Shamian (2001), 'Nurses' reports on hospital care in five countries', *Health Affairs*, **20**, 43–53.

APS (2010), *Why is a strong Australian Public Service important?*, Canberra: APS.

Befort, S.F. (2012), 'Public-sector employment under siege', *Indiana Law Journal*, **87** (1), 231–8.

Brown, K. (2004), 'Human resource management in the public sector', *Public Management Review*, **6** (3), 303–9.

CIPD (2010), *Delivering More with Less: The People Management Challenge*, UK: Chartered Institute of Personnel and Development.

Dolcos, S. and D. Daley (2009), 'Work pressure, workplace social resources, and work–family conflict: the tale of two sectors', *International Journal of Stress Management*, **16** (4), 291–311.

Duckett, S.J. (2005), 'Health workforce design for the 21st century', *Australian Health Review*, **29** (2), 201–10.

Dugan, J., E. Lauer, Z. Bouquot, B.K. Dutro, M. Smith and G. Widmeyer (1996), 'Stressful nurses: the effect on patient outcomes', *Journal of Nursing Care Quality*, **10**, 46–58.

Farnham, D. and S. Horton (1996), 'Continuity and change in the public services', in D. Farnham and S. Horton (eds), *Managing People in the Public Services*, Basingstoke: Macmillan, 3–42.

Goldfarb, M. (2010), 'Britain: a new era begins with government spending', *GlobalPost*, 20 October 2010.

HSE (2005), *Survey of Workplace Absence Sickness and (Ill)Health*, UK: Health and Safety Executive.

Ibsen, C.L., T.P. Larsen, J.S. Madsen and J. Due (2011), 'Challenging Scandinavian employment relations: the effects of new public management reforms', *The International Journal of Human Resource Management*, **22** (11), 2295–310.

Korunka, C., D. Scharitzer, P. Carayons and F. Sainfort (2003), 'Employee strain and job satisfaction related to an implementation of quality in a public service organization: a longitudinal study', *Work & Stress*, **17**, 52–72.

Noblet, A.J. and J.J. Rodwell (2009), 'Integrating job stress and social exchange theories to predict employee strain in reformed public sector organisations', *Journal of Public Administration Research and Theory*, **19** (3), 555–78.

OECD (2011), *Government at a Glance 2011*, Paris: Organisation for Economic Co-operation and Development (OECD).

Osborne, S.P. and K. McLaughlin (2002), 'The new public management in context', in K. McLaughlin, S.P. Osborne and E. Ferlie (eds), *New Public Management: Current Trends and Future Prospects*, London: Routledge, pp. 7–14.

Shierholz, H. (2012), *The Labor Market is Treading Water*, USA: Economic Policy Institute.

SSA (2011), *State of the Public Sector in Victoria 2010-11*, Melbourne: State Services Authority.

Williams, H.M., J. Rayner and C.W. Allinson (2012), 'New public management and organisational commitment in the public sector: testing a mediation model', *International Journal of Human Resource Management*, **23** (13), 2615–29.

PART I

Approaches to human resource management in the public sector

2. The distinctiveness of human resource management in the public sector

Catherine Truss

The global economic crisis that began in 2008 triggered successive waves of transformational reform within the public services of many nations around the globe. Bach (2011) notes that within the UK, for instance, some government departments are witnessing budget cuts of 25 per cent with the public sector expected to shed 330 000 jobs. UK local authorities are being asked to secure savings of 30 per cent over four years, and it is likely that significant numbers of jobs will be lost in all areas of the public sector, with some activities being drastically cut back, and others completely halted (Bach, 2011; HM Treasury, 2010). The situation in many other economies, including Greece, Italy, Portugal and Spain, is even more serious.

As governments around the world seek to impose rapid and drastic curbs on public spending, by not only cutting jobs but also introducing substantially less favourable pay and conditions for those remaining, mass union protests have taken place in many countries with more inevitably to follow, signalling an era of increasingly adversarial relations between government and public sector workers (Bach, 2011; OECD, 2008).

Public sector human resource (HR) managers have long been used to attracting charges of inefficiency and ineffectiveness. Traditionally associated with aspirations towards being a 'model employer', focused more on the fair and equitable treatment of staff than on managing for performance, it may come as no surprise to beleaguered public sector HR professionals that they are being blamed in some quarters for contributing to the current economic woes. For example, the UK's Chartered Institute of Personnel and Development recently argued that public sector organizations had failed to invest in people management skills, and further commented:

> Truly productive, well-managed workplaces should be capable of responding to such challenges while remaining agile, innovative and productive – as many private sector organizations have shown through the current recession.

However, in the UK public sector, too many workplaces appear to be the exact opposite of productive (CIPD, 2010: 3).

HR professionals within public services today are being called upon to manage substantial change and redundancy programs, and at the same time downsize themselves and address demands to improve their own performance. Bach (2011), for instance, reports that the UK central government anticipates reducing the size of their HR departments by half through the introduction of shared services.

Although faced with similar pressures to reform, research evidence suggests that the starting-point for these changes in public sector HRM around the globe varies considerably (Bach and Bordogna, 2011). There are also wide variations in the relationship between the public and the private sectors in different nation states (Meyer and Hammerschmid, 2010). Thus, rather than the application of globally similar reform initiatives, we are likely to witness the evolution and implementation of divergent solutions which will exert a differential impact on public sector staff and HR departments around the world (Bach and Bordogna, 2011; OECD, 2005).

In order to contextualize these developments, this chapter will focus on the question of what is different and unique about human resource management (HRM) in the public sector, as compared with the private sector, and how this might vary between nations, and even within nations. First, we will consider the composition of the public sector workforce and explore how differences between public and private sector employees may be relevant for HRM. We will then examine the question of HRM, and what is distinctive about HRM in the public sector as opposed to the private sector. Finally, we will move on to the role of the HR department itself, and consider how HR departments are situated and operate within public services.

PUBLIC SECTOR EMPLOYMENT PATTERNS

Studies have shown that, around the world, the public sector remains a significant employer in the majority of countries, comprising around 20 per cent of the workforce in the UK, for instance (Prowse and Prowse, 2007). However, recent decades have witnessed a decline in the number and proportion of public sector workers (albeit with a few counter-examples such as France, Germany and the USA), a trend set to continue in light of the present economic situation (Bach and Bordogna, 2011).

The nature and composition of the public sector workforce differs substantially from that of the private sector in most nations. Public sector workers are significantly older than those in the private sector (OECD, 2007; 2009). For example, in the US, 60 per cent of the federal civil service workforce is over 45 (and only 3 per cent is under 25), compared with 31 per cent in the private sector; in Denmark, almost one-third of the public sector workforce is over 50 and, in Canada, up to 50 per cent could retire within seven years (Deloitte, 2007). In the UK, 47 per cent of local government staff are over 44 and only 5.8 per cent are under 24 (Local Government Employers and LGA, 2009).

In terms of gender composition, the situation varies between countries. In the UK, there are nearly twice as many women as men employed in public services, whereas the reverse is true within the private sector (Millard and Machin, 2007; Golden, 2011). However, the OECD (2009) notes that women represent fewer than 50 per cent of public sector workers in countries such as Portugal, Ireland and New Zealand. Around the world, women are significantly under-represented at senior levels, and in no country do women hold over 40 per cent of senior posts (OECD, 2009). For instance, in the US, women represent 44.2 per cent of the federal workforce, but occupy only 29 per cent of executive positions. In countries such as Switzerland, Korea and Japan, the figure is below 10 per cent.

More detailed studies within the UK have shown that the proportions of staff from different ethnic groups and those with disabilities are broadly comparable across the public and private sectors. UK public sector workers are more likely to have a degree than those in the private sector, 32 per cent as compared with 19 per cent, and more public sector workers are classified as professional, associate professional, technical and administrative workers than in the private sector, 64 per cent and 32 per cent respectively (Millard and Machin, 2007). In terms of patterns of work, Millard and Machin (2007) found in the UK that levels of part-time work are similar in both sectors, with 71 per cent and 76 per cent respectively working full-time, but that only 14 per cent of public sector workers reported working over 45 hours per week as compared with 22 per cent in the private sector. Public sector workers were also more likely to stay with their employer for longer, 40 per cent had over 10 years of service compared with 28 per cent in the private sector.

Public sector workers continue to be more likely than their private sector counterparts to belong to a union (OECD, 2005). In the UK, 56.3 per cent of public sector workers are union members, three times more than in the private sector (Office for National Statistics, 2010; Bach and

Givan, 2008), and 90 per cent of public sector workplaces recognize unions as compared with 16 per cent of private sector workplaces (Bach et al., 2009; Roper et al., 2007; Kersley et al., 2006). In the US, trade union density is 37 per cent compared with 8 per cent in the private sector (US Bureau of Labor Statistics, 2009).

However, there is evidence that the proportion of public sector workers who are union members is declining. Hicks et al. (2005) note that public sector trade union density in the UK fell from 72 per cent to 59 per cent between 1995 and 2005. Contributory factors here are the growing fragmentation of public service delivery, the decline of nationalized industries, the transfer of staff from the public to the private sector through initiatives such as outsourcing and privatization, together with societal-level factors such as the general decline of collective forms of representation (Bach, 2011; Morris and Farrell, 2007).

The available data would therefore suggest that there are various factors in the composition of the public sector workforce that are relevant from an HRM perspective. First, the public sector workforce differs in terms of its demographic composition from that of the private sector, for example, in terms of age and educational attainment. The relatively older age of many public sector workers creates a challenge for employers due to the impending retirement of large swathes of the workforce (Millard and Machin, 2007). There are clearly also differences in terms of rates of unionization, which are relevant for pay determination processes and the management of the employment relationship. Third, whilst there are some areas of similarity between countries, for instance, in terms of the relative age of public sector workers, there are also areas of important difference, for instance, in gender composition and union roles.

Looking to the future, researchers have argued that rising levels of expectation in terms of the quality of public service provision, coupled with the increasing fragmentation of public service delivery mechanisms taking place within a climate of significant retrenchment, are combining to create substantial challenges for the public sector. As Deloitte (2007: 2) argue: 'the aging government workforce, a shrinking talent pool, different job expectations of younger generations and the need for a new set of skills in the public sector, will soon create a gap between the supply of and demand for skilled government workers in many Western countries'. Thus, despite the need to reduce the size of the public sector workforce, there remain the important issues of the recruitment, retention and deployment of skilled workers able to meet the increasing demands of service delivery.

HUMAN RESOURCE MANAGEMENT APPROACHES IN THE GLOBAL PUBLIC SECTOR

Commentators have long argued that HRM in the context of the public sector differs in important ways from that of the private sector (Boyne et al., 1999). Traditionally, public sector HRM has been associated with the aspiration to be a 'model employer', based on the ideals of justice, fairness, equality, transparency and stability, manifest in HRM activities that focus on high levels of job security, regular and predictable salary increments, generous pensions, promotion based on seniority, a focus on equal opportunities, and paternalistic and collectivist approaches to managing the employment relationship (Morgan and Allington, 2002; OECD, 2005). This has been set within the context of the traditional Weberian bureaucratic model prevalent in public services, featuring centralization, hierarchical structures, and rule-based decision-making, affording little scope for strategizing at a local level (Brown, 2004; Roper et al., 2007). Although it has been argued that this 'traditional' view of public sector HRM is an oversimplification, it does provide a useful starting point.

When New Public Management (NPM) emerged during the 1980s, this traditional approach to managing people came under attack for being outmoded, for undermining organizational performance, and for demoralizing staff who were not sufficiently rewarded or recognized for their contribution (Truss, 2008). Although NPM is a contested construct, there has been some convergence of views around its underlying ethos (Bach and Bordogna, 2011). Right-wing governments in the UK and the US in particular were of the view that the public sector needed a much stronger focus on performance, efficiency and effectiveness, and sought to introduce a raft of measures aimed at the marketization of public services. These measures include the creation of putative internal markets in order to foster competition, efforts to devolve strategy to the local level, an increased focus on managerialism, and interventions to promote performance management (Bach and Givan, 2011; Roper et al., 2007). The overall aim was to try to encourage the public sector to be 'more like' the private sector.

One implication of these reforms has been to challenge the traditional public sector approach to managing people; instead emphasizing the importance of managing people strategically through such approaches as differentiated pay and promotion based on performance rather than seniority, the use of performance appraisals, a focus on the individualization of the employment relationship, and the development of overarching organizational HR strategies aimed at supporting the general strategic aims and objectives of the organization (Bach and Givan, 2011). Farnham and Horton (1996) term this 'New People Management'. The pressures to effect significant change to the nature of the employment relationship within the public sector have intensified substantially since the start of the economic crisis (Bach, 2011); the UK's Chartered Institute of Personnel and Development (CIPD, 2010), for example, have recently argued that the traditional public sector approaches are no longer tenable.

However, there is evidence that the uptake and extent of reform to public sector HRM approaches varies considerably (Gould-Williams, 2004; Pichault, 2007). There are a number of inter-related reasons for this.

One factor is the variability of national settings. Bach and Kessler (2007) identify two dominant modes of public services employment regulation that have emerged since World War II; the 'sovereign employer' model found in countries such as France and Germany, where terms and conditions of employment are determined unilaterally by government with no collective bargaining and where industrial action is prohibited; and the 'model employer' approach, found in countries such as the UK, with a focus on areas such as conditions of work, employee voice and collective bargaining.

NPM represents a challenge to both of these modes of employment regulation, and its uptake has led to changes common to countries in both categories, such as a decreasing share of employment within public services, decreasing numbers of staff with 'special' employment status as public sector workers, the erosion of job security, the wider diffusion of voluntary pay bargaining, more decentralization, and less support for unions and collectivist criteria for pay determination (Bach and Kessler, 2007).

Overlaid on this is the dichotomy between liberal market economies on the one hand, and coordinated market economies on the other (Hall and Soskice, 2001; Bach and Givan, 2011). For instance, the UK and the US have been bracketed together as liberal market economies, which are supposedly more receptive to reform initiatives; however, these two countries have been found to vary substantially in the nature and operation of their public services. The UK, with a 'model employer' heritage, is highly centralized with no separate body governing public service employment relations, and is focused on the State 'setting a good example' to private sector employers. In the US, there is a 'sovereign employer' heritage, in contrast, there has been a strong tradition of state autonomy and a written constitution with a formal separation between legislative, executive and judicial branches of government. There is a system of election to posts which are appointed in the UK, such as school boards. Thus, the State takes more direct control over the public sector with strong rules governing bargaining and dispute resolution, alongside significant differences between public and private sector employment law, so that public sector employees enjoy more beneficial employment rights than those in the private sector; for instance, once public servants have completed their probationary period, they cannot have their contracts terminated.

Bach and Bordogna (2011) conclude that existing institutions and structures act as a filter for reform initiatives, leading to the emergence of complex patterns of similarity and dissimilarity in approaches to HRM between countries and between sectors. Thus, although NPM may appear to be a unified construct, its application within the context of public sector organizations has not given rise to a consistent public sector approach to managing people around the world. Other researchers support this view, and further suggest that public sector institutions are particularly resistant to change, with the more traditional approaches persisting in the face of NPM reforms (Boyne et al., 1999; Harel and Tzafrir, 2001; Jaconnelli and Sheffield, 2000; Soni, 2004). This has been attributed in part to the continued dominance of Weberian bureaucratic structures inherent in public sector organizations that legitimize and reinforce approaches to people management aligned to stable hierarchies (Hales, 2002). The OECD found in 2009 that the pressure on the public sector around the world to be a 'model employer' persists in many countries despite the rhetoric of NPM. One example is their finding that public service employers express a strong will to pursue diversity policies as much for the public sector values of fairness, transparency and equity, as for reasons of efficiency and effectiveness.

Pichault (2007) concludes that reforms to public sector HRM within Europe have been piecemeal and ad hoc, and identifies four domains where lack of coherence is significant. First, there is a lack of coherence between 'new' and 'traditional' approaches, leading to patchy investment in some initiatives but not others. Second, there is a lack of coherence in terms of the strategic direction of the reforms; for instance, the introduction of standardized pay rating scales in some countries does not constitute a step towards enhancing the individualization of the employment relationship. Third, there is a lack of coherence between the content and the context of reform leading, for instance, to unsuccessful efforts to impose enhanced flexibility within a hierarchical system. Finally, there is a lack of coherence between the content of reforms and the processes by which they are introduced, for instance, seeking to impose decentralization through a process that is imposed and monitored top-down.

SIMILARITIES AND DIFFERENCES BETWEEN PUBLIC AND PRIVATE SECTOR HRM

Having considered HRM in public services at a macro level, we now move on to examine in more detail some of the specific areas of HRM that are especially pertinent in the public sector; and to explore the questions of whether, and how, public sector approaches may differ from those of the private sector, as well as how these vary around the world.

One of the greatest distinctions between the public and the private sectors in all countries is the level of direct government control exerted over public sector organizations, which serves to limit the degree of discretion available to individual employers in the management of people. In many countries, the government-level push for a more strategic approach to HRM that has emerged since the 1980s has been accompanied by a range of measures designed both to encourage and to compel public sector employers to become more strategic. Thus, for instance, in the UK local government sector, the government introduced their Workforce Strategy in 2007 in order to provide guidance and an overarching framework for employers, accompanied by the 'best value' auditing scheme to check on its adoption (Entwhistle et al., 2007). The success of these initiatives has however been mixed.

Historically, public sector workers in many countries have enjoyed a special status as 'public servants', as distinct from their private sector counterparts, which offers them particular privileges and rights, for instance, Beamten in Germany and titulaires in France, whose terms and conditions of work are centrally determined by government. Bach and Bordogna (2011: 2287–2288) note that many governments have sought to reduce the rights of these public servants and align their terms and conditions of work more closely with those of the private sector. However, these efforts have met with more success in some countries than others. Countries such as New Zealand and Italy effectively removed the special status of public sector workers some time ago, Germany has witnessed a partial reduction of the privileges of public servants, and France has not witnessed any substantive change. The OECD (2004) found that 13 of their member states had changed the status of their civil servants to some degree, a move characterized by a shift away from a 'career based' system offering job security and stable career progression, towards a 'position based system' with a greater emphasis on external recruitment, accompanied by reduced levels of job security. Bach and Bordogna's (2011: 2288) research further shows how this can vary within countries as well: in the US, for instance, efforts to remove the special status of public sector workers have met with more success at the state level than at the federal level.

Alongside this, there is evidence that the changing form and structure of the public sector has led to a greater fragmentation of the employment base, and to more use of flexible employment contracts. For instance, Prowse and Prowse (2007) point to the increased use of non-permanent subcontracted staff in the public sector between 1984 and 1998, especially those on fixed term contracts. Bach and Bordogna (2011) found that the number and proportion of staff on fixed term contracts and other atypical forms of employment had increased in many countries.

One area within which the most difference between the public and the private sectors has traditionally been seen, and which NPM reforms have sought to address, is the area of pay determination. Recent years have witnessed an increasing call for public sector organizations to adopt a more strategic approach to pay determination that is less reliant on either central government or on collective bargaining processes, but is rather based on organizational strategy, the local labour market, and rewarding for performance rather than tenure (Pichault, 2007; Bach, 2011).

Roper et al. (2007) note that there are three constituencies which are important in terms of systems of public sector pay determination: the State; individual employers; and trade unions. The balance of power between these three constituent groups has varied over time, between different countries and within countries between individual sectors. An OECD survey in 2005 for instance found that in many countries, unions continue to play an important role in determining pay levels, particularly in Norway, Sweden, Austria, Belgium, Denmark and Italy, but that in other countries, including Australia, Hungary, Spain and the Slovak Republic, union involvement is weak. In the UK, collective pay bargaining has been a longstanding feature of pay determination. Bach (2011) found that collective pay agreements still cover 64.5 per cent of public sector staff, albeit that this represents a fall of 9.7 per cent since 2000 (Achur, 2010). In the US, collective bargaining is less entrenched and there is a greater variety of approaches within different states and sectors (Bach and Givan, 2011). Bach and Bordogna (2011) conclude that there is evidence of a divergence between the role played by unions in the public and private sectors. This varies between countries, with those in the Nordic area collaborating more closely with government and employers over public sector reform than those in the UK and the US, where the relationship has been more adversarial.

Overall, Bach and Bordogna (2011: 2289) note that there is evidence of an increasing level of individualized pay determination in many countries, including those such as France, where more collectivized approaches have previously been used. However, there is evidence of variation within different sectors of the same country. In the UK, for example, pay determination for the NHS has been partially centralized, and in local government, pay bargaining has taken place at the national level, with some degree of local determination (Prowse and Prowse, 2007). Despite these trends, Bach and Bordogna (2011: 2289) conclude that trade unions have maintained their general levels of standing and influence 'far more effectively than [their] counterparts in the private sector', and argue that in many cases, the gap is in fact widening.

A significant feature of NPM rhetoric has been the focus on performance management at both the organizational and the individual levels, including the adoption of regular performance appraisals, performance-related pay, and promotion based on performance rather than tenure. Historically, the public sector has been characterized by lower pay levels than the private sector, but higher levels of job security, assured progression through regular salary increments and generous pension provision. However, studies have shown that the extent to which the move towards performance management has been achieved has been mixed. A study by Chiumento (2006) found that almost two-thirds of public sector workers felt their organization turned a blind eye to poor performance.

In 2005, the OECD found that almost all member countries had a performance management or performance appraisal system in place in their civil service, except Greece, Iceland, Japan, Luxembourg and Spain. They also found that over the previous five years, most countries had reformed their performance management and performance appraisal systems around targets and objectives. They also found that the real extent to which pay for performance had been adopted in member states was difficult to determine, but that there was some evidence of differentiated pay for performance in some countries, particularly those with a 'position-based' system. Countries such as Australia, Canada, Denmark, Finland, Italy, Korea, New Zealand, Sweden, Switzerland, the UK and the US placed relatively greater emphasis within the civil service on monetary incentives, whilst other countries, such as Austria, France, Poland and Portugal placed more emphasis on career promotion opportunities (OECD, 2005). Within the UK, Bach and Givan (2011) found that there has been substantial resistance to performance-related-pay (PRP), which has been introduced in a limited way in the civil service but is not widely adopted elsewhere. However, Bach et al. (2009) did find evidence that there has been increased adoption of performance-oriented HR practices such as appraisal and formal grievance processes more akin to those used in the private sector, and the Employers Organisation for Local Government (2004) found that 90 per cent of UK local authority staff received a regular performance appraisal.

Generally, it would seem that there has been some move towards the adoption of performance management approaches; however, Perkins and White (2010: 255) conclude: 'it is hard to detect serious management efforts to dramatically change the effort-reward bargain in public services'.

The current economic climate has caused attention to focus not only on the public sector pay bill, but also on pensions entitlements for public sector workers. Even in 2007, before the start of the crisis, the OECD noted that member countries were seeking to reduce public sector pensions and move from defined benefits to funded defined contribution schemes in order to help manage the rising cost of public sector employment. In 2010, the CIPD argued that the UK's public sector pension bill was untenable, and governments around the world have announced their intention to undertake fundamental reforms to their public sector pension arrangements. These developments suggest that we will witness an erosion of traditional public sector pension entitlements, alongside the other far-reaching changes that are being proposed to employment levels and pay and conditions.

THE ROLE OF THE HR DEPARTMENT

Another important consideration is the role played by the HR department itself. Research over the past three decades into HR departmental roles has distinguished between tasks that have a primarily strategic orientation, and those that are mainly concerned with administration (Marchington and Wilkinson, 2005; Caldwell, 2003; Ulrich, 1998). Several commentators have suggested that public sector HR professionals have historically lacked credibility to a greater degree than their private sector counterparts, and have also lacked power compared with other, more persuasive groups, making it more difficult for public sector HR professionals to 'act strategically' (Horton, 2003; Lupton and Shaw, 2001; Corby and Higham, 1996). Recent years have witnessed increasing calls for public sector HR departments to be 'more like' their private sector counterparts, and move towards a more strategically-oriented approach, in order to undertake the necessary changes to HRM processes and practices required to support NPM reforms.

However, this is problematic from several perspectives. First, although the prevailing view is that moving towards a more strategic role is highly desirable, the conclusion from much of the empirical literature is that most HR departments even within the private sector continue in any event to fulfil a largely administrative role (Lawler and Mohrman, 2003; Guest and King, 2004). Second, there is such a variety of different forms and functions for the HR department, that there is no one predominant model that could easily be adopted within the public sector (Harris, 2004; Truss et al., 2002). Third, studies have repeatedly highlighted the role conflict experienced by HR departments, torn as they often are between the competing demands of employers and line managers, the needs of employees, legal requirements and professional norms, creating an environment where strategizing becomes a highly contested activity (Caldwell, 2003; Legge, 1995).

A fourth important factor is that there are substantive contextual differences between the public and the private sectors that impact on HR's potential role (Truss, 2008). Public sector organizations have been shown to be more open to their environment, to be subject to higher levels of public scrutiny and monitoring, to have a broader range of stakeholders and a multiplicity of objectives and priorities compared with their private sector colleagues (Harris, 2004; Ring and Perry, 1985). Equally, HR departments in the public sector are generally subject to a greater degree of control over their activities than private sector firms, through processes such as target setting and centralized resource allocation. Thus, the degree of control and scope for strategizing that individual public sector organizations may have over their HR operations may be significantly limited compared with the private sector. Public sector values centred around fairness, openness, transparency, equity and equality also set parameters within which HR departments operate. In such a context, a traditional, top-down strategic orientation may be less appropriate or possible (Harris, 2002). This is rendered all the more pertinent as HR departments themselves experience significant cutbacks in the current rounds of public sector spending reviews, further curtailing their available resources.

One area that has attracted considerable interest from comparative HRM scholars has been the extent to which decision-making for HRM has been devolved or decentralized. The NPM literature has suggested that increasing levels of devolution of HRM away from central government is highly desirable if public sector organizations are to become more strategic, efficient and effective (Meyer and Hammerschmid, 2010). Centralized systems, whereby most HRM policy and strategy is determined by central government, on the other hand, arguably have the advantage of guaranteed neutrality, standardized approaches, and economies of scale, whilst also avoiding the risk of fragmentation and loss of a civil service ethos.

Studies have highlighted the range of national administrative traditions that prevail within Europe (Kickert, 2005; Pollitt and Bouckaert, 2004). Meyer and Hammerschmid (2010) distinguish between an Anglo-Saxon tradition (found in the UK, Ireland and Malta), a Continental European Rechtsstaat approach (found in Austria, Belgium, France and Germany), a Southern European approach (found in Cyprus, Greece and Italy), a Scandinavian model (Denmark, Estonia, Finland), and an Eastern European model (Bulgaria, the Czech Republic, Poland, Romania). Each of these models represents a very different way of organizing public services. Within the Anglo Saxon tradition, administration is guided by principles of public interest founded in common law, creating a climate where concepts such as decentralization and marketization can more readily gain a foothold (Wollmann, 2000). The Rechtsstaat approach, on the other hand, is more dominated by the Weberian bureaucratic model, whereby the State operates as a central integrating force within society. Scandinavian approaches are more consensual and have sophisticated systems of interest representation, whilst Southern European models have a history of unstable democratic political systems and authoritarian, formalized regimes. Eastern European models are differentiated due to legacy factors.

Considering 15 different areas of decision making, Meyer and Hammerschmid (2010) found that centralized approaches continue to predominate, although no one country was either fully centralized or fully decentralized. Overall, there were strong links between administrative traditions and the organization of HRM functions. Continental European, Southern European and Eastern European countries demonstrated significantly higher levels of centralization than the Anglo Saxon model. They conclude:

> While initiatives to decentralize HRM have been reported by most countries and seem to have a high symbolic appeal, the current picture of administrative practice throughout Europe – especially Continental, Eastern and Southern European countries – is still rather centralized, with limited autonomy or even involvement of line managers in decision making. Empirical studies suggesting a trend towards HR decentralization are often based on data from the United States (Meyer and Hammerschmid, 2010: 472).

It would therefore be premature to conclude that NPM has led to a clear trend towards the decentralization of HRM decision-making to individual organizations.

In 2005, the OECD conducted a survey of the role of HR departments within the civil service of member organizations. They uncovered three prevailing trends. First, they found evidence of a transfer of responsibility for HRM from central bodies to ministries and departments. Second, they found a trend towards the simplification of rules and procedures, with overarching policy set at the centre with operational aspects devolved to individual departments. Third, they found the development of more flexible HRM policies. Overall, they found that central government retained significant control over policy development and direction, particularly in the areas of the management of top civil servants, equal opportunities, health and safety, the determination of overarching approaches to being a 'good employer', and issues concerned with the code of conduct, disciplinary procedures and redundancies. Some countries, including the UK, Canada, New Zealand, Denmark, Finland, the Netherlands and Sweden devolved more HR responsibility to departments and units than others. The most common areas of devolution were recruitment, mobility, flexible working, job classification and pay. Some countries still determined pay centrally for their civil servants: including France, Greece, Hungary, Italy, Japan, Korea, the Netherlands, Portugal, the Slovak Republic and Spain.

The overall conclusion from this research into the role of the HR department at the macro level has been that decision-making around HRM practice still tends, in many countries, to be centrally-driven, rather than strategically determined at a local level, a tendency that runs counter to the ideals of NPM.

Some studies have also been undertaken at a more micro level, examining the role played by particular HR departments and HR professionals in a variety of public sector organizations. The rhetoric of NPM, in some countries at least, has exerted coercive pressure on HR functions to act more strategically (Massey and Pyper, 2005). Alongside this, HR professionals and senior managers themselves often express the wish to perform a more strategic role (Truss, 2008).

However, evidence at this level has also been equivocal as to the extent to which HR departments have actually become more strategic. Some have argued that there is no evidence of an increasingly strategic role (Selden, 2005; Teo and Crawford, 2005; Jaconelli and Sheffield, 2000; Boyne et al., 1999; Kessler, 2000). However, Kelly and Gennard (1996), in a study of HR directors in the UK Health Service, found that many were involved in strategic level work. Within case-study research in three sectors of the UK public services, some interesting differences have been highlighted which suggest that, despite similar contexts, the will to act strategically on the part of HR professionals could lead to very different outcomes (Truss et al., 2002; Truss, 2008).

Comparing and contrasting six matched-pair HR departments in the police, local authorities and hospitals, Truss (2008; 2009) found that different approaches to HRM were possible and that, within each pair, one organization emerged as having a much more strategic approach than the other. Although the implementation of central government initiatives and upstream initiatives within the organization did serve to circumscribe the extent of strategic choice open to the individual departments (Kessler et al., 2000), there was clearly also scope for innovation at a local level.

Research at both the macro and the organizational level on the role played by HR functions therefore suggests a complex picture of divergence and dissimilarity between countries, and between sectors. Di Maggio and Powell's (1983) new institutionalist framework suggests that, over time, organizations in similar contexts will tend towards similar solutions due to a combination of coercive, mimetic and normative isomorphism. Thus, you would expect public sector HR departments, situated as they are within a context that emphasizes NPM style solutions, to be converging over time towards a more strategic model.

However, research studies have shown that the situation is not so clear-cut. Alongside the NPM rhetoric, national models of public sector HR delivery need to be considered. As Meyer and Hammerschmid (2010) note, there are different models even within Europe that provide settings with varying degrees of receptiveness towards strategic HR functional approaches. Overlaid on this is the variation between different sectors even within the same country and, at a micro level, the degree of strategic choice and influence exercised by individual HR departments (Truss, 2009). Thus, through a process of negotiated evolution, HR departments can develop into different forms, despite similar settings (Truss, 2009).

CONCLUSIONS

Public sector organizations around the world are under pressure as never before to deliver an increasing range of exceptional public services with rapidly diminishing resources. HR departments, in turn, are being asked to manage large-scale change programs, including significant redundancies, alterations to workers' pay and conditions, and new ways of working, whilst at the same time managing headcount reductions and outsourcing of their own activities. These most recent demands represent the culmination of many years of pressure to reform public sector HRM in light of the NPM ethos that emerged during the 1980s, and was associated with the desire for public sector HRM to develop into a model more akin to that of the private sector.

However, as we have seen, the picture that has emerged is one full of complexities and ambiguities. It is difficult to talk of a single clear-cut 'traditional' public sector HRM model, just as there is little real agreement over the status and meaning of NPM, or indeed any single model of HRM prevalent in the private sector that the public sector could seek to adopt. The evidence from around the world, and even from within individual sectors in one country, is that HRM in the public sector exhibits substantial levels of variety, predicated upon a complex range of contextual, historical and structural factors. As Bach (2011: 16) concludes: 'the

traditional model of a uniform pattern of public service employment relations was never fully accurate and has been ebbing away for many years'.
Nevertheless, a number of important themes have emerged.

First, traditional approaches to HRM in the public sector exhibit some
fundamental commonalities, although the precise form and expression
of these will vary between countries. In particular, these include a special
employment status for some key public sector workers that means they are
managed under a different set of terms and conditions as compared with
private sector workers (and some other public sector workers). A second
feature is that public sector workers tend to be older than their private
sector counterparts due, to a large degree, to the fact that public sector
employees tend to stay with their employers for longer. A third feature is
that levels of unionization are higher in the public sector than the private,
and that unions tend to play a more significant role in the public sector in
particular in the area of pay determination (Bach and Bordogna, 2011).
The fourth feature is that the employment relationship within public
services in all countries is more closely regulated and controlled by the
State than is the case in the private sector. Finally, HRM approaches in
the public sector of most countries are underpinned by a set of values concerned with justice, fairness and equality (OECD, 2009).

Another theme that has emerged is that there are some fundamental
differences in approaches to managing people in the public sector across
various countries, notwithstanding the similarities outlined above. Whilst
some have differentiated between liberal market economies and coordinated market economies (Hall and Soskice, 2001), others have suggested
that the key difference is between the 'sovereign employer' and the 'model
employer' traditions (Bach and Kessler, 2007), or between those countries
adopting a 'position-based' as opposed to a 'career-based' system (OECD,
2005), or between 'NPM enthusiasts' and the rest (Bach and Bordogna,
2011). Each typology is helpful in disaggregating and explaining the substantial differences between the public sector HRM approaches evident
around the world. However, the appearance of different groups of countries within each of the various typologies means that no one typology
adequately captures the full extent of variability in approach to public
sector HR management around the world.

The third theme is that, due in large part to the complex heritage of
public sector management around the world, the reform trajectories witnessed under NPM, and indeed more recent reform initiatives arising from
the financial crisis, are being implemented and managed in different ways
in different countries, further contributing to the pattern of complexity
described above. Whether this is leading to the increasing convergence
of public sector HR management towards a private sector approach is

difficult to say. The overall conclusion of many researchers is that NPM style initiatives have been adopted in a piecemeal and ad hoc fashion in different countries, and that no one country has systematically implemented a set of strategic initiatives in order to move public sector HR management into line with a cohesive NPM model, should such a model exist. However, Bach (2011: 16) concludes that, in the case of the UK at least, the recent changes constitute a significant threat to the traditional public sector ethos.

Looking to the future, the current pressures to downsize the public sector and reduce pay and benefits, coupled with the growing trend towards fragmentation and the shifting boundaries of service delivery, create a climate of uncertainty and change for HR professionals. Approaches such as outsourcing and subcontracting are likely to become more prevalent, possibly leading to the kind of deteriorating employment conditions and rising levels of work intensification described by Rubery and Urwin (2011). The encouragement of 'Big Society' style initiatives in countries such as the UK, and the rising levels of involvement of third sector organizations in public service delivery will pose additional challenges, such as the status and management of a volunteer workforce, coupled with the growing involvement of large multinational firms in the delivery of public services (Bach, 2011).

REFERENCES

Achur, J. (2010), *Trade Union Membership 2009*, London: Dept for Business Innovation and Skills.

Bach, S. (2011), *A New Era of Public Service Employment Relations? The Challenges Ahead*, ACAS Discussion Paper, August.

Bach, S. and L. Bordogna (2011), 'Varieties of new public management or alternative models? The reform of public service employment relations in industrialized democracies', *International Journal of Human Resource Management*, **22** (11), 2281–94.

Bach, S. and R. Givan (2008), 'Public service modernisation and trade union reform: towards managerial led renewal', *Public Administration*, **86** (2), 1–17.

Bach, S. and R. Givan (2011), 'Varieties of New Public Management? The reform of public service employment relations in the UK and USA', *International Journal of Human Resource Management*, **22** (11), 2349–66.

Bach, S., R. Givan and J. Forth (2009), 'The public sector in transition', in W. Brown, A. Bryson, J. Forth and K. Whitfield (eds), *The Evolution of the Modern Workplace*, Cambridge: Cambridge University Press, pp. 307–331.

Bach, S. and I. Kessler (2007), 'Human resource management and the new public management', in P. Boxall, J. Purcell and P. Wright (eds), *The Oxford Handbook of Human Resource Management*, Oxford: Oxford University Press, pp. 469–88.

Boyne, G., G. Jenkins and M. Poole (1999), 'Human resource management in the public and private sectors: an empirical comparison', *Public Administration*, **77** (2), 407–20.

Brown, K. (2004), 'Human resource management in the public sector', *Public Management Review*, **6** (3), 303–9.

Caldwell, R. (2003), 'The changing roles of personnel managers: old ambiguities, new uncertainties', *Journal of Management Studies*, **40** (4), 983–1004.

Chiumento (2006), *Tough Love*, Research Report, Slough: Chiumento, accessed 5 October 2009 at http:\\www.chiumento.co.uk/Attachments/Tough per cent-0love_2006.pdf.

CIPD (2010), *Building Productive Public Sector Workplaces. Delivering More With Less: The People Management Challenge*, Wimbledon: CIPD.

Corby, S. and D. Higham (1996), 'Decentralisation of Pay in the NHS: diagnosis and prognosis', *Human Resource Management Journal*, **6** (1), 49–65.

Deloitte Public Sector Industry Group (2007), *Aging Snapshot: The Graying Government Workforce*, New York: Deloitte.

Di Maggio, P. and W. Powell (1983), 'The iron cage revisited: institutional isomorphism and collective rationality in organizational fields', *American Sociological Review*, **48**, 147–60.

Employers' Organisation for Local Government (2004), *People Skills Scorecard*, London: Employers' Organisation for Local Government.

Entwhistle, T., M. Marinetto and R. Ashworth (2007), 'Introduction: new labour, the new public management and changing forms of human resource management', *International Journal of Human Resource Management*, **18** (9), 1569–74.

Farnham, D. and S. Horton (1996), 'Managing public and private organisations', in D. Farnham and S. Horton (eds), *Managing the New Public Services*, London: Macmillan.

Golden, M. (2011), *The Nature, Implementation and Impact of Human Resource Practices in London Borough Councils*, Unpublished PhD Thesis, London: King's College.

Gould-Williams, J. (2004), 'The effects of "high commitment" HRM practices on employee attitude: the views of public sector workers', *Public Administration*, **82** (1), 63–81.

Guest, D. and Z. King (2004), 'Power, innovation and problem-solving: the Personnel Manager's three steps to heaven', *Journal of Management Studies*, **41**(3), 401–23.

Hales, C. (2002), 'Bureaucracy-lite and continuities in managerial work', *British Journal of Management*, **13**, 51–66.

Hall, P. and D. Soskice (2001), *Varieties of Capitalism: The Institutional Foundations of Comparative Advantage*, Oxford: Oxford University Press.

Harel, G. and S. Tzafrir (2001), 'HRM practices in the public and private sectors: differences and similarities', *Public Administration Quarterly*, Fall, 316–55.

Harris, L. (2002), 'The future for the HRM function in local government: everything has changed – but has anything changed?', *Strategic Change*, **11** (7), 369–78.

Harris, L. (2004), 'UK Public Sector Reform and the "Performance Agenda" in UK local government – HRM challenges and dilemmas', Paper to the HRM and Performance Conference, Bath University, April.

Hicks, S., A. Walling, D. Heap and D. Livesely (2005), *Public Sector Employment Trends*, London: ONS.

HM Treasury (2010), *Spending Review*, accessed August 2012 at http:\\www.hm-treasury.gov.uk/spend_index.htm.

Horton, S. (2003), 'Participation and involvement: the democratisation of new public management', *International Journal of Public Sector Management*, **16** (6), 403–11.

Jaconelli, A. and J. Sheffield (2000), 'Best value: changing roles and activities for human resource managers in Scottish local government', *International Journal of Public Sector Management*, **13** (7), 624–44.

Kelly, J. and Gennard, J. (1996), 'The role of personnel directors on the board of directors', *Personnel Review*, **25** (1), 7–24.

Kersley, B., C. Alpin, J. Forth, A. Bryson, H. Bewley, G. Dix and S. Oxenbridge (2006), *Inside the Workplace: Findings from the 2004 Workplace Employment Relations Survey*, Oxford: Routledge.

Kessler, I., J. Purcell and J. Coyle Shapiro (2000), 'New forms of employment relations in the public services: the limits of strategic choice', *Industrial Relations Journal*, **31** (1), 17–34.

Kickert, W. (2005), 'Distinctiveness in the study of public management in Europe. A historical-institutional analysis of France, Germany and Italy', *Public Management Review*, **7** (4), 537–63.

Lawler, E. and S. Mohrman (2003), 'HR as strategic partner: what does it take to make it happen?', *Human Resource Planning*, **26** (3), 15–30.

Legge, K. (1995), *Human Resource Management: Rhetorics and Realities*, Basingstoke: MacMillan.

Local Government Employers and Local Government Association (LGA) (2009), 'Local Government Workforce, Demographic Profile', UK.

Lupton, B. and S. Shaw (2001), 'Are public sector personnel managers the profession's poor relations?', *Human Resource Management Journal*, **11** (3), 23–38.

Marchington, M. and A. Wilkinson (2005), *Human Resource Management at Work*, CIPD: London.

Massey, A. and R. Pyper (2005), *Public Management and Modernisation in Britain*, Basingstoke: Palgrave MacMillan.

Meyer, R. and G. Hammerschmid (2010), 'The degree of decentralization and individual decision making in central government human resource management: a European comparative perspective', *Public Administration*, **88** (2), 455–78.

Millard, B. (2007), 'Regional analysis of public sector employment', *Economic and Labour Market Review*, **1** (3), 33–9.

Millard, B. and A. Machin (2007), 'Characteristics of public sector workers', *Economic and Labour Market Review*, **1** (5), 46–55.

Morgan, P. and N. Allington (2002), 'Has the public sector retained its model employer status?', *Public Money and Management*, January-March, 35–42.

Morris, J. and C. Farrell (2007), 'The post-bureaucratic public sector organization. New organizational forms and HRM in 10 public sector organizations', *International Journal of Human Resource Management*, **18** (9), 1575–88.

OECD (2004), *Trends in Human Resources Management Policies in OECD Countries: An Analysis of the Results of the OECD Survey on Strategic Human Resources Management*, Paris: OECD.

OECD (2005), *HRM Working Party Report*, Paris: OECD.

OECD (2007), *Ageing and the Public Service: Human Resource Challenges*, Paris: OECD.

OECD (2008), *The State of the Public Service*, Paris: OECD.

OECD (2009), *Fostering Diversity in the Public Service. Public Employment and Management Working Party Report*, Paris: OECD.

Office for National Statistics (2010), *Labour Force Survey*, London: HMSO.

Perkins, S. and G. White (2010), 'Modernising Pay in the UK public services: trends and implications', *Human Resource Management Journal*, **20** (3), 258–76.

Pichault, F. (2007), 'HRM-based reforms in public organisations: problems and perspectives', *Human Resource Management Journal*, **17** (3), 265–82.

Pollitt, C. and G. Bouckaert (2004), *Public Management Reform*, Oxford: Oxford University Press.

Prowse, P. and J. Prowse (2007), 'Is there still a Public sector model of employment relations in the United Kingdom?', *International Journal of Public Sector Management*, **20** (1), 48–62.

Ring, P. and J. Perry (1985), 'Strategic management in public and private organizations: implications of distinctive contexts and constraints', *Academy of Management Review*, **10** (2), 276–86.

Roper, I., P. Higgins and P. James (2007), 'Shaping the bargaining agenda: the Audit Commission and public sector reform in British local government', *International Journal of Human Resource Management*, **18** (9), 1589–1607.

Rubery, J. and P. Urwin (2011), 'Bringing the employer back in: why social care needs a standard employment relationship', *Human Resource Management Journal*, **21** (2), 122–37.

Selden, S. (2005), 'Human resource management in American counties, 2002', *Public Personnel Management*, **34** (1), 59–84.

Soni, V. (2004), 'From crisis to opportunity: human resource challenges for the public sector in the twenty first century', *Review of Policy Research*, **21** (2), 157–78.

Teo, S. and J. Crawford (2005), 'Indicators of strategic HRM effectiveness: a case study of an Australian public sector agency during commercialization', *Public Personnel Management*, **34** (1), 1–16.

Truss, C. (2008), 'Continuity and change: the role of the HR department in the modern public sector', *Public Administration*, **86** (4), 1071–88.

Truss, C. (2009), 'Changing HR functional forms in the UK public sector', *International Journal of Human Resource Management*, **20** (4), 717–37.

Truss, C., L. Gratton, V. Hope-Hailey, P. Stiles and J. Zaleska (2002), 'Paying the piper: choice and constraint in changing HR functional roles', *Human Resource Management Journal*, **12** (2), 39–63.

Ulrich, D. (1998), 'A new mandate for human resources', *Harvard Business Review*, **76** (1), 124–34.

US Bureau of Labor Statistics (2009), *Union Affiliation of Employed Wage and Salary Workers by Occupation and Industry*, US.

Wollmann, H. (2000), 'Comparing institutional development in Britain and Germany: (persistent) divergence or (progressing) convergence?', in H. Wollmann and E. Schroeter (eds), *Comparing Public Sector Reform in Britain and Germany*, Aldershot: Ashgate, pp. 1–26.

3. Human resource management in the public sector in developing countries

Christopher J. Rees

INTRODUCTION

In this chapter, we consider aspects of the nature of human resource management (HRM) specifically in the public sector of developing countries. In relatively recent years, writings in the field of HRM have adopted a more international perspective in recognition of, for example, emerging global economic trends and the increasingly influential nature of multinational companies (MNCs) and agencies such as international non-governmental organizations (INGOs) (Almond, 2011; Jackson, 2009). Yet this international focus has tended to be fixed upon Western industrialized societies, as Budhwar and Debrah (2005: 259) succinctly state: in relative terms, '. . . very little work on HRM research in developing countries has been done'. The relative lack of research on HRM in the public sector in developing countries is even more apparent.

In introducing this chapter, it is highlighted that, at the level of functionality, key HRM-related tasks in developing countries are likely to mirror the functional tasks undertaken by HRM professionals operating in developed countries (Punnett, 2012). That is, just as large privately-owned technologically advanced organizations operating out of the heart of mainland Europe or North America are required to devise and implement HRM policies which provide a workforce capable of achieving organizational objectives, so too do public sector organizations based in developing countries in, say, sub-Saharan Africa. The objectives, stakeholders, and values of these different types of organizations are likely to be radically different as are the challenges and constraints to which they are exposed; however, organizations based in developing and developed countries are likely, over a period of time, to engage in broadly similar functional HRM activities such as recruitment and selection, training and development, performance management, health and safety management, and workforce restructuring. This point is exemplified by a study of HRM practices in organizations in Nigeria which found that, in the context of this developing country, HRM practices such as: '. . . recruitment and selection, training and development, performance appraisal, monitoring/evaluation of HRM practices, compensation and benefits and termination/layoff', were all in place, as were additional human resource activities including 'welfare services, union/labor relations and health and safety issues' (Okpara and Wyn, 2008: 70). While these core HRM activities may mirror the types of activities carried out by organizations in developed countries such as the USA and the UK, Okpara and Wyn (2008) found that, in the case of Nigeria, HRM practitioners were facing context-specific challenges linked to tribalism, AIDS, government regulation, and corruption.

Recognizing the similarities that are likely to exist between core HRM activities in both developed and developing countries, the primary focus of this chapter has not been placed upon functional HRM activities undertaken in developing countries. Rather, within the parameters of this book, the main aim of the chapter is to consider ways in which national policies can exert a major influence on the nature of HRM which is practiced at the local level in public sector organizations in developing countries. This aim is in accord with the position of Budhwar and Debrah (2001) who state that the influence of national factors is a key issue which needs to be addressed in relation to the development of the theory and practice of HRM in developing countries.

The chapter is structured as follows. First, the phrase 'developing countries' is examined and clarified with reference to the manner in which it has been used in various literature. The discussion then centers on two examples of quite different national policies which have influenced HRM in the public sector of many developing countries. These policies are: (1) decentralization; and (2) nationalization (or localization). The rationale for the choice of these policies is that, as a result of their widespread adoption across developing countries, they exemplify how national policy can, in many different ways, affect HRM and hence offer insights into HRM theory and practice in the public sector of developing countries. The chapter is concluded with a general discussion of the main themes which emerge from the analysis.

THE TERM 'DEVELOPING COUNTRY'

The classification of countries in terms of the extent to which they are developed is a time-honored yet problematic activity (Sandford and Sandhu, 2003). In areas such as international development, country-based classification systems play an important role in the prioritization of need and the targeting of international aid. Yet there is neither a universally accepted system for ranking countries on a scale of development nor agreement as to the measures that should be used to score countries on such as scale. For example, potential measures of development are diverse and may include economic indicators such as gross domestic product (GDP) and gross national income (GNI) per capita, health indicators such as life expectancy at birth, and educational indicators such as mean years of schooling. One specific set of development indicators has been provided by the United Nations in the form of their millennium development goals (MDGs). These goals, designed to promote social and economic development in relatively poor countries, are accompanied by a set of wide-ranging development targets in areas such as employment rates, hunger, gender equality, child mortality, primary education, maternal health, environmental sustainability and combating disease (United Nations, 2001). It is notable, however, that the nature of these development indicators and the extent to which they can be measured have both been called into question (Attaran, 2005).

In serving to compound definitional issues, terms such as 'third world', 'underdeveloped', 'transitional', 'emerging', 'less developed' and 'low human development' have all been applied to countries which, against one or more measures, compare relatively unfavorably to other countries. Arguably, the plethora of these types of terms, some of which are used synonymously, only adds to the confusion in this area. Hence, from the outset of this discussion on HRM in the public sector in developing countries, it must be highlighted that the term 'developing country' is wide-ranging and problematic. Not only is there no universally accepted theoretical or operational definition of what constitutes a developing country but, also, the very the use of this term has been criticized by some for implying '. . . the inferiority of a "developing country" compared to a "developed country"' (White, Smith and Currie, 2011: 2). Nevertheless, while ultimately dependent upon the measures selected to determine the extent of a country's development, it is difficult to dispute that some countries are more developed than other countries and, further, that a country may score relatively highly on one measure of development but score relatively badly on another measure.

Despite the problematic nature of the term 'developing country', international organizations and agencies such as the World Bank and the United Nations Development Programme (UNDP) have found it necessary to classify countries in terms of their development relative to other countries (UNDP, 2011). Thus, the World Bank states that the term developing economies 'has been used to denote the set of low and middle income economies' though immediately provides the caveat that the term 'developing economies does not imply either that all the economies belonging to the group are actually in the process of developing, nor that those not in the group have necessarily reached some preferred or final stage of development' (World Bank, 2012).

The International Monetary Fund's classification system divides the world's economies into two major groups, that is, advanced economies and emerging/developing economies (IMF, 2011). The IMF (2011: 169) openly acknowledges that: 'This classification is not based on strict criteria, economic or otherwise, and it has evolved over time'. Nevertheless, the classification does provide a useful indication of the relative development of nearly all countries of the world. It identifies 34 advanced economies including the Group of Seven (G7), that is, United States of America, Japan, Germany, France, Italy, the United Kingdom and Canada. Further, a total of 150 economies are classified as emerging and developing; these are drawn from regions including Central and Eastern Europe, the Commonwealth of Independent States (including Russia), developing Asia (including India and China but excluding the 'Hong Kong Special Administrative Region' and 'Taiwan Province of China'), Latin America and the Caribbean (including Brazil and Mexico), the Middle East and North Africa, and Sub-Saharan Africa.

When examining the list of countries which are classified by bodies such as the IMF as 'developing', it quickly becomes apparent that these countries vary widely in terms of factors such as geographical location, population statistics, economics, language, religion and culture. For example, although both are classified as 'developing', the commonalities shared between the Kingdom of Saudi Arabia and Zambia are not altogether obvious. This observation serves to: (1) emphasize the difficulty of conducting cross-continental research into HRM in developing countries; and (2) explain, in part at least, the rationale for literature on this subject that is focused on either specific countries such as China (Cooke, 2012) and India (Budhwar and Bhatnagar, 2009) or regions such as Latin America (see Davila and Elvira, 2009); the Middle East (see Budhwar and Mellahi, 2006; Metcalfe and Mimouni, 2012), and Africa (Kamoche et al., 2004). Thus, while one may concur with the lament of Budhwar and Debrah (2005: 260) that: 'apart from a few single-country journal articles and the work of a few researchers ... relatively little has been written about HRM in developing nations', the challenges facing researchers who are seeking to undertake cross-continental comparative research in developing countries should not be underestimated. Aside from the fact that developing countries are, at times, associated with uncertainty, unpredictability and danger (Jackson, 2002a: 220), the sheer range and variability of factors associated with a category labeled as 'developing countries' pose major obstacles for researchers, especially those seeking to undertake cross-national and cross-continental research projects (Jackson, 2002b). It is therefore seen by many to be apposite to research in-country, or more questionably, regional and case-study units in order to understand and advance HRM practices within and across developing countries.

GLOBALIZATION AND HRM IN DEVELOPING COUNTRIES

This discussion on HRM in the public sector in developing countries recognizes that, by their very nature, global economic and employment trends inevitably exert an impact on organizations in developing as well as developed countries. As a result, globalization has emerged as a ubiquitous focus of attention in international HRM research. Attempts have been made in international HRM literature, to clarify the nature of globalization and identify, in general terms, the main challenges faced by global HRM functions as a result of globalization processes. For example, Sparrow, Brewster and Harris (2004: 17) citing Brawley (2003) posit that globalization from an economic perspective is seen mainly as a process whereby markets and production in different countries become increasingly interdependent. This process leads to the movement of factors of production across national borders, the integration of financial markets, and '. . . the creation of a global market based on high levels of cross-border flows of labor, migration, trade, communication, transport of goods and other items'. It is argued by these authors that the corollaries of globalization, in turn, present specific challenges for global HR functions operating in and out of many different countries around the world. Sparrow et al. (2004: 12) state that globalization presents a challenge to the global HR function to: provide insights into the organization development during the rapid startup of international operations; learn how to use formal and informal global HR networks; and how to manage situations where the ideas of one group of HR professionals are being overridden by those of others originating from other countries and business systems. What is emphasized here is that the process of globalization impacts upon HR functions in countries around the world to create a series of challenges that need to be faced by HR professionals. Clearly, this is intended to be a broad-brush approach for the precise impact of globalization on HR functions on specific organizations is likely to vary tremendously depending upon factors such as the sector and size of an organization, its products and services, its trading partners, and the locations out of which it operates. Nevertheless, globalization is seen to impact both directly and indirectly upon HR functions in both developed and developing countries.

Although these challenges of globalization are well documented, the discourses of both international HRM and the closely aligned discourse of international human resource development (HRD) have tended to eschew the public sector. Indicative evidence for this statement can be found in both the chapter headings and the indexes of well-reputed textbooks in the field of international HRM (see Jackson, 2002a; Harzing and Pinnington, 2011; Scullion and Collings, 2006; Scullion and Linehan, 2005). It is noteworthy, however, that international developments in public sector administration have attracted attention in wider literature on subjects such as public administration and economics. For example, writing in the *International Journal of Public Sector Management*, Common (2011: 421) explores international developments in public administration in post-soviet states which have targeted bureaucratic structures. He notes that, through the application of HRM techniques and methods developed in private settings, there have been attempts across the globe to '. . . provide and encourage greater flexibility and discretion to officials in the management of human resources'. Similarly, Poór et al. (2009; 202), writing in *Acta Oeconomica*, draw international comparisons between HRM practiced in private and public sector organizations: they conclude that, in relation to ex-socialist countries in Eastern Europe:

> . . . time has come for human resource management to become much more conscious . In the future the public sector can handle domestic, European Union and global challenges only if it adopts and establishes modern management structures and improves in this field.

The focus of the current discussion is centered upon HRM in the public sector in developing countries. Given this parameter and the perceived neglect of the public sector in international HRM literature, it is argued that comparative and national outlooks on HRM are likely to be more relevant than global outlooks which tend to be slanted heavily towards Anglo-American accounts and the operations of MNCs. In contrast, comparative HRM&D and national HRM&D are broad terms that concern processes which address the formulation and practice of HRM systems, practices and policies at the organizational and societal levels (Metcalfe and Rees, 2005: 455). They can incorporate comparative analyses of HRM approaches across nations and also addresses how societies develop national HRM policies (see Figure 3.1).

The extent to which comparative and national analyses apply specifically to HRM in the public sector in developing countries becomes more apparent when the precise nature of public sector HRM is considered. When discussing HRM in public sector organizations in Latin America

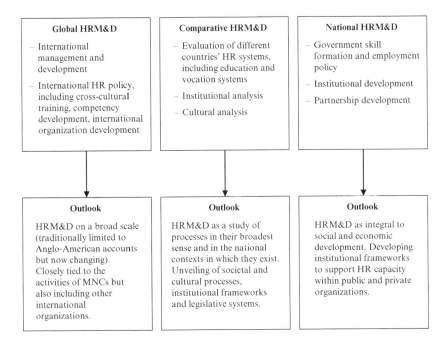

Source: adapted from Metcalfe and Rees (2005).

Figure 3.1 Mapping the boundaries of HRM&D

and the Caribbean, Klingner and Pallavicini (2002: 362) helpfully define 'public HRM' as follows:

> Public HRM is the: (1) functions needed to manage human resources in public agencies, (2) process by which scarce public jobs are allocated, (3) seven symbiotic and competing values (political responsiveness, efficiency, individual rights, and social equity under the traditional pro-government model; and individual accountability, downsizing and decentralization, and community responsibility under the emergent anti-government model) over how public jobs should be allocated, and (4) personnel systems (the laws, rules, and regulations) used to express these abstract values.

This is a wide-ranging definition which the authors themselves recognize merits further explanation for, while key HRM functions such as recruitment and selection are commonly undertaken across the full range of public sector organizations across the world, within sector differences in approaches to HRM are likely to emerge when comparisons are drawn between HRM policies and practices in developed and developing countries. This position is implied in the authors' definition of 'public HRM' which places a heavy emphasis on factors such as political responsiveness, individual rights, and social equity. Reference to the descriptions and definitions of developing countries discussed above leads one to conclude that there are likely to be stark cross-national differences between both the interpretation of these values and their application through HRM policies and systems. Thus, these authors state that:

> the development of administrative systems in general (and public personnel systems in particular) in less developed countries tends to evolve along a single track toward the model of increased rationality and transparency valued by international lenders as indicators of effective government and economic development. With respect to public HRM systems, this generally involves a sequential transition from statehood to patronage, from patronage to civil service, and from civil service to a range of alternative personnel systems. Development is a complex process affected more by economic, political and social conditions within each country, and their impact on civic culture, government and public administration (Klingner and Pallavicini-Campos, 2002: 362).

Nevertheless, despite pressure from international lenders and donors to introduce public sector reform, the political, social, economic, educational, health and environmental problems which often exist simultaneously in developing countries inevitably result in the inadequate delivery of public services. More specifically, public sector organizations in developing countries are likely to lack the human capacity to deliver essential services and these inadequacies emerge in HRM policies and practices. At a general level, Tessemam and Soeters (2006: 88) summarize HRM in the public sector in developing countries as follows:

> ... low salary levels, lack of effective performance standards, inability to fire people, too few rewards for good performance, recruitment procedures that do not attract appropriately trained people, promotion patterns based too much on seniority or patronage and too little on performance, slow promotion and lack of reward for hard work and initiative, inadequate and demoralizing management by supervisors (ineffective leadership), underemployment and lack of stimulating assignments.

This stark summary highlights the critical importance of designing effective HRM policies and practices when attempting to improve service delivery, reform public sector organizations, and ultimately contribute to the overall development of a country. Further, it raises questions as to whether centrally-driven public sector reform policies can radically change HRM practices at the local level, given the pressure exerted by the host of culturally-based norms and customs which exist in villages, towns, districts, cities, and provinces across the developing world.

Budhwar and Debrah's (2001) leading work on HRM in developing countries emphasizes the importance of national (as opposed to global) factors when considering HRM in developing countries. For example, their analytical framework of HRM in developing countries refers to four factors (that is, national culture, national institutions, the dynamic business environment and industrial sector) that are central to HRM practices in developing countries. As a result of the interaction between these factors, they assert that the nature of HRM in developing countries: '. . . tends to be "context-specific" and as such there is considerable diversity in the way "culture bound" and "culture-free" factors impact on, and determine the nature of HRM systems in different countries' (Budhwar and Debrah, 2001: 239). Unfortunately, not only is there a relative dearth of studies in international HRM literature which have examined the impact of national policies in developing countries on local HRM policies and practice in public sector organizations, there are also few studies which have explored, in comparative terms, the design and implementation of national policies in relation to the practice of HRM in developing countries. The reason for this lack of research may be attributable to some of the factors identified above including the lack of cultural similarity between many of the countries labeled as 'developing'. Nevertheless, although there are few obvious commonalities shared between the 150 economies which the IMF (2011) classify as 'emerging and developing', an analysis of broader literature in areas such as economics, international management, and international development, provides some evidence that certain trends and influences which impact upon HRM in the public sector can be found across a wide range of these countries. For example, structural readjustment, public sector reform, privatization, good governance, regulation and competition, are overlapping strategies which have, albeit in different forms, been applied in many developing countries in different regions of the world.

It is within the scope of this chapter to identify two examples of these nationally-driven trends and initiatives in order to more fully consider their potential impact at the local level. Thus, subsequent sections of this chapter will highlight and explore, from comparative and national perspectives, two public policy interventions and their potential influence on HRM in the public sector of a range of developing countries. These interventions are: (1) decentralization; and (2) nationalization (or localization). As indicated above, the choice of these interventions is intended to be indicative of the potential impact, at the local level, of national policy on HRM in the public sector of developing countries rather than representing a summative overview of relevant national policies which have affected HRM practices in developing countries.

DECENTRALIZATION

Decentralization has become a dominant theme of New Public Management (NPM); in the words of Faguet (2004), it has become 'one of the broadest movements, and most debated policy issues, in the world of development' even though its precise nature tends to vary according to the context in which it is practiced (Dawson and Dargie, 1999). In their review of decentralization in developing countries Rees and Hossain (2010: 582) state that:

> decentralization programs were rolled out across countries in Africa, Asia and Latin America ... Given the diversity of the governments, agencies and academics connected in one way or another to decentralization, the degree of this consensus was quite remarkable.

The proliferation of decentralization programs in the public sector in developing countries is evident when one refers to development management and public administration literature where decentralization has been discussed and promoted by its advocates. These advocates, including the World Bank (1981) and United Nations (1962) saw decentralization as a means by which the highly '... centralized, bureaucratic, hierarchical, organizational strategy dominant since independence in Third World administration' (Wunsch, 1991: 431) could be adapted by the devolution of authority and resources from centralized authorities to local units.

The potential scope of decentralization is wide-ranging. For example, Polidano and Hulme (1999: 125–126) distinguish between 'management decentralization' and what they term 'political decentralization' which, they argue, was heavily associated with democratization in Latin America and Africa in the 1990s and, further, in their words, 'falls outside' NPM. In terms of standard usage, however, decentralization in developing countries involves empowering local public sector entities and their managers with the authority to exert greater managerial control over decision-making and resources than in more centralized systems of governance. Dawson and Dargie (1999: 463) argue that decentralization approaches draw from a conceptual framework which encompasses public choice, rational choice, and new institutional economics. Further, there are numerous research studies which, taken together as a body of evidence, reveal the extent to which policymakers have adopted this conceptual framework in the form of decentralization. Decentralization as a nationally determined policy has been widely implemented, albeit in various forms and to various degrees, across the developing regions of the world as classified by the IMF (2011), that is, in Asia (for example, see Bagchi, 2003; Green, 2005; Qiao et al., 2008), the C.E.E. (for example, see, Meyer and Hammerschmid, 2010; Rees, Järvalt and Metcalfe, 2005), the C.I.S, (for example, see Barisitz, 2008; Freinkman, 2009; Latin America and the Caribbean (for example, see Bonet, 2006) the Middle East and North Africa (for example, see OECD, 2010) and Sub-Saharan Africa (for example, see Antwi and Analoui, 2008).

When discussing types of decentralization in developing countries, Rees and Hossain (2010) draw on the influential work on Rondinelli and Nellis (1986: 6–10). Rondinelli and Nellis identified major types of decentralization, including deconcentration, delegation, and devolution. Deconcentration mainly involves shifting some authority or responsibility from centrally located offices and staff to, for example, local administrative units outside of the national capital. Delegation mainly involves 'the transfer of managerial responsibility for specifically defined functions to organizations outside the regular bureaucratic structure' though ultimate responsibility is retained by the central authority. Devolution involves the creation or strengthening of local units of government which can, to a large extent, operate outside of the direct control of the central authority. Privatization involves governments transferring some of their responsibilities to private organizations and/or voluntary organizations. In later work, The World Bank (2003) summarized these three types of decentralization with reference to their political, fiscal, and administrative features (see Table 3.1).

The extent to which decentralization initiatives involve HRM considerations is apparent from the contents of Table 3.1. Decentralization policies in the public sector directly involve issues such as; the role of the HRM function at local level and its relationship with central HRM function, equity and compensation, the development of performance management systems at the local level, management development at the local level, competition for human resources between public sector bodies, skills shortages, recruitment and selection (for example, the establishment of local selection boards to replace national selection centers), redundancy programs, the revision of reorganizational structures including job descriptions and reporting relationships with central authorities, developing and maintaining HRM information systems, and extending the remit of relationships with trade unions at the local level. This centrality of HRM to decentralization initiatives is recognized by The World Bank (2003: 190) when summarizing the complexity of this area:

Table 3.1   Key political, fiscal, and administrative features of decentralization and the accountability for service delivery

Degree of decentralization	Political features	Fiscal features	Administrative features
Deconcentration (minimal change)	– No elected local government – Local leadership vested in local officials such as a governor or mayor, but appointed and accountable to the center – Voice relationships are remote and possibly weak	– Local government is a service delivery arm of the center and has little or no discretion over how or where services are provided – Funds come from the center through individual central ministry of department budgets – No independent revenue sources	– Provider staff working at local level are employees of center and accountable to center, usually through their ministries; weak local capacity is compensated for by central employees – Accountability remains distant
Delegation (intermediate change)	– Local government may be led by locally elected politicians, but is still accountable, fully or partially, to the center – Voice relationships are more local and proximate but can be overruled by the center	– Spending priorities are set centrally, as well as program norms and standards; local government has some management authority over allocation of resources – Funding is provided by the center through transfers – No independent revenue sources	– Providers could be employees of central or local government, but pay and employment conditions are typically set by the center – Local government has some authority over hiring and location of staff, but is less likely to have authority over firing – Both long and short routes of accountability are potentially stronger

Table 3.1   (continued)

Degree of decentrali-zation	Political features	Fiscal features	Administrative features
Devolution (substantial change)	– Local government is led by locally elected politicians expected to be accountable to the local electorate – Voice relationships can be very strong, but also subject to capture by elites, social polarization, uninformed voting, and clientelism	– Subject to meeting nationally set minimum standards, local government can set spending priorities and determine how best to meet service obligations – Funding can come from local revenues, revenue-sharing arrangement and transfers from center – A hard budget constraint is imperative for creating incentives for accountable service delivery	– Providers are employees of local government – Local government has full discretion over salary levels, staffing numbers and allocation, and authority to hire and fire – Standards and procedures for hiring and managing staff may still be established within an overarching civil service framework – Potentially the strongest long and short routes of accountability

Source: abridged from World Bank (2003: 189).

The twin tasks of devolving administration and building local capacity can be daunting even under ideal conditions of budget and stakeholder support ... National pay scales, rigid collective bargaining agreements, and disagreements with national labor unions can severely circumscribe the flexibility that subnational governments have in rationalizing employment, as seen in many Asian, African, and Latin American countries ... At the same time, administrative devolution needs to strike a balance between autonomy and uniformity to allow for desirable features such as interjurisdictional mobility for highly skilled staff in short supply (World Bank, 2003: 190-191).

Similarly, Antwi and Analoui (2008: 601) state that good local governance and the effective delivery of public service by means of decentralization is contingent upon the: '... institutional, technical and human resource development capacity arrangements governing its implementation'.

Studies of decentralization in public sector organizations in developing countries confirm the complexity of HRM-related problems resulting from nationally-driven decentralization policies. For example, at sector level, Dieleman, Gerretsen and van der Wilt (2009: 5) explored primary research studies of HRM interventions in relation to health workers' performance in low and middle income countries. They note that 'hardly any attention' has been paid to the question of how the decentralization might bring about positive outcomes for HRM functions and in which contexts; though they conclude that two studies conducted in China (Liu et al., 2006) and Mozambique (Saide and Stewart, 2001) suggest that decentralization could have a positive impact on HRM functions but required complementary interventions: 'such as management training, changes in bureaucratic procedures, and appropriate preparation in structures and staffing' to counter negative influences, for example, political interference in the transfer of workers, and nepotism in activities such as recruitment and selection.

In another study, Pallangyo and Rees (2010) examined, in detail, the impact of decentralization on HRM activities in local government authorities (LGAs) in Tanzania using a case study analysis. They found some positive impacts on HRM at the local level as a result of decentralization. For example, the nationally devised decentralization policy for LGAs brought with it, new organization structures, strategic plans, and the increased involvement of employees in decision-making and cultural change initiatives at the local level. Unfortunately, public sector officials working at the local level encountered major HRM problems when attempting to implement decentralization within their organizations. For example, the study found that LGAs were making unsuitably qualified employees redundant but subsequently were failing to fill these vacancies due to local shortages of skilled labor. These LGAs were then forced to contract, at additional cost, human resource capacity from ministries, universities, and private consultancies. Other HRM-related problems which emerged involved political interference from the national level, local customs which encouraged employees to take part-time jobs to supplement full-time positions in the LGAs, the 'poaching' of staff from one LGA to another, and community pressure exerted via councilors to bend bylaws and employment procedures. One of the main themes that emerged from this study was the extreme extent to which the specific contexts in which HRM was practiced varied even though the study was limited to one type of public sector organization (LGAs) in one developing country (Tanzania).

From the discussion above, it can be seen that decisions taken at a national level to implement decentralization policies, not only rely on effective HRM but also exert a profound impact on HRM practices in public sector organizations. As Kim (2008: ii) states, 'Decentralization itself does not render increased government effectiveness in public service provision. Instead, the effectiveness of government largely depends on the quality of human capital and institutions'. As such, HRM should be seen as an essential component in the design of decentralization rather than a separate, stand-alone process (Green, 2005: 129). Yet in many instances: '. . . decentralization has proceeded without explicit staffing strategies and a central civil service typically coexists with subnational and local government' (World Bank, 2003: 190).

NATIONALIZATION

The nationally-driven decentralization policies discussed above involve attempts to empower decision-makers operating at the local level in public sector organizations across the developing world. It has been argued that decentralization policies have a profound effect on the practice of HRM in the public sector in development countries. At this juncture, attention is drawn to another set of national policies which have also exerted a major influence on day-to-day HRM in the public sector of many of these developing countries. Variously labeled using terms such as nationalization (of labor as opposed to industries), localization and indigenization, these policies, which are primarily designed to ensure that workers from indigenous populations are not overlooked, if not actively favored, in matters of employment, have been widely and formally implemented in developing countries for over 50 years. It is stressed that these nationalization policies go beyond strategic attempts by MNCs, in countries such as China and Thailand, to employ local workers because MNCs consider them to have better knowledge and understanding of the local culture and people when compared to expatriate workers (Kaosa-ard, 1991; Law, Wong and Wang, 2004). It is also highlighted that nationalization policies contrast with the decentralization policies discussed above; nationalization policies represent a form of centralization as a result of which organizations in both the private and public sectors in developing countries face nationally formulated directives, restrictions, and sanctions, in relation to the types of workers them employ.

Nationally-driven nationalization policies seek to address specific issues connected to the employment of members of a country's indigenous population. In the case of the continent of Africa, this issue is mainly discussed in relation to colonialism; thus, nationalization policies, commonly referred to as 'Africanization', while taking a variety of different forms, have sought to transform public sector institutions, which had been constructed, led and owned by foreigners, into entities which are pre-dominately led and managed by indigenous people (however defined) in accordance with their more traditional cultural heritage (Marsden, 1991; Morris-Jones and Fischer, 1980). In addition to the objectives of achieving political independence, economic advantages and the conservation of foreign exchange, Africanization policies, had, at their heart, the desire to manage one's own affairs (Cunningham, Lynham and Weatherly, 2006; Robinson, 1990). Thus, writing about Africanization in Kenya, Sian (2007: 840) states:

> The aim of the Africanisation policy was to deconstruct the social barriers, to reverse the underdevelopment of the colonial era and to transfer economic power into the hands of Africa . . . there were moral, political, social and economic underlying justifications for such a programme . . . was a part of the greater drive for self-determination, a declaration of intent to break free from the shackles of colonialism and to show that Africans were capable of managing their own affairs.

Outside of Africa, nationalization strategies have also been adopted by countries in order to enhance the labor market in favor of the indigenous population. For example, in Asia, Malaysia implemented a system of visas and work permits to discourage the employment of foreign workers. Ruppert (1999: 12) states that, in conjunction with these strict immigration rules, policymakers in Malaysia:

> introduced several nationalization measures in an effort to encourage firms to hire Malaysian citizens instead of foreign workers. Under the Seventh Malaysia Plan (1996-2000), labor market policies focus on promoting local (i.e. Malaysian) workers through flexible work arrangements and the re employment of qualified retirees. Additional measures include incentives to increase labor mobility toward areas with excess labor demand by providing transportation, for example, and to encourage the replacement and repatriation of expatriate workers.

In other regions, such as the Middle East, governments have designed nationalization policies in a concerted attempt to control employment and immigration and, in effect, to favor indigenous workers through positive action employment programs. Unlike the context of Africa, where nationalization policies are seen to counter the history of colonial rule and its dominance of the majority, governments in the Middle East introduced nationalization policies partly as a response to increasing levels of anxiety about the scale of reliance on foreign workers. For example, indigenous workers in countries such as the United Arab Emirates have become heavily outnumbered by expatriates in the workforce (Forstenlechner,

2010). As a result, nationalization is now a widespread and influential aspect of employment policy in the Middle East. Various countries in the region have developed their own styles of nationalization and named these policies accordingly, for example, Bahrainization, Emiratization, Omanization, and Saudization (Rees, Mamman and Bin-Braik, 2007). These nationalization policies, which are enacted through mechanisms such as legislation, quotas for the employment of nationals, record-keeping and enforcing agencies, have no obvious parallels in more developed countries such as the USA, the UK and France. In the Middle East, nationalization policies apply to both the private and public sectors though their impact on the private sector is more obvious. This is because members of the indigenous workforce generally prefer to work in public sector organizations due to the relatively favorable terms, conditions and status of employment, which have resulted from the investment of oil and gas revenues in public sector organizations. In contrast, private sector organizations in the Middle East have tended to turn to expatriate workers for both skilled and unskilled workers (Rees, Althakhri and Mamman, 2012).

Evidence is emerging from the Middle East that nationally-driven nationalization policies are facing resistance from some organizational leaders and employees especially in the private sector (Rees, Mamman and Bin-Braik, 2007). In general terms, Forstenlechner (2008: 82) notes that:

> there are mainly two ways of approaching [nationalization]: one is an effort geared at producing statistics for PR or avoidance of negative consequences, the other is a serious commitment to the integration of . . . nationals into the workforce . . . the choice between these two ways determines the chances for successful [nationalization].

Rees, Althakhri and Mamman (2012: 139–40) cite a number of reasons for this resistance. They highlight that the private sector in this region relies heavily on relatively cheap foreign manual labor; locals are more expensive to employ despite new policies and regulations which, for example, elevate the costs of issuing and renewing work permits for foreign workers. In addition, managers within the private sector may hold the view that indigenous workers compare unfavorably to expatriates in terms of the skills and attitudes necessary to perform effectively in the workplace; thus, expatriates may be easier to control and compliant due to fear of dismissal and hence deportation from the host country. A further problem is that successful nationalization programs often require cooperation from the very expatriates whose employment is under threat from nationalization initiatives (Rees, Mamman and Bin-Braik, 2007: 51).

It can be seen from the above that, as with decentralization, nationally-driven nationalization policies, in the various forms that they take in developing countries, are inextricably associated with HRM. In fact, it would be extremely difficult to discuss nationalization without reference to key HRM practices. Nationalization is centered on issues such as recruitment and selection, training and development, performance management and the management of reward systems. Further, even in regions such as the Middle East, where nationalization policies are seen to affect mainly private sector organizations (Al-Dosary, 2004; Al-Lamki, 2005; Forstenlechner and Mellahi, 2011), the influence of these policies permeates HRM in public sector organizations as well. The application of mechanisms such as quota systems creates a supply and demand driven employment market for indigenous workers, which drastically affects HRM practices at the organizational level. In effect, indigenous workers become a relatively valuable commodity to public as well as private sector organizations. For example, in order to retain indigenous workers, public sector organizations are required to consider how best to design performance management, career management, mentoring and reward systems. Such workers may be sought by other organizations, not necessarily because of their work-related skills and contribution but, in part or whole, because of their nationality.

The interplay between nationally-driven nationalization policies and cultural variables at the local level becomes more apparent when one widens the discussion to include factors such as workers' perceptions of public sector employment, locally-held perceptions of expatriates and local workers, the local influence of families and tribes in employment and family settings, and low levels of job mobility for women for social and religious reasons. This interplay may help to further explain the different attitudes held about nationalization and the resistance that the HRM-related aspects of nationalization policies have encountered in various settings.

CONCLUSION

This chapter has discussed the varied nature of countries which have been classified as developing by organizations such as the IMF. The discussion has also reinforced calls in literature for country-specific studies which examine the impact of national policies on HRM. It is suggested in this chapter that one way of informing such analyses is to first identify nationally-driven policies which have been implemented across a range of developing countries and then, second, to examine how these policies have impacted upon HRM practices at the local level. It was within the scope of this chapter to highlight and explore two such policies, namely decentralization and nationalization, both of which have been implemented in public sector organizations in various forms and in many developing countries as elements of their reform agendas. One of the conclusions drawn is that nationally driven reform policies such as decentralization and nationalization will not necessarily result in effective HRM in public sector organizations at the local level, but rather, such policies may well serve as enabling mechanisms to reinforce local cultural norms. In the case of decentralization in public sector organizations, it is impossible for national policy-makers to take into account all local considerations – such as the local labor markets, local transport infrastructures, and local wage rates. However, the cascading down of decision-making authority from central institutions provides opportunities for local decision-makers to practice variations of HRM to fit local contexts. This local HRM is likely to be formulated with reference to the local cultural norms with which these decision-makers have successfully interacted in the past in order to reach positions of responsibility within their organizations.

Given the number of countries classified as 'developing', the complex issues facing developing countries, the various types of public sector organizations that exist, the relatively wide scope of HRM activities and the interactions between all of these factors; it is not possible, in a chapter of this nature, to provide a cross-national comparative analysis of HRM in developing countries or indeed an in-depth discussion of the differences that are likely to exist in the different types of public sector organizations in areas such as local government, education, and health. In fact, one of the themes to emerge from this chapter is the scale of the challenges facing those researching this subject area. Encouragingly, at the general level, it has been emphasized that public sector organizations in both developed and developing countries will inevitably engage in similar HRM activities such as recruitment and selection, performance management, and training and development, as these activities are essential to the staffing and operation of all organizations. That is, all organizations need workers and these workers are required to perform tasks in particular ways for rewards of some kind or other. These similarities between developed and developing countries, in relation to HRM activities, and to an extent, HRM terminologies, are likely to prove helpful to researchers seeking to construct research frameworks and to engage in comparative HRM work. However, what has also been emphasized is that essential HRM practices are adapted by public sector organizations in developing countries with reference to the cultural norms which are prevalent at the local level. If, for example, nepotism is a cultural feature in a local context, HRM practices (such as recruitment and selection) and HRM activities undertaken in that context are likely to reflect that particular cultural characteristic of the locality. Thus, another conclusion drawn from this discussion is that care should be taken by researchers and practitioners when using HRM-related terms, for example, 'fair selection', 'discipline', 'leadership' and 'reward'. Such terms may carry meanings and assumptions in developed countries which are radically different from the meanings and assumptions associated with these terms in some developing country contexts.

Finally, given the varied nature of developing countries, the conclusion is drawn that great caution should be taken when generalizing about HRM in public sector organizations in these countries. In general terms, it may well be accurate to summarize the employment contexts of developing countries using terms such as 'patronage', 'widespread absenteeism', 'demoralizing management', 'lack of reward for hard work', 'petty corruption', and 'moonlighting' (Tessemam and Soeters, 2006: 88; 99). The types of economic, educational and health indicators used to classify countries as developing would alone justify generalized summaries of this nature. Nevertheless, these summaries should not form the basis for assumptions about specific public sector contexts in developing countries anymore than it should be assumed that problems such as low pay, corruption and bribery are absent from public sector organizations in developed countries.

REFERENCES

Al-Dosary, A.S. (2004), 'HRD or manpower policy? Options for government intervention in the local labor market that depends upon a foreign labor force: the Saudi Arabian perspective', *Human Resource Development International*, **7** (1), 123–35.
Al-Lamki, S.M. (1998), 'Barriers to Omanization in the private sector: the perceptions of Omani graduates', *International Journal of Human Resource Management*, **9** (2), 377–400.
Al-Lamki, S.M. (2005), 'The role of the private sector in Omanization: the case of the banking industry in the sultanate of Oman', *International Journal of Management*, **22** (2), 176–88.
Amishadai, A. (1965), *The Civil Service in New African States*, London, UK: Allen & Unwin.
Almond, P. (2011), 'The sub-national embeddedness of international HRM', *Human Relations*, **64** (4), 531–51.
Antwi, K.B. and F. Analoui (2008), 'Challenges in building the capacity of human resource development in decentralized local governments: evidence from Ghana', *Management Research News*, **31** (7), 504–17.
Attaran, A. (2005), 'An immeasurable crisis? A criticism of the millennium development goals and why they cannot be measured', *PLoS Medicine*, **2** (10), 955–61.
Bagchi, A. (2003), 'Rethinking federalism: changing power relations between the center and the states', *Publius: The Journal of Federalism*, **33**, 21–42.

Barisitz, S. (2008), *Banking in Central and Eastern Europe 1980-2006: A Comprehensive Analysis of Banking Sector Transformation in the Former Soviet Union*, Oxon, UK and New York, USA: Routledge.

Brawley, M. (2003), *The Politics of Globalization: Gaining Perspective, Assessing Consequences*, Ontario, Canada: Broadview Press.

Bonet, J. (2006), 'Fiscal decentralization and regional income disparities: evidence from the Colombian experience', *Annals of Regional Science*, **40**, 661–76.

Budhwar, P. and J. Bhatnagar (2009), *The Changing Face of People Management in India*, Oxon, UK and New York, USA: Routledge.

Budhwar, P. and Y. Debrah (2001), 'Introduction', in P. Budhwar and Y. Debrah (eds), *Human Resources in Developing Countries*, Oxon, UK: Routledge, pp. 1–3.

Budhwar, P. and Y. Debrah (2005), 'International HRM in developing countries', in H. Scullion and M. Linehan (eds), *International Human Resource Management: A Critical Text*, Hampshire, UK: Palgrave Macmillan, pp. 259–78.

Budhwar, P. and K. Mellahi (2006), *Managing Human Resources in the Middle East*, Oxon, UK and New York, USA: Routledge.

Common, R. (2011), 'International trends in HRM in the public sector: reform attempts in the Republic of Georgia', *International Journal of Public Sector Management*, **24** (5), 421–34.

Cooke, F.L. (2012), *Human Resource Management in China: New Trends and Practices*, Oxon, UK and New York, USA: Routledge.

Cunningham, P.W., S.A. Lynham and G. Weatherly (2006), 'National human resource development in transitioning societies in the developing world: South Africa', *Advances in Developing Human Resources*, **8** (1), 62–83.

Davila, A. and M. Elvira (2009), *Best Human Resource Management Practices in Latin America*, Oxon, UK and New York, USA: Routledge.

Dawson, S. and C. Dargie (1999), 'New public management', *Public Management: An International Journal of Research and Practice*, **1** (4), 459–81.

Debrah, Y. and C.J. Rees (2011), 'The development of global leaders and expatriates', in A.W. Harzing and A. Pennington (eds), *International Human Resource Management* (4th Edition), New York: Sage, pp. 375–14.

Dieleman, M., B. Gerretsen, and G.J. van der Wilt (2009), 'Human resource management interventions to improve health workers' performance in low and middle income countries: a realist review, *Health Research Policy and Systems*, **7** (7), 1–13.

Faguet, J.P. (2004), 'Does decentralization increase government responsiveness to local needs? Evidence from Bolivia', *Journal of Public Economics*, **88** (3/4), 867–93.

Forstenlechner, I. (2008), 'Workforce nationalization in the UAE: image versus integration', *Education, Business and Society: Contemporary Middle Eastern Issues*, **1** (2), 82–91.

Forstenlechner, I. (2010), 'Workforce localization in emerging Gulf economies: the need to fine-tune HRM', *Personnel Review*, **39** (1), 135–52.

Forstenlechner, I. and K. Mellahi (2011), 'Gaining legitimacy through hiring local workforce at a premium: the case of MNEs in the United Arab Emirates', *Journal of World Business*, **46** (4), 455–61.

Freinkman, L. (2009), 'Fiscal decentralization in rentier regions: evidence from Russia', *World Development*, **37** (2), 503–12.

Green, E.A. (2005), 'Managing human resources in a decentralized context', in

East Asia Decentralizes: Making Local Government Work, Washington DC, USA: World Bank, pp. 129–53.

Harzing, A.W. and A. Pinnington (2011), *International Human Resource Management* (3rd Edition), London, UK: Sage Publications.

IMF (2011), World Economic Outlook April 2011: Tensions from the Two-speed Recovery – Unemployment, Commodities and Capital Flows, accessed 21 February 2012 at: http://www.imf.org/external/pubs/ft/weo/2011/01/.

Jackson, T. (2002a), *International HRM: A Cross-Cultural Approach*, London: Sage Publications.

Jackson, T. (2002b), 'Reframing human resource management in Africa: A cross-cultural perspective', *International Journal of Human Resource Management*, **13** (7), 998–1018.

Jackson, T. (2009), 'A critical cross-cultural perspective for developing nonprofit international management capacity', *Nonprofit Management & Leadership*, **19** (4), 443–446.

Kamoche, K., Y. Debrah, F. Horwitz and G. Muuka (2004), *Managing Human Resources in Africa*, London, UK and New York, USA: Routledge.

Kaosa-ard, M. (1991), 'A preliminary study of TNCs hiring and localization policies in Thailand', *TRDI Quarterly Review*, **6** (4), 11–18.

Kim, A. (2008), 'Decentralization and the provision of public services: framework and implementation', World Bank policy research working paper, 4503, accessed 24 February 2012 at http://go.worldbank.org/0WS2I4O8O0.

Klingner, D.E. and V. Pallavicini-Campos (2002), 'Building public HRM capacity in Latin America and the Caribbean: what works and what doesn't?', *Public Organization Review*, **2**, 349–64.

Law, K.S., C. Wong and K.D. Wang (2004), 'An empirical test of the model on managing the localization of human resources in the People's Republic of China', *International Journal of Human Resource Management*, **15** (4/5), 635–48.

Liu, X., T. Martineaux, L. Chen, S. Zhan and S. Tang (2006), 'Does decentralization improve human resource management in the health sector? A case study from China', *Social Science and Medicine*, **63**, 1836–45.

Marsden, D. (1991), 'Indigenous management', *International Journal of Human Resource Management*, **2** (1), 21–38.

Metcalfe, B. and F. Mimouni (2012), *Leadership Development in the Middle East*, Cheltenham, UK: Edward Elgar.

Metcalfe, B.D. and C.J. Rees (2005), 'Theorizing advances in international human resource development', *Human Resource Development International*, **8** (4), 449–65.

Meyer, R.E. and G. Hammerschmid (2010), 'The degree of decentralization and individual decision making in central government human resource management: a European comparative perspective', *Public Administration*, **88**, 455–78.

Morris-Jones, W. and G. Fischer (1980), *Decolonization and After: The British and French Experience*, Totawa, NJ: Frank Cass.

OECD (2010), *Progress in Public Management in the Middle East and North Africa: Case Studies on Policy Reform*, Paris, France: OECD.

Okpara, J.O. and P. Wynn (2008), 'Human resource management practices in a transition economy: challenges and prospects', *Management Research News*, **31** (1), 57–76.

Pallangyo, W. and C.J. Rees (2010), 'Local government reform programmes and human resource capacity building in Africa: evidence from LGAs in Tanzania', *International Journal of Public Administration*, **33** (12/13), 728–39.

Polidano, C. and D. Hulme (1999), 'Public management reform in developing countries', *Public Management: An International Journal of Research and Theory*, **1** (1), 121–32.

Poór, J., ZS. Karoliny, B.V. Musztyné-Bártfai, ZS. Pótó and F. Farkas (2009), 'Similarities and differences of human resource management in private and public sector organizations in the light of new public management: an international comparison', *Acta Oeconomica*, **59** (2), 179–206.

Punnett, B.J. (2012), *Management: A Developing Country Perspective*, Oxon, UK and New York, USA: Routledge.

Qiao, B., J. Martínez-Vázquez and Y. Xu (2008), 'The tradeoff between growth and equity in decentralization policy: China's experience', *Journal of Development Economics*, **86**, 112–28.

Rees, C.J., R. Althakhri and A. Mamman (2012), 'Leadership and organizational change in the Middle East', in B. Metcalfe and F. Mimouni (eds), *Leadership Development in the Middle East*, Cheltenham, UK: Edward Elgar.

Rees, C.J. and F. Hossain (2010), 'Perspectives on decentralization and local governance in developing and transitional countries', *International Journal of Public Administration*, **33** (12/13), 581–7.

Rees, C.J., J. Järvalt and B. Metcalfe (2005), 'Careers in transition: HR themes from the Estonian civil service', *Journal of European Industrial Training*, **29** (7), 572–92.

Rees, C.J., A. Mamman and A. Bin Braik, (2007), 'Emiratisation as a strategic HRM change initiative', *International Journal of Human Resource Management*, **18** (1), 33–53.

Robinson, D. (1990), *Civil Service Pay in Africa*, Geneva: ILO.

Rondinelli, D.A. and J.R. Nellis (1986), 'Assessing decentralization policies in developing countries: the case for cautious optimism', *Development Policy Review*, **4**, 3–23.

Ruppert, E. (1999), 'Managing foreign labor in Singapore and Malaysia: are there lessons for GCC countries?', World Bank policy research working paper, no. 2053, accessed 28 February 2012 at http://ssrn.com/abstract=597250.

Saide, M.A.O. and D.E. Stewart (2001), 'Decentralization and human resource management in the health sector: a case study (1996-1998) from Nampula province, Mozambique', *International Journal of Health Planning and Management*, **16**, 155–68.

Sanford, J.E. and A. Sandhu (2003), *Developing Countries: Definitions, Concepts and Comparisons*, Hauppage, New York, USA: Nova Science Publishers Inc.

Scullion, H. and D. Collings (2006), *Global Staffing*, Oxon, UK and New York, USA: Routledge.

Scullion, H. and M. Linehan (2005), *International Human Resource Management: A Critical Text*, Hampshire, UK and New York, USA: Palgrave Macmillan.

Sian, S. (2007), 'Reversing exclusion: the Africanisation of accountancy in Kenya, 1963–1970', *Critical Perspectives on Accounting*, **18**, 831–72.

Sparrow, P., C. Brewster and H. Harris (2004), *Globalizing Human Resource Management*, London, UK and New York, USA: Routledge.

Tessemam, M.T. and J.L. Soeters (2006), 'Challenges and prospects of HRM in developing countries: testing the HRM–performance link in the Eritrean civil service', *International Journal of Human Resource Management*, **17** (1), 86–105.

Tosun, M.S. and S. Yilmaz (2008), 'Centralization, decentralization, and conflict in the Middle East and North Africa', World Bank policy research working paper, no. 4774, accessed 24 February 2012 at http://ssrn.com/abstract=1300269.

United Nations (1962), *Decentralization for National and Local Government*, New York, USA: United Nations.

United Nations (2001), 'Road map towards the implementation of the United Nations Millennium Declaration: Report of the Secretary General', no. A/56/326, accessed 5 March 2012 at http://www.un.org/millenniumgoals/sgreport2001. pdf?OpenElement.

UNDP (2011), *The Human Development Index*, accessed 21 February 2012 at http://hdr.undp.org/en/media/HDR_2011_EN_Table1.pdf.

White, L., H. Smith, and C. Currie (2011), 'OR in developing countries', *European Journal of Operational Research*, **208** (1), 1–11.

World Bank (1981), *Accelerated Development in Sub-Saharan Africa: An Agenda for Action*, Washington, DC: World Bank.

World Bank (2003), *World Development Report 2004: Making Services Work for Poor People*, Washington, DC: World Bank.

World Bank (2012), *How We Classify Countries*, accessed 21 February 2012 at http://data.worldbank.org/about/country-classifications.

Wunsch, J.S. (1991), 'Institutional analysis and decentralization: developing an analytical framework for effective third world administrative reform', *Public Administration and Development*, **11** (5), 431–51.

Yacob, S. (2009), 'Hidden disciplines in Malaysia: the role of business history in a multi-disciplinary framework', *Australian Economic History Review*, **49**, 302–24.

PART II

Assessing and addressing the health and
well-being of public sector employees

4. Psychosocial risk factors for stress and stress claim differences between the public and private sectors

Tessa S. Bailey, Sarven S. McLinton and Maureen F. Dollard

INTRODUCTION

The issue of work stress is a global concern (Leka and Jain, 2010). Within Australia workers' compensation claims for mental stress are higher in the public sector. Does this mean that the public sector is more stressful to work in? Is it the case that claims are overrepresented in the public sector, or simply underrepresented in the private sector? This chapter sets out to examine these questions, by scrutinizing psychosocial risk factors in the workplace as predictors of workers' compensation claims, and exploring differences between sectors as possible explanations for the observed claim rates.

Context

Within Australia, relative to other serious compensation claims, mental stress claims are significantly more costly, on average costing $16,800 per claim, over twice the cost of other kinds of serious claims. Further, workers claiming compensation for stress take more time off work (11.4 weeks versus 4 weeks). Work stress is clearly costly to insurers and employers, and to injured workers in health terms.

Workers' compensation data claim rates for mental stress show significantly different prevalence rates between the public and private sector. At a national level rates of serious claims for worker compensation for mental disorders caused by mental stress are higher in the public sector (57 per cent) than in the private sector (43 per cent) as reported by Safe Work Australia 2009–10, and this trend has been evident for years (since 2005–06). According to the Australian Bureau of Statistics (2010) there was over 1.8 million Australians employed in the public sector including employees from commonwealth, state and local government organizations. This represents 16 per cent of the Australian workforce. Clearly worker's compensation claim rates for mental disorders are disproportionately higher among public sector workers, fuelling speculation in the media of stress in the public sector in epidemic proportions (Lewig and Dollard, 2001). However compensation rates are a lag indicator of the problem. From a strategic human resource management perspective, it is important to identify risk factors at work that may predispose workers to psychological injury. Empirical evidence suggests that these factors may be used to predict or forecast psychological injury and claims, and hence should be targeted to improve the mental health and engagement of the workforce.

The aim of this chapter is to examine whether there are differences between the public and private sector on risk factors that could explain the compensation rates. We refer to these factors as psychosocial risk factors, defined as 'work design and the organization and management of work, and their social and environmental contexts that have the potential for causing psychological or physical harm' (Cox, Griffiths and Rial-Gonzalez, 2000: 14). First we examine whether the psychosocial factors are related to worker compensation for work stress in the sample. Second we examine whether psychosocial factors and the psychological health of the workers by sector, to determine if this could account for the claim rate differences by sector. Third we explore other contextual factors that could explain the compensation rates.

Public Versus Private Sector Differences

Public sector workers are responsible for developing, implementing, monitoring and maintaining essential social and economic services within the community (Fogarty et al., 1999). These services are enacted through a structured and systematic coordination of rules and regulations. It is often suggested that this rule laden role served by the public sector is mirrored within their own organizations' work environments, which can be restrictive and overly burdened by bureaucracy (Aungles and Parker, 1992; Martin and Parker, 1997; Pirie, 1988).

Some argue that the private sector varies from the public sector as it is more directly driven by profit making. This leads to more financial rewards and incentives for employees with fewer constraints. Some suggest that these arrangements ultimately result in better productivity and employee health outcomes (Scott and Falcone, 1998). Whereas the private and public sector have been perceived as distinctly different in nature and structure, in the last decade or so differences have become blurred because the public sector is increasingly influenced by a trend towards economic rationalism, with its focus on cost cutting, competition, and a reduction of the welfare state (Noblet, Rodwell and McWilliams, 2006).

Consequently both the public and private sectors now share similarities such as downsizing, outsourcing and competition (Koukoulaki, 2002; Caulfield et al., 2004; Dollard, 2006; Dollard and Knott, 2004; Polanyi and Tompa, 2004; Stebbins, Thatcher and King, 2005). In Australia, downsizing is evident in public sector employment trends which previously represented 26 per cent of the working population in 1984 but now represents approximately 16 per cent (Kryger, 2006).

Work Stress: Implications for Public and Private Sectors in Australia

Clearly these macro-sector factors may influence workplace psychosocial risk factors and the health of the workforce by sector. Empirical studies investigating the differences between private and public sector workplace conditions and employee health outcomes are not always consistent. Although it is sometimes suggested that there are higher levels of work stress in the public sector this theory is not always supported by research results. An Australian study of 105 private sector and 559 public sector workers found that private sector workers were more at risk than public sector workers on a range of workplace psychosocial risk factors including job demands and job control as well as managerial and social support (D'Aleo et al., 2007). Interestingly, the obverse was found in relation to bullying; 28 per cent of public sector employees advised that they were 'always', 'often' or 'sometimes' bullied at work compared to 10 per cent reported by private sector workers.

In another Australian study of 84 private sector and 143 public sector workers, differences in psychosocial risk factors and psychological distress were investigated (Macklin, Smith and Dollard, 2006). Results did not show a significant difference between the two sectors in the experience of psychological distress or job satisfaction. However, public sector workers reported significantly more job control but there were no differences by level of demand and social support.

Recent data indicates that in Australia there has been a slight decline in prevalence rates for Commonwealth public sector psychological injury claims since 2006–07 (Safe Work Australia, personal correspondence, 15th November 2011). Rather than this being the result of better prevention or intervention practices, it may be due to changes to the *Safety, Rehabilitation and Compensation Act* introduced in April 2007. These changes effectively resulted in reduced worker access to compensation benefits for psychological injury (Cotton, 2008). Due to the relationships that have been demonstrated between workplace stress and physical injury claims, Cotton (2008) suggests that changing legislation to restrict access benefits may actually result in other symptoms such as increased musculoskeletal symptoms, absenteeism and turnover, thus having little effect on reducing the actual costs associated with workplace stress.

Even with the general decline in the Commonwealth public sector stress claim statistics, the National Data Set for Workers' Compensation Claims in the 2009–10 financial year show a higher number of mental stress claims in the public sector with 3750 claims reported, compared to 2855 claims reported in the private sector (ratio 57:43) (Safe Work Australia, personal correspondence, 15th November 2011). Compared to national employment figures the ratio should be 16:84, therefore the rate of claims in the public sector is 3.8 times higher than expected: Chi-square test (df = 1) = 125.07, $p < 0.0001$. In addition, in 2009–10 the median cost for each mental stress claim was also substantially higher in the public sector ($18,000) compared to the private sector ($15,600). Both sectors reported similar time loss due to mental stress claims, with a median time lost in the public sector at 11 weeks, compared with a median time loss of 11.8 weeks in the private sector.

It is possible that variance in rates of claims may be due to other factors such as differences in union membership, legislation and organizational policy which lead to more public than private sector employees seeking compensation (Dollard and Walsh, 1999). It is also possible that many 'at risk' occupations are contained within the public service such as education, correctional services, policing and community welfare, all of which have been identified as high risk employment occupations (O'Mara, 1991; Work Health Authority, 1991). These roles can often involve exposure to client hostility, verbal aggression, physical danger and emotional strain (Australian National Audit Office, 1997; McKenna, 1995).

International Insights into Psychosocial Risk in the Public and Private Sectors

International research also shows inconsistent results for the differences between public and private workers. A US study examined workplace pressures and resources involving 2648 private and public sector employees (Dolcos and Daley, 2009). The researchers found that public sector employees reported significantly more demands but they also experienced higher levels of supervisor and organizational support.

There are a number of theories that attempt to explain the reasons for differences in psychosocial risk found between public and private sector organizations. Results potentially vary due to gender differences in the experiences of work related demands, resources and health outcomes

(Macklin, Smith and Dollard, 2006). For example, gender studies have found that women are more likely to be stressed by workplace relationships, while men are more affected by workplace change and workload. Gender differences may explain some inconsistencies in research results between private and public sectors, particularly if participants are predominantly one specific occupation or industry that is dominated by one gender.

Evidence gathered using multiple data collection techniques can provide a deeper understanding of how psychosocial risk factors manifest in the public and private sector. Interesting insights were revealed in a UK study involving staff from two social service public sector departments with data collected via multiple methods (Coffey, Dugdill and Tattersall, 2009). The study included surveys ($N = 1237$) and focus groups ($N = 4$) providing both qualitative and quantitative information. Workplace factors were assessed for relationships with stress, and differences were found between the two divisions. Staff working in the children and families division specifically reported the poorest levels of wellbeing, highest levels of organizational constraints and highest levels of absenteeism. Over 54 per cent of staff in this division reported being off sick in the previous six months (Coffey, Dugdill and Tattersall, 2009).

In the same study results from focus groups suggested a wide range of psychosocial risk factors contributed to stress including rigid timescales, clients with challenging behaviours, and threat of complaints or litigation (Coffey, Dugdill and Tattersall, 2009). Organizational factors such as lack of recognition, harsh management practices, an authoritarian management style, lack of information, poor communication, lack of support, and lack of participation in decision making were identified by the focus groups as more influential sources of stress rather than factors that are intrinsic to the nature of the job. The researchers also noted that an accelerated level of organizational change occurring within social services may also have been contributing to perceptions of work related stress.

Organizational Factors and Leading Indicators of Work Stress

The academic literature determining the exact nature of psychosocial risk differences between private and public sectors is somewhat unclear. However, evidence consistently implies that differences in organizational factors may be responsible for relationships between psychosocial risk factors and employee health outcomes regardless of belonging to either the public or private sector. Recent Australian investigations have found that a significant direct relationship exists between organizational climate factors and worker's compensation claim statistics (Cotton, 2008).

Psychosocial safety climate (PSC) research has also found that organizational policy and management practices for psychological health, directly influencing psychosocial risk factors that lead to poorer employee health outcomes (Dollard and Bakker, 2010).

PSC theory addresses a gap in the literature because many of the current work stress theories refer only to job design elements as the triggers for work stress. PSC theory identifies antecedent factors in an organization, embedded within the development and implementation of policies, practices and procedures that act to protect employee psychological health and promote positive wellbeing (Dollard and Bakker, 2010). These features logically turn out to be leading indicators of psychosocial risk, so called 'causes of the causes'. If managers are concerned about their worker's health and well-being they will ensure demands are appropriate and that resources are adequate to safeguard against psychological injury as well as bolster motivation among employees. The theory is multi-level because organizational level factors, precipitate other organizational and job design factors, and individual level outcomes (i.e. psychological health, engagement, compensation claims).

The theoretical basis of the PSC model may be conceived as a multi-level extension of the job demands-resources (JD-R) model (Demerouti et al., 2001). The JD-R model considers job demands and resources to be significant predictors of employee health and productivity outcomes via health erosion and motivation pathways (Bakker and Demerouti, 2007). When job demands are chronic and there are inadequate job resources, psychological health problems are likely to develop via a kind of health erosion process. Adequate job resources are likely to bolster motivation and engagement, via a motivation pathway.

PSC theory proposes two major extensions to the JD-R model: (1) we propose an extended health erosion path – in this mediated path, work demands carry the effect of PSC onto psychological health problems and this has been shown empirically in several studies (Dollard and Bakker, 2010; Idris Dollard and Winefield, 2011; Law et al., 2011); (2) the extended motivational pathway – in this mediated path, work resources carry the effect of PSC on engagement and this has been shown empirically in several studies (Dollard and Bakker, 2010; Law et al., 2011); and (3) a cross links pathway, whereby PSC is related to resources that in turn relate to health problems (Schaufeli and Bakker, 2004). We expect that each of these paths will also lead to stress claims.

In previously reported Australian Workplace Barometer (AWB) research we found that PSC components were positively related to all of the demand measures; negatively related to all of the resource measures; negatively related to the psychological health measures; positively related

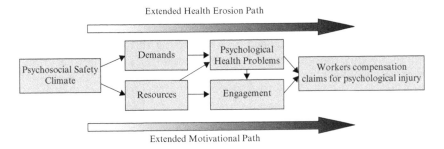

Figure 4.1   Psychosocial safety climate model

to engagement; and negatively related to work stress claims (Bailey and Dollard, in review).

In this chapter we use the PSC theoretical framework and extend the AWB research to consider the factors that might lead to worker compensation claims, and as an explanatory framework for considering sector differences. We consider that the psychosocial safety climate, because of its expected relationship with both demands and resources, will be associated with psychological health problems, engagement and workers' compensation claims. Fundamentally PSC is expected to be a leading indicator of psychosocial risk, health, engagement and claims.

Method

The Australian Workplace Barometer (AWB) project involved a national surveillance of psychosocial factors at work in Australia. Computer assisted telephone interviews were conducted in 2010 and 2011. Participants were from NSW (N = 725), Western Australia (N = 804), South Australia (N = 1143), Australian Capital Territory (N = 255), Tasmania (N = 416), and the Northern Territory (N = 170). Of these N = 1276 were employed in the public sector (commonwealth, state or local government department or agency), N = 231 were employed in a not-for-profit, religious, or community organization, and N = 1999 were employed in a private sector company. Most were permanent employees (N = 2101 fulltime, and N = 818 part-time) and N = 494 were casual/temporary (no annual sick leave), and N = 98 were on a fixed term contract. The remainder did not provide a response for these categories.

To reduce potential selection bias data was weighted based on Australian Labour Force Statistics to more accurately reflect the population of interest. The number of workers by age and sex for each state and territory was determined and used to weight the data. In addition the probability of selection by how many people in the household aged over 18 years was used in the weighting process.

The AWB tool was developed from combining various well-known and internationally recognized psychometric measures. The following measures were employed in the present study.

Psychosocial Safety Climate

The PSC–12 (Hall, Dollard and Coward, 2010) comprises four domains each with three items: (1) senior management commitment and involvement in relation to stress prevention practices; (2) management priority measures employee perceptions of how management values employee psychological health and safety in comparison to productivity goals; (3) organizational communication, encompasses processes for employees to provide feedback on psychological wellbeing; (4) organizational participation, which relates to consultation regarding psychological health and safety issues with employees' unions and OHS representatives. Responses were made on a 5-point Likert scale from 1 (strongly disagree) to 5 (strongly agree).

Organizational Demands

Job demands

Job demands were measured with the job content questionnaire (JCQ 2.0) which includes the following subscales; physical demands (six items), work pressure (five items), and emotional demands (four items). Self-report data was recoded on reverse scored items to reflect the 4-point Likert scale from 1 (strongly disagree) to 4 (strongly agree).

Organizational change

The JCQ 2.0 was also used to measure organizational change. Five items were included, rated on the same 4-point Likert scale, asking participants to report the extent to which the given statement reflects their experiences at work. For example, 'In your company/organisation, there have been changes such as restructuring, downsizing, and layoffs that have significantly affected your job'.

Organizational harassment

A seven item scale employed by Richman, Flaherty and Rospenda (1996) was used to measure organizational harassment in the present study. Participants were asked to respond with the frequency that they experienced a variety of harassment situations (for example, sexual, physical) in their workplace, from 1 (very rarely/ never) to 5 (very often/ always).

Bullying

A clear definition of bullying was given in the present study as individual explanations of the term have differed in existing research. The following was provided for the participant: 'Bullying is a problem at some work-places and for some workers. To label something, as bullying, the offensive behaviour has to occur repeatedly over a period of time, and the person confronted has to experience difficulties defending him or herself. The behaviour is not bullying if two parties of approximate equal "strength" are in conflict or the incident is an isolated event' (Lindström et al., 2000). Further, the bullying had to take place at least once a week for at least half a year or more (Leymann, 1993; Zapf and Gross, 2001). Thus, the following three questions were asked: 'Have you been subjected to bullying at the workplace during the last 6 months?' (answer yes or no); 'How often were you exposed to these bullying behaviours overall?' (5-point scale from 0 (never) to 4 (daily)); and 'How long were you exposed to these bullying behaviours overall?' (5-point scale from 1 (less than one month) to 5 (more than 2 years)).

Work–family conflict

Work–family conflict was measured by asking participants about how work affected their home lives. Five items measuring time and strain-based conflict from Netemeyer, Boles and McMurrian's (1996) work-family conflict scale were selected for use in the present study. An example of the former includes 'My job produces strain that makes it difficult to fulfil family duties', whilst the later included 'The amount of time my job takes up makes it difficult to fulfil my family responsibilities'. Responses to the items were made on a 7-point Likert scale from 1 (strongly disagree) to 7 (strongly agree).

Organizational Resources

Job control

Scales from the JCQ 2.0 were also used to measure the following three job control constructs: skill discretion (6 items, for example, 'I have an opportunity to develop my own special abilities'); decision authority (4 items, for example, 'My job allows me to make decisions on my own'); and macro-decision latitude (3 items, for example, 'In my company/ organisation, I have significant influence over decisions made by my work team or department'). Likert response format was used for all items, with responses ranging from 1 (strongly disagree) to 4 (strongly agree).

Social support
Measures were taken from the JCQ 2.0 to measure both supervisor social support (3-item scale, for example, 'My supervisor/manage is helpful in getting the job done'), and co-worker social support (3-item scale, for example, 'I am treated with respect by my co-workers'). Responses ranged from 1 (strongly disagree) to 4 (strongly agree), plus an alternate option to complete if the participant did not have a supervisor or co-workers.

Organizational justice
The JCQ 2.0 was again used to measure organizational procedural justice using a total of four items, scored on a 4-point Likert scale, ranging from 1 (strongly disagree) to 4 (strongly agree). An example item from this scale includes: 'In my company/ organization, procedures are designed to provide opportunities to appeal or challenge a decision'.

Organizational rewards
The effort-reward imbalance scale (ERI) (Siegrist, 1996) was sourced to measure organizational rewards. Four specific items were selected for use in the present study taken from the esteem reward component (1 item), the job promotion reward component (2 items), and the job security reward component (1 item). Responses were made on a 4-point Likert scale to be consistent with above measures (1 (strongly disagree) to 4 (strongly agree)).

Health Outcomes

Emotional exhaustion
Emotional exhaustion was measured through a selection of five items from the Maslach burnout inventory (MBI) (Schaufeli et al., Jackson, 1996). Items such as 'I feel tired when I get up in the morning and have to face another day on the job' were answered on a 7-point scale, ranging from 1 (never) to 7 (always).

Psychological distress
All 10 items from the Kessler 10 (K10) (Kessler and Mroczek, 1994) were included to measure psychological distress, which investigates the degree of anxiety and depressive symptoms that the participant has experienced over the last month. For example, 'In the past four weeks, about how often did you feel everything was an effort?'. Responses were scored on a 5-point scale, from 1 (none of the time) to 5 (all of the time).

Depression

Depression was measured using all items from the patient health question-naire (PHQ–9) (Spitzer, Kroenke, and Williams, 1999). These nine items apply to the nine criteria for clinical diagnoses of depressive episodes in the DSM-IV, for example 'During the last month, how often were you bothered by little interest or pleasure in doing things?'. These items are all scored on a 4-point Likert scale 1 (not at all) to 4 (nearly every day).

Union membership

Participants who were members of a union or employee organization that looks after employee's interests (for example, Nursing Federation, Police Association) were identified with a single item response: yes = 1, no = 0, don't know and refused.

Motivational Outcomes

Engagement

Nine items from the Utrecht work engagement scale – shortened version (UWES–9) (Schaufeli, Bakker and Salanova, 2006) were employed to measure work engagement. The three subscales each consist of three items to measure a different facet of engagement; vigour, for example, 'At my work, I feel bursting with energy'; dedication, for example, 'My job inspires me'; and absorption, for example, 'I get carried away when I am working'. These items were all measured on a 7-point scale which ranged from 1 (never) to 7 (every day).

Stress Claims

Respondents were asked 'Have you ever put in a worker's compensation claim?'. If they answered 'yes', the subsequent question followed 'Was this claim for a stress or psychological injury related problem?'. Responses were coded 0 (no claim), 1 = (stress claim). Participants were also offered the opportunity to refuse.

Analysis Strategy

We used multivariate analysis of variance to test the difference between public and private sectors on a range of variables, PSC, demands, resources, psychological health, engagement and work outcomes. Since trivial effects may become significant with large samples, we assessed effect sizes using partial eta-squared which assesses the proportion of variance due to the factor while partialling out variance from other factors

Table 4.1   AWB national data on stress claims by sector (weighted)

	Public		Private	
	N	%	N	%
No stress claim	939	97.2	1585	97.8
Stress claims	27	2.8	36	2.2
Total	966	100	1621	100

(Pierce, Block and Aguinis, 2004). We used the following eta squared (η^2) effect sizes classification as recommended by Cohen (1992): 0.01 for a small effect, 0.06 for a medium effect and 0.14 for a large effect.

RESULTS

Stress Claims

First, the rate of reported stress claims were analyzed to identify whether these were overrepresented in either the public or private sector. Permanent full-time and part time workers' responses were used, with the category 'no stress claim' including both non-stress related worker's compensation claims and also no claims at all. The results are presented in Table 4.1.

The proportions of public and private workers reporting making stress claims was in proportion to their numbers in the sample. There was no significant association between claims and the sector using a Chi-square test.

Table 4.2 indicates that the propensity for stress claims is related to different variables within different sectors. Overall, a poor PSC in a private sector environment is more likely to be related to an increased frequency of stress claims being lodged. The same is also true for private sector workers experiencing poor psychological health. In the public sector an individual experiencing greater demands at work, higher exhaustion or lower engagement is also more likely to lodge a stress claim.

For resources the relationship with stress claims is not distinct. Decision authority, skill discretion, macro-decision latitude and being a member of a union display no significant relationship with stress claims in either sector. Organizational justice and co-worker social support appear to have a similar relationship with stress claims in both sectors whereas organizational rewards demonstrates a weak-moderate relationship with stress claims for only private sector workers.

In terms of strength of relationships the most important factor associated with stress claims in the public sector appears to be harassment due

Table 4.2   *Correlations with stress claims for both the public and private sectors*

	Public sector	Private sector
Psychosocial safety climate		
Management commitment	−0.04	−0.22***
Management priority	−0.09	−0.19***
Org. communication	−0.14*	−0.21***
Org. participation	−0.05	−0.15**
Demands		
Emotional demands	0.21***	0.08
Work pressure	0.25***	−0.01
Physical demands	0.12*	−0.03
Work-family conflict	0.17**	0.07
Harassment	0.33***	0.04
Bullying	0.14*	0.02
Organizational change	0.08	0.06
Resources		
Rewards	−0.07	−0.22***
Organizational justice	−0.12*	−0.14**
Co-worker social support	−0.14*	−0.15**
Supervisor social support	−0.12	−0.10*
Decision authority	0.01	−0.06
Skill discretion	0.03	−0.06
Macro-decision latitude	−0.04	−0.08
Union member	0.05	−0.03
Psychological health		
Depression	0.03	0.28***
Psychological distress	0.01	0.19***
Emotional exhaustion	0.16**	0.25***
Work outcomes		
Work engagement	−0.20**	−0.10

Note: Covariates, age, gender, income; union member 1 = yes, 0 = no; data weighted; stress claim, 0 = no, 1 = yes.

to its moderate significant correlation. On the other hand, in the private sector the rate of stress claims appears to involve depression more so than other variables. There are a few trends common to both sectors, for example the importance of emotional exhaustion and the organizational communication component of PSC, in relation to stress claims.

Multivariate Analysis of Variance

Next we considered the differences between variables of interest by sector, in an attempt to identify why public sector stress claims are disproportionately higher. A multivariate analysis of variance considering all measures showed a significant effect for sector (public versus private), $F(481, 2164)$ $= 5.90$, $p < .001$ (corrected model), indicating a significant main effect worthy of further investigation. Next we looked at the specific variables.

As displayed in Table 4.3, all but one variable exhibited significant differences between sectors. However, it has long been recognized that in studies with particularly large sample sizes such as ours, correlations and F values are often found to be significant regardless of actual meaningful relationships. Thus, reporting the effect size is a more meaningful indication of the degree of those differences.

The largest differences between sectors are moderate effects in emotional demands, work pressure, work-family conflict and work engagement. The first three of these moderate effects demonstrate consistently that the private sector is a less demanding workplace psychologically, emotionally and for strain on family relationships. The fourth difference, on the other hand, indicates that public sector workers are more engaged despite their demanding environment.

Numerous small effects were observed. In relation to other demands, most of these were significantly higher in the public sector in specific harassment, bullying and organizational change. Another small effect was observed, with physical demands being significantly lower in the public sector, making this the only characteristic that is less demanding on public sector workers.

It is immediately apparent that resources are readily available in the public sector with organizational rewards, justice, decision authority, skill discretion and support received from supervisors all displaying higher levels than in the private sector. More public sector workers appeared to be union members, although macro-decision latitude is higher in the private sector.

In relation to PSC, the subscales management commitment to stress prevention, and priority for psychological health were both significantly higher in the private sector as small effects. Alternatively the PSC subscales, organizational participation and organizational communication were significantly higher in the public sector.

Of the psychological health problems, emotional exhaustion and distress are more prevalent in the public sector. In contrast depression levels are higher in the private sector. All of these effects are at a small but not negligible level.

Table 4.3 *Multivariate analysis of variance in both the public and private sectors*

Psychosocial safety climate	Mean			Standard deviation		F corrected	Partial eta squared	Effect size
	Public N = 916		Private N = 1722	Public N = 916	Private N = 1722			
Management commitment	10.26	↑	10.54	3.00	2.79	8.47***	0.045	s
Management priority	9.89	↑	9.97	3.10	3.02	3.85***	0.021	s
Org. communication	10.03 ↑		9.79	2.48	2.60	3.28***	0.018	s
Org. participation	10.15 ↑		9.49	2.48	2.80	3.23***	0.018	s
Demands								
Emotional demands	11.11	↑	9.70	2.50	2.26	8.27***	0.061	m
Work pressure	31.89 ↑		30.60	5.47	5.03	3.56***	0.063	m
Physical demands	10.14		10.54	2.75	3.10	3.19***	0.026	s
Work-family conflict	19.57	↑	18.23	8.37	8.52	5.41***	0.070	m
Harassment	8.79	↑	8.50	2.35	2.20	3.28***	0.025	s
Bullying	0.64	↑	0.33	2.41	1.73	3.00***	0.016	s
Organizational change	7.72	↑	7.01	1.69	1.64	4.12***	0.033	s
Resources								
Rewards	11.55 ↑		11.46	1.65	1.71	3.31***	0.021	s
Organizational justice	10.96 ↑		10.74	1.90	2.10	3.94***	0.050	s
Co-worker social support	9.69		9.71	1.29	1.27	1.29	0.005	–
Supervisor social support	9.22 ↑		9.09	1.58	1.59	5.98***	0.040	s
Decision authority	34.46 ↑		34.40	5.78	6.28	2.52**	0.012	s

Table 4.3 (continued)

Psychosocial safety climate	Mean		Standard deviation		F corrected	Partial eta squared	Effect size
	Public N = 916	Private N = 1722	Public N = 916	Private N = 1722			
Resources							
Skill discretion	35.40 ↑	33.22	4.98	5.13	4.84***	0.045	s
Macro-decision latitude	7.35	7.59 ↑	1.62	1.63	4.76***	0.034	s
Union member	0.55 ↑	0.20	0.55	0.40	68.26***	0.059	s
Psychological health							
Depression	3.49 ↑	3.53	3.66	3.58	4.58***	0.043	s
Psychological distress	1.48	1.46 ↑	0.46	0.46	1.78**	0.023	s
Emotional exhaustion	16.65	15.82 ↑	7.35	7.70	2.08***	0.030	s
Work outcomes							
Work engagement	51.35 ↑	49.46	8.51	10.11	3.30***	0.082	m

Note: Covariates, age, gender, income; union member 0 = no, 1 = yes; data weighted; ↑ indicates a better situation; s, small; m, medium; l, large; Org., organization.

Logistic Regression

Last, we explored which factors were most important in explaining stress claims by sector, using only the variables that displayed significant correlations with stress claims in their relevant sector (see Table 4.2). Then since there were so many variables we first determined the significant variables in clusters: PSC, demands, resources, health and engagement and their relationships to stress claims. From these analyses, we used a forward linear regression model where the most distal factors consistent with our framework were entered in steps – PSC subscales were entered first followed by demands, resources then health and engagement to observe their levels of influence in relation to stress claims. Table 4.4 shows several variables that met the inclusion criteria.

For public sector workers PSC organizational communication was entered first and was a significant contributor to stress claims. As work pressure, harassment and physical demands entered the model, PSC organizational communication was no longer significant. These results are consistent with a kind of mediation process whereby PSC is related to harassment, work pressure and physical demands that in turn relate to stress claims: for instance, PSC → demands → stress claims, consistent with a health erosion pathway.

For private sector workers, PSC subscale organizational communication first entered the model, followed by co-worker support, rewards, and then depression as the strongest contributors to the variance in stress claims. This indicates the possible existence of a mediation process with a PSC → resources → depression → stress claims pathway, consistent with a cross-paths process in the PSC model along with a main effect of PSC organizational communication.

DISCUSSION

Triggered by official stress claim rates that differed by sector, this chapter set out to explore whether work in the public sector was more stressful work in the private sector, or whether claims are overrepresented in the public sector and/or underrepresented in the private sector. Our guiding framework was the PSC theoretical framework. Previous population based research across sectors with the AWB data set shows results consistent with this framework (Bailey and Dollard, in review).

Extending this work we set out to answer the question about whether conditions varied between the sectors. First we considered differences in levels of risk between the sectors, then we considered which variables were

Table 4.4   Regression of stress claims on associated variables

Model	β	Std. error	Wald
Public sector-step 1			
Constant	−1.57	0.69	5.29*
PSC: org. communication	−0.66	0.23	8.43**
Public sector-step 2			
Constant	−5.71	1.16	24.41***
PSC: org. communication	−0.27	0.24	1.30
Harassment	0.29	0.06	24.01***
Public sector-step 3			
Constant	−9.29	1.72	29.24***
PSC: org. communication	−0.16	0.25	0.41
Harassment	0.22	0.06	11.80**
Work pressure	0.12	0.04	9.69**
Public sector-step 4			
Constant	−10.71	1.88	32.36***
PSC: org. communication	−0.11	0.25	0.18
Harassment	0.21	0.07	10.35**
Physical demands	0.15	0.07	4.71*
Work pressure	0.11	0.04	8.36**
Private Sector-step 1			
Constant	−0.77	0.48	2.55
PSC: org. communication	−1.03	0.18	33.29***
Private sector-step 2			
Constant	1.86	0.80	5.38**
PSC: org. communication	−0.70	0.21	11.30**
Rewards	−0.34	0.09	14.47***
Private sector-step 3			
Constant	5.22	1.46	12.81***
PSC: org. communication	−0.65	0.21	9.63**
Co-worker support	−0.40	0.15	7.61**
Rewards	−0.31	0.09	11.12**
Private sector-step 4			
Constant	3.40	1.48	5.24*
PSC: org. communication	−0.62	0.22	8.24**
Co-worker support	−0.40	0.14	8.11**

Table 4.4　(continued)

Model	β	Std. error	Wald
Private sector-step 4			
Rewards	−0.23	0.10	5.16*
Depression	0.15	0.03	25.49***

Note:　Stress claims response format; no = 0, yes = 1.

most important for stress claims. Consistent with the notion of the public sector being more stressful, public sector employees reported significantly higher levels of demands than private sector workers, with medium effect sizes indicating public sector workers experienced substantially more emotional demands, work pressure and work-family conflict. Smaller effects were noted for a number of other demands (for instance, bullying, harassment, organizational change). The situation was always worse in the public sector, with only one exception – physical demands were higher for private sector workers.

This result is not entirely consistent with research previously conducted in Australia. For instance, D'Aleo et al. (2007) found private sector workers reported higher job demands than public sector employees. However the results from their study showed higher levels of bullying reported in the public sector, which is consistent with our results. Our results also align with those found in a US study (Dolcos and Daley, 2009) which found that public sector employees report significantly more demands compared to private sector workers. It is possible that these results support theories of a changing trend towards higher demands in the public sector.

The theory of changing trends is further supported by the results showing significantly higher levels of organizational change reported by public sector workers in this sample, which is consistent with UK research showing significantly higher levels of organizational change in public sector employees (Coffey, Dugdill and Tattersall, 2009). This also may be an indicator of change in the public sector consistent with theories suggesting a growing trend towards economic rationalism that includes downsizing, outsourcing and increased the focus on cost cutting and competition, moving away from the welfare state (Noblet et al., 2006).

Results for resources appeared at first not to be consistent with the notion of the public sector being more stressful because levels were in general higher in the public sector. Our results for job resources were consistent with other research outcomes where public sector employees reported significantly higher levels of resources compared to the private sector workers. Similar results were found for public sector workers in Australia (D'Aleo et al., 2007; Macklin et al., 2006) and the US (Dolcos and Daley, 2009).

In relation to PSC we found interesting differences between the public and private sectors for PSC sub-measures. Although the effects were small, PSC organizational communication and participation were significantly higher in the public sector whereas management commitment and priority were higher in the private sector. This pattern potentially portrays the differences in the public and private sector cultures where public sector organizations embrace organizational level processes to address occupational health and safety issues in consultation with workers, and unions. Alternatively in the private sector management may be perceived as having a greater influence, when compared to the wider organization, with regard to the protection of employee mental health and wellbeing.

In relation to distress, consistent with the notion of the public sector as being more stressful, we found that emotional exhaustion and distress were significantly higher in the public sector. In contrast, however, depression was higher in the private sector.

Taking all of the results together it appears that the higher stress claims in the public sector may be explained via pathways suggested in the PSC model. The scenario that explains higher stressfulness and therefore claims, is that there are higher demands in the public sector caused by poor PSC, particularly relating to poor communication regarding psychosocial risks, and not heeding inputs from workers in psychological health policies. Harassment in particular may be a really big explanatory factor. There is much evidence to support the devastating effects of harassment at work (Law et al., 2011). In fact Law et al., found that harassment and bullying, over and above demands such as work pressure, and emotional demands, showed the strongest relationship to psychological health problems. In combination with bullying, harassment accounts for 15 per cent of the total stress claims reported in Australian workers' compensation data.

Work pressure also had an effect within the public sector and this may be reflected in larger proportion of national stress claims, 22 per cent due to work pressure. These demands then have an eroding effect on health over and above other factors such as resources. If it is the case that the public sector is more stressful then although public sector workers receive higher levels of resources these do not offset the effects of pressure and harassment.

Within the private sector the stress claim process was consistent with the framework in that it related to a cross-links pathway whereby PSC → resources → depression → stress claims pathway, as well as a direct effect of PSC on claims.

On balance the psychosocial risk factors and health outcome measures do support the conclusion about the stressfulness of the public sector environment, and the observation of a higher claim rate in the public sector.

Implications

These results have several important implications. Theoretically the results reported here and in Bailey and Dollard (2012) support several propositions of PSC theory. Its explanatory power in explaining claims rates between sectors is possibly through nuanced effects of PSC on demands and resources between sectors.

Practically, the results suggest that actions within organizations to prevent stress should be effectively focused on the organization, and be well upstream from the claim submission component. Actions including improving communication about psychological safety issues; bringing information about workplace psychological well-being to workers attention by managers and supervisors; and listening to the contributions of employees in resolving occupational health and safety concerns in the organization for instance should be effective in the public sector. This might reduce work pressure and harassment. If not new policies would need to be developed to control harassment and reduce demands (Bond, Tuckey and Dollard, 2010). For both private and public sectors (based on correlations) aspects such as employee involvement with major organizational decisions, perceptions of fairness within the organization, co-worker support and levels of work pressure as well as emotional exhaustion have an important influence on stress claims. Interventions focusing on these aspects would likely improve mental health outcomes and reduce stress claims for both the public and private sectors.

Another implication relates to the use of lead or lag indicators to tackle this public health issue. Access to workers' compensation for psychological injury is a fair entitlement for workers. Researchers suspect that public sector workers may feel more supported to report injuries due to aspects such as significantly higher union membership, organizational communication and participation in the public sector (Dollard and Walsh, 1999). Research has previously highlighted the stigma attached to the submission of workers' compensation claims, and therefore the possibility of under-representation of claims, particularly in the private sector (Dollard, Winefield and Winefield, 1999; LaMontagne, et al., 2008). The fact that depression was related to stress claims in the private sector, may indicate that a more severe form of psychological injury is required to trigger a claim in that sector.

The possible anomalies between actual stressfulness and claims leads to the conclusion that compensation claims are not the best indicator of the experience of stress. A superior approach to understanding and preventing work stress is to examine lead indicators, such as PSC, rather than lag indicators such as stress claims.

Limitations and Future Research

Although we have been talking in terms of stress claim predictors, in any cross-sectional research such as this, relationships with stress claims are in fact retrospective. This is because the stress claim has already occurred. Another way of interpreting the results is to consider the situation for those who have had a stress claim. In this reversed scenario, for example, those in the public sector who have submitted a stress claim still report higher work pressure, and higher harassment those who have not put in a claim. This reversed perspective is also a troubling situation.

In our study, stress claim rates per sector were proportionate to sample representation (an even rate) but were at odds with official rates. There are several possible reasons for this. First, the sample itself may underrepresent stressed workers in the public sector – they may have left employment (been paid out) and therefore may not be in our sample. Second, official figures represent accepted claims, whereas our data may represent attempted claims. Results may in fact reflect that in the private sector it is harder to have claims accepted even though claim submissions appear to be even by sector. This issue about claim acceptance rates could be followed up in future research with insurers.

Future intervention research that focuses on modifying the PSC of work organizations will provide invaluable information about causal paths illustrated in the PSC model Figure 4.1, for instance, whether improvements in PSC predict changes in psychosocial risk factors, reduced distress, improve engagement and decreased stress claims. Longitudinal data such as that gathered in future waves of the AWB study will enable investigations of such casual relationships.

Further, future research could examine the possibility that risk factors interact differently between the sectors. In their Australian study Macklin, Smith and Dollard (2006) further explored the process via which psychosocial risk factors affected psychological distress, in particular the interactions between risk factors. Taking the sectors together, support for the classic demand X control interaction (Karasek and Theorell, 1990) was found. However researchers found a significant four way interaction effect, demand X control X support X sector, indicating differences in the form of the interaction by sector. In particular they found the classic

DXC interaction in the public sector only at low levels of support and in the private sector at high levels of support. The results suggested a kind of compensation process whereby the presence of at least one or the other resource could reduce the effect of demands on distress. For the private sector, high levels of support, enabled job control to be utilized to manage demands. Whereas in the public sector overly high support when there is high control and high demands may lead to higher levels of distress, possibly the result of higher work load and responsibility.

Conclusion

In summary, this chapter provided a demonstration of the importance of surveillance and monitoring of psychosocial risks and their effects in the workplace in both public and private sectors. The coverage and content of the AWB risk assessment tool helped to identify differences and similarities between sectors in Australian workplaces. These were used to answer a pertinent question: is the public sector a more stressful environment to work in? Results indicate that differences do exist, lending weight to the conclusion that it is more stressful to work in the public sector because of significantly higher demands, despite higher levels of resources. Further, the environment in the private sector may not be supporting processes to address mental health issues resulting in an underrepresentation of stress claim acceptances for these workers. Results supported the PSC model, an extension of JDR theory, and this provided a process framework for considering multi-level antecedents to stress claims in both sectors. Leading indicators such as PSC should be a target for intervention and this will likely lead to results such as decreases in demands in the public sector, increases in resources in the private sector and improving health outcomes and reducing stress claims in both. Longitudinal data in the future can show how changes in PSC and psychosocial risk factors can influence better health outcomes and reduce worker stress claims in both public and private sectors.

REFERENCES

Aungles, S. and S.R. Parker (1992), *Work, Organisations and Change: Themes and Perspectives in Australia* (2nd Edition), St Leonards, New South Wales: Allen & Unwin.
Australian Bureau of Statistics (2010), *Employment and Earnings, Public Sector, Australia, 2009–2010*, accessed at http://www.abs.gov.au/ausstats/abs @.nsf/ ProductsbyReleaseDate/4D418C2BAE75A796CA25796C0014351E?OpenDocument.

Australian National Audit Office (1997), *The Management of Occupational Stress in Commonwealth Employment*, audit report, no. 8, Canberra, ACT: AGPS.

Bailey, T.S. and M.F. Dollard (in review), 'Psychosocial safety climate (PSC) in Australia', in M.F. Dollard and T.S. Bailey (eds), *Australian Workplace Barometer: Psychosocial Safety Climate and Working Conditions in Australia*, Melbourne: Australian Federation Press.

Bakker, A.B. and E. Demerouti (2007), 'The job demands-resources model: state of the art', *Journal of Managerial Psychology*, **22**, 209–328.

Bond, S.A., M.R. Tuckey and M.F. Dollard (2010), 'Psychosocial safety climate, workplace bullying, and symptoms of posttraumatic stress', *Organization Development Journal*, **28**, 37–56.

Caufield, N., D. Chang, M.F. Dollard and C. Eshlaug (2004), 'Stocktake of work stress interventions in Australia', *International Journal of Stress Management*, **11**, 149–66.

Coffey, M., L. Dugdill and A. Tattersall (2009), 'Working in the public sector: a case study of social services', *Journal of Social Work*, **9** (4), 420–42.

Cohen, J. (1992), 'A power primer', *Psychology Bulletin*, **112**, 155–9.

Cotton, P. (2008), *Psychological Injury in the Workplace*, accessed 13 March 2012 at http://www.psychology.org.au/inpsych/psych_injury/.

Cox, T., A. Griffiths and E. Rial-Gonzalez (2000), *Research on Work Related Stress*, Luxembourg: Office for Official Publications of the European Communities.

D'Aleo, N., P. Stebbins, R. Lowe, D. Lees and D. Ham (2007), 'Managing workplace stress: psychosocial hazard risk profiles in public and private sector Australia', *Australian Journal of Rehabilitation Counselling*, **13** (2), 68–87.

Demerouti, E., F. Nachreiner, A.B. Bakker and W.B. Schaufeli (2001), 'The job demands-resources model of burnout', *Journal of Applied Psychology*, **86**, 499–512.

Dolcos, S. and D. Daley (2009), 'Work pressure, workplace social resources, and work-family conflict: the tale of two sectors', *International Journal of Stress Management*, **16** (4), 291–311.

Dollard, M.F. (2006), 'Throwaway workers', *InPsych*, **28** (3), 8–12.

Dollard, M.F. and A.B. Bakker (2010), 'Psychosocial safety climate as a precursor to conducive work environments, psychological health problems, and employee engagement', *Journal of Occupational and Organizational Psychology*, **83**, 579–99.

Dollard, M.F. and V. Knott (2004), 'Incorporating psychosocial issues into our conceptual models of OHS', *Journal of Occupational Health and Safety Australia and New Zealand*, **20** (4), 345–58.

Dollard, M., J. Saebel, S. Chrisopoulos, M. Tuckey and T. Winefield (2007), *Resources, Workload and Well-Being in Frontline Police Officers: A Survey Preliminary Feedback*, South Australia: Centre for Applied Psychological Research, Work and Stress Group, University of South Australia.

Dollard, M.F. and C. Walsh (1999), 'Illusory correlation: is work stress really worse in the public sector?', *Journal of Occupational Health and Safety*, **15** (3), 219–31.

Dollard, M.F., H.R. Winefield and A.H. Winefield (1999), 'Predicting "stress leave" compensation claims and return to work in welfare workers', *Journal of Occupational Health Psychology*, **4**, 279–87.

Fogarty, G.J., M.A. Machin, M.J. Albion, L.F. Sutherland, G.I. Lalor and S. Revitt (1999), 'Predicting occupational strain and job satisfaction: the role of stress, coping, personality, and affectivity variables', *Journal of Vocational Behaviour*, **54**, 429–52.

Hall, G.B., M.F. Dollard and J. Coward (2010), 'Psychosocial safety climate: development of the PSC–12', *International Journal of Stress Management*, **4**, 353–83.

Idris, M.A., M.F. Dollard and A.H. Winefield (2011), 'Integrating psychosocial safety climate in the JD-R model: a study among Malaysian workers', *South African Journal of Industrial Psychology*, **37**, 1–11.

Karasek, R. and T. Theorell (1990), *Healthy work: Stress, Productivity, and the Reconstruction of Working Life*, New York: Basic Books.

Kessler, R.C., C. Barber, A.L. Beck, P.A. Berglund, P.D. Cleary, D. McKenas, P.S. Wang (2003), 'The World Health Organization health and work performance questionnaire (HPQ)', *Journal of Occupational and Environmental Medicine*, **45**, 156–74.

Kessler, R. and D. Mroczek (1994), *Final Version of our Non-specific Psychological Distress Scale*, memo 3 October 1994, Ann Arbor, MI: Survey Research Centre of the Institute for Social Research.

Koukoulaki, T. (2002), 'Stress prevention in Europe: review of trade union activities – obstacles and future strategies', *TUTB Newsletter*, **19–20**, 4–9.

Kryger, T. (2006), *The Incredible Shrinking Public Sector*, Report, Australia: Information and Research Services, Parliamentary Library.

La Montagne, A., T. Keegel, D. Vallance, A. Ostry and R. Wolfe (2008), 'Job strain-attributable depression in a sample of working Australians: assessing the contribution to health equalities', *BMC Public Health*, **8**, 1–9.

Law, R., M.F. Dollard, M.R. Tuckey and C. Dormann (2011), 'Psychosocial safety climate as a lead indicator of workplace bullying and harassment, job resources, psychological health and employee engagement', *Accident Analysis and Prevention*, **43**, 1782–93.

Leka, S. and A. Jain (2010), *Health Impact of Psychosocial Hazards at Work: An Overview*, Geneva: WHO.

Lewig, K.A. and M.F. Dollard (2001), 'Social construction of work stress: Australian news-print media portrayal of work stress 1997–98', *Work & Stress*, **15**, 179–90.

Leymann, H. (1993), *Mobbing – Psychoterror am Arbeitsplatz und wie man sich dagegen wehren kann* [Mobbing – psychoterror in the workplace and how one can defend oneself], Reinbeck, Germany: Rowohlt.

Lindström, K., A.L. Elo, A. Skogstad, M. Dallner, F. Gamberale, V. Hottinen, E., Ørhede et al. (2000), *User's Guide for QPSNordic. General Nordic Questionnaire for Psychological and Social Factors at Work*, Copenhagen: Nordic Council of Minister.

Macklin, D., L. Smith and M.F. Dollard (2006), 'Public and private sector work stress: workers compensation, levels of distress and the demand-control-support model', *Australian Journal of Psychology*, **58** (3), 130–43.

Martin, S. and D. Parker (1997), *The Impact of Privatisation*, London: Routledge.

McKenna, D. (1995), 'Trade union perspectives on occupational stress', in P. Cotton (ed.), *Psychological Health in the Workplace: Understanding and Managing Occupational Stress*, Carlton, Victoria: The Australian Psychological Society, pp. 103–10.

Netemeyer, R.G., J.S. Boles and R. McMurrian (1996), 'Development and validation of work-family conflict and family-work conflict scales', *Journal of Applied Psychology*, **81**, 400–10.

Noblet, A., J. Rodwell and J. McWilliams (2006), 'Organizational change in the public sector: augmenting the demand control model to predict employee outcomes under new public management', *Work & Stress*, **20**, 335–52.

O'Mara, N. (1991), *A Study of Work Stress Among Government Employees*, Perth, WA: Murdoch University.

Pierce, C.A., C.A. Block and H. Aguinis (2004), 'Cautionary note on reporting eta-squared values from multifactor ANOVA designs', *Educational and Psychological Measurement*, **64**, 916–24.

Pirie, M. (1988), *Privatization: Theory, Practice, and Choice*, London: Wildwood House.

Polanyi, M. and E. Tompa (2004), 'Rethinking work-health models for the new global economy: a qualitative analysis of emerging dimensions of work', *Work: Journal of Prevention, Assessment & Rehabilitation*, **23** (1), 3–18.

Richman, J.A., J.A., Flaherty and K.M. Rospenda (1996), 'Perceived workplace harassment experiences and problem drinking among physicians: broadening the stress/alienation paradigm', *Addiction*, **91**, 391–403.

Rush, A.J., M.H. Trivedi, H.M. Ibrahim, T.J. Carmody, B. Arnow and D.N. Klein (2003), 'The 16-item quick inventory of depressive symptomatology (QIDS), clinician rating (QIDS-C), and self-report (QIDS-SR): a psychometric evaluation in patients with chronic major depression', *Biological Psychiatry*, **54**, 573–83.

Schaufeli, W. B., and A. B. Bakker (2004), 'Job demands, job resources, and their relationship with burnout and engagement: A multi-sample study', *Journal of Organizational Behavior*, **25**, 293–315.

Schaufeli, W.B., A.B. Bakker and M. Salanova (2006), 'The measurement of work engagement with a short questionnaire: a cross-national study', *Educational and Psychological Measurement*, **66**, 701–16.

Schaufeli, W.B., M.P. Leiter, C. Maslach and S.E. Jackson (1996), 'Maslach burnout inventory-general survey', in C. Maslach, S.E. Jackson and M.P. Leiter (eds), *The Maslach Burnout Inventory: Test manual* (3rd Edition), Palo Alto, CA: Consulting Psychologists Press, pp. 22–6.

Scott, P.G., and S. Falcone (1998), 'Comparing public and private organizations: an exploratory analysis of three frameworks', *The American Review of Public Administration*, **28**, 126–45.

Siegrist, J. (1996), 'Adverse health effects of high-effort/low-reward conditions', *Journal Occupational Health Psychology*, **1**, 27–41.

Spitzer, R., K. Kroenke and J. Williams (1999), 'Validation and unity of a self-report version of PRIME-MD: The PHQ primary care study', *Journal of American Medical Association*, **282**, 1737–44.

Stebbins, P., S. Thatcher and R. King (speakers) (2005), *Work Related Stress: HR, OH&S and Legal Strategy* [CD], Brisbane: PsyHealth Media.

Ware, J.E. and C.D. Sherbourne (1992), 'The MOS 36-item short-form health survey (SF–36): I. Conceptual framework and item selection', *Medical Care*, **30**, 473–83.

Warr, P., J. Cook and T. Wall (1979), 'Scales for the measurement of some work attitudes and aspects of psychological well-being', *Journal of Occupational Psychology*, **52**, 129–48.

Winwood, P.C., A.H. Winefield, D. Dawson and K. Lushington (2005), 'Development and validation of a scale to measure work-related fatigue and recovery: the occupational fatigue exhaustion recovery scale (OFER)', *Journal of Occupational and Environmental Medicine*, **47**, 594–606.

Work Health Authority (1991), *Stress Management in the Public Sector*, Canberra, ACT: Workcover Corporation.

Zapf, D. and C. Gross (2001), 'Conflict escalation and coping with workplace bullying: a replication and extension', *European Journal of Work and Organizational Psychology*, **10**, 497–522.

5. Building more supportive and inclusive public sector working environments: a case study from the Australian community health sector

Andrew J. Noblet, Kathryn Page and Tony LaMontagne

SUMMARY

The aim of this chapter is to explore the strategies (policies, systems, practices) that could enhance perceptions of control and support experienced by healthcare professionals working in the publicly funded, community services sector. Working conditions that facilitate employee control and support not only make significant contributions to the levels of stress experienced by public sector employees working in the health and human services, but also represent key features of high performing work systems. Identifying the specific policies, processes and practices that can enhance the support and control experienced by employees could therefore contribute to the development of healthier and more effective human service working environments. The current study involved a series of focus groups with front-line community health workers working in an Australian community health service. The group discussions were organized around the participating agency's three major work areas and, based on participant responses, strategies designed to enhance support and control need to be directed at systems and practices existing within: (1) individual work areas (e.g. selecting team leaders carefully and making sure they have the interpersonal and team-development skills required to lead and manage people); and (2) the organization overall (e.g. increasing the level of face-to-face contact between executive-level personnel and ensuring agency management have a more in-depth understanding of employees' needs). There was also considerable variation in the types of support and control-based practices utilized in each work area and the comments from participants indicate that higher levels of satisfaction and joint commitment can be achieved when these practices are consistent with more contemporary HR systems. Finally, there was notable overlap between the support and control-oriented strategies. This suggests that initiatives that aim to enhance support for employees may also offer valuable opportunities for increasing control and decision latitude.

BACKGROUND LITERATURE

Community health services (CHSs) are at the forefront of illness prevention and health promotion and play a critical role in helping to maintain an effective, well-integrated healthcare sector (PHAA, 2005). Although the specific healthcare services provided by CHSs vary between countries and jurisdictions, they generally include medical, allied health and dentist services, child and family counseling (including drug and alcohol), psychiatric disability support and, health promotion and education (Brown, 2000). The demands placed on community-centered health services are growing at a rapid rate, with larger proportions of acute and sub-acute care now being undertaken by community-based health services. This burden is further complicated by the ageing of the population and the increasingly complex health and social needs of communities (Kemp et al., 2002; Department of Health and Ageing, 2009). CHSs have also experienced significant cost-containment reforms over the past two decades. The on-going pressure to 'do more with less' has raised concerns regarding the sector's capacity to meet growing demands (Baum, 1996; Leggat et al. 2006; Noblet et al., 2007).

In addition to the broader socio-economic challenges affecting the sector, concerns regarding the capacity of CHSs to meet community needs include the already disproportionally high levels of job stress experienced in health and community services, current and projected shortages in medical and allied health professionals, and the lack of progressive human resource management systems throughout the healthcare industry. In the case of job stress, health and community services has the highest number of stress-related workers' compensation claims at both national and state/ territory levels, accounting for 20 per cent of psychological distress claims nationally (Dollard et al., 2007). Dollard and colleagues also undertook a review of studies assessing the levels of distress experienced by various public health and human service professions. Results indicated that rates of distress in this sector were two to three times that of the Australian adult population. In relation to workforce shortages, the well-publicized shortfall in qualified healthcare professionals is as prominent in Australia as it is in many other countries (Scott, 2009). However labor shortages in healthcare are generally expected to impact more heavily on those areas experiencing rapid increases in demand (Duckett, 2005). As Australian governments have turned to community and home-based care as a key strategy for reducing the enormous costs associated with institutionalized healthcare (Kemp et al., 2002; Department of Health and Ageing, 2009), community-based healthcare agencies would appear to be particularly vulnerable to labor shortages over the coming years.

One factor that is thought to affect the capacity of healthcare agencies to cope with rising community demands and to better attract and retain staff, is the extent to which the sector has adopted more progressive, high performing work systems (HPWSs) (Leggat et al., 2011). HPWS, which are also referred to as high-involvement or high-commitment work practices, are designed to enhance employees' level of skill, motivation, information and empowerment. This is achieved by dispersing information and decision-making power throughout the organization, investing in staff development initiatives that can expand task and organization-related knowledge, and introducing more supportive leadership styles that promote joint problem solving, trust and teamwork (Guthrie, 2001; Butts et al., 2009). Importantly, research examining the impact of high involvement management practices have identified links with a range of outcomes that are important for employees (for example, job satisfaction, workplace safety), organizations (for example, reduced labor turnover, enhanced performance) and clients (for example, improved customer satisfaction, enhanced patient outcomes) (Arthur, 1994; West et al., 2006; Mendelson et al., 2011).

Despite the benefits of HPWPs, Australian healthcare agencies have generally been slow to introduce management methods that promote high employee involvement (Bartram et al., 2007). In a recent study involving 132 public hospitals and community health services based in Victoria, Australia, participating organizations reported a general lack of HPWSs. This study also identified a gap between HRM policy and practice; while CEOs of healthcare organizations reported high levels of strategic HRM (including HPWPs), senior managers indicated that HPWSs were distinctly lacking (Leggat et al., 2011). Other research focusing on the use of participatory decision-making (PDM) in Australian healthcare services found that there was considerable disparity between the rhetoric of PDM and the reality in practice (O'Donoghue et al., 2011). While this particular study was limited to three agencies, the findings support the view that effective PDM systems are not well executed within the Australian healthcare sector and that much of the success of participatory mechanisms hinge on the extent to which managers support these initiatives and believe that the benefits are worthwhile.

Intuitively, the lack of high involvement people management strategies in the health sector would appear to be a major weakness, especially in terms of addressing stress and retention-related issues. At a conceptual level, the core features of HPWSs (participatory decision-making, capacity building and supportive leadership styles) closely resemble key characteristics of widely used job stress models, including the demand-control-support (DCS) model (Karasek and Theorell, 1990) and the job demands-resources (JD-R) model (Demerouti et al., 2001). According to the DCS, job control (including decision-making influence and skill discretion) and support from supervisors and colleagues (in the form of information, guidance, feedback and direct assistance) represent influential work-based resources that employees can draw on to modify demanding workloads or to alleviate their impact. The proposition underpinning the JDR is very similar, although in this case, resources include any personal or work-based characteristics (for example, coping styles, decision-making influence) while the definition of job demands goes beyond workloads to include any threatening situation or condition faced by employees.

From an empirical perspective, the extent to which HPWSs are linked to job stress is only just emerging. In one of the few investigations to examine this relationship, a study involving 1723 retail employees in the US found that high involvement work practices were negatively associated with job stress and positively associated with employee attitudes (job satisfaction, organizational commitment) and self-rated job performance (Butts et al., 2009). The authors also investigated the underlying mechanisms through which the high involvement strategies were linked to stress-related outcomes. Consistent with the DCS and JD-R, empowerment mediated the relationship between the participatory work practices and the target variables. At the same time, perceived support from the organization moderated the relationship between organizational practices and the outcome measures, such that the positive effects of empowerment were stronger when perceived organizational support was high rather than low. Although it is difficult know whether these same relationships would apply in the state-funded health and community services, the results of this research suggest that high involvement work practices may provide valuable opportunities for addressing the high levels of job stress in the health and community services sector. They may also contribute to improved attitudinal outcomes, especially in terms of job satisfaction and organizational commitment.

The potential for high involvement work practices to combat job stress and enhance employee attitudes within health and community services is supported, to some extent, by research focusing on the psycho-social working conditions experienced by various medical and allied health personnel (Dollard et al., 2007; Noblet et al., 2007). These studies did not measure HPWSs directly, however findings indicate that several of the underlying conditions, particularly decision-making control and social support, were closely associated with a number of health and attitudinal outcomes. For example, a study involving five Australian-based CHSs (Noblet et al., 2007) found that job control and support from supervisors and colleagues were predictive of psychological distress, job satisfaction and commitment to the organization. By comparison, the effect sizes associated with job demands and other job stressors specific to the community health context were relatively small. These findings are similar to those identified in a review of 25 international and 10 Australian studies undertaken between 1999 and 2004 (Dollard et al., 2007). All investigations examined the sources of job stress experienced by health and community services personnel and the overall results indicate that a lack of job control and poor social support were common sources of stress across these studies.

While there are strong indications that stressors involving job control and social support are prominent throughout community-based and other health services, and that HPWSs may offer valuable mechanisms for addressing these stressors, the lack of uptake of participatory mechanisms and other HPWSs within this sector suggest further research is required to better understand how these initiatives should be designed to increase uptake and more effectively address stress-related working conditions. Previous research involving Australian-based healthcare services has shown that, of the few organizations that have adopted HPWSs, such practices have been well accepted by both managers and staff (O'Donoghue et al., 2011). A key aim of the current investigation is to build on this earlier research and explore those strategies (policies, systems, practices) that can enhance the psychosocial working conditions experienced by community health service employees.

METHODS

Sample and Research Context

The current study involved healthcare professionals working in an Australian-based CHS. The agency was located in a large Australian city and employed a range of healthcare personnel, including general practitioners, community health nurses, dentists, physiotherapists, speech pathologists, occupational therapists, social workers, drug and alcohol counselors and health education specialists. Like many community health services in Australia, the agency had experienced considerable growth in the preceding three to five years, especially in terms of the geographical areas served, the number of services and programs provided and the size of the healthcare workforce. The demographic profile of the community accessing the CHS was very diverse (in relation to age, ethnicity, educational background, employment status and income levels) and, based on agency records, there had been a steady increase in both the volume and complexity of cases over the previous five years.

Three open-ended, semi-structured focus groups were undertaken to explore employees' perceptions of the specific psycho-social working conditions experienced within this agency. Qualitative approaches are noted for their ability to elicit detailed, contextual descriptions of the issues under investigation (Dewe, 1989), with group discussions being particularly useful for facilitating interaction between participants and for gaining diverse perspectives of both formal and informal practices (Ritchie and Herscovitch, 1995; Hawe et al., 1998). The focus groups were organized around the major work areas within the participating agency with the purpose of providing insights into systems and practices that exist within specific departments as well as across the overall organization. One of these work areas was comprised solely of administrative personnel (executive officers, finance, human resource management, IT staff) and given that the current study focuses on the working conditions experienced by healthcare personnel, the results involving administration staff have been excluded. The actual names of the work areas discussed in the results have been changed to protect agency confidentiality and will hereafter be referred to as clinical services, primary care, community services and corporate services.

The focus group discussions were undertaken in response to an employee health and wellbeing survey that had been undertaken in the organization in the months leading up to the current study. The purpose of the survey was to assess the levels of psychological health, job satisfaction and commitment among employees and to identify the psychosocial conditions that were closely associated with these outcomes as well as the intention to quit. The survey also sought to assess the extent to which the outcome measures and the predictor variables varied between work areas within the organization and to help identify those groups that were particularly vulnerable to low levels of satisfaction, commitment and wellbeing.

Almost three-quarters of agency staff took part in the organization-wide survey (n = 187). By-and-large, the results were similar to those identified in research involving other Australian-based CHSs (Noblet et al., 2007). Social support was predictive of all four outcome measures, while job control was closely associated with all the target variables except intention to quit. Furthermore, the overall effect sizes associated with the generalized working conditions – job demands, job control, and social support – were much stronger than those attributed to the CHS-specific stressors (as reflected in the adjusted R2). While the organization-wide means on the outcome measures compared favorably with other CHSs, comparisons between work areas indicated that these levels were not uniformly distributed throughout the organization. Participants from the clinical services area, and to a lesser extent primary care, appeared to be particularly vulnerable to poorer outcomes and reported the lowest levels of psychological wellbeing, job satisfaction, and organizational commitment. Clinical services also recorded the lowest mean scores for social support and job control, the two working conditions that were closely associated with the outcome measures. In contrast, the community and corporate service areas reported relatively high mean scores on both the outcome measures and the working conditions.

From the participating agency's perspective, a key aim of the focus group discussions was to use the views and ideas of employees to develop recommendations for dealing with the specific stress-related conditions identified in each work area. In the context of the current investigation, organizing these discussions around the work areas also gave the researchers the opportunity to explore how the specific conditions involving control and support varied between the work areas, and whether these contributing factors were linked to specific characteristics of the work area (for example, leadership style of manager, nature of work undertaken by group) and/or the organization overall (agency-wide communication and decision-making systems). The work area discussions also provided the opportunity to compare the low support-control work areas with the high support-control work areas and identify the particular policies, systems or practices that undermined or enhanced the support and control received by employees. It was expected that the results of these comparisons would provide particularly valuable insights into the specific HPWSs that could foster higher levels of support and control within a community-based healthcare agency.

Procedures

The three focus groups involving clinical services, primary care and community services were facilitated by Andrew Noblet, the first-named author of this chapter, and consisted of 8–12 non-managerial staff. Participants represented a cross-section of employees based in each work area on the basis of key demographic characteristics (work role, tenure and full/part-time status). Each focus group started with an introduction that outlined the objectives of the study (including how the focus groups would build on the information gained in the employee survey), the nature of the questions to be posed, how the information would be used and steps taken to protect participant confidentiality. Participants were also provided with a summary of the survey results that related to their specific work area and were given an explanation of how their results compared to the organization-wide means.

The schedule of questions began by asking participants to comment on the extent to which the work area results reflected their perceptions of working in that area. This question was designed primarily as a means of assessing member validity, but also as a way of encouraging participants to begin reflecting on their working environments. The subsequent questions required participants to consider the extent to which: (1) their needs for support and control were being met; and (2) to describe the specific factors (policies, systems, practices) that either enhanced or undermined the support and control-based resources they received. The final questions asked participants to consider how the conditions involving support and control could be improved.

Participant responses to the questions were recorded on large sheets of paper that had been fixed to mobile white-boards. To enhance the accuracy of recorded notes, participants were asked to check the facilitator's interpretation of the responses and make sure these matched their intended meaning. Further, a series of general probes were used to encourage participants to reflect broadly on their experiences (for example, to consider the support provided by professional associations), with specific elaboration probes being used to ensure members provided detailed, unambiguous descriptions of the system, policy or practice they were referring to (Bernard, 1988; Hudleson, 1994).

RESULTS

General Responses to Survey Results

Generally, focus group participants felt that the survey results for their work areas accurately reflected their experiences of working in those areas. In the case of clinical services, participants agreed that levels of satisfaction and wellbeing were low in their units with some being surprised that their scores were not even lower. When asked why the levels of satisfaction and wellbeing were considerably lower than other areas within the organization, participants generally felt that this was due to a combination of the nature of their work (constant contact with ill and disadvantaged patients, long waiting lists) as well as the conditions in which they work (reliance on clinical-based funding yet still required to complete a relatively large number of non-clinical tasks, chronic under-resourcing and insufficient space).

Focus group participants from primary care also thought that the results were consistent with their experiences. The relatively high level of psychological distress was something that resonated strongly with participants from this area. In counseling, for example, one respondent reported that some colleagues wanted to move away from those roles involving high-level contact with severe cases, such as family violence, and would prefer to have a client-base where the needs varied and where they had some respite between the emotionally challenging cases. The client-base was also mentioned as a key reason why psychological and emotional demands are higher in this area, with many clients living crisis-driven lives and experiencing extreme hardship (unemployment, homelessness, drug addiction and/or relationship breakdown).

Participants from community services also reported high level contact with disadvantaged groups and recognized that this could be draining at times. However, they also felt that they had a supportive team environment and that this support helped them to work through the difficult times. In addition, participants in this focus group mentioned that they received a high level of advice, guidance and assistance from their team leader and that this helped them deal effectively with challenging clients.

Enhancing Social Support

The second part of the group discussions aimed to identify and explore those policies, systems and practices that undermined or enhanced the support received by employees. The discussions involving clinical services and primary care were very similar and tended to revolve around those aspects of social support that were lacking. In contrast, discussions involving participants from community services focused more heavily on those practices that were having a positive influence on their perceived support. In view of the similarities in the responses from clinical services and primary care, the results of these particular discussions have been presented together.

Clinical services and primary care
Several participants from the clinical services and primary care focus groups mentioned that more senior personnel such as team leaders and program managers were considered a potentially valuable source of support since they are often the ones who have the authority and the

knowledge to address the specific work-related needs of employees. However some focus group members also felt that support from more senior personnel was lacking in their areas. At a team level, a number of participants expressed difficulty in confiding in their team leader regarding work-related concerns. They perceived this difficulty to stem from the organization's tendency to recruit team leaders from within existing teams, and that such people were inadequately prepared or trained to take on their leadership role. Others felt that external EAP-style support should be provided as a standard service (not just in the case of acute incidents) and that confidential, externally-based support should be available irrespective of the supportive capacities of the team leader.

Limited access to professional supervision was identified as another support-related concern, especially for those working in multi-disciplinary teams or in areas involving rapid change. Participants explained that the five-day training quota was not flexible enough, both in terms of the timing (for example, people sometimes require more and do this on their rostered leave days) and the content (for example, the required training does not always match 'approved' training).

Team meetings were identified as an important forum for giving and receiving support. However several members of the focus groups involving clinical services and primary care representatives believed these were held too infrequently to be of real benefit. Similarly, participants lamented the lack of attention given to team development initiatives, which limited the extent to which workers could support each other. Focus group participants also expressed concern regarding the organization's approach to training and development and the emphasis placed on informal peer-to-peer training. Heavy client loads and the ongoing pressure to address community needs made it difficult for staff to invest time in teaching new colleagues, especially in areas where there had been a gradual influx of new employees and/or steady turnover of existing staff.

The difficulties faced by group members appeared to be exacerbated by the lack of support from the CHSs management. Generally, participants in the clinical services and primary care focus groups believed that senior personnel in the organization took little interest in their areas and that they rarely had contact with executive members of the organization. These groups were also concerned about the 'top-down' approach to managing the organization and that the lack of two-way communication made it difficult to express their needs and concerns.

It should be noted that not all participants in the clinical services and primary care focus groups shared the same concern regarding centre management. One particular member believed their unit had regular contact with executive personnel and that leading members of the organization took a genuine interest in their group's activities. However, these views appeared to be in the minority. Overall, the mood of the focus groups involving clinical services and primary care was negative. Members were pessimistic about the organization's ability to manage increasing community demands and, although the agency had experienced considerable growth in response to these rising needs, focus group participants reported that this growth had come at the expense of effective communication and decision-making systems. There were also serious doubts raised regarding the organization's ability to physically house an expanded workforce in facilities that were already over-crowded and out-of-date.

Community services

Comments from the focus group involving community services were generally in contrast to those raised in the focus groups involving clinical services and primary care. Participants in this group readily acknowledged the challenges they faced in terms of the difficult nature of their work and the limited resources available to address these demands. However, unlike employees in the previously discussed groups, these employees were confident in their capacity to meet these challenges. According to some participants, this confidence was partly attributed to the level of support provided by colleagues and team leaders. One particular member mentioned that their team has a 5–10 minute 'stand-up' meeting at the beginning and end of each day. These meetings helped to ensure there was a high level of communication within the group. Others recognized that the team meetings, in combination with the ongoing informal and impromptu peer-to-peer discussions, were an important opportunity to debrief on complex cases, to ensure that issues were not internalized and to identify and deal with problems quickly. They were also happy with the level of professional supervision they received (in one group this was once a fortnight) and felt that the use of workload planners and training calendars enabled them to better manage their workloads while also addressing their ongoing need for professional development.

Participants in the community service focus group also recognized that camaraderie and teamwork were key strengths of their work area and that workers readily helped each other out. Further, new members reported being warmly welcomed into the group and appreciated the guidance and assistance they received from colleagues and team leaders. Likewise, more experienced members felt that the flexible team culture and workers' willingness to cover for each other enabled them to achieve a better balance between professional and personal responsibilities. The high level of communication and teamwork within these groups was due, in a large part, to the leadership style adopted by team leaders. Both utilized participatory management styles and employed two-way communication as a way of better understanding the needs of their group members, whilst also fulfilling important organizational objectives. There also appeared to be a higher level of interaction with program managers and the groups overall felt that they were supported to think creatively, to take risks and look for innovative ways of achieving their team's objectives.

Increasing Employee Control

The third and final component of the group discussions focused on job control (for instance, involvement in decision-making and skill discretion). Overall, participants' comments revealed a similar trend to that involving social support. Participants from the clinical and primary care focus groups tended to concentrate on where decision-making systems and skill discretion was deficient, while community services emphasized the conditions that supported their sense of control. The following is a summary of the responses from these particular discussions.

Clinical services and primary care
Members from all three focus groups indicated that they had a relatively high level of professional autonomy and that they could control, to a large extent, the specific methods used to complete their work. However, participants from the clinical services and primary care generally felt they had less influence over the way their units were run and had limited input into operational matters.

In clinical services, for example, participants indicated that they had little control over the amount of non-clinical work they were involved in and felt relatively powerless to change influential policies (for example, relating to training provisions) or other aspects of their work settings (for example, state of their facilities and equipment). In relation to facilities, staff understood that even the CHS had limited control over the physical conditions in which they worked, however several participants believed that relatively small changes could make a significant difference and that the control over these changes could be devolved down to the work area level.

In primary care, several participants believed that decision-making within the organization was more centralized than it should be and that workers tended to do what they were required to do, not what they thought could be more effective. They also felt that the more distant approach adopted by CHS management undermined staffs' ability to develop a working understanding of the agency's vision and, in turn, restricted their ability to make meaningful contributions to the goals of the organization. Participants from both the clinical service and the primary care focus groups also felt that their level of control was hampered by the lack of information regarding other programs and that the agency's intranet lacked accurate, up-to-date information and specific guidance. Further, participants re-emphasized their concern regarding the speed at which the agency was growing and the need for systems (communication, information dissemination) to keep pace with this growth.

Community services

The views expressed by members of the community services focus group were somewhat different to those raised in the clinical services and primary care groups. Members certainly felt that a lack of adequate work space – not just for completing work tasks but also for rest and reflection – diminished people's sense of control and that failing infrastructure, especially IT systems, was a further barrier. Concern was also expressed regarding the tendency to hold meetings in the central sites (geographically). Participants believed that in order to maintain involvement from all sections of the organization, meetings needed to be spread among the various sites. Despite these concerns, members of the community services focus group generally felt that the organization adopted an inclusive approach to decision-making and that there were numerous committees, as well as other forums, where people could have their say. They also believed that these forums offered genuine opportunities for input into decision-making and that their views were taken seriously. At a more immediate work area level, participants in this focus group believed that their level of decision-making authority generally matched the level of responsibility they had and staff were not held accountable for work they had little control over.

Other opportunities for boosting employee control were identified in discussions involving employee support (see previous sub-section). For example, more open and supportive leadership styles, where managers actively seek and engage the views of employees, would provide staff with the opportunity to have greater influence over their working environments. Similarly, more frequent staff meetings could not only provide staff with timely information and guidance, but also allow them further opportunities for influencing how their work is organized, and for developing more effective ways of addressing the demanding nature of their work. The greater face-to-face contact with management was also seen as a way of enabling workers to gain a better understanding of what is happening across the organization, particularly in terms of new programs. More visible management would also provide workers with the opportunity to learn more about the organization's vision and to have input into how this vision could be realized.

DISCUSSION

The overall aim of the current investigation was to explore those strategies (policies, systems, practices) that could enhance the support and control-based working conditions experienced by community health service employees. The types of strategies identified in the focus groups varied between work areas and tended to reflect the levels of support and control reported in the organization-wide survey undertaken prior to the current research. Participants taking part in the focus group discussions believed that there were numerous opportunities for enhancing social support and job control within their organization. Some of the strategies for building a more supportive workplace included ensuring that agency management develop a more in-depth understanding of the needs and demands experienced by employees; selecting team leaders and program managers carefully and making sure they have the interpersonal and team-development skills required to lead and manage people; enhancing intra-unit communication by running staff meetings that provide staff with meaningful opportunities for giving and receiving support and; providing staff with ongoing access to EAP-style support, especially for those involved in emotionally demanding work.

The strategies suggested for improving employee control and involvement included ensuring that all staff with people management responsibilities are aware of the importance of job control in shaping employee health and satisfaction and using selection and training as avenues for developing more inclusive management capacities; encouraging all senior personnel (executive staff, program managers and team-leaders) to monitor the employees' roles and responsibilities and ensuring that they have enough decision-making influence to address these demands; reviewing current organization-wide consultative mechanisms and determining if there are groups who lack access to these mechanisms and; developing a more inclusive culture within the agency by ensuring that there is greater face-to-face contact between executive-level personnel and front-line staff.

One of the benefits of the focus group responses is that they can help explain the reasons why support and control figured so prominently in previous job stress research involving CHSs (Noblet et al., 2007). As healthcare professionals working in a community-based service, participants were more accepting of the demanding nature of their work environment and readily acknowledged that the volume and complexity of the demands faced were heavily influenced by the needs of their clients and communities. The agency itself had very little control over community needs and therefore could not be expected to modify these demands. However a recurring theme reflected in the focus groups (especially those from the low support-control work areas) is that organizational leaders can have more influence over the way in which internal resources are managed, particularly in relation to support and control-based resources. A lack of decision-making influence and support were evident in numerous comments made by participants from the clinical and primary care work areas (for example, inadequate input into decisions involving agency goals, poor or inappropriate supervisory support) and was a major source of frustration and dissatisfaction for those involved. In contrast, where necessary levels of support and control were available, staff could use these to deal with complex cases, to engage in more creative problem solving, and to generate higher levels of communication and teamwork.

The strategies recommended by focus group participants also reinforce the use of high performance work systems in CHSs. Participatory decision-making systems, leadership styles, training and development programs, teamwork, methods of communication and other initiatives typically addressed in HPWS were all highlighted in suggestions for improving control and support-based conditions. As the comments from the community services work area indicate, CHSs do have the capacity to adopt practices that are consistent with HPWSs and that, where such practices are well executed and managed, they can have a positive influence on employee attitudes and behavior. These results are consistent with other research involving HPWSs and indicate that multi-disciplinary, community-based healthcare services should carefully consider utilizing HPWSs as a way of addressing high levels of job stress within the sector (West et al., 2006; Butts et al., 2009).

The focus group discussions have also provided useful insights into the levels at which HPWSs should operate within a community health context. For the current organization, conditions involving support and control appeared to be heavily influenced by both work area factors and organization-wide systems and approaches. In the case of work areas, comments from participants suggest that the skills, attitudes and actions of supervisors and team leaders can have a major influence on the level of support and control experienced by group members. This finding is consistent with research indicating that management support for participatory decision-making and their perceived benefits were the most important factors in determining whether healthcare agencies adopted this style of decision-making (O'Donoghue et al., 2011). An important implication of these findings is that in order to enhance employee control and support, agencies first need to ensure mid-level managers have the necessary skills and motivation to adopt HPWSs (through selection, training and/or other developmental opportunities). At an organization-wide level, the systems and processes adopted by executive personnel also influenced the support and control experienced by organizational members. The specific comments reported in the focus groups indicate that there is a need for executive level staff to continually assess their decision-making and communication systems to ensure they are engaging with and supporting all sections of the workforce.

Although the breadth of strategies mentioned in the focus groups suggest that fostering conditions that build employee support and control would be time-consuming, labor intensive and potentially disruptive to introduce, the level of overlap between strategies indicates that this may not be the case. A number of the opportunities for boosting social support (for example, developing more open and supportive leadership styles, more timely staff meetings that offer opportunities for information sharing and collaborative problem-solving) also provide opportunities to enhance employee control. This synergy between support and control-based strategies reinforces the early job stress research (House, 1981; Karasek and Theorell, 1990) and indicates that the mechanisms for enhancing decision latitude can also create more supportive workplaces (and vice-versa). From a pragmatic organizational change perspective, this co-dependence may make support and control strategies more appealing for organizations, especially given the resource constraints of community-based healthcare agencies.

Limitations and Future Research

There are a number of limitations that need to be kept in mind when interpreting the results of the current investigation. One of the key limitations is that the sample consisted of a cross-section of employees from one Australian-based CHS. Although there may be many similarities between this agency and other small, state-funded organizations operating in the health and human services, there are also likely to be differences – both within the internal and external environments. There needs to be close alignment between people management initiatives (including job stress prevention/reduction strategies) and the needs, capacities and strategic direction of the organization involved and hence the context-specific nature of the strategies identified in the current investigation restrict the generalizability of the findings.

Although the idiosyncratic nature of the participating organization is a clear limitation, the methods used to develop these strategies are likely to have broader applicability. Combined quantitative-qualitative approaches are not widely used in job stress research, especially within the behavioral sciences. However, as demonstrated in the current study, qualitative methods such as semi-structured focus groups can complement quantitative methods. In comparison to the employee survey, the responses from focus group participants were particularly useful for providing a more detailed understanding of the often complex reasons why conditions involving support and control were important for staff and helped to uncover the specific strategies for improving these conditions. In addition, the combined quantitative-qualitative methods provided greater scope for drawing on the views and ideas of employees. This appeared to generate greater enthusiasm for introducing strategies that could enhance the effectiveness of people-management systems and practices.

Another important limitation of the current research is that the focus groups consisted entirely of front-line community health workers. Supervisors, team leaders and other managerial personnel were excluded from the group discussions, to ensure that their involvement did not influence participant responses. However as the attitudes and actions of supervisors and managers had a large influence on the psycho-social working conditions experienced by participants (positive and negative), research is needed to identify the reasons why they adopted certain styles or practices and to consider the types of support mechanisms that are required to facilitate the development of more effective and less stressful people management strategies. Previous public sector research involving middle managers has found that supervisors and team leaders often have day-to-day responsibility for implementing directives from more senior personnel and government officials, while at the same time dealing with the reactions of subordinates (Butterfield et al., 2004). Not only can the constant pressure of playing 'piggy in the middle' be a key source of stress for junior and middle managers, but the sheer workload volume can limit the extent to which they are able to interact with staff. Any initiatives designed to enhance psycho-social working conditions in public sector services should therefore take into account the needs and capacities of this group.

Conclusion

The responses from the focus groups have provided a detailed description of the many factors that contribute to employees' experiences of support and control in a state funded community health service. The nature of these factors, as well as the types of systems and practices required to enhance support and control-based working conditions, varied according to whether the work area reported higher or lower levels of social support and job control. Many participants also indicated that, in contrast to work demands, the agency has considerable influence over how it organizes work and manages people and strategies for enhancing support and control need to operate at both a work area level and an organizational level. Finally, the results from the current investigation support the view that HPWSs can operate effectively in a CHS and, where they do, these initiatives can not only improve stress-related working conditions such as job control and social support, but can also have a positive influence on the attitudes and wellbeing of employees.

REFERENCES

Arthur, J. (1994), 'Effects of human resource systems on manufacturing perform-ance and turnover', *Academy of Management Journal*, **37**, 670–87.

Bartram, T., P. Stanton S. Leggat, G. Casimir and B. Fraser (2007), 'Lost in trans-lation: exploring the link between HRM and performance in healthcare', *Human Resource Management Journal*, **17** (1), 21–41.

Baum, F. (1996), 'Community health services and managerialism', *Australian Journal of Primary Health Interchange*, **2** (4), 31–41.

Bernard, R. (1988), *Research Methods in Cultural Anthropology*, Beverly Hills: Sage Publications.

Brown, R. (2000), 'Community health within the context of health reform', *Australian Journal of Primary Health Interchange*, **6** (1), 85–96.

Butterfield, R., C. Edwards and J. Woodall (2004), 'The new public manage-ment and the UK police service: The role of the police sergeant in the imple-mentation of performance management', *Public Management Review*, **6** (3), 395–415.

Butts, M.M., R.J. Vandenberg, D.M. DeJoy, B.S. Schaffer and M.G. Wilson (2009), 'Individual reactions to high involvement work processes: investigat-ing the role of empowerment and perceived organizational support', *Journal of Occupational Health Psychology*, **14** (2), 122–36.

Demerouti, E., A.B. Bakker, F. Nachreiner and W.B. Schaufeli (2001), 'The job demands-resources model of burnout', *Journal of Applied Psychology*, **86** (3), 499–512.

Department of Health and Ageing (2009), *Primary Healthcare Reform in Australia: Report to Support Australia's First National Primary Healthcare Strategy*, Canberra.

Dewe, P. (1989), 'Examining the nature of work stress: individual evaluations of stressful experiences and coping', *Human Relations*, **42**, 993–1013.

Dollard, M.F., A.D. LaMontagne, N. Caulfield, V. Blewett and A. Shaw (2007), 'Job stress in the Australian and international health and community services sector: a review of the literature', *International Journal of Stress Management*, **14** (4), 417–45.

Duckett, S.J. (2005), 'Health workforce design for the 21st century', *Australian Health Review*, **29** (2), 201–210.

Guthrie, J. (2001), 'High-involvement work practices, turnover, and productivity: evidence from New Zealand', *Academy of Management Journal*, **44** (1), 180–90.

Hawe, P., D. Degeling and J. Hall (1998), *Evaluating Health Promotion: A Health Worker's Guide*, Sydney: MacLennan and Petty.

House, J.S. (1981), *Work Stress and Social Support*, London: Addison-Wesley Publishing Company.

Hudleson, P. (1994), *Introduction to Qualitative Research. Qualitative Research for Health Programmes*, Geneva: Division of Mental Health, World Health Organization, pp. 1–10.

Karasek, R. and T. Theorell (1990), *Healthy Work: Stress, Productivity, and the Reconstruction of Working Life*, New York: Basic Books.

Kemp, L., E. Comino, E. Harris and D. Killian (2002), 'A decade of change in a community health service: a shift to acute and short-term services', *Australian Health Review*, **25** (6), 148–55.

Leggat, S.G., T. Bartram and P. Stanton (2006), 'People management in Victorian community health services: an exploratory study', *Australian Journal of Primary Health*, **12** (3), 59–65.

Leggat, S.G., T. Bartram and P. Stanton (2011), 'High performance work systems: the gap between policy and practice in healthcare reform', *Journal of Health, Organization and Management*, **25** (3), 281–297.

Mendelson, M.B., N. Turner and J. Barling (2011), 'Perceptions of the presence and effectiveness of high involvement work systems and their relationship to employee attitudes: a test of competing models', *Personnel Review*, **40** (1), 45–69.

Noblet, A., C. Cooper, J. McWilliams and A. Rudd (2007), 'Wellbeing, job satisfaction and commitment among Australian community health workers – the relationship with working conditions', *Australian Journal of Primary Health*, **13** (3), 40–8.

O'Donoghue, P., P. Stanton and T. Bartram (2011), 'Employee participation in the healthcare industry: the experience of three case studies', *Asia Pacific Journal of Human Resources*, **49** (2), 193–212.

PHAA (2005), *Public Health Association of Australia Policy Statements: Health Services Development (Section 8), Primary Healthcare*, accessed 19 September 2006 at http://www.phaa.net.au/policy/contents.htm.

Ritchie, J. and F. Herscovitch (1995), 'From Likert to love it: engaging blue collar workers in focus group inquiries', *Journal of Occupational Health and Safety – Australia and New Zealand*, **11** (5), 471–9.

Scott, I. A. (2009), 'Healthcare workforce crisis in Australia: too few or too disabled?', *Medical Journal of Australia*, **190** (12), 689–92.

West, M., J. Guthrie, J. Dawson, C. Borrill and M. Carter (2006), 'Reducing patient mortality in hospitals: the role of human resource management', *Journal of Organizational Behavior*, **27**, 983–1002.

6. Work engagement among public and private sector dentists

Arnold B. Bakker and Jari J. Hakanen

INTRODUCTION

Dentistry is a stressful occupation (Blinkhorn, 1992; Wilson et al., 1998). Several studies have shown that burnout (for instance, a job stress syndrome characterized by emotional exhaustion, depersonalization, and reduced personal accomplishment) is by no means rare among dentists (for example, Gorter et al., 1998; Gorter, Eijkman and Hoogstraten, 2000; Humphries, 1998; Osborne and Croucher, 1994). Research has identified several job demands associated with job stress and burnout in the dentistry profession. In his review of the literature, Gorter (2000) concluded that demanding patient interactions, workload, time pressure, physical demands, and inflicting pain or fear are all possible causes of job stress in dentistry. How do dentists manage to cope with their job demands and stay engaged in their work? In the present chapter, we answer this question by investigating the working conditions of Finnish dentists.

In this respect, the difference between the public and private sector is important. The dental law reforms carried out in Finland in the early 2000s are of particular concern for dentists working in the public sector. The reforms meant that, since December 2002, every Finnish citizen has the right to receive dental healthcare support. It was legislated that dental healthcare support should be provided through two channels: (i) clients can use the services of private dentists and get health insurance compensation; or (ii) clients can use the community dental healthcare services. However, clients' financial responsibility is clearly higher in the private sector. Consequently, the dental services in the public sector have become congested. In addition, there has been a shift from preventive work towards acute and emergency care, and the work pace of dentists in the public sector has increased after the reform. For example, 43 per cent of dentists employed in the public sector (as compared with 5 per cent in the private sector) reported that since the reform, acute and emergency care has increased by a large extent. At the same time, 48 per cent of the dentists in the public sector (17 per cent in the private sector) stated that the demand for dental services has increased (Hakanen, 2004).

The central goal of this chapter is to compare the levels of work engagement and performance of dentists working in the public and private sector. Moreover, we will investigate whether dentists in the public sector are exposed to different levels of job demands and job resources compared to dentists working in the private sector. We will use the job demands-resources (JD-R) model (Bakker and Demerouti, 2007, 2008; Demerouti et al., 2001) as a theoretical framework.

WORK ENGAGEMENT AND PERFORMANCE

Kahn (1990) was one of the first to theorize about work engagement. He described engaged employees as being fully physically, cognitively and emotionally connected with their work roles. Engagement refers to focused energy that is directed toward organizational goals (Macey et al., 2009). Engaged employees are more likely to work harder through increased levels of discretionary effort than those who are disengaged. There are several definitions of engagement (see Albrecht, 2010; Bakker and Leiter, 2010), but Schaufeli et al. (2002: 74) proposed what is arguably the most often used definition: '. . . a positive, fulfilling, work-related state of mind that is characterized by vigor, dedication and absorption'. In essence, work engagement captures how people experience their work: as stimulating and energetic and something to which they really want to devote time and effort (the 'vigor' component); as a significant and meaningful pursuit ('dedication'); and as engrossing and something on which they are fully concentrated ('absorption') (Bakker et al., 2008a).

Work engagement is different from job satisfaction in that it combines high work pleasure (dedication) with high activation (vigor, absorption); job satisfaction is typically a more passive form of employee well-being. Research has shown that engaged employees are highly energetic, self-efficacious individuals who exercise influence over events that affect their lives (Bakker, 2011). Due to their positive attitude and high activity level, engaged employees create their own positive feedback, in terms of appreciation, recognition, and success. Engaged employees are not addicted to their work. They enjoy other things outside work. Unlike workaholics, engaged employees do not work hard because of a strong and irresistible inner drive, but because for them working is fun (Schaufeli, Taris and Bakker, 2006). Not surprisingly then, work engagement is a better predictor of job performance than job satisfaction or workaholism.

The number of studies showing a positive link between employee work engagement and job performance is steadily increasing. For example, Bakker, Demerouti and Verbeke (2004) showed that engaged employees received higher ratings from their colleagues on in-role performance (those officially required outcomes and behaviors that directly serve the goals of the organization) and extra-role performance (discretionary behaviors on the part of an employee that are believed to directly promote the effective functioning of an organization, without necessarily directly influencing a person's target productivity). These findings indicate that engaged employees perform well and are willing to go the extra mile. Further, in their study of employees working in Spanish restaurants and hotels, Salanova, Agut and Peiró (2005) showed that employee ratings of work engagement and service climate were positively related to customer ratings of employee performance.

In their quantitative diary study of Greek employees working in fast-food restaurants, Xanthopoulou et al. (2009) expanded this research and made a compelling case for the predictive value of daily work engagement for daily job performance. Participants were asked to fill in a survey and a diary booklet for five consecutive days. Consistent with hypotheses, results showed that employees were more engaged on days that were characterized by many job resources. Daily job resources like supervisor coaching and team atmosphere contributed to the employees' personal resources (daily levels of optimism, self-efficacy and self-esteem), which, in turn, contributed to daily engagement. In addition, the higher employees' levels of daily engagement were, the higher their objective financial returns were. For a meta-analysis of the link between work engagement and performance, we refer to Christian, Garza and Slaughter (2011).

THE JD-R MODEL

During the past decade, the JD-R model (Bakker and Demerouti, 2007, 2008; Demerouti and Bakker, 2011; Demerouti et al., 2001) has been used to predict a wide range of work-related experiences. The model has been used to predict job burnout (for example, Bakker et al., 2008b; Demerouti et al., 2001), organizational commitment, work enjoyment (Bakker, Van Veldhoven and Xanthopoulou, 2010), connectedness (Lewig et al., 2007), and employee work engagement (Bakker and Demerouti, 2008; Bakker et al., 2007; Hakanen, Bakker and Schaufeli, 2006). In addition, the JD-R model has been able to predict the consequences of these work-related experiences including objective sickness absenteeism (for example, Bakker et al., 2003; Clausen et al., 2012; Schaufeli, Bakker and Van Rhenen, 2009), other-ratings of job performance (Bakker, Demerouti and

Verbekke, 2004), and objective sales performance (for example, Bakker et al., 2008a).

One important reason for the popularity of the JD-R model is its flexibility. According to the model, all working environments or job characteristics can be modeled using two different categories, namely job demands and job resources. Thus, the model can be applied to all work environments and can be tailored to the specific occupation under consideration. Job demands refer to those physical, psychological, social, or organizational aspects of the job that require sustained physical and/or psychological effort and are therefore associated with certain physiological and/or psychological costs (Demerouti et al., 2001). Examples are a high work pressure and emotionally demanding interactions with patients or clients. Although job demands are not necessarily negative, they may turn into hindrance demands when meeting those demands requires high effort from which the employee has not adequately recovered (Meijman and Mulder, 1998). Job resources refer to those physical, psychological, social, or organizational aspects of the job that either/or: (1) are functional in achieving work goals; (2) reduce job demands and the associated physiological and psychological costs; and (3) stimulate personal growth, learning and development (Bakker, 2011; Bakker and Demerouti, 2007). Hence, resources are not only necessary to deal with job demands, but they are also important in their own right. Whereas meaningful variations in levels of certain specific job demands and resources can be found in almost every occupational group (like work pressure, autonomy), other job demands and resources are more unique. For example, although physical demands are still very important job demands nowadays for road workers and nurses, cognitive demands are much more relevant for scientists and engineers, and emotional demands are more important for dentists.

According to the JD-R model, job demands and resources are the triggers of two fairly independent processes, namely a health impairment process and a motivational process. Thus, whereas job demands are generally the most important predictors of such outcomes as exhaustion, psychosomatic health complaints, and RSI-complaints (e.g. Bakker, Demerouti and Schaufeli, 2003; Hakanen et al., 2006), job resources are generally the most important predictors of work enjoyment and engagement (Bakker et al., 2007; 2010). The reasons for these unique effects are that, in basic terms, job demands cost effort and consume energetic resources, whereas job resources fulfill basic needs – like the needs for autonomy, relatedness, and competence (Deci and Ryan, 2000). Longitudinal research in dentistry has shown that job demands predict future burnout, which in turn predict depression, whereas job resources predict reduced burnout and increased levels of work engagement and commitment (Hakanen et al., 2008b).

Moreover, related research among dentists has shown that job resources are predictors and outcomes of work engagement and personal initiative (Hakanen, 2008a). This indicates that job resources stimulate engagement and personal initiative. Simultaneously, engaged dentists proactively change their work environment so that their job resources increase. This phenomenon is also known as 'job crafting' (Bakker, 2011).

One important proposition put forward by the JD-R model is that job demands and resources interact in predicting occupational well-being. There are two possible ways in which demands and resources may have a combined effect on well-being. The first interaction is the one where job resources buffer the impact of hindrance job demands on well-being. Several studies have shown that job resources like social support, job autonomy, performance feedback, and opportunities for personal development can mitigate the undesirable impact of job demands (work pressure, emotional demands, etc.) on well-being, including burnout (for example, Bakker, Demerouti and Euwema, 2005; Xanthopoulou et al., 2007). The second interaction is the one where job challenges amplify the positive impact of job resources on motivation. Thus, research has shown that job resources become salient and have the strongest positive impact on work engagement when job challenges are high.

Hakanen et al. (2005) tested the latter interaction hypothesis in a sample of Finnish dentists employed in the public sector. It was hypothesized that job resources (for example, variability in the required professional skills, peer contacts) are most beneficial in maintaining work engagement under conditions of high job demands. The dentists were split into two random groups in order to cross-validate the findings. A set of hierarchical regression analyses resulted in 17 out of 40 significant interactions (40 per cent), showing, for example, that variability in professional skills boosted work engagement when qualitative workload was high, and mitigated the negative effect of qualitative workload on work engagement. Importantly, the lowest levels of engagement were found under conditions of high job demand and low job resources.

Conceptually similar findings have been reported by Bakker et al. (2007). In their study among Finnish teachers working in elementary, secondary and vocational schools, they found that job resources act as buffers and diminish the negative relationship between pupil misbehavior and work engagement. In addition, they found that job resources particularly influence work engagement when teachers are confronted with high levels of pupil misconduct. A series of moderated structural equation modeling analyses resulted in 14 out of 18 possible two-way interaction effects (78 per cent). Particularly supervisor support, innovativeness, appreciation and organizational climate were important job resources for teachers that helped them cope with demanding interactions with students. Again, the lowest levels of engagement were found under conditions of high job demands and low job resources.

In summary, previous research with the JD-R model clearly indicates that job resources are the most important predictors of employee work engagement, and that this effect is particularly found when job demands are high. The worst working environments are those that are characterized by high job demands and low job resources, because workers who are confronted with such environments do not have the resources to cope with their high job demands. We will now turn to the work of dentists to investigate which demands and resources may play a role in determining work engagement.

THE PRESENT STUDY

In Finland, like for example in Sweden, half of the dentists work in the public sector and the other half in the private sector. In addition, a majority of dentists do not work alone but in smaller or larger dental clinics employing other dental staff as well. In the public sector, most dentists in Finland are employed in municipal healthcare centers, and, to a lesser extent, in hospitals and in universities. Traditionally, dentists in the private sector are self-employed but in bigger private clinics there are also employed dentists. Regardless of the sector, the work of dentists is a challenging combination of various job demands, such as emotional (meeting a fearful patient), cognitive (choosing the right procedure), physical (difficult work postures), and quantitative (limited time for each patient) demands (for example, Gorter, 2000; Hakanen et al., 2008b). In addition, dentistry includes several possible job resources, such as positive patient contacts, clinical autonomy, seeing the immediate and long-term results of one's work, and supportive colleagues (e.g., Gorter et al., 2006; Hakanen et al., 2008a and b). In the present study, we focused on a total of eight job demands and eleven job resources in dentistry. We also investigated the levels of engagement and self-reported job performance: in-role and extra-role performance and personal initiative. On the basis of our overview of the literature and the JD-R model, we formulated the following hypotheses:

Hypothesis 1: Public sector dentists have fewer job resources than private sector dentists.

Hypothesis 2: Public sector dentists have higher job demands than private sector dentists.

Hypothesis 3:   Public sector dentists report lower work engagement than private sector dentists.

Hypothesis 4:   Public sector dentists report lower levels of performance than private sector dentists.

METHOD

Procedure and Participants

The study reported in this chapter is part of a longitudinal research project focusing on well-being and health in dentistry in Finland. In 2010, a questionnaire including validated scales was sent to (1) all dentists who participated in two previous study waves and that could be reached for the third wave ($N = 2275$), and (2) those Finnish dentists that did not respond to earlier surveys or who had become dentists after the second wave in 2006 ($N = 2015$). The response rates were 86 per cent ($N = 1964$) for those who had participated in the panel study, and 44 per cent ($N = 933$) for the new participants, respectively. The present study consists of 1632 dentists employed in the public sector and 1124 dentists working in the private sector. Note that the sector could not be defined unambiguously for 141 participants, most typically because these dentists worked evenly in both sectors. The participants account for approximately 49 per cent of the dental profession in Finland.

Measures

Job resources
We assessed five general job resources and six dentist-specific job resources. We first describe the general job resources.

Decision authority ($\alpha_{pub} = .84$ and $\alpha_{pri} = .81$): was measured with Karasek's (1985) job content instrument. It includes three items, such as 'My job allows me to make a lot of decisions on my own'. The items are scored on a five-point scale, ranging from 1 = strongly agree to 5 = strongly disagree. *Role clarity* ($\alpha_{pub} = .81$ and $\alpha_{pri} = .73$): was measured with the Finnish version of the Nordic questionnaire for psychological and social factors at work (QPS Nordic) (Dallner et al., 2000). The scale comprises three items, such as 'Do you know what your responsibilities are?' Items were judged on a five-point scale ranging from 1 = very seldom or never to 5 = very often or always. The positive organizational climate and innovative climate were derived from the healthy organization barometer (HOB) (Lindström, 1997; Lindström, Hottinen and Bredenberg, 2000).

Positive organizational climate (α_{pub} = .83 and α_{pri} = .85): was assessed with three items, such as 'What is the climate in your work unit? . . . Encouraging and supportive of new ideas' (1 = strongly disagree, 5 = strongly agree).

Innovative climate (α_{pub} = .74 and α_{pri} = .72): consisted of three items, for example 'How often do the following aspects occur in your work? . . .We continuously make improvements concerning our jobs' (1 = hardly ever, 5 = very often).

Work-to-family enrichment (α_{pub} = .79 and α_{pri} = .82): was assessed using three items from Grzywacs and Marks (2000). An example item is 'The things you do at work help you deal with personal and practical issues at home' (1 = never, 5 = all the time). Profession-specific job resources were assessed using five scales from the dentists' experienced job resources scale (DEJRS) (Gorter et al., 2006), which is specifically aimed at identifying and investigating job resources in dentistry. The DEJRS is based on previous studies that have identified job resources in dentistry, and has been validated among large samples of dentists in The Netherlands (Gorter et al., 2006), and also in Finland (Hakanen, 2004).

Craftsmanship (α_{pub} = .67 and α_{pri} = .70): consisted of three items comprising the opportunity to work with one's hands, being creative and combining medical and technical aspects.

Pride in the profession (α_{pub} = .77 and α_{pri} = .78): included five items covering aspects such as pride, problem-solving, and the nature of the profession itself.

Direct and long-term results (α_{pub} = .89 and α_{pri} = .87): consisted of six items covering, for example, good treatment results, making a successful restoration, gaining patients' trust, and patients using their teeth without problems.

Peer contacts (α_{pub} = .81 and α_{pri} = .78): was measured with four items, for example, interacting with colleagues and opportunities for advanced training.

Positive patient contacts (α_{pub} = .67 and α_{pri} = .55): included three items, for example, the enthusiasm and spontaneity of children. The items for these five scales were formulated such that the respondents could indicate the extent to which they perceived the descriptions (items) as personal resources at work (1 = very little or not at all, 5 = very much).

Cooperation with one's assistant (α_{pub} = .75 and α_{pri} = .72): finally, the sixth profession-specific job resource was based on a four-item scale (Hakanen, 2004). The items, such as 'Does cooperation with your assistant run smoothly?' were rated on a five-point scale ranging from 1 = very rarely to 5 = very often/ always.

Job demands
We assessed eight job demands – four general demands and four dentistry-related demands. We first describe the general job demands.

Quantitative workload (α_{pub} = .79 and α_{pri} = .74): was assessed with three items developed by Karasek (1985). The items were scored from 1 = strongly agree to 5 = strongly disagree and reversed so that high scores were indicative of high workload.

Physical environment (α_{pub} = .79 and α_{pri} = .78): consisted of eight items measuring the perceived adversity of different aspects (for example, 'chemicals', 'noise' and 'quality of indoor air') in the physical work environment (Hakanen, 2004). The five-point scale ranged from 1 = not at all to 5 = very much.

Emotional dissonance (α_{pub} = .88 and α_{pri} = .87): is a scale developed by Zapf et al. (1999), and the scale included four items, such as 'How often in your job do you have to display feelings that do not agree with your actual feelings towards the clients?' (1 = very rarely/never, 5 = very often/several times an hour).

Work to family conflict (α_{pub} = .85 and α_{pri} = .86): was measured with four items developed by Grzywacz and Marks (2000), such as 'My job makes me feel too tired to do the things that need attention at home' (1 = never, 5 = all the time).

Impact of the law changes (α_{pub} = .83 and α_{pri} = .84): of the specific scales developed for dentistry this is a six-item scale developed by Hakanen (2004) to measure the impact of the law reform on one's work and work-site. The topics covered items such as the need to prioritize services, division of labor in the work-unit, increased demand for services, and an increase in acute care. The impact could be indicated on a five-point scale (1 = very little, 5 = very much). Three other specific job demands for dentists were based on the dentists' experienced work stressors scales (DEWSS) developed by Gorter et al. (1999).

Work contents (α_{pub} = .85 and α_{pri} = .86): the respondents were requested to indicate the stressfulness of six scenarios, such as 'the risk of making mistakes' and 'inflicting pain'.

Negative patient contacts (α_{pub} = .77 and α_{pri} = .77): comprised five items, including, for example, 'Physically and/or mentally aggressive patients' and 'unreasonably demanding patients'.

Financial aspects (α_{pub} = .75 and α_{pri} = .87): was assessed with four items, such as the 'rise of practice expenses' and 'insecurity concerning economic subsistence'. In all these three scales, the respondents were requested to indicate the stressfulness of each demand from 1 = very little to 5 = very much.

Work engagement

Work engagement was assessed with the three subscales of the Utrecht work engagement scale (UWES) (Schaufeli et al., 2002).

Vigor (α_{pub} = .75 and α_{pri} = .74): was assessed with six items, including 'At my job I feel strong and vigorous'.

Dedication (α_{pub} = .83 and α_{pri} = .83): was assessed with five items, such as 'I am enthusiastic about my job'.

Absorption (α_{pub} = .84 and α_{pri} = .82): was measured with six items, including 'I am immersed in my work'. The participants could respond to each item using a seven-point scale (0 = never, 6 = daily).

Job performance

Job performance was measured with three scales.

In-role performance (α_{pub} = .89 and α_{pri} = .88): was assessed with nine items.

Extra-role performance (α_{pub} = .86 and α_{pri} = .87): was assessed with seven items proposed by Goodman and Svyantek (1999). Example items are 'I demonstrate expertise in all job-related tasks' (in-role performance), and 'I am willing to attend functions not required by the organization, but which help its overall image' (extra-role performance). The items were scored on a scale ranging from 1 = strongly disagree to 7 = strongly agree.

Personal initiative (α_{pub} = .77 and α_{pri} = .77): was measured with four items adapted from Frese et al.'s (1997) instrument. One example is 'Whenever there is a chance to get actively involved, I take it' (1 = hardly ever or never, 5 = very often or always).

Statistical Analysis

We used multivariate analyses of variance (MANOVA) to test whether the two groups of dentists (the public sector versus the private sector) scored differently regarding job resources, job demands, work engagement and job performance. Pillai's trace was used as a test statistic. After finding that there were differences between the two groups, separate univariate analyses of variance (ANOVAs) were conducted for all the study variables.

RESULTS

Inter-correlations between the study variables among dentists employed in the public and private sector are presented separately in Table 6.1. The pattern of relationships between the study variables in both sectors was similar.

MANOVA results showed that there were differences between public and private sector dentists regarding all four sets of variables. The groups scored differently on job resources $F(11, 2356) = 98.04, p < .001$, job demands $F(8, 2558) = 236.15, p < .001$, work engagement $F(3, 2688) = 33.14, p < .001$), and job performance $F(3, 2633) = 72.27, p < .001$.

A closer look at the differences in job resources showed that the two groups had different levels of job resources in 10 out of 11 job resources (see Table 6.2). Dentists in the private sector had higher levels of decision authority, role clarity, positive climate, innovative climate, co-operation with assistants, pride in the profession, craftsmanship, immediate and long-term results and work-to-family enrichment. However, dentists in the public sector reported more positive patient contacts. The groups did not differ regarding peer contacts. It is noteworthy that private sector dentists reported more task resources and work-family enrichment experiences than public sector dentists. In sum, Hypothesis 1 was generally supported. Public sector dentists have fewer job resources than private sector dentists, although there are some exceptions.

With respect to job demands, we found differences between the two groups of dentists in the levels of all eight measured demands (Table 6.3). Compared with dentists working in the private sector, dentists working in the public sector reported a higher quantitative workload, more problems in work content and in the physical work environment, more negative patient contacts and emotional dissonance, more work-to-family conflict, and a stronger negative impact of the law changes. Financial demands were the only demands that dentists in the private sector faced more often than dentists in the public sector. Thus the results support Hypothesis 2. Public sector dentists have higher job demands than private sector dentists.

As predicted in Hypothesis 3, the results show that dentists in the public sector score lower on each dimension of work engagement than private sector dentists: for instance, vigor, dedication and absorption (see Table 6.4). Consistently, they also reported lower in-role and extra-role performance, as well as less personal initiative. This is consistent with Hypothesis 4.

Table 6.1   *Pearson correlations between the study variables among public sector (N = 1632) and private sector dentists (N = 1124)*

Variables	1	2	3	4	5	6	7	8	9	10	11	12
1. Decision authority	–	0.33	0.37	0.30	0.18	0.15	0.17	0.06	0.16	0.07	0.16	−0.25
2. Role clarity	0.27	–	0.32	0.44	0.12	0.15	0.19	0.16	0.20	0.11	0.23	−0.15
3. Positive climate	0.37	0.24	–	0.49	0.20	0.18	0.18	0.08	0.27	0.07	0.23	−0.24
4. Innovative climate	0.18	0.28	0.49	–	0.25	0.16	0.20	0.08	0.27	0.08	0.30	−0.15
5. Work to family enrichment	0.05	0.09	0.12	0.21	–	0.23	0.31	0.13	0.29	0.22	0.14	−0.16
6. Craftsmanship	0.14	0.19	0.16	0.26	0.27	–	0.59	0.49	0.43	0.40	0.22	−0.02
7. Pride in profession	0.18	0.26	0.19	0.29	0.33	0.64	–	0.53	0.52	0.43	0.22	−0.01
8. Immediate and long-term results	0.26	0.26	0.21	0.20	0.20	0.48	0.61	–	0.40	0.53	0.18	0.02
9. Peer contacts	0.07	0.17	0.20	0.35	0.26	0.40	0.52	0.43	–	0.38	0.27	−0.02
10. Positive patient contacts	0.02	0.17	0.15	0.21	0.25	0.41	0.46	0.42	0.42	–	0.19	−0.01
11. Co-operation with assistant	0.15	0.23	0.24	0.41	0.24	0.30	0.27	0.24	0.27	0.24	–	0.00
12. Quantitative job demands	−0.11	0.00	−0.13	0.05	−0.08	0.06	0.01	0.01	0.03	0.02	0.02	–
13. Physical demands	−0.21	−0.14	−0.25	−0.18	−0.06	−0.09	−0.11	−0.06	−0.02	−0.04	−0.17	0.28
14. Emotional dissonance	−0.18	−0.15	−0.15	−0.05	−0.09	−0.11	−0.15	−0.09	−0.09	−0.16	−0.12	0.22
15. Work to family conflict	−0.10	−0.08	−0.22	−0.09	−0.18	−0.14	−0.15	−0.07	−0.05	−0.10	−0.09	0.49
16. Impact of law changes	−0.22	−0.12	−0.11	0.05	0.08	0.05	0.00	−0.06	0.13	0.07	−0.02	0.16
17. Work contents	−0.14	−0.14	−0.14	−0.16	−0.06	−0.18	−0.16	−0.03	−0.05	−0.03	−0.12	0.25
18. Negative patient contacts	−0.17	−0.17	−0.14	−0.06	0.01	−0.05	−0.07	−0.10	0.05	−0.02	−0.05	0.12

13	14	15	16	17	18	19	20	21	22	23	24	25
−0.27	−0.20	−0.26	−0.20	−0.28	−0.24	−0.18	0.24	0.28	0.15	0.25	0.14	0.16
−0.20	−0.18	−0.22	−0.07	−0.18	−0.19	−0.14	0.24	0.30	0.10	0.24	0.14	0.15
−0.29	−0.16	−0.28	−0.10	−0.17	−0.13	−0.16	0.18	0.23	0.09	0.17	0.15	0.13
−0.22	−0.13	−0.16	0.03	−0.13	−0.07	−0.08	0.20	0.24	0.15	0.18	0.24	0.20
−0.10	−0.13	−0.21	0.02	−0.11	−0.07	−0.05	0.30	0.33	0.25	0.16	0.22	0.24
−0.01	−0.16	−0.14	0.04	−0.16	−0.09	0.07	0.38	0.44	0.34	0.28	0.24	0.31
−0.02	−0.18	−0.10	0.08	−0.12	−0.09	0.04	0.43	0.54	0.35	0.30	0.31	0.34
0.13	−0.15	−0.05	0.12	0.09	0.07	0.04	0.28	0.34	0.23	0.17	0.19	0.14
−0.04	−0.14	−0.09	0.07	−0.06	−0.04	0.03	0.33	0.41	0.29	0.23	0.32	0.30
0.07	−0.19	−0.11	0.16	0.03	−0.02	−0.05	0.28	0.33	0.25	0.07	0.19	0.20
−0.13	−0.12	−0.13	0.01	−0.17	−0.10	0.01	0.23	0.25	0.16	0.22	0.27	0.26
0.29	0.21	0.51	0.25	0.29	0.23	0.22	−0.10	−0.12	0.06	−0.24	0.02	0.02
–	0.29	0.35	0.26	0.42	0.42	0.27	−0.21	−0.20	−0.07	−0.19	−0.09	−0.15
0.24	–	0.34	0.13	0.36	0.37	0.16	−0.24	−0.24	−0.11	−0.22	−0.08	−0.15
0.32	0.31	–	0.19	0.45	0.30	0.27	−0.29	−0.24	0.02	−0.32	−0.06	−0.15
0.27	0.20	0.19	–	0.25	0.27	0.15	−0.04	−0.04	0.03	−0.16	0.01	0.00
0.41	0.28	0.36	0.14	–	0.50	0.18	−0.31	−0.26	−0.08	−0.48	−0.13	−0.28
0.31	0.27	0.18	0.30	0.33	–	0.32	−0.21	−0.21	−0.07	−0.24	−0.07	−0.16

Table 6.1   (continued)

Variables	1	2	3	4	5	6	7	8	9	10	11	12
19. Financial aspects	−0.08	−0.05	−0.12	−0.08	−0.11	−0.02	−0.05	−0.03	−0.08	−0.06	−0.03	0.34
20. Vigor	0.14	0.26	0.20	0.27	0.24	0.40	0.45	0.38	0.30	0.31	0.24	0.03
21. Dedication	0.20	0.26	0.22	0.26	0.29	0.45	0.57	0.45	0.39	0.34	0.23	−0.05
22. Absorption	0.07	0.13	0.08	0.19	0.25	0.33	0.36	0.26	0.26	0.20	0.18	0.15
23. In role performance	0.14	0.25	0.18	0.20	0.11	0.33	0.37	0.25	0.19	0.20	0.19	−0.07
24. Extra-role performance	0.15	0.24	0.23	0.37	0.16	0.31	0.32	0.26	0.33	0.25	0.30	0.13
25. Personal initiative	0.12	0.25	0.14	0.31	0.25	0.36	0.37	0.28	0.28	0.26	0.27	0.10

Note: Numbers above the diagonal refer to public sector dentists and numbers below the diagonal refer to private sector dentists. For public sector dentists, correlations < 0.08 are statistically significant at $p < 0.001$; correlations between 0.07-0.08 are statistically significant at p < 0.01; correlation 0.06 is statistically significant at p < 0.05. For private sector dentists, correlations > 0.10 are statistically significant at $p < 0.001$; correlations between 0.08–0.10 are statistically significant at $p < 0.01$; correlation 0.07 is statistically significant at $p < 0.05$.

Table 6.2   *Differences in mean scores for job resources among dentists in the public sector (N = 1632) versus the private sector (N = 1124)*

	Public sector		Private sector		*p*-value
	M	SD	M	SD	
Decision authority	3.91	0.77	4.64	0.50	***
Role clarity	4.05	0.77	4.42	0.58	***
Positive organizational climate	3.64	0.87	4.11	0.75	***
Innovative climate	3.04	0.77	3.20	0.77	***
Work to family enrichment	2.40	0.75	2.56	0.81	***
Craftsmanship	3.66	0.80	3.92	0.74	***.
Pride in the profession	3.79	0.62	3.96	0.59	***
Direct and long-term results	4.30	0.58	4.50	0.49	***
Peer contacts	3.81	0.70	3.78	0.71	n.s.
Positive patient contacts	3.71	0.79	3.35	0.74	***
Cooperation with one's assistant	3.51	0.65	3.62	0.62	***

Note: *** $p < 0.001$; and n.s. – not significant.

13	14	15	16	17	18	19	20	21	22	23	24	25
0.35	0.22	0.36	0.21	0.39	0.32	–	−0.05	−0.06	0.06	0.00	0.09	0.04
−0.17	−0.18	−0.20	−0.02	−0.25	−0.13	−0.15	–	0.75	0.54	0.43	0.37	0.49
−0.17	−0.18	−0.18	0.01	−0.22	−0.10	−0.17	0.75	–	0.53	0.37	0.34	0.40
0.00	−0.05	0.05	0.03	−0.04	−0.01	0.03	0.48	0.50	–	0.20	0.29	0.38
−0.16	−0.09	−0.19	−0.03	−0.47	−0.06	−0.17	0.43	0.40	0.18	–	0.32	0.40
−0.07	−0.08	0.00	0.06	−0.10	−0.06	0.04	0.31	0.30	0.22	0.31	–	0.52
−0.09	−0.13	−0.12	0.03	−0.18	−0.04	−0.07	0.44	0.38	0.29	0.35	0.42	–

Table 6.3   Differences in mean scores for job demands among dentists in the public sector (N = 1632) versus the private sector (N = 1124)

	Public sector		Private sector		p-value
	M	SD	M	SD	
Quantitative workload	3.33	0.91	2.64	0.82	***
Physical environment	2.52	0.62	2.24	0.57	***
Emotional dissonance	2.57	0.83	2.37	0.83	***
Work to family conflict	2.72	0.72	2.49	0.71	***
Impact of the law changes	2.78	0.85	1.82	0.69	***
Work contents	2.77	0.76	2.51	0.77	***
Negative patient contacts	2.27	0.83	1.61	0.66	***
Financial aspects	1.74	0.65	2.10	0.79	***

Note: *** $p < 0.001$.

DISCUSSION

In the present study, we compared the levels of work engagement and performance of dentists working in the public sector with those working in the private sector. The results show that dentists in the public sector score lower on work engagement and performance. We used the JD-R model (Bakker and Demerouti, 2007, 2008; Demerouti et al., 2001) to identify

Table 6.4   *Differences in mean scores for work engagement and job performance among dentists in the public sector (N = 1964) vs. the private sector (N = 928)*

Work engagement	Public sector		Private sector		p
	M	SD	M	SD	
Vigor	4.46	0.98	4.82	0.87	***
Dedication	4.88	0.98	5.10	0.91	***
Absorption	3.70	1.35	3.96	1.33	***
Job performance					
In-role performance	4.99	0.93	5.45	0.75	***
Extra-role performance	5.08	0.91	5.44	0.90	***
Personal initiative	3.59	0.66	3.79	0.63	***

Note: *** $p < 0.001$.

the possible reasons for the differences between both groups. As hypothesized, public sector dentists were exposed to higher job demands and lower job resources than private sector dentists. Thus, our findings offer support for the JD-R model and indicate which job demands and resources should be targeted in order to increase the work engagement and performance among public sector dentists.

The results are consistent with previous findings in the literature showing that the combination of high job demands and low job resources undermines work engagement (Bakker et al., 2007; Hakanen et al., 2005) and fosters burnout (Bakker et al., 2005; Xanthopoulou et al., 2007). Thus, the present study adds to the knowledge base, but also indicates that the JD-R model can be fruitfully used to identify possible unique correlates of work engagement among specific groups of workers. Such information can be used as a starting point for interventions.

Compared to dentists in the private sector, dentists in the public sector reported lower levels of decision authority, role clarity, positive climate, innovative climate, co-operation with assistants, pride in the profession, craftsmanship, immediate and long-term results, and work-to-family enrichment. All these resources have the potential to fuel work engagement, since they can satisfy dentists' basic needs for relatedness, competence and autonomy (Van den Broeck et al., 2008). Thus, whereas decision authority may satisfy dentists' need to have control over how they perform their work (need for autonomy), information about the immediate and long-term results of their work may satisfy dentists' need for competence.

In a similar vein, a positive and innovative climate and good collaboration during practice may satisfy dentists' need for relatedness. Since public sector dentists had less access to these job resources than private sector dentists, their levels of vigor, dedication and absorption (for instance, work engagement) were lower as well.

In addition, public sector dentists were exposed to higher job demands than private sector dentists. Public sector dentists reported a less favorable physical environment, a higher quantitative workload, more stressful work, and more negative contacts with patients. Consistently, they experienced more emotional dissonance as a result of faking emotions in their interactions with patients. In addition, public sector dentists were more negatively affected by the changes in the Finnish law than private sector dentists. Thus, public sector dentists were confronted with an increased demand for services, and with an increase in acute care. It is not surprising that these demands coincide with increased levels of work-family conflict. Whereas confrontation with a high workload and time pressure can lead to time-based work interference with family life (being too late at home to take care of one's family responsibilities), emotionally demanding interactions with patients may foster strain-based work-to-family conflict (ruminating in the evening about what has happened at work during the day). Moreover, previous research has shown that particularly the combination of high demands and low job resources leads to work-family conflict (Bakker et al., 2011), and undermines work engagement (Bakker et al., 2007; Hakanen et al., 2005). Public sector dentists presumably have too few resources to cope with their daily job demands. In what follows, we will discuss what public dentists can do in order to improve their levels of work engagement and performance.

Interventions

In Finland, in collaboration with the Finnish Dental Association and by applying the JD-R model, several measures have been taken in order to improve working conditions and the well-being of dentists – particularly in the public sector. The primary aim of these activities has been to help dentists to identify and promote actual and potential job resources in their workplaces. For example, a guideline for creating good workplaces for dentists has been published and posted to all members of the Finnish Dental Association, which is sent to every dentist in Finland. In addition, a letter enclosed with fact sheets about preventing burnout and promoting work engagement has been sent to every Finnish dental manager employed in the public sector. Further, numerous seminars, workshops, leadership trainings, and popular articles in professional journals have focused on the strengths, resources, and positive gain spirals related to the work of dentists in order to raise awareness of the motivating potential of job resources and work engagement in dentistry and to encourage innovativeness in the midst of changes in this sector.

More generally, when it comes to interventions in an organizational context, it is useful to differentiate organizational level interventions from individual-level interventions. Whereas efforts to optimize the work environment and employee work-life balance can be considered as organizational interventions; efforts to optimize employees' personal resources or to ask them to engage in proactive job crafting behaviors can be seen as individual interventions (Bakker, Oerlemans and Ten Brummelhuis, 2012). In this chapter, we discuss one organizational level and one individual level intervention that aims at building work engagement.

At the level of the organization, dentists can use the JD-R model as a tool to optimize work engagement. After having identified the relevant job demands and resources for the dentist profession, dentist organizations can use the questionnaire to conduct a *quantitative* analysis of the job demands and job resources that play a role in the development of engagement. The analysis could focus on differences between practices, in terms of job demands, resources, engagement and its consequences. Dentists could also participate in engagement workshops before the start of the study, so that they can learn how to use the information that will become available. The subgroup analyses can provide clear indications for interventions to foster engagement in the workplace, since they highlight the strengths and weaknesses of practices. Tailor-made interventions are then possible, aimed at reducing the identified (hindrance) job demands, and increasing the most important job resources, which, in turn, may increase the likelihood of work engagement and high job performance.

In addition, we have developed Internet applications of the JD-R model – called the *JD-R Monitor* and the *Engagement App* – in which workers who fill in an electronic version of the questionnaire receive online and personalized feedback on their computer or smartphone about their most important job demands and resources. The feedback includes histograms of the specific demands and resources identified as important for engagement, and the participants' scores are compared with a benchmark (comparison group). In addition, the feedback mode is interactive, such that participants can click on the histograms and receive written feedback about the meaning of their scores on the demands and resources. In a similar way, feedback about work engagement has been included in these web-based tools. The PDF-report that can be generated at the end of the program can be used as input for interviews with consultants or personal coaches. In this way, it becomes possible to optimize the working environment for individual employees.

Dentists may also actively change the design of their jobs themselves by choosing tasks, negotiating different job content, and assigning meaning to their tasks or jobs (Parker and Ohly, 2008). This process of workers shaping their jobs has been referred to as job crafting (Wrzesniewski and Dutton, 2001). Job crafting is defined as the physical and cognitive changes individuals make in their task or relational boundaries. Physical changes refer to changes in the form, scope or number of job tasks, whereas cognitive changes refer to changing how one sees the job. Changing relational boundaries means that individuals have discretion over whom they interact with while doing their job. According to Wrzesniewski and Dutton (2001), job crafting focuses on the processes by which employees change elements of their jobs and relationships with others to revise the meaning of the work and the social environment at work. Thus, job crafting is about *changing* the job in order to experience the enhanced meaning of it. As a consequence, employees may be able to increase their person-job fit and thereby increase their work engagement (Tims, Bakker and Derks, 2012).

A job crafting intervention could be designed as follows. Participants who are enrolled in the program are instructed through the internet and are followed for four weeks. At the start of each week, they receive an e-mail explaining the goal of the program: 'The goal of this assignment is to ensure that your work fits (even) better with your specific knowledge, skills, and personal needs. You will do this by personally changing your work or your work environment. Perhaps you have not looked at your work like this before, but research shows that it is possible to derive more satisfaction from life if you proactively align your work with your skills and needs. Please try to use this way of working during this week.' Participants can be provided with examples, such as changing the way they work, when they work, with whom they work (clients, colleagues), changing the frequency of feedback and coaching, simplifying their work versus looking for more challenges, and carrying out additional tasks. The instruction could additionally provide clear examples of employees in certain jobs who mobilized their job resources or increased/reduced their job demands (see Bakker et al., 2012, for more interventions).

Conclusion

Our study focused on job resources, job demands, work engagement and job performance among a large and representative sample of Finnish dentists working in the public or private sectors. The results supported the JD-R model by showing that dentists in the public sector, who were exposed to higher job demands and had fewer job resources than dentists working in private sector, also reported lower levels of work engagement and poorer job performance. By using individual-level and organizational interventions it is possible to enhance work engagement and guarantee high-quality performance – also in the public sector.

REFERENCES

Albrecht, S. (ed.) (2010), *Handbook of Employee Engagement: Perspectives, Issues, Research and Practice*, Cheltenham, UK and Northampton, MA, USA: Edward Elgar Publishing.

Bakker, A.B. (2011), 'An evidence-based model of work engagement', *Current Directions in Psychological Science*, **20**, 265–9.

Bakker, A.B. and E. Demerouti (2007), 'The job demands-resources model: state of the art', *Journal of Managerial Psychology*, **22**, 309–28.

Bakker, A.B. and E. Demerouti (2008), 'Towards a model of work engagement', *Career Development International*, **13**, 209–23.

Bakker, A.B., E. Demerouti, E. de Boer and W.B. Schaufeli (2003), 'Job demands and job resources as predictors of absence duration and frequency', *Journal of Vocational Behavior*, **62**, 341–56.

Bakker, A.B., E. Demerouti and M.C. Euwema (2005), 'Job resources buffer the impact of job demands on burnout', *Journal of Occupational Health Psychology*, **10**, 170–80.

Bakker, A.B., E. Demerouti and W.B. Schaufeli (2003), 'Dual processes at work in a call centre: an application of the job demands – resources model', *European Journal of Work and Organizational Psychology*, **12**, 393–417.

Bakker, A.B., E. Demerouti and W. Verbeke (2004), 'Using the job demands-resources model to predict burnout and performance', *Human Resource Management*, **43**, 83–104.

Bakker, A., J.J. Hakanen, E. Demerouti and D. Xanthopoulou (2007), 'Job resources boost work engagement, particularly when job demands are high', *Journal of Educational Psychology*, **99**, 274–84.

Bakker A. B. and M.P. Leiter (eds) (2010), *Work engagement: A Handbook of Essential Theory and Research*, New York: Psychology Press.

Bakker, A.B., W. Oerlemans and L.L. Ten Brummelhuis (2012), 'Becoming fully engaged in the workplace: what individuals and organizations can do to foster work engagement', in R. Burke and C. Cooper (eds), *The Fulfilling Workplace: The Organization's Role in Achieving Individual and Organizational Health*, UK: Gower.

Bakker, A.B., W.B. Schaufeli, M.P. Leiter and T.W. Taris (2008a), 'Work engagement: an emerging concept in occupational health psychology', *Work & Stress*, **22**, 187–200.

Bakker, A.B., L. Ten Brummelhuis, J.T. Prins and F.M.M.A. Van der Heijden (2011), 'Applying the job demands–resources model to the work-home interface: a study among medical residents and their partners', *Journal of Vocational Behavior*, **79**, 170–180.

Bakker, A.B., H. Van Emmerik and P. Van Riet (2008b), 'How job demands, resources, and burnout predict objective performance: a constructive replication', *Anxiety, Stress, and Coping*, **21**, 309–24.

Bakker, A.B., M.J.P.M. Van Veldhoven and D. Xanthopoulou (2010), 'Beyond the demand-control model: thriving on high job demands and resources', *Journal of Personnel Psychology*, **9**, 3–16.

Blinkhorn, A.S. (1992), 'Stress and the dental team: a qualitative investigation of the causes of stress in general dental practice', *Dental Update*, **19**, 385–7.

Christian, M.S., A.S. Garza and J.E. Slaughter (2011), 'Work engagement: a quantitative review and test of its relations with task and contextual performance', *Personnel Psychology*, **64**, 89–136.

Clausen, T., K. Nielsen, I. Gomes Carneiro and V. Borg (2012), 'Job demands, job resources and long-term sickness absence in the Danish eldercare services: a prospective analysis of register-based outcomes', *Journal of Advanced Nursing*, **68**, 127–36.

Dallner, M., A.L. Elo, F. Gamberale, V. Hottinen, S. Knardahl, K. Lindström, A. Skogstad and E. Ørhede (2000), *Validation of the General Nordic Questionnaire (QPSNordic) for Psychological and Social Factors at Work*, Copenhagen: Nordic Council of Ministers.

Deci, E.L. and R.M. Ryan (2000), 'The "what" and "why" of goal pursuits: human needs and the self-determination of behavior', *Psychological Inquiry*, **11**, 227–68.

Demerouti, E. and A.B. Bakker (2011), 'The job demands–resources model: challenges for future research', *South African Journal of Industrial Psychology*, **37**, 1–9.

Demerouti, E., A.B. Bakker, F. Nachreiner and W.B. Schaufeli (2001), 'The job demands-resources model of burnout', *Journal of Applied Psychology*, **86**, 499–512.

Frese, M., D. Fay, T. Hilburger, K. Leng and A. Tag (1997), 'The concept of personal initiative: operationalization, reliability and validity in two German samples', *Journal of Occupational and Organizational Psychology*, **70**, 139–61.

Goodman, S.A. and D.J. Svyantek (1999), 'Person-organization fit and contextual performance: do shared values matter?', *Journal of Vocational Behavior*, **55**, 254–75.

Gorter, R.C. (2000), 'Burnout among Dutch dentists: identification and prevention', Doctoral thesis, Amsterdam, The Netherlands: University of Amsterdam.

Gorter, R.C., G. Albrecht, J. Hoogstraten and M.A. Eijkman (1998), 'Work place characteristics, work stress and burnout among Dutch dentists', *European Journal of Oral Sciences*, **106**, 999–1005.

Gorter, R.C., G.H. Albrecht, J. Hoogstraten and M.A. Eijkman (1999), 'Measuring work stress among Dutch dentists', *International Dental Journal*, **49**, 144–52.

Gorter, R.C., M.A. Eijkman and J. Hoogstraten (2000), 'Burnout and health among Dutch dentists', *European Journal of Oral Sciences*, **108**, 261–7.

Gorter, R.C., J.H. te Brake, M.A. Eijkman and J. Hoogstraten (2006), 'Job resources in Dutch dental practice', *International Dental Journal*, **56**, 22–8.

Grzywacz, J.G. and N.F. Marks (2000), 'Reconceptualizing the work-family interface: an ecological perspective on the correlates of positive and negative spillover between work and family', *Journal of Occupational Health Psychology*, **5**, 111–26.

Hakanen, J.J. (2004), *Hammaslääkäreiden työhyvinvointi Suomessa* [Work-related well-being among Finnish dentists], Helsinki: Finnish Institute of Occupational Health.

Hakanen, J.J., A.B. Bakker and E. Demerouti (2005), 'How dentists cope with their job demands and stay engaged: the moderating role of job resources', *European Journal of Oral Sciences*, **113**, 479–87.

Hakanen, J.J., A. Bakker and W.B. Schaufeli (2006), 'Burnout and engagement among teachers', *Journal of School Psychology*, **43**, 495–13.
Hakanen, J.J., M. Peeters and R. Perhoniemi (2011), 'Enrichment processes and gain spirals at work and at home: a three-year cross-lagged panel study', *Journal of Occupational and Organizational Psychology*, **84**, 8–30.
Hakanen, J.J., R. Perhoniemi and S. Toppinen-Tanner (2008a), 'Positive gain spirals at work: from job resources to work engagement, personal initiative and work-unit innovativeness', *Journal of Vocational Behavior*, **73**, 78–91.
Hakanen, J.J., W.B. Schaufeli and K. Ahola (2008b), 'The job demands-resources model: a three-year cross-lagged study of burnout, depression, commitment, and work engagement', *Work & Stress*, **22**, 224–41.
Humphries, G. (1998), 'A review of burnout in dentists', *Dental Update*, **25**, 392–96.
Kahn W.A. (1990), 'Psychological conditions of personal engagement and disengagement at work', *Academy of Management Journal*, **33**, 692–724.
Karasek, A. (1985), *Job Content Instrument Users Guide, Revision 1.1 March 1985*, Los Angeles: University of Southern California, Department of Industrial and Systems Engineering.
Lewig, K.A., D. Xanthopoulou, A.B. Bakker, M.F. Dollard and J.C. Metzer (2007), 'Burnout and connectedness among Australia volunteers: a test of the job demands-resources model', *Journal of Vocational Behaviour*, **71**, 429–45.
Lindström, K. (1997), 'Assessing and promoting healthy work organizations', in P. Seppälä, T. Luopajärvi, C. Nygård and M. Mattila (eds), *From Experience to Innovation*, Helsinki: Finnish Institute of Occupational Health, pp. 504–506.
Lindström, K., V. Hottinen and K. Bredenberg (2000), *The Healthy Organization Barometer*. [Työilmapiiri- ja hyvinvointibarometri], Helsinki: Työterveyslaitos.
Macey, W.H., B. Schneider, K. Barbera and S.A. Young (2009), *Employee Engagement: Tools for Analysis, Practice, and Competitive Advantage*, London, England: Blackwell.
Meijman, T.F. and G. Mulder (1998), 'Psychological aspects of workload', in P.J.D. Drenth and H. Thierry (eds), *Handbook of Work and Organizational Psychology: Vol. 2. Work Psychology*, Hove, UK: Psychology Press, pp. 5–33.
Osborne, D. and R. Croucher (1994), 'Levels of burnout in general dental practitioners in the south-east of England', *British Dental Journal*, **177**, 372–7.
Parker, S.K. and S. Ohly (2008), 'Designing motivating jobs', in R. Kanfer, G. Chen and R. Pritchard (eds), *Work Motivation: Past, Present, and Future*, NewYork: Routledge, pp. 233–384.
Salanova, M., Agut, S. and J.M. Peiró, (2005), 'Linking organizational resources and work engagement to employee performance and customer loyalty: the mediation of service climate', *Journal of Applied Psychology*, **90**, 1217–27.
Schaufeli, W.B., A.B. Bakker and W. Van Rhenen (2009), 'How changes in job demands and resources predict burnout, work engagement, and sickness absenteeism', *Journal of Organizational Behavior*, **30**, 893–917.
Schaufeli, W.B., M. Salanova, V. Gonzalez-Roma and A.B. Bakker (2002), 'The measurement of engagement and burnout: a two-sample confirmatory factor analytic approach', *Journal of Happiness Studies*, **3**, 71–92.
Schaufeli, W.B., T.W. Taris and A.B. Bakker (2006), 'Dr. Jekyll and Mr. Hide: on the differences between work engagement and workaholism', in R. Burke (ed.), *Research Companion to Working Time and Work Addiction*, Northhampton, UK: Edward Elgar, pp. 193–217.

Tims M., A.B. Bakker and D. Derks (2012), 'The development and validation of the job crafting scale', *Journal of Vocational Behavior*, **80**, 173–86.

Van den Broek, A., M. Vansteenkiste, H. De Witte and W. Lens (2008), 'Explaining the relationships between job characteristics, burnout and engagement: the role of basic psychological need satisfaction', *Work & Stress*, **22**, 277–294.

Wilson, R.F., P.Y. Coward, J. Capewell, T.L. Laidler, A.C. Rigby and T.J. Shaw (1998), 'Perceived sources of occupational stress in general dental practitioners', *British Dental Journal*, **184**, 499–502.

Wrzesniewski, A. and J.E. Dutton (2001), 'Crafting a job: revisioning employees as active crafters of their work', *Academy of Management Review*, **26**, 179–201.

Xanthopoulou, D., A.B. Bakker, E. Demerouti and W.B. Schaufeli (2009), 'Work engagement and financial returns: a diary study on the role of job and personal resources', *Journal of Occupational and Organizational Psychology*, **82**, 183–200.

Xanthopoulou, D., A.B. Bakker, M.F. Dollard, E. Demerouti, W.B. Schaufeli, T.W. Taris and P.J.G. Schreurs (2007), 'When do job demands particularly predict burnout? The moderating role of job resources', *Journal of Managerial Psychology*, **22**, 766–86.

Zapf, D., C. Vogt, C. Seifert, H. Mertini and A. Isic (1999), 'Emotion work as a source of stress: the concept and development of an instrument', *European Journal of Work and Organizational Psychology*, **8**, 371–400.

7. Emotional labor, job satisfaction and burnout: how each affects the other

Mary E. Guy and Meredith A. Newman

Cool heads, warm hearts. That is what we want when public workers meet citizens. Achieving that combination requires cognitive labor *and* emotional labor. In this chapter we explain what the term 'emotional labor' means, how it pertains to the delivery of public services, and how it contributes to job satisfaction. Strategies are then discussed for dealing with the downside of emotionally intense work. The chapter concludes with a discussion of how human resource functions such as job analysis, selection, training and performance appraisal can contribute to the performance of 'emotion work' so that it brings more job satisfaction and less burnout.

The term 'emotional labor' refers to the management of one's own feelings as well as those of the person with whom the worker is interacting. Its purpose is to enable 'getting the job done'. Such work has multiple facets, ranging from authentic expression of the worker's own emotions, and the suppression of emotions that are felt but not expressed, to requiring workers to don masks and display an emotion that they do not actually feel – such as when they must seem nicer-than-nice or, conversely, tougher-than-tough.

More specifically, emotional labor comes into play during communication between workers and citizens and it requires the rapid-fire execution of:

1. Emotive sensing, which means detecting the affective state of the other.
2. Assessing one's own affective state.
3. Judging how alternative responses will affect the citizen, then selecting the response that is likely to elicit the desired response.
4. Behaving, such that the worker suppresses or expresses an emotion in order to elicit the desired response (Newman, Guy and Mastracci, 2009).

At varying levels of intensity, emotional labor plays a role in nearly all government jobs. Frontline workers deal with the day-to-day needs of an increasingly demanding public; management handles the inter- and intra-agency demands of subordinates and superiors on everything from budget and staffing to agency turf battles. Of particular interest in this chapter is the emotional labor performance when the state meets citizen, in other words, when public workers are interacting directly with citizens.

The subject of emotional labor is relatively new in the public service literature and there is confusion about terminology. Here is a clarification: service exchanges between the worker and the citizen require the worker to sense the right tone and medium for expressing a point and/or feeling and then to determine whether, when and how to act on that analysis. As a theoretical construct, those who possess higher levels of 'emotional intelligence' are more capable of sensing emotive states and engaging in 'emotional labor'. While emotional intelligence is a trait inherent to the individual, emotional labor is a requirement of the job, analogous to cognitive labor or physical labor. In this discussion we also use the term 'emotion work'. That is another way of referring to performance that requires emotional labor. Thus, the relationship is as follows: Those with higher levels of emotional intelligence do well in jobs that require emotional labor. Emotion work is what the worker does.

A preponderance of public service work is with people in vulnerable situations. This is due to the very nature of services that are provided by the state: disaster response, regulatory compliance, law enforcement, assistance to needy individuals and families, and emergency services, among others. These activities proceed more smoothly when there is rapport and trust between the official and the citizen. It is emotional labor that enables this transaction.

Emotional labor shares similarities as well as differences with cognitive and physical labor – all require skill and experience and are subject to external controls and divisions of labor. Compared to cognitive and physical labor, however, the purpose of emotional labor is to affect how the citizen feels. Law enforcement needs citizens to be deferential and to trust their authority. Social services need citizens to feel that there is a constructive way to deal with their problems. Emergency responders need citizens to trust their expertise and be confident of their actions. In these terms, the jobs of a social worker and correctional officer can be viewed as opposite poles. One employs a smile and requires its incumbents to be 'nicer than natural'. The other employs toughness and requires 'tougher than natural' behavior. Acting in a neutral manner also demands emotion work as workers suppress their true feelings in order not to under- or over-react and to present an air of fairness and lack of bias.

Emotion work requires workers to manage their own emotions as well as the emotions of the citizen. There are two forms of emotion management in the context of employment: 'other-focused' and 'self-focused' (Pugliesi, 1999). Other-focused emotional labor refers to efforts to help others manage distress, enhance or protect their self-esteem, and to mediate conflicts. In contrast, self-focused emotional labor refers to the suppression or masking of one's own emotions so as to present a demeanor that is appropriate to the situation. In terms of display rules, mandates to express or suppress particular types of feelings, meaning 'what-to-do' rules, cause clerks to wear a smile and close the transaction with a friendly wish that customers 'have a nice day'. 'What-not-to-do' rules result in hiding or faking true emotions. For example, emergency medical responders must try to calm victims and must suppress their own horror when dealing with a badly wounded victim. Law enforcement officers must manage their own reactions to tragedy. Weeping is not an option when they are dealing with someone whose loved one has just been killed. In other words, emotional labor often requires workers to suppress the emotion they are experiencing and to display a different emotion. It requires them to wear a mask. This is called 'false-face acting'. It is as important to job performance as forthright expressions of emotion are. But this aspect of emotional labor is riskiest for workers because it is the form of emotion work that is most likely to result in burnout.

RELATING EMOTIONAL LABOR TO JOB SATISFACTION AND BURNOUT

Emotionally intense work may contribute to burnout but it definitely contributes to job satisfaction. This was demonstrated empirically by the work of Hsieh, Jin and Guy (2011). They surveyed public service workers in a variety of jobs, including human service providers in social service settings, attorneys and detectives in investigative jobs, educators, prison officials, emergency call takers, and workers who receive citizen complaints about faulty consumer products. In other words, some were first responders who interact with citizens for only a few minutes and receive no feedback about the results of their actions. Some were professionals who work with the same citizen for years. And some were clerical staff whose work is fairly routine and for which they learn the outcome of every case they work. The common thread of these varied jobs is that each required the worker to be in direct communication with the citizen, providing a service that is unique to government. Their results showed that emotional labor has a positive, direct effect on job satisfaction. The more it is performed, the higher the worker's job satisfaction is. Workers who

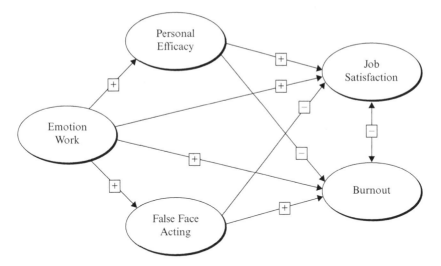

Note: This figure has been reproduced with permission from M.E. Sharpe. It appeared in Mastracci, Guy and Newman (2011: 38).

*Figure 7.1   Relationship of emotion work to personal efficacy, false face
acting, job satisfaction and burnout[1]*

are more efficacious – more capable of managing their emotions while also managing the emotional state of the other – score higher in terms of their job satisfaction and score lower in terms of burnout. The results also show that those who identify the need for emotion work and who perform it are also more skilled in false face acting. The downside of their ability to pretend to feel one way when actually feeling another is that this is the sort of emotional labor that results in higher levels of burnout and lower levels of job satisfaction.

Figure 7.1 shows how these three variables are related. This diagram results from the structural equation model that Hsieh, Jin and Guy (2011) generated from the survey results previously discussed. The figure shows that emotional labor is positively related to both job satisfaction and burnout and that there are two moderating variables. Personal efficacy, meaning an individual's ability to perform emotional labor, contributes to satisfaction and minimizes burnout. This means that the more capable someone is of managing their own emotions as well as the emotions of citizens with whom they are working, the less likely it will be that they suffer burnout. The figure also shows that false face acting contributes to burnout and is inversely related to job satisfaction. This is the type of work where workers must suppress their true feelings while expressing an emotion they do not actually feel. It also shows that the more workers must mask their true feelings, the greater the likelihood is that they will suffer burnout and the less likely it is that they will have high levels of job satisfaction. Notwithstanding the deleterious effect of false face acting, the figure shows that emotion work is likely to result in higher levels of job satisfaction.

Job Satisfaction

Job satisfaction derives from workers' engagement in the jobs they perform. Engagement is defined as a persistent, positive, motivational state of fulfillment that is characterized by vigor, dedication and absorption. It is particularly related to job resources, such as autonomy, feedback, and learning opportunities. In the best of circumstances, emotional labor provides all of these. For example, interviews with experienced workers at the front lines of public service gives a voice to these qualities in their jobs. An emergency medical technician (EMT) explains how emotionally intense work motivates him (Mastracci, Guy and Newman, 2011: 34): 'When you save people's lives and you make a difference, it's the most amazing thing'. A member of a search and rescue team on assignment following the disastrous Haitian earthquake of 2010 tells how it feels to search for survivors:

> We didn't know exactly where this girl was and it was getting late at night. We drilled a hole [through multiple slabs of concrete] and they take a camera in and put it through and we had one of our chiefs who was an interpreter speaking to her and it was interesting. He said to go toward [the light]. She's been in there four days. So he said try to move towards the light where the camera went to the hole and the light and we're looking at it and suddenly her hand just pops up in front of the camera . . . it's one of those things we'll never forget. Because we have simulators, we have manikins, we have the whole thing, but you're watching it in the camera and it's just rubble and then someone's hand comes in front of it and starts shaking. It's one of those moments you'll never forget (Mastracci, Guy and Newman, 2011: 35).

Examples such as the EMT's success story and the earthquake rescue demonstrate that great emotional intensity results in great reward. And for people in human service professions, helping others gives a sense of meaning. Other workers speak about their sense of personal and professional accomplishment, of an ability to 'juggle twelve balls in the air all at once', and of 'good exhaustion'.

> I must be just emotionally drained, but in the same token when we've done something really great here, nothing beats that feeling. You go home and it's like, wow, I've really accomplished something . . . you can't beat . . . this feeling

... Here you see the fruits of your labor ... I directly impact their lives and it's for the better and ... it's a euphoric feeling (Guy, Newman and Mastracci, 2008: 56).

Engagement is the enthusiasm a counselor feels towards her job:

> I absolutely love my job and I love being able to calm them down when they need to calm down or be stern when I need to be ... I love every minute of it ... they're so appreciative for what I do for them and they tell me they are ... I guess I get some affirmation from them that I'm doing my job ... So I'm just so darn appreciative for ... what I get to do every day (Guy, Newman and Mastracci, 2008: 29).

These quotes are emblematic of workers who are engaged in their work, derive personal meaning from it, feel that they are making a difference in other people's lives, and are motivated to go back to work day after day and do the same thing again. Job satisfaction derives from their emotional labor. In contrast to job satisfaction, there is a downside that can occur and when it does, it is hurtful to employee well-being and to productivity. It is called burnout and is the antithesis of engagement.

Burnout

The performance of emotional labor implicates the 'self' more directly than other types of work. Because of this it has distinct benefits for workers but it can also have psychological costs. While engagement is characterized by the 'wow' factor and a feeling of personal success, burnout is like 'heart death' for workers. Intense exposure to protracted emotive experiences in the absence of positive outcomes can result in post-traumatic stress as well as vicarious trauma. Absenteeism, turnover, physiological symptoms, compensation for health claims, psychological withdrawal, aggression, alienation, depersonalization, and dysfunctional coping mechanisms, such as relying on alcohol as a 'coping drug', combine to raise the price of getting the job done. Workers who 'flame out' become mechanical in their discussions with co-workers. They start blaming the victim or referring to cases as if each situation is an unfortunate but emotively sterile event.

The term 'burnout' was popularized by psychiatrist Herbert Freudenberger in 1974. It has been variously defined as a psychological syndrome occurring among individuals who do 'people work', an affliction of 'those who care', the numbing of emotions to the point of being unable to feel any emotion, a disease of over-commitment or under-stimulation, and a state of physical, emotional and mental exhaustion caused by chronic emotional stresses resulting from intense, emotionally demanding involvement with people. Workers in 'high-touch' jobs, such as emergency response teams, case workers, law-enforcement officers and lawyers in legal aid offices, must frequently spend considerable time in intense involvement with troubled people, and these exchanges may be charged with feelings of anger, embarrassment, frustration, fear or despair. The resulting chronic tension and stress can be emotionally draining, which leaves the worker feeling 'empty' and 'burned out' (Golembiewski, Munzenrider and Stevenson, 1986; Maslach, 1981). Emotional exhaustion, cynicism and ineffectiveness are the principal dimensions of burnout. A description of each follows.

Emotional exhaustion

Exhaustion is the main symptom of burnout and its most obvious manifestation. It refers to feeling overextended and depleted of one's emotional and physical resources. Workers feel drained and unable to unwind and recover. They experience a general malaise that accompanies a paradoxical combination of weariness and sleep problems. Although burnout victims are tired during the day, they are unable to sleep at night because of tormenting thoughts or nightmares. The overwhelming exhaustion coupled with an incapacity to disengage from the job even in sleep is expressed in the following way:

> I'm tired . . . I mean I really have to say I just don't want to do this anymore. I don't sleep well at night . . . I dream about this place, and it's not even romantic. It's just work, you know, problems that pop up . . . I do find I dream about this place a lot. Not every night, but frequently (Guy, Newman and Mastracci, 2008: 105).

Within the human services, the emotional demands of the work can exhaust a service provider's capacity to be involved with, and responsive to, the needs of recipients. Moreover, workers who perform emotional labor under conditions of low job autonomy and high job involvement are more at risk of emotional exhaustion than others. This means that burnout is a serious risk in extraordinarily difficult jobs: such as in family services agencies in the US, where caseworkers have huge caseloads, little discretion, and service budgets that cannot possibly cover all needs.

Those who work in prisons give further examples of how exhaustion can occur. Dangerous working conditions and the lack of support from public opinion combine to produce enormous emotional labor demands on these workers. Emotion management is the *modus operandi* for correctional workers as they wear a mask every day:

Our jobs are far more difficult emotionally because you have to overcome your own feelings and their [the prisoners'] feelings and try to make something happen at the same time . . . One thing I do really stress for myself is not flying off the handle, but remaining calm and that takes a great deal out of me. Sometimes I go home at night and I'm just exhausted because I've had to be professional when I sometimes would like very much not to be . . . All that tension just goes right into you. And it's like you carry it around with you. Because I'm not allowed to shout, scream, yell, carry on like a fool, it just kinda goes around with you (Guy, Newman and Mastracci, 2008: 30).

Cynicism

People use cognitive distancing to protect themselves from repeated emotional demands that are overwhelming. In colloquial terms, they become 'crispy' in that they are negative, callous or excessively detached from their jobs. They are 'absent on the job', going through the motions in a detached, uncaring, even robotic manner. They depersonalize the citizens they work with, treating them as objects and they become mechanical in their discussions with coworkers. An example of this protection mechanism discussed in the following.

To protect themselves from the emotional intensity of what they are seeing, emergency response workers may become detached from the people they are called upon to help. The chief of an emergency medical rescue team explains:

We had a news camera crew riding with us. They were looking at developing this TV show about paramedics, and we had a call where this car had crossed the center line and hit directly head on into another vehicle . . . It was a very bad accident. The mother that I was taking care of was in terrible shape and pinned in the car . . . we worked for probably forty-five minutes to cut her out of the car to get her to the hospital, and after the call I look over and the camera man has his head in his hands, he had just thrown up, he was wrecked and he said he had never seen anything like that and he doesn't know how we even deal with that. We got back to the station and he put the video in to show us what he had shot and it hit me. I realized it. I mean he was focusing in. I couldn't even tell you what that woman looked like. I never personalize it – I never put a face with the person. I think we just block everything out . . . and it hit me, he personalized it. He was zooming in on her face, on my face . . . he was making it much more personal and I think we separate ourselves from that (Mastracci, Guy and Newman, 2011: 92).

Public service occupations generally, and helping professions especially, suffer a built-in non-reciprocal balance of giving. The worker gives, the citizen takes. Depersonalization is a means of overcoming the lack of reciprocity by withdrawing psychologically from the citizen. Detachment becomes permanent and the person is chronically unable to feel what he or she should feel.

Ineffectiveness

This is the third dimension of burnout. It is the tendency to evaluate one's work negatively. The belief that one is no longer able to achieve one's goals is accompanied by feelings of inefficiency, poor professional self-esteem, and a growing sense of inadequacy. For many public service workers who spend each day working with citizens who are in dire need, they may feel that no matter how hard they try and what actions they take, they will not have a lasting impact. This causes a discouraging sense of fatalism. And seeing so much need and deprivation on a daily basis can make it difficult to maintain a professional edge and psychic balance. Here is how the supervisor of a family services agency captures this:

> As awful as it is, you have to have a strong enough constitution that you have to deal with whatever is there, and at the same time not be so blunted that it doesn't matter anymore. If you begin to think that every house should have green plastic bags with dirty laundry and garbage all over the place and you begin to think that's the norm, you're in deep trouble and then you need to leave. I think you have to be able to still be appalled and annoyed and shocked without going over the bend with it (Guy, Newman and Mastracci, 2008: 72).

As trying as emotionally intense work can be, there are strategies that help to mitigate its toxic effects. The next section discusses techniques that are useful in forestalling or dealing with burnout.

STRATEGIES FOR DEALING WITH BURNOUT

From multiple perspectives – employee wellness, quality of work life, citizen trust, service outcomes – management has an important role to play ensuring that the emotive aspects of work are acknowledged and that there are systems in place to prevent or minimize its downside. The following sections describe five strategies that are effective for avoiding or minimizing the effects of burnout: critical incident debriefings, self-care plans, job redesign, time outs and ways of thinking about emotionally intense events.

Critical Incident Debriefings

A strategy used frequently by law enforcement, firefighters and emergency rescue squads is called 'critical incident debriefings' or 'critical stress debriefings'. These meetings serve a valuable function in dealing with vicarious trauma and post-traumatic stress by helping workers deal with the intense emotions they suppressed while the work was ongoing or afterward. The debriefings may be required or voluntary. They provide an opportunity to talk with peers and/or trained professionals about lingering images, memories and emotions in a manner that suits the workplace culture. They may be one-on-one with a counselor or they may be group meetings that involve all the workers who were involved in the incident. A firefighter describes it in the following way:

> And then there is critical stress debriefing – personnel that we have come up to the fire stations and they talk about it and anytime we have any type of situations like that we do sit down and we talk with them and they say okay, how are you feeling? I know I've had to do it one or two times but I've also learned how to deal with it . . . Could we have done better? Could we have gone in this window instead of this door to get to that child? So, you know, you try your best to adapt – you try your best to find that avenue of peace where you're able to say okay, you know what? I've done all that I was capable of doing (Mastracci, Guy and Newman, 2011: 43).

An opportunity to 'talk shop' and to vent feelings with co-workers is an important source of social support. Such sessions are only effective when those attending are responsive, however. Masculine cultures such as among police and firefighters are known to discourage expression of emotions other than those that are tough and self-confident. Officers are reluctant to express doubts, fears, or regrets because they fear ostracism by their peers. For instance, a detective said that: 'The problem is that the officers can go in there and choose not to participate or participate minimally and so it doesn't get addressed; then it's just a box that is ticked off' (Mastracci, Guy and Newman, 2011: 43). Critical incident debriefings are designed to overcome this block to an honest exchange of feelings but to be successful, they require support and encouragement from supervisors and directors. It is often preferable for management to require debriefings rather than letting them be 'on demand'. This way, workers must attend and they do not lose face or appear 'weak' by requesting a session.

Self-care Plans

Another strategy that is effective in helping workers prevent burnout is a self-care plan. Used predominantly among female dominated workforces such as victim assistance workers and domestic violence workers, the purpose of a self-care plan is to serve as a preemptive means for keeping employees healthy. It may be required by the employer or it may be optional. Where most effective, the plan requires employees to specify personal goals for themselves on an annual basis. The goals may or may not be work-related and always relate to personal growth. The ultimate purpose of the plan is to remind workers that their lives and personal growth are separate from, and more important than, any one crisis on the job.

When workers have their annual performance appraisal, they are evaluated on their progress toward achieving goals in their self-care plan, just as they are evaluated on the various dimensions of their specific job. A plan includes personal stretch goals in the area of physical, emotional, financial, intellectual and/or spiritual health. Within the first 30 days of employment, workers are required to create their plan and state it in measurable, outcome oriented terms. An employer who has institutionalized this technique at the agency she directs says 'it's amazing what people get done in a year and how great they feel about it. It is a large part of why some of the staff say that they have remained at the agency for such a long period' (personal interview with Cathy Phelps, June 14, 2010). She explains, 'We are witness to horrible things that we have to be able to absorb and work with. You can't do that if you're not practicing self-care and if you don't have an environment that supports that practice.' She reports that the agency reaps benefits from this requirement because there is less sick leave, lower absenteeism and fewer worker's compensation claims.

Emotionally intense work is performed in some venues that are not anticipated and strategies are just as necessary in these settings as in those where it is well understood. For example, in large urban areas translators must be on staff in the public hospital's emergency room and they may need to accompany police officers and victim assistance counselors as they intervene with crime victims. When translating, interpreters speak in the voice of the victim: In the words of one translator, 'We're the ones that are speaking in the first person—*I* was raped, *I* was, you know—and nobody's recognizing what that does to *us*' (Mastracci, Newman and Guy, 2011: 45).

From the standpoint of employee well-being, self-care plans have much to commend them. They acknowledge that the worker is a whole person and they legitimate the acknowledgement that it is the whole person who performs the job, not just a truncated remnant of a human being as Ralph Hummel (1987) asserts. The plans are unobtrusive and can be as private or public as the employee wishes. Because they are attached to the worker's performance appraisal, the goals become far more than soon-to-be-forgotten New Year's resolutions.

Job Redesign

Another major point of intervention is the redesign of jobs to relieve emotional pressure on workers. One way of doing this is to rotate responsibilities so that the individual alternates between work that is intensely involved with citizens and administrative work that removes the worker from the emotive demands of daily face to face contact. For example, at a correctional facility in Illinois, correctional officers and counselors routinely divide their time between interacting with inmates in the housing units and performing administrative tasks in offices in a different building (Guy, Newman and Mastracci, 2008). Administrators can also reduce demands on workers by varying the work load as described in the next section.

Time Outs

The concept of 'time out' is relevant for any work that involves a high degree of stress. Managers can structure 'time-outs' that enable workers to temporarily escape from usual job demands, giving them a change of pace during which they 'recharge their batteries'. Time-outs are opportunities for staff to voluntarily choose to do less stressful work while others take over their responsibilities with service recipients. What makes this form of withdrawal a positive one is that continuity of care can be maintained even while the professional is getting a temporary emotional breather. When physical distancing is impossible, workers use emotional withdrawal as a respite from the stressors of their work. The dysfunctional side of time out includes 'absence behavior' and 'time abuse', such as taking longer breaks, calling in sick, spending more time on paperwork, leaving work early and tardiness, all of which are examples of withdrawal by means of spending less time on the job. However, if there is a proactive schedule that provides for time outs, the break can fit within the patterns of the organization.

One of the important ways that self-awareness plays out for emotional laborers is that it helps them situate themselves, doing the type of work that is most rewarding. This changes over the course of their careers. A counselor who works at a domestic violence shelter gives this explanation for why she started her career in direct services, then moved into administration, then moved back to direct services:

> I've gone from management back to direct service and then back to management. That was good for me because that's part of my self-care . . . To do this work is to pay attention to what you need and where you can be most effective right now for yourself . . . I mean, I had people question me when I went back to direct service. Why did you do that? But that's just where I needed to be. I just needed that contact again, and it was good that I did it. It energized me (Mastracci, Guy and Newman, 2011: 52).

This person used a protracted time out from direct service and then a time out from administration. This is an example of how organizations benefit by accommodating the worker's well being. When large enough to provide lateral moves from one department to another, organizations have the advantage of being able to flexibly respond to workers' needs without losing a well trained, knowledgeable employee.

Habits of the Mind

In addition to strategies that the employer controls, there are, for lack of a better term, habits of the mind – ways of thinking – that help workers move beyond the intensity of their on-the-job experiences. In other words, it is not what happens that matters, as much as it is how workers *think* about what happened. Hobbies and other outside interests help workers decompress, taking their attention away from work experiences and focusing their energy and thoughts on something totally different.

When dealing with critical incidents, responders who learn to treat bad outcomes as learning opportunities seem to succeed in avoiding burnout. This is aided by being able to talk about their experience and feelings to someone whom they trust, whether it is a supervisor, teammate or a spouse. There is a general consensus among those who work in emotionally intense jobs that a strong bond of trust among team members is very helpful. A police officer explains the police culture and why dealing with traumatic experiences is difficult:

> I think we have a lot [who] don't know why they survive, but they do, and a lot of that has to do with they are able to make some sense out of the meaninglessness of whatever they encounter . . . We're all human beings and so we all pretty much respond pretty similarly. We just have been given this power and authority by the public and so that kind of jacks with our perception sometimes and makes us close down or hold that much closer to the vest than we need to (Mastracci, Guy and Newman, 2011: 46).

This quote reveals how officers can manage the emotional intensity of their jobs when they can prevent themselves from becoming jaded by the grisly experiences they encounter. At the same time, because the state imbues them with power and authority, they are uncomfortable expressing feelings that make them appear weak. Keeping feelings bottled up so as not to show weakness is taxing and takes a toll on them unless they can think about their experiences in a way that is not toxic.

These five strategies, critical incident debriefings, self-care plans, job redesign, time outs and 'habits of the mind', are means by which the pitfalls of emotional labor can be avoided or burnout at least can be minimized. Discussion now turns to the human resource management

(HRM) functions that can enable the performance of emotional labor in a constructive, productive manner.

HRM FUNCTIONS THAT ENABLE SUCCESSFUL EMOTION WORK

Drawing and redrawing organizational charts, writing and rewriting organizational rules, and reviewing and revising procedures in an effort to perfect them are only a part of management's job. Thinking that this is sufficient to guarantee public service outcomes is to treat human processes like computer code. In computer programming, getting the zeroes and ones right will produce a particular outcome every time; however, people are not zeroes and ones. Agencies should be screening, training, evaluating and rewarding employees on the quality not just of their cognitive (technical) skills but also of their emotive skills and on their ability to mitigate overloads when the stress is too much. The development of more accurate and complete job descriptions, selection mechanisms with high goodness of fit between job demands and worker characteristics, effective training and meaningful performance appraisals, are necessary steps toward placing the right person with the right skills in the right job.

Job Analysis and Job Description

Interpersonal skills and emotional labor are at the heart of most public service jobs. Ironically, most job descriptions fail to mention the emotive skills that are necessary. For instance, those who respond to job ads for emergency call takers are often surprised to learn that in addition to being familiar with electronic dispatch systems, they must also be personally equipped to handle the panicked emotional state of callers. It is this aspect of the work that sticks with them after work hours, long after they have removed the headphones and turned away from the dispatch console.

Job analyses that include the position's cognitive component as well as emotional component provide a more accurate depiction of the necessary skills. An accurate job analysis then makes it easy to write an accurate job description. An accurate job description makes it easier for prospective applicants to determine whether the job is right for them and it paves the way for hiring authorities to consider all requisite skills when reviewing applicants.

Selection

Self awareness is an essential trait when selecting workers who must engage in emotionally intense work. Employers seek job applicants who are aware of their own reactions to emotive states and are cognizant of the need to deal openly with the emotional intensity of their experiences. This trait enables workers to take stock of their own performance and to process their emotions. The director of an agency that serves crime victims describes her search for employees this way:

> I'm looking for self-awareness, self-management. We ask what strategies do you use to cope with stress and the answers are amazing. Some people think the answer is to tell us that they don't have any stress. That that's it. 'Oh, I don't get stressed'. Impossible. Others think, Wow! That's a good question. Let me think about it . . . Self-awareness is huge. Self-management is huge. That's at the top of my list (Mastracci, Guy and Newman; 2011: 47).

Training and Supervision

The importance of training and supervision cannot be overemphasized. Agencies that do a good job of training are those that treat emotive skills as being as important as cognitive skills and offer training accordingly. Working in emotionally intense jobs has a cumulative effect. Sensitizing workers to this helps to ward off burnout. Those who work with crime victims, for example, encounter vicarious trauma on a daily basis. As they counsel victims, they hear more detail than their imaginations can bear. Although not victims themselves, this takes a toll over time. Here is how a victim services coordinator explains this situation to workers:

> I live upstairs in a condo. So if I go grocery shopping and I have ten bags that I have to carry up the stairs I have two choices. I can make ten trips up and down the stairs and carry a bag each time. Or I can load those puppies up in my arms and make one hideous trip up the top of the stairs. Either way, I am going to be exhausted when I get done. Whether I run up and down ten times or whether I am carrying a heavy load once. The impact physically is going to be the same. I'm going to be exhausted. That's what it's like with vicarious trauma. You can either be called to a homicide where it's horrible and horrific and just raw emotion out there, or you can do five or six milder callouts in a row. In the end, you're going to be impacted on an emotional level. It's the same thing. So you want to be aware of that and have a heightened sense of self-awareness. How are you feeling? Are you cranky? Are you snapping at your kids and you're kicking the dog? Stop and think about, okay, what have I done? What am I reacting to here? (Mastracci, Guy and Newman, 2011: 49.)

Another dimension to training workers who will be in emotionally intense situations is to prepare them for managing their own emotional overload. A firefighter warns that, when approaching a burning building, you have to make sure it's safe to act: 'It's very easy to get tunnel vision because of the adrenalin that's going on and it's like the moth to the fire and so that does take training to learn to get those parts of your emotions under control – the adrenalin-junkie emotions – because those are the ones that tend to get people seriously hurt' (Mastracci, Guy and Newman, 2011: 50).

Training sessions and workshops organized to discuss and exercise emotion management practices, and protocols that set forth rules of emotional display and expression serve to legitimize and institutionalize this work. Organizational culture dictates which emotions are appropriate to display and which ones are not and this is why training is most effective when provided in the context of the workplace. Whether norms are formally or informally expressed, they influence whether the worker disguises emotional expression or not. The police culture is one of those with restrictive display rules, even when in conversation with one another. The secretive culture makes it difficult for officers to discuss their experiences openly and deal with them constructively. Fields whose workforces are predominantly female, however, have an easier time addressing the emotive aspects of the job during training.

There is also preemptive training that can forestall or prevent the downside to emotion work. Alerting workers that it is normal to experience intense, lingering images of horrific scenes helps them to understand that their reaction is predictable, rather than being a sign of weakness. We have long acknowledged that workers must be well trained in the technical aspects of their jobs. However, they must also be trained in the emotive aspects of their work. And supervisors must be sensitive to these aspects of their work.

Performance Appraisal

Skillful performance of emotional labor should be rewarded just as skillful performance of cognitive labor is rewarded; however it rarely is. In a study conducted by Mastracci, Newman, and Guy (2006), they reported their examination of performance appraisal forms used by a number of public agencies. The goal of their review was to determine what percentage of forms included items pertaining to the employee's proficiency in performing the emotional labor component of the job. Of all instruments reviewed, 86 per cent identified the performance of emotion work at only a perfunctory level or less. The lack of acknowledgement renders such labor invisible, fails to reward the worker for that aspect of their performance that gives them the greatest satisfaction and fails to reward those workers who know how to balance the stress of the job such that it does not wear them down.

Properly conducted job analyses that include the emotive component of the work overcome the silence of current performance appraisal forms. Once tasks are identified in the analysis, they can be included in the job description and the performance appraisal. This then leads to a more accurate job description, which leads to appraisals that will include consideration of this important aspect of the job.

The implications for emotional labor in public service are thus: through selective recruitment of applicants who are technically skilled and emotionally self-aware, the workforce is better equipped to deliver public services. Training that enhances worker knowledge about emotional labor and the feelings that are normal in such work will advance the performance of emotion work and proactively reduce its downside. Supervisors that are knowledgeable about emotive tasks as well as cognitive tasks are better equipped to train, motivate and provide support to workers.

SUMMARY

In some ways, the vernacular 'street smart' captures what emotional labor is. The worker 'reads' the emotive state of the citizen and accommodates it in order to effectuate a transaction. The emphasis in bureaucratic theory on cognitive rationality and the de-emphasis on feelings often causes the emotion work aspects of public service to be viewed as irrelevant and 'not work'. This causes feelings – the management of one's own feelings and feelings of others – to remain out of bounds. Yet Chris Argyris (1964: 273) long ago remarked that emotionality and interpersonal competence would become as important as the values of rationality and intellectual competence in the organization of the future.

Argyris' forecast is still on the horizon. There is a lag between theory and practice. Employee well-being, more often than not, is sacrificed at the altar of 'countable' work, while that aspect of the job that provides the greatest meaning to the worker is overlooked. If the citizen needs to be calmer, it is up to the worker to achieve that. If the citizen is angry, it is up to the worker to resolve that anger. If the citizen is panicked, it is up to the worker to calm the situation and cause the citizen to gain control. If citizens are belligerent, it is up to the worker to engage them in such a way that they agree to comply. Emotional labor is by its very commission, spontaneous and unique to each situation and each citizen's interaction with the state. It is very real and it is not programmable. Workers must be trained to use their own discretion using guiding principles as their boundaries. In the words of those who perform it, emotional labor gives meaning to workers' lives. A firefighter describes what it feels like after retirement:

> After you retire you think you're not gonna miss it and there's not a day that goes by that you don't – you know everybody needs to be needed. Some people just need to help (Mastracci, Guy and Newman, 2011: 40).

Whether civil servants come in contact with citizens over a reception desk, at the tax assessor's office, at a zoning hearing, or in an emergency, emotional labor will be required. All public servants would do well to have at their disposal self-care plans, time outs, critical incident debriefings, and the flexibility to redesign the job so that there is a pressure release valve in some form. Even though most workers operate in an atmosphere of conference calls and emails, face to face transactions between the state and the citizen are important and will continue to be; and with these transactions comes the emotive component of the job.

In emotion work, the highs are high and the lows can be very low. Employers and supervisors are advised to acknowledge the highs and anticipate the lows. They can do this by providing mechanisms that celebrate the upside while not ignoring the downside and not leaving individuals to rebound on their own. In the absence of strategies for coping with haunting recollections long after the job is done, workers too often turn 'crispy', engaging in dysfunctional behaviors, losing interest in their work and seeking work elsewhere. Losing trained, competent workers is expensive and, with forethought, avoidable.

REFERENCES

Argyris, C. (1964), *Integrating the Individual and the Organization*, New York: John Wiley & Sons.

Golembiewski, R.T., R.F. Munzenrider and J.G. Stevenson (1986), *Stress in Organizations: Toward a Phase Model of Burnout*, New York: Praeger.

Guy, M., M.A. Newman and S. Mastracci (2008), *Emotional Labor: Putting the 'Service' in Public Service*, Armonk, NY: M.E. Sharpe.

Hsieh, C.-W., M. Jin and M.E. Guy (2011), 'Consequences of work-related emotions: analysis of a cross-section of public service workers', *American Review of Public Administration*, February 21, 2011.

Hummel, R. (1987), *The Bureaucratic Phenomenon*, NY: St. Marten's Press.

Maslach, C. (1981), 'Burnout: a social psychological analysis', in J.W. Jones (ed.), *The Burnout Syndrome: Current Research, Theory, Interventions*, Park Ridge, IL: London House Press, pp. 30–53.

Mastracci, S., M. Guy and M.A. Newman (2011), *Working on the Razor's Edge: Emotional Labor and Crisis Response*, Armonk, NY: M.E. Sharpe.

Mastracci, S., M.A. Newman and M.E. Guy (2006), 'Appraising emotion work: determining whether emotional labor is valued in government jobs', *American Review of Public Administration*, **36** (2), 123–38.

Newman, M.A., M.E. Guy and S.H. Mastracci (2009), 'Beyond cognition: affective leadership and emotional labor', *Public Administration Review*, **69** (1), 6–20.

Pugliesi, K. (1999), 'The consequences of emotional labor: effects on work stress, job satisfaction, and well-being', *Motivation and Emotion*, **23** (2), 125–54.

PART III

Human resource management challenges in the public sector

8. Management and leadership development in public service organizations

Patrick McGurk

INTRODUCTION

The question of how to raise the quality of management and leadership in public service organizations (PSOs) has been central to reform efforts in recent decades. One response has been to recruit inspirational senior executives to help transform PSOs, such as local government or civil service departments, schools and hospitals (see Borins, 2000; Boyne et al., 2008; Storey, 2004a: 13). Another has been the identification of management and leadership 'competences', which are then used to direct managers' behaviour in the public services and professions (Burgoyne et al., 2004: 13–16; Horton, 2002). A third response, though one which has received less academic scrutiny, has been a surge in management and leadership development (MLD) initiatives, designed to improve the knowledge, skills and capabilities of public managers.

The international trend of increasing investment in MLD for the public sector has been widely recognized (Guest and King, 2005: 248–49; Raffel et al., 2009; Lawler, 2008: 22; Storey, 2004b: 4–6). But little is known about the actual impact of MLD initiatives on modernization and change in PSOs (Charlesworth et al., 2003; Burgoyne et al., 2004: 70), not least because this type of intervention is notoriously difficult to quantify (see Tamkin et al., 2002; Martineau, 2004). Investment in MLD is most easily identifiable in the provision of formal training and development programmes that lead to recognized management qualifications, or in the creation of public organizations that promote MLD (such as the UK's Council for Excellence in Management and Leadership or Sweden's National Council for Quality and Development). However, at the level of the individual organization, MLD necessarily takes a number of forms (Mabey and Finch-Lees, 2008; Burgoyne et al., 2004; Mole, 2000; Mumford and Gold, 2004). It may constitute informal as well as formal activity, it may be individual or collective in orientation, and it may concentrate on 'leadership' rather than 'management' (see Gold et al., 2003). This chapter makes sense of the diversity of MLD activity in PSOs and offers a contextualist explanation for why some interventions may be more effective than others.

The chapter has three sections. The first section of the chapter analyses the changing nature of the demand for management and leadership in PSOs. The second section explains the main approaches to MLD that may be adopted at an organizational level. Three broad types of MLD are differentiated: management development, leader development and leadership development (Day, 2001). The third section presents findings from three UK-based case studies of the outcomes of MLD and the obstacles to its effectiveness in PSOs (from McGurk, 2009; 2011; 2010). The cases represent three quite different types of strategic organizational challenge that shape MLD options and outcomes. Based on these findings, the chapter concludes that the effectiveness of MLD's contribution is contingent upon the organization's structural context and direction of change.

THE CHANGING DEMAND FOR MANAGEMENT AND LEADERSHIP IN THE PUBLIC SERVICES

> Efficient management is a key to the revival ... And the management ethos must run right through our national life – private and public companies, civil service, nationalized industries, local government, the National Health Service (Speech in 1980 by Michael Heseltine, UK government minister, cited in Pollitt (2003: 169)).

Such pronouncements by policy-makers in the 1980s signalled a change in the prevailing perceptions of the roles of senior staff in PSOs. The public manager became increasingly identified as the key agent through whom the efficiency and quality of public services would be improved. 'The right of the manager to manage', free from the constraints of central bureaucratic control, was a central tenet of managerialism (Clarke and Newman, 1997; cited in Lawler, 2008: 22) and an important aspect of the ideological shift from the 'old public administration' to the 'new public management' (NPM) (Dunleavy and Hood, 1994).

The demand for individual managers in PSOs to possess generic managerial knowledge and skills, largely derived from private sector models (Dingwall and Strangleman, 2005: 478–80), was an important aspect of the first main wave of public service reform from the 1980s to the mid-1990s. The main intention was that public managers would ensure efficient resource-allocation through more effective management of self, operations, finance, people, information and strategy. The amount of subsequent management training and development in the public sector is not easily measured or open to international comparison. However, some indication of the growth in MLD activity during this period is provided by Mabey (2004b), who reports that the time spent on management training and development in European firms almost doubled from approximately 5 to 9 days per year in the years 1992–2004. From earlier studies it is reasonable to assume a similar trend in the public sector (see Thomson et al., 2001, which included PSOs in the sample).

An important trend in the public sector, particularly in the Anglo-Saxon world, has been the growth of competence-based management (Horton, 2002; Hondeghem, 2002). Instead of defining management according to broad job roles, competence-based management involves a detailed codification of what managers 'should know and be able to do' and 'how they should behave' at different levels of the management hierarchy. This approach proved influential in the design of management training and development across various public services and professions, including social work, teaching and the civil service. Although the competence movement appears to have 'lost some of its impetus' (Guest and King, 2005: 242), competence-based management development has nevertheless remained important in the UK and US public services (OECD, 2001: 22), especially in the design of management qualifications for various sectors and professions (Burgoyne et al., 2004: 15).

During the second wave of public service reform from the late-1990s onwards, as the efficiency priorities of NPM began to give way to the quality, innovation and governance concerns of modernization (Dunleavy et al., 2006; Newman, 2002; Osborne, 2006), there was a gradual change in policy-makers' emphasis: from management towards leadership. The theoretical distinction between managers and leaders – in which managers implement decisions through the exercise of formal authority, while leaders inspire and motivate staff to innovate and commit to organizational goals (see Kotter, 1990; Zaleznik, 1992) – has been a matter of considerable dispute among academics (see Storey (2004a) for a review of the key arguments). However, the management-leadership dichotomy has been influential for policy-makers who sought to address the new and more complex challenges of modernization (Storey, 2004b: 7; O'Reilly and Reed, 2010; Milner and Joyce, 2005: 71; Lawler, 2008: 22).

North American models of leadership, emphasizing an individualistic and entrepreneurial approach to reforming the public services (see Osborne and Gaebler, 1992), were an important early influence on policy-makers. However, a counterbalance was provided by more conservative European models, which conceptualized the public leader as the 'steward' of public services and protector of the processes and values that ensure their democratic legitimacy (see Denis et al., 2005: 451). Despite such definitional diversity, policy-makers continued to be attracted away from the more mundane and predictable notion of management towards the less tangible but more dynamic idea of leadership. A 2001 report by the Organisation for Economic Co-operation and Development (OECD) illustrates this. The report conceded that '[i]n all countries, structural and management reform in the public sector has been used to better align public services with the needs of contemporary society' (OECD, 2001: 12). Yet it went on to argue that 'something was missing', namely 'a lack of dedication to the underlying values of public service cultures and the public interest'; this 'something' was to be 'fixed' through leadership (OECD, 2001).

The underlying reasons for policy-makers' growing preoccupation with the emotional and psychological aspects of the public manager's role, as opposed to its more functional and task-related aspects, are clarified by Hughes (2007: 320–1):

> The emergence of concepts of leadership in the public sector should be seen as a reassertion of individual and personal attributes in management, and, as a corollary, a reduction in the emphasis on management by formal rules. Giving a manager real responsibility to achieve results means that he or she must then deliver and their part of the organization must also deliver. The staff involved need to achieve and the manager needs to lead them. A good manager must not only deliver results, but somehow get subordinates to agree with the general parameters of the vision and to be inspired to achieve themselves, for the overall benefit of the organization.

The gradual reassertion of the personal and relational dimension of management, as described by Hughes, is also reflected in the evolution of the UK's *National Occupational Standards in Management and Leadership*. These standards originated in 1991 and were then revised in 1997, 2004 and 2008. They continue to be widely used as the basis of qualifications and competence-based development in the UK public sector. The 1991 standards were restricted to the areas of managing operations, finance, people and information. However, in the 2008 version, the standards were clustered around the six broader-ranging areas of 'managing self and personal skills', 'providing direction, 'facilitating change', 'working with people', 'using resources' and 'achieving results' (Burgoyne et al., 2004: 15; MSC, 2008). That the first four of the six new clusters demonstrate a relational rather than task emphasis is illustrative of an general trend to include leadership competences alongside more traditional management competences (see Salaman, 2004). Alongside the changing competence profile in the UK, the research and consultancy work of Alimo-Metcalfe and Alban-Metcalfe has also been influential in re-focusing policy-makers' attention on the motivational role of the public manager (see Alimo-Metcalfe and Alban-Metcalfe, 2004; The Real World Group, 2011). In particular, Alimo-Metcalfe and Alban-Metcalfe (2004: 174–76) have highlighted the importance of attending to the psychological wellbeing of staff in the light of stress caused by rapid change and new employment insecurities in PSOs.

Beyond the individualized dimension of leadership, policy-makers have shown an interest in more collectivized concepts of leadership for the promotion of innovation and organizational development (see for example, Mulgan and Albury (2003); Performance and Information Unit (2001: 15–18)). This derives from the analysis that public managers are increasingly faced with more complex governance arrangements and have to rely on partnerships and collaborative networks to stimulate innovations and deliver personalized services to users (see Denis et al., 2005: 452–62). In this perspective, leadership is less about developing motivational relationships with one's subordinates, and more about the processes of collaboration across organizations to develop the collective capacity for change. Collectivist conceptions of leadership therefore emphasize the distributed nature of power and influence across organizations and projects, which managers in PSOs need to learn to navigate in order to be effective (see Gronn, 2000; Hall and Janmen, 2010; MacBeath, 2005; Spillane et al., 2001).

Clearly there have been a number of interpretations of public service leadership over the years (see also Milner and Joyce, 2005). As an overall idea, however, leadership became pervasive during the second wave of public service reform. The OECD (2001) shows how it has inspired recent investments in public leadership centres and leadership development initiatives in the UK, US, Germany, Sweden, Norway and Mexico. At the United Nations Development Programme, leadership was recently identified as one of the four key drivers of its mission (UNDP, 2011). In the UK alone, the last decade has witnessed the establishment of the NHS Leadership Centre for the health service, the National College for School Leadership, and the Leadership Centre for Local Government. Some commentators suggest that leadership has come to be seen as a 'panacea that may cure the widespread and often long-term ills of the public sector' (Grugulis, 2007: 145; citing Storey, 2004b: 7).

It is indeed questionable how much practical difference policy-makers' demands for more effective leadership have made. For example, Charlesworth et al. (2003) found in a survey of 1900 middle and junior public sector managers that a low organizational priority was in fact placed on leadership development activity. Similarly, it may be argued that the tendency to promote leadership at the expense of management has served to distort understanding of public managers' real contribution in organizations, and has led to confused demands for change. Notably Mintzberg (2009: 9) has maintained that leadership should never have been treated as different to management, but simply as 'management practiced well'. He also argues that the 'cult' of leadership has had a destructive effect on the public services by diverting managerial priorities away from their natural organizational context (Mintzberg, 1996: 80; see also Mintzberg 2004: 1).

In the search for a model of what senior staff in PSOs should do and how they should behave, it seems that the management-leadership debate has 'now served its purpose' (Burgoyne et al., 2004: 13). However, for the question how best to *develop* managers, the management-leadership distinction is still valuable. As Day (2001: 581) argues, much 'conceptual confusion' underlies MLD practice. For a more precise understanding of how MLD contributes to strategic change in PSOs, it is necessary to unpick the range of available MLD methods and their underlying aims.

MANAGEMENT AND LEADERSHIP DEVELOPMENT OPTIONS IN ORGANIZATIONS

The academic literature is abundant with descriptions of the various approaches to management training and development that are employed in organizations (see Burgoyne and Reynolds, 1997; Mumford, 1997; Mumford and Gold, 2004; Storey and Tate, 2000; Mole, 2000; Guest and King, 2005; Mabey and Finch-Lees, 2008). Distinctive among them is Day's (2001) typology, which allows linkages to be established with specific strategic organizational priorities. This enables clarity regarding the different types of contributions that MLD may make in PSOs.

Day distinguishes between management development, leader development and leadership development. Management development, according to Day (2001: 582), has 'an emphasis on acquiring specific types of knowledge, skills and abilities to enhance task performance in management roles'. He maintains that management development has 'mainly a training orientation' and characterizes it as 'the application of proven solutions to known problems' (Day, 2001). For example, line-managers need to be competent in the implementation of staff absence and discipline policies so that basic performance standards are maintained. Similarly, they need to be competent in the management of financial resources to ensure that departmental budgets are not over-spent. For such reasons, organizations frequently invest in standard management development programmes, typically delivered in a classroom setting with well-defined objectives and expected learning outcomes, in order to ensure that managers are equipped with the knowledge and skills to maintain organizational performance and implement business plans.

In contrast, leader development is described by Day as developing the individual manager 'to think and act in new ways' (2001: 584). Leader development is more concerned with the psychological and emotional aspects of work in organizations, and is not necessarily related to a specific managerial position. It is about understanding one's own character and personality, how one fits into the broader strategic organizational picture, and how one's behaviour is perceived and impacts on others. For example, a manager might discover that colleagues perceive him or her to be sympathetic but overly submissive in his or her interactions with others. Alternatively it may be learnt that he or she is perceived as decisive but overly dominant. Leader development is designed to address such issues and work with the individual to become more effective in social interactions. It tends to have less prescribed learning outcomes than management development and uses individualized methods such as 360-degree feedback, coaching, mentoring and personal development plans. Leader development activities are often included as the self-development or self-management element of standard management development programmes, designed to encourage managers to learn about how they can improve their relationships with others and influence their teams more effectively to commit to strategic goals.

Leadership development is described by Day (2001: 582) as a collective process for 'building capacity in anticipation of unforeseen challenges'. It involves networking, action learning and special project assignments, which include both planned and ad hoc group activities, designed to guide and draw upon interactions between managers so that solutions to organizational problems may emerge. Due to its emphasis on collective learning and relationship-building between managers, leadership development is concerned with the creation of 'social capital'. This is to be distinguished from 'human capital', which is the concern of leader development (Day, 2001: 583–84). The development of social capital involves efforts to increase mutual understanding, trust, commitment and obligation between managers to 'enhance cooperation and resource exchange in creating organizational value' (Day, 2001: 585; see also Nahapiet and Goshal, 1998). Such activities have a strong association with 'organizational capacity-building' (Tyler 2004; O'Connor and Quinn, 2004), communities of practice (Lave and Wenger, 1991; Brown and Duguid, 1991) and organizational learning (Argyris and Schön, 1978).

In practice, there are overlaps between the different types of MLD activity in organizations (Day, 2001: 584; Gold et al., 2003: 7). Indeed

Day (2001: 605) argues that any one approach to MLD 'is incomplete by itself' and that the keys to effectiveness are 'consistent and intentional implementation . . . [and] . . . linking initiatives across organizational levels and in terms of an overall developmental purpose within the context of a strategic business challenge' (Day, 2001: 606). Yet empirical evidence is sparse regarding the specific types of MLD actually practiced in organizations and 'what works and when' (Burgoyne et al., 2004: 1, 82). Mabey (2004b: 506) reports a clear preference across European firms for in-house development activities, rather than sponsorship for external courses. However, this does not mean that personalized leader development or ad hoc leadership development activities are necessarily preferred over group-based and standardized management development. Management development may, in fact, be the best description for the bulk of in-house activity in organizations; perhaps especially in PSOs, which are subject to greater regulation and standardization than private sector firms. UK surveys certainly suggest that the majority of MLD activity in organizations constitutes standardized management development programmes, or elements of them, and that the remainder of MLD activity is mostly in the form of leader development (Gold et al., 2003; Burgoyne et al., 2004: 22). Moreover Gold et al. (2003: 9–10) claim that leadership development activities, in the form described above, are actually rare.

Some combination of the three main MLD approaches may then be expected to be found in PSOs. However, more precise expectations about the orientation of an organization's MLD investment may be deduced by exploring in greater detail the connection between MLD options and organizational strategic goals. As Boxall and Purcell (2008: 20) point out, organizations typically pursue a range of broad human resource management (HRM) goals simultaneously: on the one hand, organizational stability is sought through the maintenance of operational efficiency and by securing the on-going trust and confidence of the workforce; on the other hand, organizations pursue more dynamic goals by trying to ensure greater workforce flexibility and organizational capacity for the future. Given this simultaneous pursuit of stability and change, it is logical to expect that organizations will pursue different blends of MLD practices according to their strategic priorities.

Day's typology may be usefully developed by deducing the broader HRM goals and intended organizational outcomes that underlie the three main MLD options. The goals driving management development, leader development and leadership development may be respectively derived as: (1) efficient and effective management; (2) effective leading of staff; and (3) adaptive capacity. The organizational outcomes to which the three

MLD options are intended to contribute may be respectively derived as: (1) organizational stability; (2) planned strategic change; and (3) emergent strategic change.

These theoretical linkages require some further elaboration, taking each MLD option in turn. Firstly, management development may be said to be driven by the requirement for efficient and effective management and thus is intended to support organizational stability in terms of the viable, on-going provision of the organization's services to customers and the smooth implementation of the organization's business plans. Secondly, leader development is driven by the concern to ensure the effective leading of staff; it aims to do this through activities that enhance individual managers' abilities to take the initiative and to influence others to commit to longer term, strategic goals. In this sense, leader development is intended to support the overall organizational goal of deliberate and planned strategic change (see Mintzberg and Waters, 1985). Thirdly, leadership development is driven by the concern to build greater adaptive capacity in the organization; it aims to do this through activities that foster relationships and help generate shared knowledge amongst managers in pursuit of the overall goal of improving the organization's future flexibility. In this sense, leadership development is intended to contribute to emergent strategic change (see Mintzberg and Waters, 1985).

The above differentiation of the MLD options according to three broad organizational goals necessarily underplays the overlaps that are likely to exist between MLD interventions in practice. For example, management development interventions may contribute to planned strategic changes as well as to the continuity of service to customers. The value of this novel framework, however, is to clarify the linkages between various strategic HRM goals, associated MLD interventions and intended organizational outcomes. The linkages are illustrated in Table 8.1.

The relationships depicted in Table 8.1 represent a theoretical framework that enables a rich, contextualized analysis of MLDs contribution in organizations. There is a clear need for this type of MLD research (see Thomson et al., 2001: 178; Mabey, 2002: 1156). The most extensive recent studies of the impact of MLD (Mabey, 2002; 2004a) provide important insights into the variables that determine its effect on improving organizational performance. However, they do not capture the detail of the different MLD methods used in organizations, how these are experienced by different stakeholders, and how they relate to strategic organizational context. Nor has much attention been paid to date to the specific context of PSOs. The case study approach (Yin, 1994) is well suited to addressing this gap, by providing the opportunity to examine how MLD has been used as an instrument of strategic change in contemporary PSOs.

Table 8.1   MLD goals, options and intended organizational outcomes

Strategic HRM goals ⟶	Associated MLD intervention ⟶	MLD activities ⟶	Contributes to intended organizational outcomes ⟶
Efficient/ effective management	Management development	Prescribed learning programmes: e.g. work-related assignments, management qualifications	Continuity of service for customers Effective implementation of business plans
Effective leading of staff	Leader development	Individualized learning activities: e.g. 360-feedback, coaching, mentoring, personal development plans	Planned strategic change
Adaptive capacity	Leadership development	Collective learning activities: e.g. networking, special project assignments, action-learning	Emergent strategic change

THREE CASE STUDIES OF MANAGEMENT AND LEADERSHIP DEVELOPMENT IN PUBLIC SERVICE ORGANIZATIONS

The case studies that follow illustrate the role played by MLD across three important types of organizational changes in public service reform. The first case demonstrates the use of management development and leader development in a privatized train operating company, which sought to improve its customer service in line with the government regulator's demands. The second case demonstrates the use of management development and leader development in a fire brigade, a traditional public sector bureaucracy, which sought to professionalize its service. The third case demonstrates the use of management development, leader development and leadership development in a local authority adult social care department, a professional bureaucracy (Mintzberg, 1979) which sought greater operational flexibility through partnerships and projects with local care-related services. The case organizations are all large PSOs in the south east of England, reputed in their sectors for their MLD practice, and studied during the same time period of 2000–7, during which the Labour Government pursued its modernization policies.

Management and Leadership Development in a Privatized Train Operating Company

The first organization originated as an independent franchise in the British Rail privatization of 1996. It experienced a series of industrial disputes and fines from the government regulator for poor performance in its first five years, with employment relations problems coming to a head with a strike by station staff in 2002. This prompted the board of directors to introduce a new 'employee-centred strategy', which was principally designed to reduce staff absence and improve customer service on the front-line, and was accompanied by a heavy investment in MLD.

The lion's share of MLD investment from 2002–5 went to management development, represented by a suite of compulsory line-management courses. These courses were principally focused on training managers to implement the company's new HRM policies on staff attendance and discipline, but they also included training in the 'softer' dimension of line-management in the form of regular one-to-one development discussions with staff. Although line-managers from the non-operational side of the business tended to complain about the compulsory 'sheep-dipping' approach, managers responsible for operational stations, fleet depots and driver depots generally responded enthusiastically to the training. There was strong evidence from staff attendance records and staff and customer satisfaction surveys to suggest that this investment in standardized management development made a significant contribution to securing and maintaining organizational stability following the poor start to the franchise (see McGurk, 2009: 472, 476).

The rest of the MLD investment went to leader development. The first leader development intervention was a two-day course in 2003, called 'The Wow Factor', which was compulsory for all of the company's approximate five hundred managers. The course constituted a series of small-group introspective discussions, aiming to explore 'the emotional aspect of management and how people felt about themselves and, in turn, how that would impact on the way they would manage their people' (Interview with the Human Resources Directorat at the case study train operating company, 2006). The Wow Factor divided opinion and took many managers 'out of their comfort zones'. Although described by one as 'excellent', 'brave' and 'radical', another found the course 'appalling' and 'diabolical'. She explained:

> A lot of that course, I found, was about making people feel on the spot, opening up things that people may have not wanted to share at work . . . I really did walk away from those two days thinking '. . . [H]ave I learnt anything that is going to make me a more effective manager? No'. And feeling frustrated that I knew all my managers were going to be released for the same two days and thinking 'what a waste of time' (Interview with the Guards Manager at the case study train operating company, 2006).

The second leader development intervention was in 2005, in the form of a talent management programme for 50 selected 'high-performing' managers. The programme aimed to retain the selected managers in the business over the long-term and to develop them to bring about strategic improvements in business performance. The leader development activity was constituted of a 360-degree exercise, psychometric testing and personal development planning. Most managers welcomed the opportunity to be singled out for such individualized attention and the insights gained into their personal leadership style. However, the intervention was relatively inconsequential in terms of changing individual leadership practices. As one driver manager said of his personal development plan that resulted from the 360-degree feedback: 'It was quite difficult for me to find anything that I felt I couldn't do that related to the job . . .' (Interview with the Driver Depot Manager at the case study train operating company, 2006).

The lack of obvious opportunities for managers to put the lessons of leader development into practice was related to the highly regulated work environment and the constraints of the managerial job roles, particularly in the driving and fleet areas of the operation. Despite this, there was evidence that the talent management programme did succeed in making some managers more reflective about how they related to their staff. In particular, several realized the importance of softening their communication styles. As one station manager learnt from his 360-degree feedback exercise:

> [S]ome of my managers actually really appreciate the direct, blunt approach, because they know where they stand. But I had to adapt myself for some of my team, because they obviously didn't react to that particular way of management . . . (Interview with Station Manager 1 at the case study train operating company, 2006).

It was notable that specific opportunities for individual managers to 'think and act in new ways' (Day 2001: 584) were effectively limited to those managers in customer-facing environments. Notably the station managers had access to detailed and frequent customer service performance data that could be attributed to their particular station or group of stations. They could then use this data to go beyond issues of absence and behaviour in their discussions with staff, and have wider consultations about how to achieve better business performance. As one station manager related as a consequence of his leadership development:

> I was out with a guy, one of my managers, last week, just going round his group of stations and helping him see what I see, and telling him how I approach addressing looking at a station ... Just getting him to see how I approach looking at stuff, and then getting him to tell me how he approaches it and just giving him some pointers about what he could do differently (Interview with Station Manager 2 at the case study train operating company, 2006).

The train operating company case illustrates the potentially powerful contribution of traditional management training in standardized operating environments, which are common in the public services (see Rainbird et al., 2004). Yet it also illustrates how the scope of leader development and its impact might be limited in such environments. Even in commercialized, customer-orientated PSOs, in which quite narrowly-defined strategic priorities might be clear, the opportunities for individual managers to 'lead effectively' may be constrained. The case suggests that leader development is at its most effective when grounded in ways that produce meaningful opportunities for managers to practice motivation and change strategies with their staff; furthermore it suggests that such opportunities are likely to vary within the organization itself.

Management and Leadership Development in a Fire Brigade

The second case organization is a regional fire brigade that also made heavy investments in MLD as part of a wider strategy for change. In this case, however, the emphasis was less on training line managers to ensure a standardized service for customers, and more on developing senior uniformed staff to adopt a new, empowering style of management.

The increasingly complex and uncertain operating environment for the fire service, coupled with adversarial employment relations, led in the mid-2000s to a national process of professionalization (Andrews, 2010; Fitzgerald, 2005). This involved an attempt by the UK government to shift the management of fire brigades away from a traditional bureaucratic model towards a modernized, community-orientated fire safety model. The former was characterized by the government as having entrenched working practices, highly prescribed operating procedures and a reactive, command-and-control style of coordination. The latter was characterized as having more flexible working practices, a preventative approach to managing local community fire safety, and it being the responsibility of line-managers to engage with staff development so that firefighters practice a broader set of skills and become more proactive. Already moving in this latter direction, during the late-1990s the case study brigade gradually abolished the old examination-based system of promotion through the uniformed ranks and pioneered its own competence-based management and leadership system of career development. In 2001 this system was adopted nationally as part of the 'integrated personal development system' (IPDS), a new competence framework for all uniformed staff that enshrined the new management and leadership behaviours that were desired by reformers.

IPDS came to underpin most MLD activities, which at the case study brigade represented a mixture of traditional management development and more reflective leader development. Management development was represented by traditional classroom instruction in technical processes and general management theory, as well as by simulated fireground activities and the compilation of certified evidence of competence in the workplace. Leader development was represented in the more individualized and coaching-orientated parts of the simulated fireground exercises, but was also supported by various leadership workshops and secondments linked to career development plans.

Problematically, the all-embracing IPDS framework was inextricably linked with the contested modernization reforms, which challenged a long tradition of self-regulated, informal learning on fire stations. A station commander described how he built his own managerial career under the old system:

> I was at a station where there was quite a turnover of staff, one of the leading firefighters was always away on courses or secondments; there was always an opportunity. It was like that at a lot of the stations where the people who were interested in promotion would be mentored by the existing office staff, groomed in a way, in 'this is what you do'. You tended to be put on the turntable ladder . . . you would attend [fire] incidents but you wouldn't necessarily be in charge. So it was a natural thing (Interview with Station Commander 1 at the case study fire brigade, 2005).

IPDS sought to replace this 'natural' system of 'grooming' for promotion, on the grounds that such practices were unfair and opaque, ultimately serving to perpetuate the over-representation of white males in fire service management (see ODPM, 2003). Uniformed staff generally accepted the need for changes to career promotion processes, but residual resentment of the modernization reforms remained, manifesting itself in the mid-2000s in some scepticism and resistance to MLD. Most uniformed managers dismissed the new MLD system at best as irrelevant to their 'real' work and at worst as dangerous bureaucratic interference by non-specialists in the technical business of firefighting. One manager said of the new system: 'It's like the King's New Clothes. We will believe we have better people, because it says so on paper' (Interview with Station Commander 2 at the case study fire brigade, 2005).

Yet despite the political obstacles to MLD, there was some evidence of its success in promoting a more empowering and developmental approach to management. This was most true of the MLD activity that took place in practical and specialist settings. As one station commander related from a simulated fire incident on the training ground:

> One day, on the last couple of days of the . . . course, they said 'Right, on this drill . . . we want you to assess the next officer in charge . . . where do you think [he] should be standing?' I said, 'Where I am'. And it was like the heavens opened and I suddenly realized that, as a manager, you need to see the big picture, you need to step away . . . It was just changed overnight . . . For me, it was just an amazing experience (Interview with Station Commander 3 at the case study fire brigade, 2005).

The suggestion that such positive responses to MLD were then translated into more participatory approaches to management receives support from government inspection reports on the case study brigade and on the national fire service. Andrews' (2010: 609, 613) analysis of fire service performance reports in England from 2001–2006, while recognizing that reform had been controversial, concludes that IPDS (of which MLD was a central part) had clearly led to improved HRM outcomes and may have helped develop greater trust between managers and staff.

There was less evidence, however, that MLD had an impact on promoting the other main strand of the government's reform agenda for the fire service: community fire safety. With the exception of one young manager, none of the managers in this research chose to reflect on their community fire safety role, either in terms of their responsibilities for outreach activity, or as part of their MLD experience. Part of the reason for this lies in the residual resistance of managers to the government's modernization programme; however, the main explanation lies in the lack of resourcing for fire prevention activities on the front line (see Fitzgerald, 2005: 657; Andrews, 2010: 611). Even if a deep commitment to the new strategic priority of community fire safety had been stimulated through MLD, the opportunities for operational managers to enact this new professional responsibility were not fully formed at the time.

The fire brigade case illustrates the potential of combined management development and leader development, firmly grounded in the appropriate vocational context, to promote more participatory types of management in traditional bureaucratic PSOs. However, the case also highlights the limitations of MLD as an instrument of HRM when it is faced with political obstacles that produce managerial resistance. These obstacles are apparently heightened during professionalization, as this type of organizational change inevitably involves a negotiated process of identifying what constitutes managerial competence and effective leadership, and who should decide this (see Abbott, 1998; cited in Ferlie and Geraghty, 2005: 425, 426). In addition, the experience of the community fire safety initiative illustrates how MLD alone cannot be expected to effect strategic change; the organizational environment needs to provide managers with meaningful opportunities to enact their learning.

Management and Leadership Development in a Local Authority Adult Social Services Department

The final organization is the adult social services department of a large English local authority, which also responded to an employment relations crisis by investing in management and leadership development, amongst a raft of other HRM measures. Radical national reforms to social care management from the mid-1990s to the mid-2000s, combined with problems of staff recruitment and retention, particularly among social workers, presented social security departments with a range of strategic and HRM challenges. In this authority, however, between 1998 and 2007, local government and social services inspectors noted significant improvements in leadership and management, which they believed contributed to large increases in staff retention and the transformation of services from 'poor' to 'excellent'.

The largest part of the MLD investment went to traditional management development activities, which included a leader development component. This was represented by the provision of a suite of nationally-recognized management qualifications, run in-house by the authority's corporate learning and development function. Individual managers were sponsored to study for qualifications such as the Diploma in Management, the content of which was closely related to the strategic plans of the authority and the department, and to the government's social care quality standards. The diploma was clearly successful in enabling managers to align their day-to-day efforts with strategic goals. As one manager saw it:

> I'm not that far away from being a teamster myself to have forgotten what it's like to be in the team room and to be asked to do things that are not connected

to anything – it's just a task. Now at the other side of the fence I can see all of the connections, and the DM [Diploma in Management] has made me try hard to try and sell those . . . (Interview with Social Care Manager 1 at the case study local authority, 2007).

External inspection reports reinforce the interpretation that the promotion through MLD of a consistent, goal-orientated approach to management and leadership was effective in helping to ensure organizational stability and progress towards strategic goals (see McGurk, 2010: 463, 468).

In addition to the management qualifications, the authority's learning and development function provided a series of short-term leader develop-ment workshops for its middle managers in 2006–7. The three-day residen-tial workshop series, entitled 'From Good to Great' was constituted of a range of individual and group tasks that aimed to 'assist each participant to engage in future work with the wisdom and determination to act on a newly found understanding in innovative ways that will further enhance the performance of the department and the quality of your own life' (Case study local authority learning and development documentation accessed online, 2007). Some individual managers felt changed by the workshops, but it was rare that they could identify how this might have led to any substantial changes in their practice. In some cases, the transformational language of the programme was echoed in managers' own accounts of personal change. For example, one manager related her realization that she was 'strong' and 'powerful', and described the course as 'very, very freeing' in helping her adapt to the fact that her staff 'don't have my energy'. In contrast, however, another participant admitted to a type of 'leadership development fatigue', explaining that:

I have to be honest . . . I am incredibly busy in my job and I use these [courses] to reflect. So even if they sat there and played nursery rhymes, it would be something that would be good for work . . . (Interview with Social Care Manager 2 at the case study local authority, 2007).

The experiences in this case suggest that general, 'off-the-shelf' approaches to leader development may have some initial effect on increasing manag-ers' self-awareness; but the longer-term effect on organizational change will be limited if such interventions over-promise and do not address the specific organizational context in which the intervention takes place.

Finally, the department invested in a leadership development inter-vention in 2006–7. This took the form of a series of workshops called 'Inspirational Leadership'. The workshops followed a period of organiza-tional restructuring and national and local reforms, in which the author-ity began to personalize care services for clients and make greater use of partnerships with organizations in the health, employment and housing services and voluntary sector. Over a period of several months, all middle managers in the directorate participated in workshops and action-learning sets facilitated by an external trainer to help prepare for, and make sense of, the new adult care management environment. Managers' reactions to the workshop activities themselves were mixed. However, after a few sessions, the action-learning set members decided to dispense with the services of the trainer, and the meetings were converted into a semi-formal 'County District Managers Group'. This new group convened regularly and was enthusiastically attended by middle managers and other interested parties. Discussions centred on how to implement strategic plans, such as receiving electronic payments for personalized care services. One manager explained the value of the new group as follows:

> ... [W]e [the district managers] kept saying this [the new strategy] isn't going to work, and then ... we get an email from HQ saying 'You have to make this work' ... [W]e need it, because that's the future. But the actual practicalities of it, the detail, they don't want to hear ... You want the good ideas, ... but you want some time and space and some understanding of how we deliver them, really (Interview with Social Care Manager 3 at the case study local authority, 2007).

The social services case illustrates how, in a professional environment, leadership development may result in a significant contribution to strategic change. However, the effectiveness of such interventions appears to depend on conditions of operational uncertainty and on managers having the opportunity to exercise considerable discretion. These conditions were less evident in the first two organizations, which operated in more predictable environments – especially for the train operating company and to a lesser degree in the fire brigade. However, the professionalized environment of social care management demanded not only investment in management development to promote organizational stability, and leader development to stimulate staff commitment, but also in the collective activity of leadership development, which allowed the 'time and space' for managers to identify their own coordination problems and for common solutions to emerge.

CONCLUSION

The case study evidence in this chapter provides a contextualized insight into the changing demand for management and leadership in PSOs and how, at the organizational level, different types of MLD have been directed towards modernization goals. Although the idea of leadership may have been very influential on policy-makers in recent years, the evidence here suggests that PSOs, particularly those operating in standardized and traditional bureaucratic environments, have a relative preference for firm management. The observed investment in management development activity, orientated towards ensuring staff compliance, is strongly suggestive of the use of MLD to promote organizational stability over organizational change. This was most clearly illustrated in the train operating company and the fire brigade cases, but was also evident in the social services case, in which MLD was predominantly used to promote adherence to centralized targets.

Despite the relative dominance of more traditional forms of management development, the case study evidence nevertheless confirms a growing recognition in PSOs of the importance of the emotional and psychological aspects of managerial work. This was illustrated in all three cases by the significant investments in leader development, which aimed to increase the self-awareness and motivational abilities of managers. The evidence suggests, however, that in order to effect the desired strategic changes through leader development, leader development requires careful tailoring to the organizational and professional context. Managers' ability 'to lead' may be constrained by the actual opportunities to initiate change that are afforded by the organizational structure. At the very least, managers' expectations about how they might channel their newfound enthusiasm need to be managed. It is also an important reality that a PSO's strategic plan, to which leader development is expected to promote commitment, may be under-resourced and contested by stakeholders. As other research on MLD has shown, managers should not only be carefully assessed and selected for leader development, they also need to be set specific learning challenges and provided with longer-term organizational support to put their new skills into practice (see Van Velsor and McCauley, 2004). This requires considerable MLD competence and resources, in which many PSOs are unlikely to invest sufficiently.

Finally, the case study evidence suggests that leadership development, which has the strongest associations with the modernization goals of innovation and partnership-working, is most likely to be found in professional environments that are seeking to adopt more flexible, post-bureaucratic forms of coordination. It is this type of organizational change that most readily produces opportunities for MLD to contribute to emergent strategy. Nonetheless, as the social services case illustrated, the innovations which leadership development might help to stimulate are also necessarily shaped by the participant managers' job roles and by institutional regulation of the sector.

When promoting MLD initiatives in the public services, reformers would do well to appreciate organizational-level differences and the realities of public managers' job roles. The organization's structure, and the type of strategic change sought, are important in determining opportunities for public managers to put their learning into practice, and ultimately for MLD investments to be fruitful. As Pichault and others have argued (see Pichault, 2007; Pichault and Nizet, 2000; Pichault and Schoenaers, 2003), the success of HRM interventions in PSOs is likely to be contingent on the resolution of internal political tensions and a fit with the organization's structural context.

REFERENCES

Abbott, A. (1998), *The System of Professions: An Essay on the Division of Expert Labour*, London: University of Chicago Press.

Alimo-Metcalfe, B. and J. Alban-Metcalfe (2004), 'Leadership in public sector organizations', in J. Storey (ed.), *Leadership in Organizations. Current Issues and Key Trends*, London: Routledge, pp.173–202.

Andrews, R. (2010), 'The impact of modernisation on fire authority performance: an empirical evaluation', *Policy and Politics*, **38** (4), 599–617.

Argyris, C. and D. Schön (1978), *Organizational Learning: A Theory of Action Perspective*, Boston: Addison-Wesley.

Borins, S. (2000), 'Loose cannons and rule breakers? Some evidence about innovative public managers', *Public Administration Review*, **60** (6), 498–507.

Boxall, P. and J. Purcell (2008), *Strategy and Human Resource Management*, Basingstoke: Palgrave Macmillan.

Boyne, G. A., O. James, P. John and N. Petrovsky (2008), 'Executive succession in English local government', *Public Money and Management*, **28** (5), 267–74.

Brown, J.S. and P. Duguid (1991), 'Organizational learning and communities-of-practice: toward a unified view of working, learning and innovation', *Organization Science*, **2** (1), 40–57.

Burgoyne, J., W. Hirsh and S. Williams (2004), *The Development of Management and Leadership Capability and its Contribution to Performance: The Evidence, the Prospects and the Research Need*, Research Report RR560, Lancaster: Department for Education and Skills, Lancaster University.

Burgoyne, J. and M. Reynolds (eds) (1997), *Management Learning: Integrating Perspectives in Theory and Practice*, London: Sage.

Charlesworth, K., P. Cook and G. Crozier (2003), *Leading Change in the Public Sector: Making the Difference*, London: Chartered Institute of Management.

Clarke, J. and J. Newman (1997), *The Managerial State*, London: Sage.

Day, D. (2001), 'Leadership development: a review in context', *Leadership Quarterly*, **11** (4), 581–613.

Denis, J.-L., A. Langley and L. Rouleau (2005), 'Rethinking leadership in public organizations', in E. Ferlie, L.E. Lynn (Jr) and C. Pollitt (eds), *The Oxford Handbook of Public Management*, Oxford: Oxford University Press, pp.446–67.

Dingwall, R. and T. Strangleman (2005), 'Organizational cultures in the public services', in E. Ferlie, L.E. Lynn (Jr) and C. Pollitt (eds), *The Oxford Handbook of Public Management*, Oxford: Oxford University Press, pp.468–490.

Dunleavy, P. and C. Hood (1994), 'From old public administration to new public management', *Public Money and Management*, July-September, 9–16.

Dunleavy, P., H. Margetts, S. Bastow and J. Tinkler (2006), 'New public management is dead – long live digital-era governance', *Journal of Public Administration Research and Theory*, **16** (July), 467–94.

Ferlie, E. and K.J. Geraghty (2005), 'Professionals in public services organizations. Implications for public sector "reforming"', in E. Ferlie, L. E. Lynn(Jnr) and C. Pollitt (eds), *The Oxford Handbook of Public Management*, Oxford: Oxford University Press, pp.422–45.

Fitzgerald, I. (2005), 'The death of corporatism? Managing change in the fire service', *Personnel Review*, **34** (6), 648–62.

Gold, J., H. Rodgers, M. Frearson and R. Holden (2003), 'Leadership development: a new typology', Working Paper, Leeds: Leeds Business School and Learning and Skills Research Centre.

Gronn, P. (2000), 'Distributed properties: a new architecture for leadership', *Educational Management and Administration*, **28** (3), 317–38.

Grugulis, I. (2007), *Skills, Training and Human Resource Development. A Critical Text*, London: Palgrave.

Guest, D. and Z. King (2005), 'Management development and career development', in S. Bach (ed.), *Managing Human Resources*, Oxford: Blackwell, pp.237–65.

Hall, T. and K. Janmen (2010), *The Leadership Illusion: The Importance of Context and Connections,* Basingstoke: Palgrave Macmillan.

Hondeghem, A. (2002), 'Competency management: the state of the art in the public sector?', in S. Horton, A. Hondeghem and D. Farnham (eds), *Competency management in the public sector: European variations on a theme*, Amsterdam/Oxford: IOS Press, pp.173–180.

Horton, S. (2002), 'The competency movement', in S. Horton, A. Hondeghem and D. Farnham (eds), *Competency Management in the Public Sector. European Variations on a Theme*, Amsterdam: IOS Press, pp.3–15.

Hughes, O.E. (2007), 'Leadership in a Managerial Context', in R. Koch and J. Dixon (eds), *Public Governance and Leadership*, Wiesbaden: Deutscher Universitaets-Verlag, pp.319–42.

Kotter, J. (1990), *A Force for Change: How Leadership Differs from Management*, New York: Free Press.

Lave, J. and E. Wenger (1991), *Situated Learning: Legitimate Peripheral Participation*, New York: Cambridge University Press.

Lawler, J. (2008), 'Individualization and public sector leadership', *Public Administration*, **86** (1), 21–34.

Mabey, C. (2002), 'Mapping management development practice', *Journal of Management Studies*, **39** (8), 1139–60.

Mabey, C. (2004a), 'Developing managers in europe: policies, practices, and impact', *Advances in Developing Human Resources*, **6** (4), 404–27.

Mabey, C. (2004b), 'Management development in Europe: implications for research and practice', *Advances in Developing Human Resources*, **6** (4), 504–13.

Mabey, C. and T. Finch-Lees (2008), *Management and Leadership Development*, London: Sage.

MacBeath, J. (2005), 'Leadership as distributed: a matter of practice', *School Leadership and Management*, **25** (4), 349–66.

Martineau, J.W. (2004), 'Evaluating the impact of leader development', in C. McCauley and E. Van Velsor (eds), *The Center for Creative Leadership Handbook of Leadership Development*, San Francisco, CA: Jossey-Bass, pp.234–67.

McGurk, P. (2009), 'Developing "middle leaders" in the public services? The realities of management and leadership development for public managers', *International Journal of Public Sector Management*, **22** (6), 464–77.

McGurk, P. (2010), 'Outcomes of management and leadership development', *Journal of Management Development*, **29** (5), 457–70.

McGurk, P. (2011), 'The contingent role of management and leadership development for middle managers: cases of organisational change from the public services', PhD Thesis (unpublished), London School of Economics.

Milner, E. and P. Joyce (2005), *Lessons in Leadership: Meeting the Challenges of Public Services Management*, Routledge: London.

Mintzberg, H. (1979), *The Structuring of Organizations: A Synthesis of the Research*, London: Prentice Hall.

Mintzberg, H. (1996), 'Managing government, governing management', *Harvard Business Review*, May-June, 75–83.

Mintzberg, H. (2004), 'Enough leadership', *Harvard Business Review*, November, 1–2.

Mintzberg, H. (2009), *Managing*, Harlow: FT Prentice Hall.

Mintzberg, H. and J. Waters (1985), 'Of strategies deliberate and emergent', *Strategic Management Journal*, **6** (3), 257–72.

Mole, G. (2000), *Managing Management Development*, Milton Keynes: Open University Press.

MSC (2008), *National Occupational Standards in Leadership and Management*, accessed on 23 October 2009 at www.management-standards.org.

Mulgan, G. and D. Albury (2003), 'Innovation in the public sector', Discussion paper, Prime Minister's Strategy Unit, London, October.

Mumford, A. (1997), *Management Development: Strategies for Action*, London: Institute for Personnel and Development.

Mumford, A. and J. Gold (2004), *Management Development. Strategies for Action*, London: Chartered Institute for Personnel and Development.

Nahapiet, J. and S. Goshal (1998), 'Social capital, intellectual capital, and the organizational advantage', *Academy of Management Review*, **23** (2), 242–66.

Newman, J. (2002), 'The new public management, modernization and institutional change: disruptions, disjunctures and dilemmas', in K. McLaughlin, S.P. Osborne and E. Ferlie (eds), *New Public Management. Current Trends and Future Prospects*, London: Routledge, pp.77–92.

O'Connor, P.M. and L. Quinn (2004), 'Organizational capacity for leadership', in E. VanVelsor and C. McCauley (eds), *The Center for Creative Leadership Handbook of Leadership Development*, San Francisco: Jossey-Bass, pp.417–37.

O'Reilly, D. and M. Reed (2010), '"Leaderism": an evolution of managerialism in UK public service reform', *Public Administration*, **88** (4), 960–78.

ODPM (2003), *Our Fire and Rescue Service*, White Paper, June 2003, London: Office of the Deputy Prime Minister / HMSO.

OECD (2001), *Public Sector Leadership for the 21st Century*, Paris: Organisation for Economic Co-operation and Development, OECD Publishing.

Osborne, S.P. (2006), 'Editorial. The new public governance?', *Public Management Review*, **8** (3), 377–87.

Osborne, D. and T. Gaebler (1992), *Reinventing Government: How the Enterpreneurial Spirit is Transforming the Public Sector*, Reading, MA: Addison-Wesley.

Performance and Information Unit (2001), *Strengthening Leadership in the Public Sector: A Research Study by the PIU*, London: Cabinet Office.

Pichault, F. (2007), 'HRM-based reforms in public organisations: problems and perspectives', *Human Resource Management Journal*, **17** (3), 265–82.

Pichault, F. and J. Nizet (2000), *Les pratiques de gestion des ressources humaines. Approches contingente et politique*, Paris: Seuil.

Pichault, F. and F. Schoenaers (2003), 'HRM practices in a process of organisational change: a contextualist perspective', *Applied Psychology*, **52** (1), 120–43.

Pollitt, C. (2003), *The Essential Public Manager*, Maidenhead: Open University Press.

Raffel, J., P. Leisink and A. Middlebrooks (2009), 'Introduction', in J. Raffel, P. Leisink and A. Middlebrooks (eds), *Public Sector Leadership: International Challenges and Perspectives*, Cheltenham: Edward Elgar, pp.1–32.

Rainbird, H., A. Munro and L. Holly (2004), 'Exploring the concept of employer demand for skills and qualifications: case studies from the public sector', in C. Warhurst, E. Keep and I. Grugulis (eds), *The Skills That Matter*, Basingstoke: Palgrave Macmillan, pp.91–108.

Salaman, G. (2004), 'Competences of managers, competences of leaders', in J. Storey (ed.), *Leadership in Organizations*, Abingdon: Routledge, pp.58–78.

Spillane, J., J. Diamond and R. Halverson (2001), 'Towards a theory of leadership practice: a distributed perspective', Institute for Policy Research Working Paper, Northwestern University.

Storey, J. (2004a), 'Changing theories of leadership', in J. Storey (ed.) *Leadership in Organizations: Current Issues and Key Trends*, Abingdon: Routledge, pp.11–37.

Storey, J. (2004b), 'Signs of change: "damned rascals" and beyond', in J. Storey (ed.) *Leadership in Organizations. Current Issues and Key Trends*, Abingdon: Routledge, pp.3–10.

Storey, J. and W. Tate (2000), 'Management development', in S. Bach and K. Sisson (eds), *Personnel Management: A Comprehensive Guide to Theory and Practice*, Oxford: Blackwell, pp.195–217.

Tamkin, P., J. Hillage and R. Willison (2002), *Indicators of Management Capability: Developing a Framework*, London: Council for Excellence in Management and Leadership.

The Real World Group (2011), *Homepage*, accessed on 1 November 2011 at http://www.realworld-group.com/.

Thomson, A., C. Mabey, J. Storey, C. Gray and P. Iles (2001), *Changing Patterns of Management Development*, Oxford: Blackwell.

Tyler, S. (2004), 'Making leadership and management development measure up', in J. Storey (ed.), *Leadership in Organizations. Current Issues and Key Trends*, London: Routledge, pp.152–70.

UNDP (2011), *Drivers of Change*, accessed on 4 November 2011 at http://www.beta.undp.org/undp/en/home/ourwork/capacitybuilding/drivers_of_change.html.

Van Velsor, E. and C.D. McCauley (2004), 'Introduction: our view of leadership development', in E. Van Velsor and C.D. McCauley (eds), *The Center for Creative Leadership Handbook of Leadership Development*, San Francisco: Jossey Bass, pp.1–22.

Yin, R.K. (1994), *Case Study Research: Design and Methods*, London: Sage Publications.

Zaleznik, A. (1992), 'Managers and leaders: are they different?', *Harvard Business Review*, March–April, 126–36.

9. Employee turnover in public agencies: examining the extent and correlates

Mark Bradbury, Jessica E. Sowa and J. Edward Kellough

No matter how well designed an organization's human resource management (HRM) system is, a certain amount of employee turnover is to be expected in even the most effective establishment (Cho and Lewis, 2012; Kellough and Osuna, 1995; Moynihan and Landuyt, 2008; Selden, 2009; Selden and Moynihan, 2000). Turnover, when not excessive, can produce positive changes for organizations, infusing them with new ideas and bringing the latest training and technologies into the work setting (Kellough and Osuna, 1995; US Merit Systems Protection Board, 1989). Because government agencies, as the reform efforts of the past 25 years have argued, are not always the most flexible in terms of their management of people (Battaglio, 2010; Lavigna and Hays, 2004; Park and Joo, 2010; Pollitt and Bouckaert, 2000), the presence of some turnover may prevent them from becoming stagnant over time and could encourage high levels of performance. However, turnover obviously can also impose costs associated with recruiting and training replacement workers, especially when highly skilled employees leave an organization.

The importance of turnover is further emphasized by recent studies of workforce dynamics across the public, private and nonprofit sectors that have demonstrated that people are much more likely to move through several positions during their career lifetimes today than they were in the past (Bureau of Labor Statistics, 2010; Chao and Gardner, 2007; Chetkovich, 2003; Sullivan, 1999; Sutherland, 2002; Sullivan and Baruch, 2009). As a result, turnover is a fact for most agencies or organizations across sectors, and the challenge is finding ways to successfully manage it. While a certain amount of turnover is to be expected, the difficulty comes when turnover levels grow high, do not promote organizational benefits, and begin imposing significant costs on the organization.

Certainly, employee turnover is not solely a concern of government –

turnover concerns organizations in all sectors, as noted, and for all types of employees. However, turnover has been of particular concern for public service organizations, such as government agencies and nonprofit organizations, as recruiting and retaining qualified workers can be more difficult due to limited access to extrinsic rewards. In addition to well-established bodies of research in the private and public sectors, current research on non-profit organizations shows significant concerns regarding the retention of employees and volunteers (Hustinx, 2008; Jamison, 2003; Moynihan and Pandey, 2008). In addition, the anticipated wave of forthcoming retirements from the baby boomer generation further highlights the need for public service organizations, in particular government agencies, to be attentive in managing their current levels of turnover and planning for better retention strategies to maximize their existing human capital (Tobias, 2001, Cho and Lewis, 2011). Direct costs associated with employee replacement (hiring and training new employees) and indirect costs such as lower productivity as new employees adapt to their positions, along with costs associated with current employees expending time and effort orienting and training these new employees should be minimized (Davidson, Lepeak and Newman, 2007a; Kellough and Osuna, 1995; Selden, 2009). It is imperative, therefore, for organizations to monitor turnover and understand the factors that may be associated with variation in turnover rates.

This chapter explores the nature of turnover in United States federal agencies, conceptualizing turnover as the extent to which employees quit their positions in these agencies. We examine the research on turnover in organizations, focusing on the different types of turnover and empirical strategies for understanding and assessing turnover. In particular, we focus on the research on turnover in government agencies and the particular factors that influence turnover in this sector. Using data from the US Office of Personnel Management, we explore what factors predict organizational quit rates.[1] Our findings suggest that the proportions of an agency's workforce that are young (under 30 years of age), female, or in temporary positions are all positively associated with employee quit rates. Interestingly, minority employment is negatively related to quit behavior. Other factors such as organization size, the proportion of the workforce in professional or administrative positions, and the proportion in clerical positions are unrelated to agency quit rates. We conclude with a discussion of the implications of these findings, along with suggestions for future research in the area of government turnover. While scholars focusing on human resources management (HRM) in the public sector have made significant progress in terms of assessing and understanding why employees leave public agencies, there are areas for further research, both in terms of the empirical examination of turnover and the development of practical strategies for minimizing excessive turnover.

WHAT ARE THE CATEGORIES OF EMPLOYEE TURNOVER?

In examining why employees leave organizations, it is essential to begin with a clear definition of turnover and a specification of the different types of turnover. Turnover occurs whenever an employee leaves a position in an organization. However, the nature of that separation and the implications for retention strategies are important to clarify. Turnover can include voluntary separations (organizational quits), retirements, layoffs, involuntary separations (dismissals) or vacancies that occur as the result of death (Selden, 2009; Shaw et al., 1998). Scholars exploring turnover generally focus on the voluntary/involuntary turnover distinction. Understanding this distinction is essential, as voluntary turnover (quitting) is usually based on the desire to find different or preferable employment, whereas involuntary turnover (dismissal) is the product of action taken by the organization to correct performance problems, actions or deficiencies on the part of the employee. Selden (2009) argues that many researchers examining turnover and retention often view these phenomena as two sides of the same process. However, because the implications of turnover differ, depending on the type involved, that view is not entirely correct. Retention strategies are geared primarily toward reducing voluntary turnover, not involuntary turnover (Selden, 2009). While involuntary turnover has its own set of costs for an organization, the underlying assumption with voluntary turnover is that the employees in question still provide value to the organization, and, therefore, strategies should be explored in order to retain them.

Voluntary turnover is a human resource management priority at the national, state, and even local levels of government (see Boyne et al., 2011; Choi, 2009; Selden, 2006). Although career bureaucrats are the focus of most studies of turnover in the public sector, the dynamics operate much the same for the personal staff of legislators (Anderson, 1990), sheriff's officers (Kiekbusch, Price and Theis, 2007), and appointed administrators such as local government managers (Boyne et al., 2010; Clingermayer et al., 2003; Feiock and Stream, 1998; Whitaker and DeHoog, 1991). With resources becoming increasingly scarce in the public sector, developing effective strategies to reduce voluntary turnover is essential to maximize the performance of existing human capital inventories of public agencies.

The costs associated with voluntary turnover are significant, with the average overall turnover costs associated with filling vacant positions ranging from 33 per cent to 250 per cent of a vacant position's annual salary (Partnership for Public Service and Booz Allen Hamilton, 2010; Selden, 2009; Shortenhaus, 2006). As stated, these costs include the expense of recruitment, selection, and orientation efforts for new employees designed to increase the probability that they will be successful (Breaugh, 2008; Davidson, Lepak and Newman, 2007b; GPP, 2007). There is also typically a lag in time between the selection of a new hire and the attainment of full productivity, with some estimates maintaining that it can take up to five years for a new employee to reach full productivity (Partnership for Public Service and Booz Allen Hamilton, 2010). The complexity of government work across many agencies may lead to significant costs associated with new hires, both in terms of their acquisition and training and the adjustment period toward full productivity. While the direct costs of turnover are high, the indirect costs on the existing workforce are also high. Current workers may be required to handle the duties of the employees who have quit, placing increased stress on these employees. Even when vacant positions are filled and the duties reassigned, long-term workers may be tasked with orienting and training new employees. Those kinds of assignment can obviously reduce the productivity of long-term employees (Cho and Lewis, 2012; Kellough and Osuna, 1995; Moynihan and Landuyt, 2008; Selden, 2009; Selden and Moynihan, 2000). It is clear that turnover is a pressing HRM issue for government agencies; the question is how to best measure and assess turnover in the public sector.

EMPIRICAL STRATEGIES FOR UNDERSTANDING TURNOVER

A thorough review of the extant literature reveals three distinct issues that researchers must address: (1) whether the work will draw distinctions between types of turnover focusing, for example, on voluntary separations, i.e. quit behavior; (2) whether 'turnover' is an independent or dependent variable in the analysis; and (3) if turnover is a dependent variable, what independent variables will be used as predictors?

What Type of Turnover?

Perhaps the most important consideration in a given study is whether turnover is conceived to be total, voluntary, and/or involuntary. Measures of the total turnover for an organization lump together personal actions such as quitting, retiring, termination and other separations (see Balfour and Neff, 1993; Boyne et al., 2011). Although these actions are similar to the extent that they confer costs and benefits to the organization, each type of separation is influenced by a different alchemy of causes, and each implies markedly distinct prevention and coping strategies for the organization. Perhaps the essential element here is whether the employee's separation was initiated by the organization or by the employee. Few studies of public sector turnover have focused on involuntary turnover, since separation caused by reduction in forces (RIFs) or death, for example, are not readily controllable and do not lend themselves to research (Shaw et al., 1998). Dismissal, on the other hand, is a type of involuntary separation (at least from the employee's point of view), which is important to study since it implies a hiring decision in need of reversal. Notably, Selden (2006) found that states that adopt standardized discipline systems, include discipline systems in their collective bargaining contracts with labor, and put greater restrictions on the supervisors' ability to terminate an employee are less likely to dismiss employees.

The most common strategy for studying turnover is to focus on voluntary separations by the employee. Since quitting is initiated by the worker and can be somewhat unpredictable for the organization in terms of when it will occur, Kellough and Osuna (1995: 59) call this kind of separation 'the heart of the retention problem'. Not only is the employee terminating the employment contract, but it is one that the organization would presumably prefer to have continued (Selden and Moynihan, 2000). This finding leads us to study the causes of voluntary turnover so that it can be better understood, predicted and, perhaps, prevented. The research presented in this chapter focuses on voluntary turnover as measured by the number of workers who quit within an organization for a given year as a proportion of the total number of positions, i.e. the annual quit rate.

Is Turnover an Independent or Dependent Variable?

A small body of research uses turnover as an independent variable to predict various organizational phenomena. For example, turnover has been used to analyze organizational performance (Boyne et al., 2011; Meier and Hicklin, 2008), the extent of borrowing and indebtedness of local governments (Clingermayer et al., 2008), and the likelihood that a local government will contract out for services (Clingermayer and Feiock, 1997).

The preponderance of research, however, examines turnover as a dependent variable and looks for factors that are associated with it and may represent underlying causes for variation in turnover rates. Most of this work, however, does not measure turnover directly, but rather, examines employee 'intention to turnover' as measured through survey responses. Referred to by some scholars as a 'frequently used surrogate' for measuring actual turnover (Moynihan and Pandey, 2008: 207), studies of employees' intentions to leave (typically in the near future) assume that such intentions are indicative of some type of dissatisfaction with the current employer. Researchers have sought to understand the root causes of such dissatisfaction. Notable examples of probable causes of an intention to quit include concerns over inadequate training opportunities (Owens, 2006), a lack of procedural justice within an organization (Rubin, 2009), insufficient compensation levels (Lee and Jimenez, 2011; Lee and Whitford, 2008), ineffective diversity management (Choi, 2009), unsatisfactory person-organization fit (Bright, 2008), limited opportunities for advancement (Ito, 2003), insufficient public service motivation (Naff and Crum, 1999), and burnout (Chuang et al., 2003). Notably, many of these factors are based on the perceptions of employees that may or may not correlate with actual working conditions that the organization can readily manipulate (see Selden, 2009).

Despite the myriad factors that could influence one's intention to quit, such an intent is not synonymous with actual quitting. It would seem quite likely that a sizable proportion of those who indicate an intention to quit on an anonymous survey would not, and perhaps could not, take such a step due to personal, financial or professional reasons. Indeed, workers may fanaticize about quitting while knowing very well that they are unable to do so, and the indication of an intention to quit in response to a survey question could be as much a reflection of that fantasy as an actual likelihood of voluntary leaving. Alternatively, a worker may have no actual or anticipated intention of leaving, and may give no indication of such an intent on a survey, but may still voluntarily quit a job for a whole host of unforeseen reasons. The fact that a recent study found that 31 per cent of people currently employed are look for new positions and 41 per cent are passively looking suggests that the intention to quit may not be a valid 'surrogate' for actual quitting (Frincke, 2006; Selden, 2009). Thus, despite the fact that necessary data 'consumes a lot of time to collect' (Udechukwu et al., 2007: 263), measures of actual turnover are the strongest indicators of any potential retention problem.

Thankfully, a critical mass of literature does examine the actual turnover of career employees in public sector organizations (Cho and Lewis, 2012; Kellough and Osuna, 1995; Lewis, 1991; Lewis and Durst, 1995; Lewis and Hu, 2005; Lewis and Park, 1989; Llorens and Stazyk, 2011; Selden and Moynihan, 2000). Overall, these studies have affirmed that turnover is an ever-growing concern at all levels of government, though rates may vary considerably across jurisdictions (Llorens and Stazyk,

2011; Selden and Moynihan, 2000), organizations (Kellough and Osuna, 1995) and occupational types and levels (Lewis and Durst, 1995; Lewis and Hu, 2005). As with any empirical research, a key consideration is which explanatory variables are, and are not, included in these models; this is the third issue that researchers must confront.

What are the Possible Determinants of Turnover?

A myriad of factors could influence an employee to voluntarily quit. Some of these factors serve to 'push' the employee out, such as dissatisfaction with policies and supervisors, while others 'pull' the worker toward personal, financial or professional advancement in other positions or organizations (Feiock et al., 2001). These push and pull factors, in turn, can be conceived of as composing three basic categories of independent variables to predict voluntary turnover: environmental, organizational and individual. Intended to cover factors that are external to the organization, environmental variables are most relevant in models that compare turnover rates across units of government, such as the States in the US. They are not as germane to national government studies since the external environment of different agencies is relatively similar. Nevertheless, the environmental factors thought to influence turnover include geographical region, population, unemployment rate, per capita income, and a state's political ideology (Llorens and Stazyk, 2011; Selden and Moynihan, 2000). Although these factors are outside of the control of the employer, they must be accounted for in any retention strategy.

All studies of actual turnover include variables that account for characteristics of the organization and/or unit of government as a whole. These factors reflect the structural features of the employer that may be difficult to alter but nonetheless are felt by employees, and may affect, for example, the desirability of voluntarily quitting. Common examples of organizational variables include size, unionization, the degree of public-private wage equity, the range and number of occupations within particular agencies, human resource policies, salaries, and the extent to which temporary employees are used (Kellough and Osuna, 1995; Lewis and Hu, 2005; Llorens and Stazyk, 2011; Selden and Moynihan, 2000).

Finally, the characteristics of the employees themselves relate to turnover. Frequently used variables account for race/ethnicity, gender, age, experience/tenure, and the extent and focus of education (Kellough and Osuna, 1995; Lewis and Durst, 1995; Lewis and Hu, 2005; Llorens and Stazyk, 2011; Selden and Moynihan, 2000). The research model presented in this chapter uses a combination of organizational and individual

Table 9.1　Variables in the analysis

Variable	Minimum	Maximum	Mean	Std. deviation
Quit rate	0.203	13.288	3.907	2.570
Organizational size	461	764 299	49 215.950	124 535.467
Per cent young	3.401	25.248	10.206	4.450
Per cent female	26.996	68.818	50.387	10.181
Per cent minority	22.067	87.630	37.761	12.394
Per cent pro/admin	30.417	95.586	77.555	17.431
Per cent clerical	0.561	47.650	6.091	8.010
Per cent temporary	0.722	36.537	9.537	9.240

characteristics to predict voluntary turnover in US federal government agencies.

REVISITING KELLOUGH AND OSUNA (1995)

The research presented in this chapter is based upon a model developed by Kellough and Osuna (1995) to examine quit rates in the US federal Service. That model relied upon agency quit rate data provided by the US Office of Personnel Management for the years 1986, 1988, 1990 and 1992. The updated model includes data for 2009 and 2010 and uses all of the same variables, with the exception of work force unionization, which is no longer available. Thus, six independent variables, three organizational variables and three individual variables, are employed to predict agency quit rates. Table 9.1 displays descriptive statistics for all variables in the analysis.

Employee Age Distribution

Prior research has consistently found that younger workers are more likely to quit than their older colleagues (GPP, 2007; Kellough and Osuna, 1995; Lewis, 1991; Lewis and Park, 1989; Llorens and Stazyk, 2011; Meyer et al., 1979). The relationship may be curvilinear when considering voluntary turnover 'in general', however, because the oldest workers are likely to voluntarily exit the workforce by way of retirement (Lewis and Durst, 1995). Since our data codes quitting separately from retirement, we hypothesize that agencies with a relatively younger workforce will experience higher quit rates. Llorens and Stazyk (2011) argue that this is a particularly important consideration in light of the looming retirement of the baby boomer generation. Based on the presumption that those retirees will be replaced by workers who are considerably younger than their predecessors, agencies could experience considerably higher annual rates of turnover. We define young as less than 30 years old and our variable measures the proportion of an agency workforce that is in that age category.

Gender

The gender balance seen throughout a workforce reinforces the relevance of asking whether workers from either gender are more likely to quit. Here the extant evidence is inconsistent, but with a tendency toward suggesting that women are more likely to turnover voluntarily (Cotton and Tuttle, 1986; Lewis, 1991; Lewis and Park, 1989; Meyer et al., 1979). Irrespective of differences in actual quit rates between the genders, Frincke (2006) observes that males may quit for different reasons than females: males are more likely to quit to pursue alternate professional opportunities, whereas women are more likely to indicate reasons related to work/life balance (Selden, 2009). The enduring pattern of female employees being clustered at the lower grade-levels in the bureaucracy (i.e. the glass ceiling effect), however, may explain much of the observed gender-based differential in the quit rate. Nevertheless, we hypothesize that agencies with a greater proportion of female workers will experience higher quit rates.

Race/Ethnicity

Much like the complexity of isolating the impact of gender, Blau and Kahn (1981) found that one must control for other personal and job related characteristics in order to best ascertain whether black workers are more likely to quit than their white colleagues. Although it is difficult to account for at the federal level, sub-national studies could measure the relative difficulty for black workers in conducting job searches due to potentially discriminatory job markets and cultures; obviously such discrimination may deter a worker from quitting a job (Holmlund and Lang, 1985; Zax, 1989). On the other hand, the US federal government has made marked progress toward achieving a representative workforce, in part because of vigorous enforcement of equal employment opportunity policies. Although some previous work has found no significant relationship between race/ethnicity and quit rates (Kellough and Osuna, 1995; Llorens and Stazyk, 2011), we hypothesize that the continued presence of discrimination will result in lower quit rates for minority (black, Hispanic, Asian, and native American) workers as a group than for their white colleagues.

Occupational Characteristics

The sheer size of the federal bureaucracy would suggest that workers who are unhappy in their current position could seek a promotion or transfer, as opposed to quitting. Juxtaposing professional/administrative employees, on the one hand, and clerical staff on the other, it is likely that the former have greater prospects for alternative job opportunities within their agency and/or the federal bureaucracy in general. This is the dominant finding in the current literature (Kellough and Osuna, 1995; Meyer et al., 1979; Selden and Moynihan, 2000). However, the observed willingness for younger generations of professions to switch jobs, careers, and even sectors may call this seemingly settled relationship to quit rates into question. Furthermore, workers in clerical positions may have dimmer job prospects outside of the federal bureaucracy, thereby making them disinclined to quit (Lewis and Park, 1989). Relatedly, Kellough and Osuna (1995) provide the only known test for whether a higher proportion of temporary workers in an agency results in a higher quit rate. This hypothesis is based on the notion that temporary workers have less invested in the employing agency, and the employing agency has invested less in them (i.e. not offering full-time employment). With regard to occupational characteristics, then, we hypothesize that: (1) a higher proportion of clerical positions in an agency will be positively related to the quit rate; (2) a higher proportion of professional/administrative positions in an agency will be negatively related to the quit rate; and (3) there will be a positive relationship between the proportions of temporary workers and the agency's quit rates.

Organization Size

Similar to the effect of professionalization, a relatively larger organization may have more internal alternatives for current workers, thereby squelching one's inclination to quit. Consistent with the classic work on organization behavior by March and Simon (1958), the extant empirical research indicates a negative relationship between larger organizational size and quit rate (Kellough and Osuna, 1995; Selden and Moynihan, 2000; Smith, 1979), which we also hypothesize.

FINDINGS

Table 9.2 displays quit rates for 43 US federal agencies for the years 2009 and 2010.[2] The list contains 31 of the 41 agencies examined by

Table 9.2   Quit rates for selected US federal agencies 2009 and 2010

Agency	2009	2010
Agriculture Department	6.468	6.562
Broadcasting Board of Governors	1.531	1.467
Commerce Department	4.361	6.938
Commodity Futures Trading Commission	10.508	8.727
Consumer Product Safety Commission	3.905	7.255
Corporation for National and Community Service	9.540	4.430
Court Services Agency for the Dc	1.767	2.795
Defense Department	3.571	3.421
Education Department	5.192	3.241
Energy Department	2.490	2.213
Environmental Protection Agency	2.694	1.814
Equal Employment Opportunity Commission	1.785	1.887
Federal Communications Commission	3.045	3.766
Federal Deposit Insurance Corporation	3.266	3.865
Federal Trade Commission	9.643	13.288
General Services Administration	1.617	1.443
Government Printing Office	0.951	0.961
Health and Human Services Department	2.983	3.413
Homeland Security Department	3.320	2.492
Housing and Urban Development Department	4.319	3.735
Interior Department	4.819	4.793
International Development Cooperation Agency	3.733	1.481
Justice Department	1.872	1.763
Labor Department	3.160	3.359
National Aeronautics and Space Administration	0.907	1.018
National Archives	8.040	8.614
National Credit Union Administration	2.270	2.224
National Labor Relations Board	1.455	1.867
Nuclear Regulatory Commission	1.710	2.422
National Science Foundation	5.870	4.922
Office of Management and Budget	8.206	8.785
Office of Personnel Management	4.904	3.778
Pension Benefit Guaranty Corporation	3.275	3.903
Railroad Retirement Board	0.413	0.203
Securities and Exchange Commission	2.763	3.523
Small Business Administration	7.538	5.150
Smithsonian Institution	2.707	3.417
Social Security Administration	2.431	2.942
State Department	7.516	4.348
Transportation Department	1.302	1.317
Treasury Department	5.167	4.829
Veterans Affairs Department	3.404	3.439

Table 9.3   Determinants of US federal agency quit rates

Variables	B	Standard error
Agency size	−0.000001	0.000
Per cent young	0.232	0.062***
Per cent female	0.075	0.029***
Per cent minority	−0.053	0.025**
Per cent pro/admin	−0.002	0.020
Per cent clerical	−0.015	0.042
Per cent temporary	0.059	0.027**
Year	−0.240	0.475

Note: N = 84; R^2 = 0.355; ***p < 0.01; **p < 0.05.

Kellough and Osuna (1995). Due to various reorganizations, some agencies included in 1995 are omitted today while other new agencies (such as the Department of Homeland Security) are present in the current data set. In addition, the present work includes the Defense Department as a single unit, whereas Kellough and Osuna's (1995) study examined the Air Force, Army and Navy separately. Nevertheless, quit rates for 2009 and 2010 are markedly lower than those from the late 1980s and early 1990s. In Kellough and Osuna (1995), quit rates ranged from a low of 1.0 per cent for the Securities and Exchange Commission in 1990, to a high of 26.5 per cent for the Pension Benefit Guaranty Corporation in 1988. By comparison, the Securities and Exchange Commission experienced quit rates of 2.763 and 3.523 per cent in 2009 and 2010 respectively, and quit rates at the Pension Benefit Guaranty Corporation were only 3.275 and 3.903 per cent in 2009 and 2010 (see Table 9.1). Still, there is considerable variation in recent quit rates. For the agencies in Table 9.2, the minimum rate was experienced at the Railroad Retirement Board, which had a rate of 0.203 per cent in 2010. The maximum rate of 13.288 per cent was at the Federal Trade Commission in 2010. In the Kellough and Osuna (1995) data, 17 agencies experience quit rates of 10 per cent or higher, but in the current data set, only 3 agencies had quit rates that high. The lower rates for 2009 and 2010 are no doubt a reflection, at least in part, of the recent severe economic downturn which has limited alternative job opportunities.

Our data are analyzed using OLS regression with a dummy variable to control for the year;[3] the results are displayed in Table 9.3. A number of interesting findings are produced by the analysis. For example, it appears that in this sample of agencies, and during the years examined, organizational size bears no relationship to employee quit behavior. Larger agencies do not have significantly lower quit rates than smaller agencies. This result stands in contrast to that of Kellough and Osuna (1995), however, where a small but statistically significant negative relationship was found between agency size and quit rates. Our analysis also finds no relationship between quit rates and the proportion of the workforce in professional/ administrative positions or between quit rates and the proportion of clerical positions. The variable for year is also insignificant. In contrast, the earlier work by Kellough and Osuna (1995) found clerical work positively associated with quit behavior.

Relationships are found between quit rates and all other variables in our model. The proportion of the workforce that is young (less than 30 years old) is strongly and positively associated with quit rates as expected. Organizations with larger proportions of their workforces who are in this age category have significantly higher quit rates than other organizations. Similarly, the proportion of the workforce comprised of women is also significantly and positively associated with agency quit rates. With regard to minority employment, we find a negative relationship suggesting that as the proportion of the workforce held by minority group members increases, quit rates decline. The proportion of the workforce in temporary positions is strongly significant and positively associated with quit rates. Overall, the model explains approximately 40 per cent of the variance in quit rates.

AVENUES FOR FUTURE STUDY

Despite the theoretical rigor of our model of quit rates in the federal bureaucracy, other factors have been shown to relate to voluntary turnover and future research ought to endeavor to empirically test for a relationship. Notably, Kellough and Osuna (1995) included a measure of workforce unionization based on the premise that the procedural protections and alternate dispute resolution options provided by unions will result in lower quit rates in agencies that have a higher proportion of union members in their workforce. That previous study, however, found that agencies with more employees in collective bargaining units did not experience lower quit rates. We were unable to replicate the data used in the previous study because data on union membership is no longer available.

Other studies of turnover in federal agencies have employed control variables for experience and/or tenure in the federal government, education, pay and performance ratings (Cho and Lewis, 2012; Lewis and Durst, 1995; Lewis and Hu, 2005). Predictably, these studies found that the probability of quitting decreased as the years of service increased.

Although the dynamics at work for experience/tenure, and age are similar, it is important to consider these variables separately given the job mobility of younger professionals in public service (i.e. it seems increasingly likely that employees will be joining the federal workforce at an age that previously may been thought of as 'mid-career'). Although they did not use them to predict turnover, Lewis and Hu (2005) constructed variables for federal information technology employees related to their highest degree earned, the subject area of college degree, and the average performance ratings received as compared to employees at large; future studies of federal agencies could employ such variables as predictors for turnover.

Studies of turnover at the state level have employed a number of variables related to human resource management on which there is substantial variation across the states. A robust stream of research has examined the trend for states to reform their personnel systems and replace traditional civil service protections with at-will employment (Condrey and Battaglio, 2007; Hays and Sowa, 2006; Kellough and Nigro, 2005). Selden (2006) examined states that have removed civil service protections, but found that they are no more likely to terminate employees, although they take less time to complete a termination once the process has begun. Contrary to the findings of previous research, Llorens and Stazyk (2011) did not find pay equity between the public and private sectors to be a significant predictor of turnover. Selden and Moynihan (2000) found that greater training opportunities and higher pay leads to a reduced quit rate, as did the availability of on-site child care. To the extent that HRM-related data such as this can be collected for federal workers, future research should account for these types of variables.

Finally, it is misnomer to regard all federal workers as falling under the same merit system, although 'an extremely large number of federal civilian employees' are covered by the familiar General Schedule system and all are based on the same merit principles (Nigro, Nigro and Kellough 2007: 133). Nevertheless, employees in the defense intelligence community, healthcare professionals at the Department of Veteran's Affairs, the Tennessee Valley Authority, and others are covered by distinct merit systems that have their own sets of personnel rules and regulations. To the extent that transferring within the federal government is seen as an alternative to quitting, then it is important to recognize that it is easier for an employee in an agency covered by the GS system to transfer across agencies than it is for an employee in the Tennessee Valley Authority, for example, future models predicting turnover in the federal bureaucracy ought to account for these different merit systems if possible.

NOTES

1. All data are from the US Office of Personnel Management, FedScope, September 2009 and 2010, accessed online 22 November 2011 at http://www.fedscope.opm.gov.
2. Quit rates are equal to the percentage of positions in which the incumbent employee voluntarily resigned during a specified year. To avoid the inclusion of agencies with small numbers of employees, only those with 500 or more employees in at least one of the years studied are included. The smallest agency is the Consumer Product Safety Commission with 510 employees in 2010 (although it had only 461 employees in 2009). The largest agency is the massive Department of Defense which had 764 299 civilian employees in 2010.
3. Because our data are comprised of observations for 43 separate government agencies over two years (2009 and 2010), autocorrelation could be a problem. However, the year dummy variable controls for the effect of the passage of time, and the Durbin–Watson test statistic of 1.509 suggests that autocorrelation is not a problem. For this reason we utilize OLS procedures to analyze the data.

REFERENCES

Anderson, R.A. (1990), 'Patterns of staff turnover in two state legislatures', *State and Local Government Review*, 22 (3), 132–38.

Balfour, D.L. and Neff, D. (1993), 'Predicting and managing turnover in human service agencies: A case study of an organization in crisis', *Public Personal Management*, 22 (3), 473–87.

Battaglio (Jr), R. (2010), 'Public service reform and motivation: evidence from an at- will employment environment', *Review of Public Personnel Administration*, **30** (3), 341–63.

Blau, F.D. and L.M. Kahn (1981), 'Race and sex differences in quits by young workers', *Industrial and Labor Relations Review*, **38** (October), 16–25.

Boyne, G.A., O. James, P. John and N. Petrovsky (2010), 'Does public service performance affect top management turnover', *Journal of Public Administration Research and Theory*, **20**, 261–79.

Boyne, G.A., O. James, P. John and N. Petrovsky (2011), 'Top management turnover and organizational performance: a test of a contingency model', *Public Administration Review*, **71** (4), 572–81.

Breaugh, J.A. (2008), 'Employee recruitment: current knowledge and important areas for future research', *Human Resource Management Review*, **18**, (3), 103–18.

Bright, L.A. (2008), 'Does public service motivation really make a difference on the job satisfaction and turnover intentions of pubic employees?', *American Review of Public Administration*, **38**, 149–66.

Bureau of Labor Statistics, US Department of Labor (2010), 'Number of jobs held, labor market activity, and earnings growth among the youngest baby boomers: results from a longitudinal study', News Release, US Department of Labor, accessed 11 January 2012 at http://www.bls.gov/news.release/pdf/nlsoy.pdf.

Chao, G.T. and P.D. Gardner (2007), *Young Adults at Work: What They Want, What They Get, and How to Keep Them*, White Paper prepared for MonsterTRAK, accessed 11 January 2012 at http://ceri.msu.edu/publications/pdf/ yadultswk3-26-09.pdf.

Chetkovich, C. (2003), 'What's in a sector? The shifting career plans for public policy students', *Public Administration Review*, **63** (6), 660–74.

Cho, Y.J. and G.B. Lewis (2012), 'Turnover intentions and turnover behavior: Implications for retaining federal employees', *Review of Public Personnel Administration*, 32 (March), 4–23.

Choi, S. (2009), 'Diversity in the US federal government: Diversity management and employee turnover in federal agencies', *Journal of Public Administration Research and Theory*, **19** (3), 603–30.

Chuang, C.J., I. Huang and H. Lin (2003), 'The role of burnout in the relationship between perceptions of organizational politics and turnover intentions', *Public Personnel Management*, **32** (4), 519.

Clingermayer, J.C. and R.C. Feiock (1997), 'Leadership turnover, transaction costs, and exxternal city service delivery', *Public Administration Review*, **57** (3), 231–9.

Clingermayer, J.C., R.C. Feiock and C. Stream (2003), 'Governmental uncertainty and leadership turnover: influences on contracting and sector choice for local services', *State and Local Government Review*, **35** (3), 183–95.

Clingermayer, J.C., R.C. Feiock, B. Coyle McCabe and H.-J. Park (2008), 'Turnover, transaction costs, and time horizons: an examination of municipal debt financing', *American Review of Public Administration*, **38** (2), 167–79.

Condrey, S.E. and R.P. Battaglio (2007), 'A return to spoils? Revisiting radical civil service reform in the United States', *Public Administration Review*, **67** (3), 425–36.

Cotton, J.L. and J.M. Tuttle (1986), 'Employee turnover: a meta-analysis and review with implications for research', *Academy of Management Review*, **11** (January), 55–70.

Davidson, G., S. Lepeak and E. Newman (2007a), *The Impact of the Aging Workforce on Public Sector Organizations and Mission*, Alexandria, VA: International Public Management Association for Human Resources, accessed 11 January 2012 at www.impa-hr.org.

Davidson, G., S. Lepeak and E. Newman (2007b), *Recruiting and Staffing in the Public Sector: Results from the IPMA-HR Research Series*, Alexandria, VA: International Public Management Association for Human Resources, accessed 11 January 2012 at www.impa-hr.org.

Feoick, R.C., J.C. Clingermayer, C. Stream, B.C. McCabe and S. Ahmed (2001), 'Political conflict, fiscal stress, and administrative turnover in American cities', *State and Local Government Review*, **33** (2), 101–8.

Feiock, R.C. and C. Stream (1998), 'Explaining the tenure of local government managers', *Journal of Public Administration Research and Theory*, **8**, 117–30.

Frincke, J. (2006), *2006 US Job Retention*, Washington, DC: Society for Human Resource Management and CareerJournal.com.

Government Performance Project (GPP) (2007), *Survey of 50 State Governments*, Washington DC: Pew Center on the States, accessed 11 January 2012 at www.pewcenteronthestates.org/gpp_report_card.aspx.

Hays, S.W. and J.E. Sowa (2006), 'A broader look at the "accountability" movement: some grim realities in state civil service systems', *Review of Public Personnel Administration*, **26** (2), 102–17.

Holmlund, B. and H. Lang (1985), 'Quit behavior under imperfect information: searching, moving, learning', *Economic Inquiry*, **23**, 383–93.

Hustinx, L. (2008), 'I quit, therefore I am? Volunteer turnover and the politics of self-actualization', *Nonprofit and Voluntary Sector Quarterly*, **39** (2), 236–55.

Ito, J.K. (2003), 'Career mobility and branding in the civil service: an empirical study', *Public Personnel Management*, **32** (1), 1–21.

Jamison, I.B. (2003), 'Turnover and retention and volunteers in human resource agencies', *Review of Public Personnel Administration*, **23**, 114–32.

Kellough, J.E. and L.G. Nigro (2005), 'Radical civil service reform: Ideology, politics, and policy', in S.E. Condrey (ed.), *Handbook of Human Resource Management in Government* (2nd Edition), San Francisco: Jossey-Bass.

Kellough, J.E. and W. Osuna (1995), 'Cross-agency comparisons of quit rates in the federal service', *Review of Public Personnel Administration*, **15**, 58–68.

Kiekbusch, R., W. Price and J. Theis (2007), 'Causes of employee turnover in sheriff operated jails', *Public Personnel Management*, **36** (1), 51–63.

Lavigna, R.J. and S.W. Hays (2004), 'Recruitment and selection of public workers: an international compendium of modern trends and practices', *Public Personnel Management*, **33** (3), 237–53.

Lee, G. and B.S. Jimenez (2011), 'Does performance management affect job turnover in the federal government?', *American Review of Public Administration*, **41** (2), 168–84.

Lee, S. and A.B. Whitford (2008), 'Exit, voice, loyalty, and pay: evidence from the public workforce', *Journal of Public Administration Research and Theory*, **18** (4), 647–71.

Lewis, G.B. (1991), 'Turnover and the quiet crisis in the federal civil service', *Public Administration Review*, **51** (March/April), 145–55.

Lewis, G.B. and S.L. Durst (1995), 'Will locality pay solve recruitment and retention problems in the federal civil service?', *Public Administration Review*, **55** (4), 371–80.

Lewis, G.B. and Z. Hu (2005), 'Information technology workers in the federal service: more than a quiet crisis?', *Review of Public Personnel Administration*, **25**, 207–24.

Lewis, G.B. and K. Park (1989), 'Turnover in federal white collar employment: are women more likely to quit than men?', *American Review of Public Administration*, **19** (March), 13–28.

Light, P.C. (1999), *The New Public Service*, Washington, DC: Brookings Institution Press.

Llorens, J.J. and E.C. Stazyk (2011), 'How important are competitive wages? Exploring the impact of relative wage rates on employee turnover in state government', *Review of Public Personnel Administration*, **31** (2), 111–27.

March, J.G. and H.A. Simon (1958), *Organizations*, New York: Wiley.

McCabe, B.C., R.C. Feiock, J.C. Clingermayer and C. Stream (2008), 'Turnover among city managers: The role of political and economic change', *Public Administration Review*, **68** (2), 380–86.

Meier, K.J. and A. Hicklin (2008), 'Employee turnover and organizational performance: testing a hypothesis from classical public administration', *Journal of Public Administration Research and Theory*, **18** (4), 573–590.

Meyer, C.K., M.J. Beville (Jr), T.C. Magedanz and A.M. Hackert (1979), 'South Dakota state government employee turnover and work related attitudes: an analysis and recommendation', *Midwest Review of Public Administration*, June, 88–118.

Moynihan, D.P. and N. Landuyt (2008), 'Explaining turnover intention in state government: examining the roles of gender, life cycle, and loyalty', *Review of Public Personnel Administration*, **28** (2), 120–43.

Moynihan, D.P. and S.K. Pandey (2008), 'The ties that bind: social networks, person- organization value fit, and turnover intention', *Journal of Public Administration Research and Theory*, **18** (2), 205–27.

Naff, K.C. and J. Crum (1999), 'Working for America: does public service motivation make a difference?', *Review of Public Personnel Administration*, **19**, 5–16.

Nigro, L., F. Nigro and J.E. Kellough (2007), *The New Public Personnel Administration* (6th Edition), Belmont, CA: Thomson Wadsworth.

Owens, P.L. (2006), 'One more reason not to cut your training budget: the relationship between training and organizational outcomes', *Public Personnel Management*, **35** (2), 163–72.

Park, C. and J. Joo (2010), 'Control over the Korean bureaucracy: a review of the NPM civil service reforms under the Roh Moo-Hyun government', *Review of Public Personnel Administration*, **30** (2), 103–33.

Partnership for Public Service and Booz Allen Hamilton (2010), *Beneath the Surface: Understanding Attrition at Your Agency and Why it Matters*, Washington, DC: Partnership for Public Service.

Pollitt, C. and G. Bouckaert (2000), *Public Management Reform: A Comparative Analysis*, Oxford: Oxford University Press.

Price, W., R. Kiekbusch and J. Theis (2007), 'Causes of employee turnover in sheriff operated jails', *Public Personnel Management*, **36** (1), 51–63.

Rubin, E.V. (2009), 'The role of procedural justice in public personnel management: empirical results from the Department of Defense', *Journal of Public Administration Research and Theory*, **19** (1), 125–43.

Selden, S.C. (2006), 'The impact of discipline on the use and rapidity of dismissals in state governments', *Review of Public Personnel Administration*, **26** (4), 335–55.

Selden, S. (2009), *Human Capital: Tools and Strategies for the Public Sector*, Washington, DC: CQ Press.

Selden, S.C. and D.P. Moynihan (2000), 'A model of voluntary turnover in state government', *Review of Public Personnel Administration*, **20** (2), 63–74.

Shaw, J.D., J.E. Delery, G.D. Jenkins (Jr) and N. Gupta (1998), 'An organizational-level analysis of voluntary and involuntary turnover', *Academy of Management Journal*, **41** (5), 511–25.

Shortenhaus, S. (2006), *Strategies for Working with Business and High Growth Industries*, US Department of Labor, Center for Faith Based and Community Initiatives, accessed 11 January at http://www.scribd.com/doc/1657276/Department-of-Labor-DOL-CFBCI-Business-Partnerships.

Smith, C.B. (1979), 'Influence of internal opportunity structure and sex of worker on turnover patterns', *Administrative Science Quarterly*, **24** (September), 362–81.

Sullivan, S.E. (1999), 'The changing nature of careers: a review and research agenda', *Journal of Management*, **25** (3), 457–84.

Sullivan, S.E. and Y. Baruch (2009), 'Advances in career theory and research: a critical review and agenda for future exploration', *Journal of Management*, **35** (6), 1542–71.

Sutherland, J. (2002), 'Job-to-job turnover and job-to-non-employment movement: a case study investigation', *Personnel Review*, **31** (6), 710–21.

Tobias, R.M. (2001), 'An aging workforce: a time of opportunity or a time of calamity?', *The Public Manager*, **30** (2), 27–30.

Udechukwu, I.I., W. Harrington, T. Manyak, S. Segal and S. Graham (2007),

'The Georgia Department of Corrections: an exploratory reflection on correctional officer turnover and its correlates', *Public Personnel Management*, **36** (3), 247–68.

US Merit Systems Protection Board (1989), *Who is Leaving the Federal Government?*, Washington, DC: US Merit Systems Protection Board.

Whitaker, G.P. and R.H. DeHoog (1991), 'City managers under fire: how conflict leads to turnover', *Public Administration Review*, **51** (2), 156–65.

Zax, J.S. (1989), 'Quits and race', *Journal of Human Resources*, **24** (Summer), 469–93.

10. Managing human resources in the public sector during economic downturn[1]

Parbudyal Singh and Ronald J. Burke

INTRODUCTION

Human resources management (HRM) in the public sector has attracted considerable attention among academics and practitioners, especially over the past three decades (Bach, 2005). Much of this attention has been driven by the switch from a 'rule-bound culture' associated with traditional personnel administration to a 'performance-based culture' of strategic HRM and the potential benefits of such a change (Llorens and Battaglio, 2010; Morris and Farrell, 2007; Brown, 2004). Over this period, there was widespread managerial reorganization and restructuring across many parts of the world, from Anglo-Saxon countries (USA, Canada, Australia, New Zealand and the UK to continental Europe, Asia Pacific, and Latin America (Skelly, 2002). Public sector organizations, like private firms, began to focus on the need to recruit, employ, train and develop employees, while compensating and rewarding them for behaviours that help the organizations achieve their goals. It became evident, however, that managing people in the public sector had additional complexities versus the private sector. For instance, it was challenging to manage the public sector with the intent of 'achieving organizational competitiveness and business outcomes' (Brown, 2004: 305), while focusing on the public's interest at the same time. With additional pressures from the public to deliver essential (and sometimes non-essential) services, and with politicians and administrators' jobs on the line during elections, these complex tasks become even more problematic during times of economic downturn (Burke and Cooper, 2000).

In this chapter, we focus on HRM in the public sector during economic downturns, drawing on examples of how governments across the globe have sought to institute reforms. The second section of this chapter provides a brief overview of human resource management in the public sector (as this has been covered elsewhere in this book). Here we provide insights on traditional public sector management as a backdrop for subsequent public sector transformation. The third section provides a historical review of typical government responses to tough economic times. Specifically, it traces the role of Margaret Thatcher in the late 1980s and early 1990s and the new public management (NPM) model that was spawned during that period. We further examine the responses by selected governments globally and argue that some of the policy prescriptions adopted were based on the perceptions that the public sector was not cost-efficient and provided shoddy and low quality services (i.e. the ideological basis for restructuring the public sector). The fourth section explores the specific pressures of managing HR functions in the public sector during economic downturn. Since a significant percentage of the public sector budget is devoted to wages and salaries, we focus much of the discussion on related issues: including public versus private sector compensation, wage concessions, layoffs, wage freezes, and threats to pensions and other benefits. We also look at the effects on other HR functions such as training and development. The final section concludes with some suggestions on ways to manage human resources in the public sector during economic downturns.

HUMAN RESOURCES MANAGEMENT IN THE PUBLIC SECTOR: A BRIEF OVERVIEW

For centuries, the public sector has utilized a distinctive approach to HRM/personnel management, with a focus on good wages, high job security and guaranteed pensions, to name a few (Gardner and Palmer, 1997; Gray and Jenkins, 1995); this has often made public sector employment very attractive to many job seekers and even a role model for other organizations (Black and Upchurch, 1999). Over time, the traditional public sector management model has come under pressure as it was perceived as having excessive bureaucracy and tight monitoring, which slowed decision making and communication and reduced accountability (Llorens and Battaglio, 2010; Seldon, 2006; Heckscher and Applegate, 1994). Compounded by increasing debt, soaring costs for services, and the economic downturn of the late 1980s to the early 1990s, these pressures combined made governments across the globe seem too big and expensive to maintain (Skelley, 2002); this subsequently spawned widespread reform in public organizations in an attempt to achieve greater efficiencies through the implementation of effective human resource management practices (Kellough and Nigro, 2006; Kramar, 1986; Gray and Jenkins,

1995; Walker, 1992). In the 1980s and 1990s, government organizations in the developed world underwent considerable public sector transformation, known globally as the 'new public management' (Kettl, 2000; Politt and Bouckaert, 2000). While these public sector reforms were predominantly in the Anglo-American countries, it eventually spread across the European continent and most developed states of Asia and Latin America (Peters and Savoie, 1998; Kettl, 2000; Politt and Bouckaert, 2000; Skelley 2002). This period coincided with scholarly developments in the HRM field that emphasized the role of strategic HRM practices in attaining desired employee behaviours and enhanced organizational outcomes (Pfeffer, 1994; Huselid, 1995; Kaufman, 1992; Blackwell et al., 1994; Terpstra and Rozell, 1993; Wright and Snell, 1998).

Today's public sector HRM is generally characterized by less centralized control and more empowerment of managers and supervisors so that they can undertake greater responsibility for their work (Gardner, 1993; Gardner and Palmer, 1997; Shim, 2001; Brown, 2004). In many jurisdictions, a shift from personnel administration to more strategic HRM in the public sector has resulted in more multidimensional roles, restructured career paths, less use of seniority as a basis for promotion, greater emphasis on performance and productivity measures, and the removal of rigid employment categories (Llorens and Battaglio, 2010; Brown, 2004; Black and Upchurch, 1999; Gardner and Palmer, 1997; Kettl et al., 1996; Miller, 2003).

However, the reform of government organizations and associated HRM practices has been severely criticized for its erosion of working conditions and internal career opportunities (Bach, 2005; Brown, 2004), the curtailment of wages and benefits, and sometimes significant staff reduction/downsizing and ultimately changes in organizational structure and culture (Black and Upchurch, 1999; Morris and Farrell, 2007). We will examine the effects of these changes in the sections below, starting with interventions by Margaret Thatcher in England in what has come to be known as new public management (NPM).

HISTORICAL REVIEW OF TYPICAL HRM AND GOVERNMENT RESPONSES TO TOUGH ECONOMIC TIMES

As mentioned above, the changes in HRM and other management practices in the public sector in the 1980s–90s were closely linked to the notion of NPM; the espoused intent of the NPM was to make the public sector more efficient and effective in delivering services while being competitive and flexible (Llorens and Battaglio, 2010; Kim, 2000). During these two decades, 'public sector organizations adopted the NPM as ways of managing human resources as part of its reform' (Gray and Jenkins 1995: 80). These changes began in the UK in the late 1980s under then Prime Minister Margaret Thatcher and subsequently spread to the US, Canada, Australia and New Zealand, followed by Scandinavia and Continental Europe (Weikart, 2003; Lane, 2000; Skelley, 2002; Hood 1991). Eventually, Asian countries adopted the NPM as a way to survive the tough economic times facing them in the late 1990s (Kim, 2000). In reality, the NPM did not fully replace the structures of traditional public sector management, but instead added new dimensions to human resource management and governance (Lane, 2000) – these essentially focused on cost-cutting, performance measures, outsourcing/contracting out services, and efficiency.

Grounded in a performance-based approach, NPM has changed the public sector in two key ways: (1) 'by being redrawn as public sector entities which are privatized in their entirety', and (2) 'by becoming blurred as entities, which are public by definition, design and destiny, which are nonetheless reconfigured by moving certain in-house functions out to service providers and in the process establishing new contractual relationships and service delivery mechanisms that fall under the generic mantle of "outsourcing"' (Lavelle, 2006: 220). Besides, public sector organizations introduced all three elements of NPM: for instance, downsizing, delayering, and shifting boundaries of the organizations (Morris and Farrell, 2007), all in an effort to cut costs.

NPM has impacted different countries to varying degrees (Common, 2011; Skelley, 2002), as culture and established institutional mechanisms, among other factors, influenced the speed and extent to which these changes were adopted (Common, 2011). English speaking regimes were quicker to embrace NPM than Continental and Asian regimes (Skelley, 2002: 181). For example, Kettl (2000: 65) observes that in the US reforms were more rapid than in other countries, since in the US the 'integration of governance [was weaved] deeply into the very fabric of civil society'. In the US, reforms were implemented in most of the major cities, from Indianapolis under Mayor Goldsmith beginning in 1992, to New York City under Mayor Giuliani beginning in 1993 and to Los Angeles under Mayor Riordan beginning in 1993 – all with varying degrees of success or failure in terms of decreases in tax, city savings, increase in city debt and shift in expenditures (Weikart, 2003). Furthermore, the US government under Bill Clinton enacted the Government Performance and Results Act (GPRA), 'which mandated that federal agencies develop strategic plans and assess the outcomes they produce compared with those plans' (Kettl, 1997: 449).

In the UK, under the Thatcher government, there were significant layoffs of employees in public sector offices (Campbell and Wilson, 1995; Kemp, 1990). This was followed by the widespread privatization and contracting out of services (Kettl, 1997). These moves led to a decrease in civil service personnel of nearly 30 per cent over the 15 years that Thatcher was in power. With performance as the key driver, new demands/expectations were imposed on public sector managers. Additionally, in many instances, the role of unions was reduced from broader umbrella groups to unions representing more specific workplaces (Fairbrother, 1994).

New Zealand, like the UK, embarked on NPM but not until 1998; however, it has been argued that they undertook the most rapid and radical reforms amongst the Anglo-Saxon countries (Boston, 1995; Boston et al., 1996). New Zealand went to extraordinary lengths (Schick, 1998) to create and enhance an environment that was conducive to negotiating and enforcing formal contracts within the public sector (Wallis and Dollery, 2001). However, government officials were experiencing increasing fear that 'contractualism may have been pushed beyond the point at which it starts to damage the social capital' (Wallis and Dollery, 2001: 247).

Australia also fell 'in line' with reforming the public sector (Adler et al., 2008; Boston and Uhr, 1996). The Australian Labor Party, under Prime Minister Hawke, adopted a moderate version of the NPM and was not as swift to embrace the reforms as comprehensively as New Zealand (Johnston, 2000). Hawke, unlike Reagan and Thatcher, brought trade union and business leaders together to tackle unemployment (Kelly, 1994). The strongest evidence of NPM in the Australian public sector was in its 'macro-economic policies' (Johnston, 2000).

In Canada, the provincial governments attempted several reforms. For instance, the Government of Ontario's commitment to a balanced budget in the early 1990s, coupled with lower levels of financial support from the Federal government, which resulted in lower levels of funding for healthcare. It created the Hospital Services Restructuring Commission (HSRC) which conducted a study indicating that the City of Toronto should reduce the number of hospitals from 45 to 32 through mergers and amalgamation of services, hospitals closing and outsourcing and rationalization of services. Healthcare restructuring in Canada took two forms: hospital closures and mergers and bed reductions and downsizing through cuts in health human resources. By 1999, over 200 hospitals had morphed into 171 and merged hospitals had been reorganized to combine services and get rid of duplication (Burke and Greenglass, 2000).

Korea, like most other Asian countries, did not immediately embrace the NPM model. However, Korea's economic crisis of 1997, spawned by 'structural deficiency and lagging adjustment to global standards resulting in a drop in competitiveness' (Kim, 2000: 327), led to public sector reforms. There were subsequent widespread changes in its personnel management systems, from recruitment and selection to rewards and promotion and to compensation reform (Kim, 2000).

Overall, while these changes may have resulted in cost savings, several authors believe that much of public sector reform was channelled towards altering attitudes and behaviour and not transforming the fundamental premise of public sector structure and processes (Skelley, 2002; Kettl, 2000). Kettl (2000: 32) posits that 'six years of reinvention left the [US] federal government about the same size in scope and scale'. In sum, the changes may have been more ideological rather than ensuring effective HRM management.

PRESSURES ON MANAGING HR IN ECONOMIC DOWNTURNS

HRM interventions in economic downturns can result in both positive and negative outcomes for employees and organizations. On the negative side, there is the usual downsizing and layoffs and all the human costs associated with these processes and outcomes (Cascio, 2005; Chui, 2009). Dramatic reforms, however, have been embarked upon for economic survival during such periods as the Great Depression, the oil and inflationary crises of the 1970s, the debt crises of the 1980s and 1990s, the global financial crisis of 2007–09 (Chwieroth, 2010; Kamoche, 2006; Virtanen et al., 2006). It can be argued that during periods of economic downturn the 'importance of economic structures, distributive preferences, strategic agency, uncertainty, and belief systems' (Chwieroth, 2010: 2) are most recognized for their relevance to social and political stability.

Government organizations across the globe have used financial and budgetary crises as occasions to reform their internal structures in the quest for efficiency, flexibility and overall success. However, many of the difficulties faced by public sector organizations are also common in the private sector. Thus, to a great extent, public sector transformations are grounded in principles already well known in the private and commercial spheres (Emery and Giauque, 2005). However, given the inherent political nature of the public sector, these organizations' human resource policies and procedures are more politically driven, as opposed to the private sector which is market and technology driven (Harel and Tzafrir, 2001).

There is a considerable body of literature on the effects of economic downturn on organizations (see, for example, Burke and Cooper, 2000; Cameron et al., 1987; Weitzel and Jonsson, 1989). McKinley (1993) suggests two approaches that are most commonly used during such times: the 'rigidity approach' and the 'adaptation approach'. The *rigidity approach* leads to organizations instituting more stringent controls with an emphasis on enhancing efficiency, while the *adaptation approach* leads to organizations shifting gear and adapting to changes in the environment due to economic downturn (McKinley, 1993; Rosenblatt and Mannheim, 1996). The literature covered in this chapter suggests that public sector organizations around the globe have implemented both approaches.

While reforms have focused on efficiency and flexibility, it has been tough for public sector administrators to make the cuts that are sometimes needed the most; instead, they focus on cuts that are the easiest – both politically and administratively. Thus, rather than effective re-designing of jobs and management structures which are more long-term and where results are not evident within single electoral cycles, the focus has instead been on labour costs savings/cuts given that this is the largest 'cost centre' in budgets (Rothenbacher, 1997). Cuts in labour costs, through reductions in the labour force (i.e. cutbacks, lay-offs and so on) and wage concessions, have been the norm in public sector organizations since the NPM in the 1980s (Virtanen et al., 2006; Morgan and Allington, 2002; Rothenbacher, 1997). Hansen (2009: 5) states, for example, that most organizations 'are holding the line on salaries by cutting their 2009 merit increase budgets, freezing salaries or even cutting base pay in some instances'. The Canadian public sector administrators have recently mandated a wage freeze for all public sector employees, citing budget shortfall (Duncan, 2010). According to a more recent survey, while 'the hiring freezes that were put into place during the recession are beginning to thaw, especially for professional and technical workers and positions that require employees with critical skills' (Hansen, 2011: 135), the pattern is clear: focus on labour costs during economic downturns.

Managing human resources in the public sector during economic downturn has also been done through an increase in the use of part-time, fixed-term contracts and temporary employees, while decreasing the number of fulltime employees (Roche et al., 2011; Morgan and Allington, 2002). Again, the underlying principle seems to be compensation controls. This has led to sharper internal divisiveness, decreased job security and down-graded working conditions within government sectors across the globe (Virtanen et al., 2006). For example, in Finland, the unemployment rate rose sharply (by roughly 525 per cent from 3.5 to 18.4 per cent) between 1990 and 1994 (Virtanen et al., 2006); this significant drop in employment spawned a spill-over of drastically decreased tax revenues, which inevitably forced the public sector, including the municipalities, into severe financial hardships. However, while Finland's private sector employment was also negatively impacted by the rise in unemployment, the impact was not as significant as that felt in the public sector (Virtanen et al., 2006). In the same vein, when Finland's economic situation began to rebound in mid-1990's, a similar disparity could be seen – that is, the private sector employment was recorded at close to 'pre-recession levels' while employment in public sector organizations lingered far below the 'pre-recession level' (Virtanen et al., 2006: 44).

The central role of public sector compensation in economic downturns has spawned considerable debate among academics and practitioners alike (Belman and Heywood, 2004; Harel and Tzafrir, 2001). While it may be necessary to reduce wages in times of economic downturn, wages set too low can eliminate the calibre of employees needed to effectively and efficiently deliver quality services to the public. From another perspective, while it is necessary to capture top talent, wages set too high may be seen as inequitable and an improper use of public resources that could be funnelled into other government services, such as tax reduction, education, healthcare, and so on.

In the US, public sector organizations are guided by the 'Reform Act of 1962', which is a guiding instrument for sectoral wage comparisons (Belman and Heywood, 2004). The fundamental purpose of this Act is to establish a 'logical and factual basis for the setting of federal pay, ensuring equality between otherwise similar workers in the private and federal sectors, and ensuring fairness to private-sector employers by neither underpaying nor overpaying federal workers' (Belman and Heywood, 2004: 570). However, salaries of public sector employees lag way behind those of private sector workers and as such any claim to pay equality between the sectors is an ideal rather than a reality (Belman and Heywood, 2004). In other words, 'any claim to efficiency or "the market" is surely irrelevant when you can find no workers in the public sector actually earning the private-sector wage [and] even the hope of a logical and factual basis for pay setting seems not to be achieved' (Belman and Heywood, 2004). Thus, the law seems to have been somewhat ineffective in ensuring a balance between private and public sector compensation.

Within the unionized sector, there are 'efforts to adjust wage rates downwards inside unionized organizations when recession strikes', and these discussions are 'dominated by the theme of concession bargaining' (Roche et al., 2011: 6). Roche et al. (2011: 6) defines concession bargaining as involving 'union "give backs" to management in the form of freezes or even cuts in pay and benefits'. This concession, the authors argue, can be 'more successful if based on openness and transparency, equality of sacrifice and trade union gain – where companies agree to some trade union demands in return for accepting significant concessions [which] can include some form of financial participation such as profit sharing or some type of employment security programme' (Roche et al., 2011: 6). However, unions have typically resisted efforts aimed at wage concessions and downsizing, the other key element of the public sector response to tough economic times. This resistance was exemplified in the case of Wisconsin, where the government sought to roll back union gains, not only through layoffs, but an attempt to curtail collective bargaining. The Wisconsin case is symbolic, as it was the first state to grant public sector workers the right to bargain collectively in 1959; now, only half the states in the US allow such bargaining rights for public employees (Tumulty, 2011). More recently, the unions joined the Occupy Wall Street Movement to help publicize issues facing workers – both in the public and private sectors (Potter, 2011).

Training and development is another HRM function that tends to suffer when organizations – in both the public and private sectors – are faced with financial crisis; this is so even though research suggests that training and development opportunities enhance employees' performance on the job with the 'spill over effect' of better organizational performance (Jacobs and Washington, 2003). Fluctuations in training and development seem to have a direct link to economic downturn in public (and private) sector organizations. The decreased investment in training and development during economic downturn is best explained by the increase in part-time and temporary workers and the further decrease in the full-time employee complement, as organizations tend to spend less in training on part-time and temporary workers (Tregaskis and Brewster, 1998).

There are concerns at the national level about the cuts to training and development. In Australia, for instance, public sector organizations outsourced roughly 48 per cent of training and development functions in recent years (Holland et al., 2007). This decline in employer investment in training and development is problematic. The Australian Bureau of Statistics reports that between 1993 and 1996 there was a marked decline in training and development expenditure and investment. This decline was evident in the number of training hours each employee received, which amounted to a decrease in training dollars from 2.9 per cent to 2.5 per cent (as a percentage) of payroll dollars (Smith, 2003). This decline occurred in both public and private sector organizations (Peretz and McGraw, 2011).

Pensions and retirement benefits also face pressures in times of economic downturns. Pension plans can be described as monetary mechanisms set up by employers in the public and private sectors to provide participating employees with post retirement income to which employers have a legal obligation (Schneider, 2005). Pension plans have been successfully used by organizations in both sectors to attract and retain employees (Bodie and Papke, 1992). However, in the last couple of decades there has been widespread concern regarding the inadequacy or deficit faced by pension plans in both public and private sector organizations around the globe. Spawned by various financial crises and economic downturns, as well as the rise in baby boomer populations (Liadze and Weale, 2010), 'public sector debts and deficits have been the dominant public policy issue of the 1990s in Canada, and in most other industrialized economies' (Stanford, 1995: 113).

Vivekanandan (2002: 49) claims that the 'pension system in Canada is shifting from rights-based to a needs-based one. There is a move towards privatization in this sphere too. A free-market system is slowly being introduced in several areas of the pension system in Canada'. When faced with budgetary restraints, it appears to be the custom for organizations to cut spending where they can. This practice was rampant in Canada during the Mulroney era; around 1989, the government started to claw back benefits from the pensioners who they considered to be in higher income brackets, which undoubtedly watered down the pension plans, among other government programmes (Vivekanandan, 2002).

In the US, in 2005, California Governor Arnold Schwarzenegger wanted to change the pension plan from a 'defined benefit' (DB) to a 'defined contribution' (DC) systems for employees hired beginning July 1, 2007 (Kilgour, 2006). But what Schwarzenegger was proposing, while relatively new to the public sector, is common in the private sphere. The private sector utilizes more of a defined contribution model which passes the risk of investment on to the employees (Kilgour, 2006), while the public sector uses the defined benefits (DB) model which imposes the risk of public sector pension plans on the governments. The debate surrounding the question of whether to shift from the DB to the DC pension plan model is a complicated one for the public sector, to say the least. The public sector has a greater rate of employee pension coverage than do private sector organizations. For example, 'in 1995, 78 per cent of full-time US private sector employees were members of pension plans' (US Bureau of Labor Statistics, 1999), whereas virtually all full-time public sector employees were members (Schneider, 2005: 109). Thus, pressures on pension plans, especially those with defined benefits (DB) as in the public sector, will continue to be an issue – even more so for public sector employees during economic downturns when the costs of these plans become clearly visible.

CONCLUDING COMMENTS

During periods of extended or successive economic downturns, business activities tend to decline, and to deal with this decline organizations often turn to some form of restructuring, the most prominent of which is downsizing (Sheaffer et al., 2009). This turn was pronounced in the two periods of recession (1985–86 and 1990–91) when organizations, both private and public, increased their downsizing activities upwards of 25 per cent, including an additional 5 per cent reduction in the workforce (Morris et al., 1999).

This common response to economic downturns in the public sector, almost knee-jerk, has been deep and widespread. Reports indicate that during the late 1980s and 1990s, the period of widespread adaptation to the NPM model, US employers undertook extensive employee reduction schemes, to the tune of 4.4 million between 1985 and 1990, and another 2.2 million between 1990 and 1995 (Serwer, 1995). In fact, between 1989 and 1993, downsizing was undertaken by roughly 85 per cent of the top 1000 organizations in the US (Donaldson, 1994). In the most recent recession, downsizing was more global in scope, with 8.5 million layoffs in the US and more than 50 million worldwide (Cascio, in press). The public sector has not been spared; for instance, Greece has announced a cut of about 30 000 or 3 per cent of its public sector jobs through early retirements and layoffs. However, despite downsizing's widespread appeal and usage, reports indicate that it has had limited success in achieving its intended goals (Love and Nohria, 2005). In fact, in several studies, Cascio (in press; 2005) has demonstrated that organizations that downsize often do not realize significant gains; rather, they do worse.

Several authors contend that this limited success rate can be attributed to factors such as employees' attitudes and behaviours in response to downsizing, the negative impact on internal organizational practices, and the costs of employee reduction (such as severance packages and the need to recruit later on) (Mishra and Spreitzer, 1998; Pfeffer, 1998); other authors argue that downsizing is harmful to organizational learning and development and can hinder adaptation during rapidly changing environments by negatively impacting informal communication networks (Fisher and White, 2000; Lei and Hitt, 1995). Over time, these negative repercussions can decrease organizational performance and competitiveness (DeRue et al., 2008; Noer, 1993; Sheaffer et al., 2009).

While downsizing is usually concerned with organizational survival in times of recession, it is not uncommon for organizations to proactively downsize as part of a broader restructuring tactic, sometimes in anticipation of future economic downturn (Scott and Ueng, 1999; Sheaffer et al., 2009; Wayhan and Werner, 2000) or as a means of gaining competitive edge and increasing profitability (Burke and Nelson, 1998; McKinley and Scherer, 2000). In the end, organizations are guided by their economic need to reduce cost and maximize efficiency (Cascio et al., 1997) and as such are blindsided by the belief that business can be more profitable and better achieve objectives with fewer staff members (Sheaffer et al., 2009).

Organizations, public or private, can be just as successful without massive downsizing, which can have a negative impact on their performance in the long run. There is extensive work in this area (Budros, 1999; Cascio, in press; 2005; 2002; Freeman and Cameron, 1993; Tzafrir et al., in press). Ludy (2009), for instance, offers several strategies whereby organizations can reduce costs without terminating employees; essentially, using a team approach, employees are encouraged to problem-solve ways of reducing costs. Several steps are suggested in his approach: creation of a responsible organizing and management team; preparation of the team and the organization; generation of creative ideas and solutions; taking action and documenting results; and monitoring progress and following up (Ludy, 2009). Cascio (in press) notes Germany's implementation of the *Kurzarbeit* policy (short work/reduced work schedules) and reduced work weeks as institutional mechanisms at the national level – which are particularly relevant in the public sector. Along similar lines, DeWitt (in press), suggests that fixed-term employment contracts and staged retirements would allow firms to be competitive through staffing flexibility. As the common saying goes, 'an ounce of prevention is worth a pound of cure'. Such prevention may require much planning and balancing of HR supply and demand and strategically linking these to the organization's strategy, goals and objectives. That is, public sector organizations need to strategically plan for the longer term, focusing on sustainable work systems that help to serve the public in an efficient manner. This will help to ease the pain that is caused by knee-jerk cuts in economic downturns.

NOTE

1. We are grateful for the excellent research assistance provided by Paulette Burgher, a graduate student in the School of Human Resource Management, York University.

REFERENCES

Adler, P.S., S.W. Kwon, and C. Heckscher (2008), 'Professional work: the emergence of collaborative community', *Organization Science*, **19** (2), 359–76.

Bach, S. (2005), *Managing Human Resources: Personnel Management in Transition* (4th Edition), Toronto: Blackwell Publishing.

Belman, D. and J. Heywood (2004), 'Public-sector wage comparability: the role of earnings dispersion', *Public Finance Review*, **32** (6), 567–87.

Black, J. and M. Upchurch (1999), 'Public sector employment', in G. Hollinshead,

P. Nicholls and S. Tailby (eds), *Employee Relations*, London: Financial Times Management.

Blackwell, W.D., A.J. Brickley and S.M. Weisbach (1994), 'Accounting information and internal performance evaluation', *Journal of Accounting and Economics*, **17**, 331–58.

Bodie, Z. and L.E. Papke (1992), 'Pension fund finance', in Z. Bodie and A.H. Munnell (eds), *Pensions and the Economy: Sources, Uses and Limitations of Data*, Philadelphia: Wharton School of the University of Pennsylvania, Pension Research Council, pp. 49–172.

Boston, J. (1995b), 'Inherently governmental functions and the limits to conglobal revolution in public management contracting out', in J. Boston (ed.), *The State under Contract*, Wellington, New Zealand: Bridget Williams Books.

Boston, J., J. Martin, J. Pallot and P. Walsh (1996), *Public Management: The New Zealand Model*, Auckland, New Zealand: Oxford University Press.

Boston, J. and J. Uhr (1996), 'Reshaping the mechanics of government', in F. Castles, R. Gerritsen and J. Vowles (eds), *The Great Experiment*, St. Leonards, Australia: Allen and Unwin, pp. 48–76.

Brown, K. (2004), 'Human resources management in the public sector', *Public Management Review*, **6** (3), 303–9.

Budros, A. (1999), 'A conceptual framework for analyzing why organizations downsize', *Organization Science*, **10**, 69–82.

Burke, R.J. and C.L. Cooper (2000), 'The organization in crisis: downsizing, restructuring and privatization', Oxford: Blackwell.

Burke, R.J. and Greenglass, E.R. (2000), 'Organizational restructuring, identifying effective hospital downsizing processes', in R.J. Burke and C.L. Cooper (eds), 'The organization in crisis: downsizing, restructuring and privatization', Oxford: Blackwell, pp. 284–302.

Burke, R.J. and D. Nelson (1998), 'Mergers and acquisitions, downsizing, and privatization: a North American perspectiv', in M.K. Gowing, J.D. Kraft and J.C. Quick (eds), *The New Organizational Reality: Downsizing, Restructuring and Revitalization*, American Psychological Association, Washington, DC, pp. 21–51.

Cameron, K.S., D.A. Whetten and M.U. Kim (1987), 'Organizational dysfunctions of decline', *Academy of Management Journal*, **30**, 126–37.

Campbell, C. and G.K. Wilson (1995), *The End of Whitehall: Death of a Paradigm?*, Oxford, England: Blackwell.

Cascio, W.F. (2002), 'Strategies for responsible restructuring', *Academy of Management Executive*, **16** (3), 80–91.

Cascio, W.F. (2005), 'Strategies for responsible restructuring', *Academy of Management Executive*, **19** (4), 39–50.

Cascio, W.F. (in press), 'How does downsizing come about?', in C.L. Cooper, J.C. Quick and A. Pandey (eds), *Downsizing: Is Less Still More?*, Cambridge, UK: Cambridge University Press.

Cascio, W.F., C.E. Young and J.R. Morris (1997), 'Financial consequences of employment-change decisions in major US corporations', *Academy of Management Review*, **40**, 1175–89.

Chui, L. (2009), 'Managing human resources for an economic downturn', *Hong Kong Industrialist*, June, 14–17.

Chwieroth, J.M. (2010), 'How do crises lead to change? Liberalizing capital controls in the early years of new order Indonesia', *World Politics*, **62** (3), 496–527.

Common, R. (2011), 'International trends in HRM in the public sector: reform attempts in the Republic of Georgia', *International Journal of Public Sector Management*, **24** (5), 421–34.

DeRue, D.S., J.R. Hollenbeck, M.D. Johnson, D.R. Ilgen and D.K. Jundt (2008), 'How different team downsizing approaches influence team-level adaptation and performance', *Academy of Management Journal*, **51** (1), 182–96.

DeWitt, R. (in press), 'Good downsizing', in Cooper, C.L., Quick, J.C. and Pandey, A. (eds), *Downsizing: Is Less Still More?*, Cambridge, UK: Cambridge University Press.

Donaldson, G. (1994), *Corporate Restructuring*, Boston, MA: Harvard Business School Press.

Duncan, D. (2010), Budget Speech on March 25, 2010, Toronto Star website, accessed on 11 January 2012 at http://www.thestar.com/news/ontario/ontario budget/article/785340--budget-ontario-vows-freeze-on-public-sector-wages.

Emery, Y. and D. Giauque (2005), 'Employment in the public and private sectors: toward a confusing hybridization process', *International Review of Administrative Sciences*, **71** (4), 639–57.

Fairbrother, P. (1994), *Politics and the State as Employer*, London: Mansell.

Fisher, S.R. and M.A. White (2000), 'Downsizing in a learning organization: are there hidden costs?', *Academy of Management Review*, **25**, 244–51.

Flanagan, J. and S. Perkins (1995), 'Public/private competition in the City of Phoenix, Arizona', *Government Finance Review*, **11**, 7–12.

Freeman, S.J. and K.S. Cameron (1993), 'Organizational downsizing: convergence and reorientation framework', *Organization Science*, **4**, 10–29.

Gardner, M. (1993), *Human Resource Management and Industrial Relations in the Public Sector*, South Melbourne: Macmillan.

Gardner, M. and G. Palmer (1997), *Employment Relations: Industrial Relations and Human Resource Management in Australia* (2nd Edition), Melbourne: Macmillan.

Gray, A. and B. Jenkins (1995), 'From public administration to public management: reassessing a revolution', *Public Administration*, **73** (1), 75–99.

Hansen, F. (2009), 'Currents in compensation and benefits', *Compensation and Benefits Review*, **41** (3), 5–19.

Hansen, F. (2011), 'Currents in compensation and benefits', *Compensation and Benefits Review*, **43** (3), 135–45.

Harel, G.H. and S.S. Tzafrir (2001), 'HRM practices in the public and private sectors: differences and similarities', *Public Administration Quarterly*, **25** (3), 316–55.

Heckscher, C. and L.M. Applegate (1994), 'Introduction', in C. Heckscher and A. Donnelon (eds), *The Post Bureaucratic Organization: New Perspectives on Organizational Change*, London: Sage, pp. 1–13.

Holland, P., C. Sheehan and H. De Cieri (2007), 'Attracting and retaining talent: exploring human resources development trends in Australia', *Human Resource Development, International*, **10** (3), 247–62.

Hood, C. (1991), 'A public management for all seasons?', *Public Administration*, **69** (1), 3–19.

Huselid, A.M. (1995), 'The impact of human resource management practices on turnover, productivity, and corporate financial performance', *Academy of Management Journal*, **38**, 635–72.

Jacobs, R.L. and C. Washington (2003), 'Employee development and organizational performance: a review of literature and directions for future research', *Human Resource Development International*, **6** (3), 343–54.

Johnston, J. (2000), 'The New Public Management in Australia', *Administrative Theory and Praxis*, **22** (2), 345–68.

Kamoche, K.N. (2006), 'Managing people in turbulent economic times: a knowledge-creation and appropriation perspective', *Asia Pacific Journal of Human Resources*, **44** (1), 25–45.

Kaufman, T.R. (1992), 'The effects of Improshare on productivity', *Industrial and Labor Relations Review*, **45** (3), 11–322.

Kellough, J.E. and L.G. Nigro (2006), 'Dramatic reform in the public service: at-will employment and the creation of a new public workforce', *Journal of Public Administration Research and Theory*, 16, 447–66.

Kelly, P. (1994), *The End of Certainty*, St. Leonards Australia: Allen and Unwin.

Kemp, P. (1990), 'Next steps for the British Civil Service', *Governance*, **3** (April), 186–96.

Kettl, D. (1997), 'The global revolution in public management: driving themes, missing links', *Journal of Policy Analysis and Management*, **16** (3), 446–62.

Kettl, D.F. (2000), *The Global Public Management Revolution: A Report on the Transformation of Governance*. Washington: Brookings Institution Press.

Kettl, D.F. (2005), *The Global Public Management Revolution* (2nd Edition), Washington, DC: Brookings Institution Press.

Kettl, D.F., P.W. Ingraham, R.P. Sanders and C. Horer (1996), *Civil Service Reform: Building a Government that Works*, Washington, DC: The Brookings Institution.

Kilgour, J. (2006), 'Public sector pension plans: defined benefit versus defined contribution', *Compensation and Benefits Review*, **38** (1), 20–28.

Kim, P.S. (2000), 'Human resource management reform in the Korean Civil Service', *Administrative Theory and Praxis*, **22** (2), 326–44.

Kitsantonis, N. (2011), 'Greeks move to slash state jobs by 300,000', *The New York Times*, accessed 23 October 2011 at http://www.nytimes.com/2011/10/03/world/europe/greeks-move-to-slash-state-jobs-for-30000.html.

Kramar, R. (1986), 'The personnel practitioner and affirmative action', *Human Resource Management Australia*, **24** (1), 38–44.

Lane, J.-E. (2000), *New Public Management: An Introduction*, London and New York: Routledge.

Lavelle, J. (2006), 'It's all about context and implementation some thoughts prompted by: unlocking the human potential for public sector performance — the United Nations world public sector report 2005', *The Public Personnel Management*, **35** (3), 217–28.

Lei, D. and M.A. Hitt (1995), 'Strategic restructuring and outsourcing: the effects of mergers and acquisitions and LBOs on building firms' skills and capabilities', *Journal of Management*, **21**, 835–59.

Liadze, I. and M. Weale (2010), 'Economic performance under labour', *National Institute Economic Review*, **212**, R2–R14.

Llorens, J.J., and P.R. (Jr) Battaglio (2010), 'Human resources management in a changing world: reassessing public human resources management education', *Review of Public Personnel Administration*, **30** (1), 112–32.

Love, E.G. and N. Nohria (2005), 'Reducing slack: the performance consequences of downsizing by large industrial firms', *Strategic Management Journal*, 1 (26), 1087–108.

Ludy, P.J. (2009), *Profit-building: Cutting Costs Without Cutting People*, San Francisco: Berrett-Koehler.

McKinley, W. (1993), 'Organizational decline and adaptation: theoretical controversies', *Organizational Science*, **4** (1), 1–9.

McKinley, W. and A.G. Scherer (2000), 'Some unanticipated consequences of organizational restructuring', *Academy of Management Review*, **25**, 735–52.

Miller, D. (2003), '"What is best value? Virtualism – the larger context?" New managerialism and changing forms of organisational governance: governance without government', in H. Dumer (ed.), *Gouverner Les Organisations*, Paris: L'Harmatton, pp. 288–313.

Mishra, A.K. and G.M. Spreitzer (1998), 'Explaining how survivors respond to downsizing: the roles of trust, empowerment, justice and work redesign', *Academy of Management Review*, **23**, 567–88.

Morgan, P. and N. Allington (2002),'Has the Public Sector Retained its "model employer status?"', *Public Money and Management*, **22** (1), 35–42.

Morris, J.R., W.F. Cascio and C.E. Young (1999), 'Downsizing after all these years: questions and answers about who did it, how many did it, and who benefited from it', *Organizational Dynamics*, **27**, 78–87.

Morris, J., and C. Farrell (2007), 'The "post-bureaucratic" public sector organization. New organizational forms and HRM in ten UK public sector organizations', *International Journal of Human Resource Management*, **18** (9), 1575–88.

Noer, D. (1993), 'Healing the wounds: overcoming the trauma of layoffs and revitalizing organizations', San Francisco: D. Jossey-Bass.

Peretz, M. and P. McGraw (2011), 'Trends in Australian human resource development practice, 1996–2009', *Asia Pacific Journal of Human Resources*, **49** (1) 36–54.

Peters, G.B. and D.J. Savoie (1998), *Taking Stock: Assessing Public Sector Reforms*, Montreal: McGill-Queen's University Press.

Pfeffer, J. (1994), 'Competitive advantage through people: unleashing the power of the workforce', Boston: Harvard University Press.

Pfeffer, J. (1998), *The Human Equation: Building Profits by Putting People First*, Boston, MA: Harvard Business School Press.

Pollitt, C. and G. Bouckaert (2000), *Public Management Reform: A Comparative Analysis*, New York: Oxford University Press.

Potter, M. (2011), 'Unions swell ranks of Occupy Wall Street protesters', *Toronto Star*, 6 October, accessed on 24 October 2011 at http://www.thestar.com/news/world/article/1065036--unions-swell-ranks-of-occupy-wall-street-protesters.

Roche, W.K., C. Teague, A. Fahy and M. Final (2011), Report presented to the Labour Relations Commission, January 2011, pp. 1–45, accessed 2 September 2011 at http://www.lrc.ie/documents/symposium11/Exec-Summary-Human-Resources-in-the-Recession.pdf.

Rosenblatt, Z. and B. Mannheim (1996), 'Organizational response to decline in the Israeli electronics industry', *Organization Studies*, **17** (6), 953–84.

Rothenbacher, F. (1997), 'Public sector employment in Europe: where will the decline end?', *Eurodata Newsletter*, **6**, 1–11.

Schick, A. (1998), 'Why most developing countries should not try New Zealand's reforms', *World Bank Research Observer*, **13** (1), 123–31.

Schneider, M. (2005), 'The status of U.S. public pension plans: a review with policy considerations', *Review of Public Personnel Administration*, **25** (2), 107–37.

Scott, B.G. and C.J. Ueng (1999), 'Downsizing and firm long-term performance', *Proceedings of the Financial Management Association Annual Conference*, Orlando, FL, October.

Seldon, S.C. (2006), 'The impact of discipline on the use and rapidity of dismissal in state governments', *Review of Public Personnel Administration*, **26**, 335–55.

Serwer, A.E. (1995), 'Layoffs tail off – but only for some', *Fortune*, 20 March, p. 14.

Sheaffer, Z., A. Carmeli, and M.S. Zionit (2009), 'Downsizing strategies and organizational performance: a longitudinal study', *Management Decision*, **47** (6), 950–74.

Shim, D. (2001), 'Recent human resources developments in OECD member countries', *Public Personnel Management*, **30** (3), pp. 323–47.

Skelley, B.D. (2002), 'The ambiguity of results: the assessments of the new public management', *Public Administration and Management: An Interactive Journal*, **7** (2), 168–87.

Smith, A. (2003), 'Recent trends in Australian training and development', *Asia Pacific Journal of Human Resources*, **41** (2), 231–44.

Stanford, J. (1995), 'Forum: debt and disorder in the world economy: the economics of debt and the remaking of Canada', *Studies in Political Economy*, **48**, 113–35.

Terpstra, E.D. and J.E. Rozell (1993), 'The relationship of staffing practices to organizational level measures of performance', *Personnel Psychology*, **46**, 27–48.

Tregaskis, O. and Brewster, C. (1998), 'Training and development in the UK context: an emerging polarization?', *Journal of European Industrial Training*, **22** (4/5), 180–89.

Tumulty, K. (2011), 'Wisconsin governor wins battle with unions on collective bargaining', *Washington Post*, 11 March, accessed on 24 October 2011 at http://www.washingtonpost.com/wp-dyn/content/article/2011/03/10/AR2011 031005940.html.

Tzafrir, S., H.C. Ben-Gal and S. Dolan (in press), 'Exploring the aetiology of positive stakeholder behavior in global downsizing', in C.L. Cooper, J.C. Quick and A. Pandey (eds), *Downsizing: Is Less Still More?*, Cambridge, UK: Cambridge University Press.

Virtanen, P., A. Saloniemi, J. Vahtera, M. Kivimaäki, M. Virtanen and M. Koskenvuo (2006), 'The working conditions and health of non-permanent employees: are there differences between private and public labour markets?', *Economic and Industrial Democracy*, **27** (1), 39–65.

Vivekanandan, B. (2002), 'Welfare state system in Canada: emerging challenges', *International Studies*, **39** (1), 45–63.

Walker, J.W. (1992), *Human Resource Strategy*, New York: McGraw-Hill.

Wallis, J. and B. Dollery (2001), 'Government failure, social capital and the appropriateness of the New Zealand model for public sector reform in developing countries', *World Development*, **29** (2), 245–63.

Wayhan, V.B. and S. Werner (2000), 'The impact of workforce reductions on financial performance: a longitudinal perspective', *Journal of Management*, **26** (2), 341–63.

Weikart, L.A. (2003), 'Allocation patterns among the new public management mayors', *Public Performance and Management Review*, **27** (1), 37–52.

Weitzel, W. and E. Jonsson (1989), 'Decline in organizations: a literature integration and extension', *Administrative Science Quarterly*, **34** (1), 91–109.

Wright, P. and S. Snell (1998), 'Toward a unifying framework for exploring fit and flexibility in strategic human resource management', *Academy of Management Journal*, **23** (4), 756–73.

11. Motivation, job satisfaction and retention/turnover in the public sector

Wouter Vandenabeele

INTRODUCTION: WHY SHOULD WE EVEN BOTHER?

Within the framework of human resources management in the public sector, it is essential to reflect upon motivation, job satisfaction and retention as related concepts. Most public sector organizations employ large cohorts of people, without which these organizations would not be able to operate at all. For all organizations – public, private or non-profit – employees are crucial to the daily operations (Kojasteh, 1993). Moreover, contrasted to the private sector organizations, where the competitive advantage often lies in physical or financial capital that is owned by a company, this is not the case in the public sector. Next to a set of legal resources – granted by political processes – the competitive advantage (if any) of public sector organizations is often situated with its human resources. The difference between a poor-performing and a well-performing police force can often be found in its officers and similarly the difference between an effective ministry and an ineffective one is often reflected in its civil servants.

When pondering upon this observation, it is necessary to dig deeper and go beneath the surface of the human resources that form the basis of the observation. If one asks oneself why these human resources make a difference, it is very easy to arrive at the related concepts of motivation, job satisfaction and retention.

For motivation, there are several reasons why it should be considered a pivotal concept in the operations of public sector organizations.

First, in a labor market that is growing increasingly tight due to demographic shifts, individual motivation is a crucial variable. Long-term forecasts project a decrease in the labor market population over the next 20 to 30 years (Little and Triest, 2001; Muenz, 2007; Productivity Commission,

2005), which will cause the power to shift from the employer – where it has resided until recent years – to the prospective employee. Despite the labor market being a forced market where participants cannot avoid participation (Mollemans and Proos, 1990) – putting it very crudely, no employment means no food or shelter or at least a grim-position in society – it is no longer guaranteed that all demand for labor by prospective employers is satisfied. Recruiting employees is no longer a sole decision of the employers but is increasingly up to the prospective employee, the supply side of the labor market, where these resources will be allocated. It is up to the prospective employee to decide where he or she will work. Evidently, there still will be sectors or countries where the power will remain mainly or fully with the employers as the supply side of the labor market is still saturated, but more and more we will see this shift taking place, in particular in those sectors where talented or skilled people are high in demand. Employer attractiveness and employer branding – the weapons to wage this war of talent – rely greatly on the concept of motivation. The goal is to have people select a particular organization over all other contenders as a prospective employer and the way to do this is to motivate people to do so (Backhaus and Tikoo, 2004; Vandenabeele, 2008a).

Second, it is not sufficient to staff an organization. New public management has drawn attention to the (lack of) performance of public sector organizations (Aucoin, 1990; Hood, 1991). Societal changes and political ideologies have created a climate in which government and its associated organizations are no longer without scrutiny. Nowadays, public organizations have to deliver what is expected from them, they have to perform and motivation of individual employees has been identified as one of the most crucial variables in creating effective public organizations and enhancing performance (Rainey and Steinbauer, 1999; Brewer and Selden, 2000; Kim, 2005).

Third, public administration and public management is not only about doing things right, but it also about doing the right things. Whereas private sector organizations' main goal is to create return on capital – as illustrated by Alfred Sloan 'The strategic aim of a business is to earn a return on capital, and if in any particular case the return in the long run is not satisfactory, then the deficiency should be corrected or the activity abandoned for a more favourable one' (Grant, 2002: 37) – public sector organizations have to adhere to a much more complex set of principles. Government has to ensure the rights of citizens (for example, due process in the US), but also uphold general principles as the rule of law or other public values oriented toward the internal or external operation of the public sector (Jorgensen and Bozeman, 2007). As accountability mechanisms dwindle or shift due to new public management reforms, motivation of individual employees can act as a corrective (Moynihan, 2008), which again is a crucial variable when thinking about public management.

A related concept is job satisfaction, particularly from a practitioner's perspective this is also important to consider when thinking about strategy and human resources management (HRM) in the public sector. Job satisfaction is an easy to assess variable in daily management practice, at least much easier than, for example, motivation. Most reasonably sized organizations conduct annual or bi-annual job satisfaction surveys to assess the level of job satisfaction with their employees. There are a plethora of instruments available to assess its relative presence or absence – The Job Satisfaction Survey, The Job Descriptive Index, The Minnesota Satisfaction Questionnaire – in order to provide quantitative evidence (Fields, 2002). Job satisfaction, because it is so easy to assess, is often used as a proxy for other attitudes or types of behavior, thus enhancing its status as a major HR-outcome in any organization. In particular from a public sector perspective, job satisfaction is also to some extent considered to be a desirable end-state. Government has, since the 1970s been considered to be a model employer. It therefore should not merely strive to be effective in its policy, it should also explicitly strive for employee well-being (Boyne et al., 1999; Farnham and Horton, 1996). Despite the fact that, due to public management reforms, public sector organizations have to some extent lost this appeal, they are still important when considering HRM in the public sector – partly due to the collective system of labor relations.

Another related concept to consider when discussing human resources in the public sector is retention or its antithesis, turnover. Although it is also strongly related to the concepts of motivation and job satisfaction (Mobley et al., 1979; Griffeth et al., 2000), there are some important distinctions. First, it is, contrary to motivation or job satisfaction, not an attitudinal concept. Instead, it refers to actual behavior, in this case withdrawal behavior (for example, comparable to absence), and is therefore not subjective or a perception, but objective. It is a 'relatively clear-cut [act] of behavior that [has] potentially critically consequences for both the person and for the organization (Porter and Steers, 1973: 151). This makes it highly visible and therefore easy to assess, almost as a by-product of daily operations. Second, as it has 'potentially critical consequences for the organization', it is evident that this is a concept that has drawn much attention in the past and is still creating a sense of urgency with those who are involved in HRM, both in the public and private sectors.

For these reasons, it is important to address motivation and job satisfaction as well as retention when looking at practical human resources issues. These are concepts one cannot do without when discussing HRM in the public sector. Due to their interrelatedness, it is beneficial to study them simultaneously, as has been done in this chapter. First, an overview of motivational theories that apply to public sector employment will be provided. Next, job satisfaction will be discussed, both as a concept and as a correlate of motivation, and both of the former concepts will be related to turnover and retention. Finally, the relevance for practitioners is reviewed and some handles for practical application are provided.

MOTIVATION IN THE PUBLIC SECTOR: PUBLIC SECTOR MOTIVATION vs. PUBLIC SERVICE MOTIVATION

Few topics in the study of management have been addressed to the same extent as work motivation. In past decades, motivation has not only stirred psychologists, but also sociologists, economists and other social scientists to study what drives human behavior in an organizational setting. Much of the initial knowledge on what motivates people stems from research in a private sector environment (Perry and Porter, 1982). However, gradually, research on public sector organizations increased and the results demonstrated both similarities (Buelens and Van den Broeck, 2007) and differences (Rainey, 1982; Crewson, 1997; Houston, 2000) between the motivations of public and private employees. This observation led to the conclusion that, on the one hand, private sector knowledge can be useful when looking at public sector employees' motivation; but, on the other hand, some things are particular to the public sector (although some scholars dismiss this latter finding (Gabris and Simo, 1995)). This amalgam of motivations that motivate public sector employees is therefore termed 'public sector motivation' (Brewer and Selden, 1998; Perry and Hondeghem, 2008), as it refers to multiple motivations: that people have to join the public sector, work and develop their careers there. In this next section, a number of elements of this public sector motivation will be addressed. First, the more general theories, not particular to the public sector and mainly derived from private sector research, will be addressed. Second, more specific elements of work motivation in the public sector will be discussed.

General Types of Motivation

Theories of job motivation can be divided into two general groups (Rainey, 2009). Need theories or content theories are concerned with the particular needs, motives or rewards that affect motivation. They are opposed to process theories, which are more concerned with the psychological process behind motivation. First, we will address some of the more prominent need theories, followed by some of the most prominent general process theories. Evidently, the scope of this chapter does not allow for a full treatment of all available theories, but a selection has been made based on the applicability and usefulness for public sector organizations (for further reading, see Pinder (2008) or Reeve (2009)).

Need theories
One of the most widespread theories of motivation is the theory by Maslow (Rainey, 2009). The theory, which in its earliest form claims that people have five hierarchical needs: physiological, safety, social, esteem and self-actualization needs; and that a lower need should be satisfied before another higher need can be addressed, has great appeal to practitioners in various parts of society. However, despite its appeal, empirical evidence which supports the theory has, up to now (half a century later), not been provided. Whether this is due to the complexity of the theory or to the theory just being wrong remains unsettled (Pinder, 2008). However, given the lack empirical support, relying on Maslow to address motivational issues in any field would appear foolish.

Another needs theory of similar seniority is the motivator-hygiene theory by Herzberg et al. (1959). Herzberg begins with making the, later very popular, distinction between intrinsic and extrinsic factors of motivation. Intrinsic elements (motivators in his terminology) are those which are directly associated with the task at hand. Examples are growth, autonomy, achievement, etc. These enhance satisfaction, which, according to Herzberg, in their turn will enhance performance. Extrinsic elements (hygiene factors in his terminology) are not associated with the task at hand but with outcomes of the task. Examples are working conditions, security, supervision, etc. Hygiene factors prevent people from being dissatisfied, but they have only a confined role in enhancing satisfaction. Therefore, their motivational potential is limited. Despite the apparent lack of empirical evidence that also plagued this framework, the theory has more credibility that its predecessor. This is largely due to the important legacy left by Herzberg, as there are the differences between extrinsic and intrinsic motivational factors and the concepts of job design and particularly job enrichment. The theory, or some elements of it in one form or another, has also been applied within a public sector setting to explain behavior or attitudes (Moon, 2000; Vandenabeele et al., 2004).

One of the most recent and most well developed need theories is the job characteristics model (Hackman and Oldham, 1980). The model claims that there are five basic job characteristics – skill variety, task identity, task significance, autonomy and feedback from the job – that address needs which, once satisfied, render critical psychological states (meaningfulness, responsibility and knowledge of the results)which in turn render positive work outcomes (both attitudes and behavior). Although a review of the literature suggest that 'corrections and modifications are needed' (Fried and Ferris, 1987: 311), there is solid evidence that the general propositions of the theory are valid (for example, the links between job characteristics and work-related attitudes) but that the particular features (for example, the factorial structure) cannot always be corroborated (Parker et al., 2001). As the analyses have been based on the private sector, public sector and mixed samples, the model also demonstrated validity for public sector application (Fried, 1991).

Process theories
Process theories do not depart from the proposition that needs are the basis for motivation and behavior. Conversely, process theories are more concerned with the psychological processes behind motivation and as a result, they have a less normative foundation (as it does not rely on needs as compulsory drives or values as desirable end-states).

A first and very prominent theory that fits into the category of process theories is the goal-setting theory (Locke and Latham, 1990). Central to this theory is the focus on goals as determinants of behavior. Goals are anything a person tries to attain or accomplish and are therefore the aim or object of an action (Locke and Latham, 2002). The basic components of goal-setting theory are goal content and goal commitment (Latham and Locke, 1991). Goal content refers to the nature of the goal and the theory states that specific goals and difficult goals increase motivation. Goal commitment refers to both self-efficacy about achieving the goal and the actual importance of the goal to the individual. Goal-setting has been one of the most dominant motivational theories of the last decades (Latham and Pinder, 2005). It has generated a lot of empirical support, also in the field of public management. The theory has been adapted to the specifics of the public sector (Wright, 2001) and has subsequently been corroborated by empirical data (Wright, 2004; Wright, 2007), adding to its status as a valid and applicable theory in many settings.

Another theory that has gained a substantial amount of attention in the last few decades is the person-environment fit theory. Based upon the attraction-selection-attrition framework (Schneider, 1987), the theory assumes that for situations in which the individual fits with the environment or some of its elements – the job, supervisor, team, organization – motivation is enhanced and thus beneficial outcomes are rendered (Kristof et al., 2005). This fit could be either complementary (one party has something another needs) or supplementary (one party resembles another). Despite its seeming simplicity, the framework has provided consistent outcomes (Kristof, 1996; Kristof et al., 2005; Verquer et al., 2003) and it should be credited for taking the environment into account to a much larger extent than the theories previously discussed. It thus succeeds better in bridging the gap between psychology and other social science perspectives than other theories. In a public sector environment, the framework has proven its usefulness for explaining various outcomes (Moynihan and Pandey, 2008; Vigoda-Gadot and Meiri, 2007, Vigoda, 2000).

Some theories combine both process theory characteristics as well as need theory characteristics. A prime example, and one of the most promising theories in the field of management, is the self-determination theory (SDT) (Deci and Ryan, 2004). Although it did not originate as a theory of work motivation, it is making rapid progress in the field of management (Gagné et al., 2010). SDT starts from the observation that the difference between extrinsic and intrinsic motivation is not sufficient to explain self-regulated behavior. Based on the earlier work of Deci (1975), a more elaborate typology of motivation has been developed, in which the distinction is made between intrinsic motivation, on the one hand, doing things because one inherently enjoys them; and four types of extrinsic motivation, on the other hand (Gagné and Deci, 2005). An initial type of extrinsic motivation (or regulation) is external regulation, referring to the motivation of doing something because one wants to obtain an external reward or to avoid an external consequence. A second type is introjection, which refers to when a regulation has been taken in, but has not been accepted by the person. Guilt and esteem play an important role in this respect. A third type of extrinsic motivation is identified regulation, when one is motivated to do something because it is important to them and they identify with it. The final type of extrinsic motivation is integrated regulation. In this case identification does not only influence the behavior targeted at the object of identification (for example a nurse caring his/her patients) but also behavior targeted at other objects (a nurse also motivated to care for other people). The first two types of extrinsic regulation are controlled types, as individuals experience an external perceived locus of control; whereas the latter two types are autonomous, as individuals perceive an internal locus of control, as the regulation has been more internalized. The various types of motivation can be placed on a continuum from external regulation at one end, to introjection, identification and integration and finally to intrinsic motivation at the other end. The closer one gets to intrinsic motivation, the stronger the link between the type of motivation and behavior will be (Ryan and Deci, 2004). However, it must be stressed that this is not a stage-process, in which an individual moves gradually towards intrinsic motivation (Gagné and Deci, 2005). The link between process and need theories lies in the claim that, to the extent that basic psychological needs of autonomy, competence and relatedness are satisfied, individuals will become more autonomously motivated (Gagné and Deci, 2005). This not only provides a clear bridge between these two types of theory, but it also enables the theory to take into account the environment, when addressing individual motivation (Vandenabeele, 2007). It also provides links with some of the aforementioned theories, such as the goal-setting theory or the job characteristics model (Gagné and Deci, 2005). Due to its recent inception and due to the fact its roots lie elsewhere, there has only been limited evidence supporting the validity of the theory in a public sector environment. However, some recent examples demonstrate promise for public sector applications (Kuvaas, 2008; Van den Broeck et al., 2008).

A related theoretical framework, as it stems from the same theoretical predecessor, is motivation crowding theory (Frey, 1997). Like SDT, it also relies heavily on cognitive evaluation theory in addressing the question on how various types of motivation interact. The core of the theory is that external interventions may or may not be deleterious to intrinsic motivation. Based on the principles of cognitive evaluation theory (Deci, 1971), but also on psychological contract theory (Rousseau, 1995), the theory states that initial autonomous motivation (in the words of Frey 'intrinsic' motivation) will be removed and replaced by controlled motivation (in the words of Frey 'extrinsic' motivation) if the intervention is perceived as controlling (crowding-out). However, if the intervention is seen as supportive, initial controlled motivation may be replaced by autonomous motivation (crowding-in). The external intervention may refer to material or monetary rewards, but also other activities such as monitoring systems, deadlines or feedback. Frey (Frey, 1997; Frey and Regen, 2001) identifies saliency of the intervention, contingency of the intervention with the task and deadlines and intense control or threats as conditions that foster crowding-out, whereas interventions that build personal relationships, foster communication, enhance participation and stimulate crowding-in. In addition, interesting tasks are particularly prone to crowding-in processes. In a public sector environment, both crowding-in and crowding-out effects, in particular with regard to pay-for-performance and management control, have been identified (Vandenabeele, 2009b; Jacobsen and Andersen, forthcoming; Weibel et al., 2010).

Specific Types of Motivation for the Public Sector

Next to the general theories of motivation that have been presented above, practitioners and scholars alike have claimed that, due to the nature of the public sector, public sector employees are not motivated in an entirely similar way to other employees (Rainey, 1982; Wittmer, 1991). Research has demonstrated that particularly with respect to needs, public employees overall demonstrate a higher need for job security and a lower need for monetary rewards (Rainey, 1982; Wittmer, 1991; Houston, 2000; Khojasteh, 1993; Buelens and Van den Broek, 2007), without differing much on other needs.

There is however a set of needs which is systematically more prominent with public employees than with private sector employees (Mann, 2006; Houston, 2000). These needs, although around for more than two millennia (Horton, 2008), refer to what has, since the 1990s, been known as public service motivation (PSM). PSM has many definitions, but Perry and Wise (1990), who were the first to define it, describe it as 'an individual predisposition to respond to motives grounded primarily or uniquely in public institutions (368)'. As such, it refers to the 'motives [. . .] in the public domain that are intended to do good for others and shape the well-being of society' (Perry and Hondeghem, 2008: 3). There has been some debate on the dimensions of the PSM construct. Originally, Perry (1996) found four dimensions – attraction to public policy making, civic duty and public interest, compassion and self-sacrifice. Subsequent research, on the one hand, corroborated some of the dimensions; whereas, on the other hand, it supplemented or adapted the original concept (Coursey et al., 2008; Coursey and Pandey, 2007; Vandenabeele, 2008b; Kim, 2009; Ritz, 2009; Kim and Vandenabeele, 2010).

PSM theory departs from an institutional perspective (Perry, 2000; Vandenabeele, 2007) to explain why specific needs occur in a public sector environment and people act accordingly. It claims that institutions – value-based structural interaction patterns – socialize their members into identities which hold institutional values in high regard and therefore create needs particular to those institutions (Perry, 1997; Vandenabeele, 2011). However, at the same time, it relies heavily on other motivational perspectives to explain how these needs determine attitudes and behavior (Perry and Vandenabeele, 2008), thus linking institutional environment and individual motivation in a single framework. PSM has been positively related to outcomes within the public sector: such as employer attraction and job choice (Ritz and Waldner, 2011; Christensen and Wright, 2011; Vandenabeele, 2008a; Lewis and Frank, 2002; Steijn, 2008); various types of performance (Pandey et al., 2008; Brewer and Selden, 2000; Vandenabeele, 2009a; Ritz, 2009; Andersen, 2009; Bright, 2008); general work motivation (Wright, 2007) and ethical behavior (Brewer and Selden, 1998; Choi, 2004). It has also been negatively related to red tape perception (Scott and Pandey, 2005) and withdrawal behavior and attitudes

(Wright and Pandey, 2011; Steijn, 2008; Vandenabeele and Coursey, 2010). Many of these studies have applied PE-fit, goal-setting theory or self-determination theory as auxiliary frameworks in explaining the effect of PSM on the respective outcomes.

An important element to note is that, within a public sector environment, PSM operates next to other motives, being only one element of the general public sector motivation. However, it is remarkable the effects of other 'typical' needs that are found in the public sector, as job security and limited workload only seem to play a limited role in attraction processes (Vandenabeele, 2008; Ritz and Waldner, 2011; Christensen and Wright, 2011), but they are not reported in studies on the other outcomes. This observation points to the importance of autonomous motivation – and consequently PSM – when addressing these 'other' issues.

JOB SATISFACTION AND TURNOVER IN THE PUBLIC SECTOR

Research on job satisfaction has dominated the field of HRM and organizational behavior for a long time (Rainey, 2003). Although it is not a terminal outcome itself – except in the case of a prospective model employer – it has been related to various outcomes. It has been said to be related to potential effects such as job performance, motivation, organizational citizenship behavior, withdrawal behavior, burnout, psychological well-being and other outcomes that may be useful from a management perspective (Spector, 1997), although in some cases, these assumed relationships can be questionable (for example, in the case of performance, see Pinder (2008)), or at least more complex than assumed (Judge et al., 2001). Nevertheless, job satisfaction is considered to be an important indicator for signaling anything that might be wrong from a HR-perspective. This, in combination with the ease of collecting quantitative data on job satisfaction, makes the use of job satisfaction as a proxy for these types of behaviors very attractive.

Job satisfaction has been defined as 'a pleasurable or positive emotional state, resulting from the appraisal of one's job or job experiences' (Locke, cited in Gruneberg, 1979: 3). However, two approaches have developed. The first approach further elaborates the global perspective of an overall type of satisfaction, as described above. The second approach puts more emphasis on the various facets of the job and is concerned with identifying the various parts of the job that produce job satisfaction (Spector, 1997), such as pay, communication, coworkers, supervision, etc. This latter perspective makes it very hard to distinguish between antecedents of job satisfaction and the concept itself. Therefore, it will not be addressed here and job satisfaction should be understood in terms of the global, overall concept.

Whether someone is satisfied in his or her job, depends on a wide set of determinants. Spector (1997) distinguishes between environmental antecedents – job characteristics, organizational constraints such as supervision or pay, conflicts within the organizational roles, work-family conflict or other organizational determinants; and personal antecedents – personality traits, locus of control or motivation or gender. Nevertheless Rainey (2003: 275) notes that 'even so, some studies report contradictory findings for almost any antecedent'. Despite the contradictory findings, research results demonstrate that motivation has a strong correlation with job satisfaction. The above described general perspectives on motivation, as well as PSM, demonstrate clear and evident links with job satisfaction, both in the general population as well as in the public sector (Vansteenkiste et al., 2007; Wright and Davis, 2003; Wright and Pandey, 2008; Vandenabeele, 2009a).

As for the consequences of job satisfaction, similar controversy exists (Rainey, 2003). One often claimed outcome of job satisfaction is individual performance. However, this relationship – sometimes described as the 'Holy Grail' (Landy, 1989) – is much more ambiguous than it appears at first glance. A meta-analysis by Judge et al. (2001) has shown that although there is a robust correlation is most cases, there are seven possible ways to frame the relationship, and satisfaction causing performance is only one of those. Therefore, one should be hesitant in linking job satisfaction with performance without any further evidence.

However, one other outcome which is less disputed is retention, or more broadly speaking, withdrawal behavior (which also includes absenteeism). Retention, or the opposite concept of turnover, refers to voluntary staying or leaving a particular job. Retirement or unilateral dismissal by the employer cannot be considered as turnover – Porter and Steers (1973) therefore talk about avoidable turnover. Despite the many moderating and mediating factors – for example, alternatives or expectancies of future job outcomes – which weaken the direct relationship between job satisfaction and turnover (Mobley, 1977; Mobley et al., 1979), job satisfaction remains a robust predictor of turnover (Griffeth et al., 2000).

As turnover concerns potential disruptive behavior in an organization (Porter and Steers, 1973), studying job satisfaction can provide useful information to avoid such a disruption or to address it at an early stage. However, even if turnover or retention does not demonstrate itself as a critical event, it may be still useful to study turnover. After all, since it is the end of a causal chain that starts with motivation, and both motivation and job satisfaction are linked with other, perhaps even more critical types of organizational behavior, increased turnover rates may signal problems with this behavior. As turnover data is even easier to collect than job satisfaction data, it can serve as a much more cost-efficient proxy of HR-processes and outcomes (Hanisch and Hulin, 1991). Staffing numbers and headcounts are easy to come by, as they are often a by-product of other organizational or management processes and thus constitute a cheap source of information.

One problem with this use of turnover as a proxy for other concepts is that not all turnover is voluntary. In many cases, turnover is forced upon the employee. As already stated above, retirement, health problems or redundancy can make people leave the organization and thus bias the turnover as an indicator or signal function. Conversely, retention should not always be considered a good thing for an organization. People who are very dissatisfied with a job, and consequently may display a lack of motivation or behavior that is important to the organization, will not always leave the organization. A shortage of satisfactory alternatives in the job market may retain people, despite the fact that they are unhappy at their job, even to the extent that they are not productive. The public sector is prone to this kind of behavior – retaining employees as 'dead wood' (Elling and Thompson, 2008) – as it provides not only elaborate social protection due to unionization, but also delayed benefits by means of attractive retirement conditions. That is why another type of with-drawal behavior is sometimes studied: absenteeism. As with turnover, it is related to other outcomes (such as job satisfaction) and can thus be used as a proxy (Blau and Boal, 1989), being also very cost-efficient as a by-product of other human resources processes. In particular when more extreme types of withdrawal behavior are not likely to manifest them-selves, this strategy may be useful. Nevertheless, as with turnover, there are again some loopholes in this line of reasoning: there is voluntary or involuntary turnover, and only voluntary absenteeism is linked to job sat-isfaction (Sagie, 1998). Therefore, although both turnover and absentee-ism may provide useful information, excessive reliance on both concepts as critical indicators, without collecting additional information, may be counter-productive.

VALUE FOR PRACTITIONERS

When addressing the practicalities of HRM in the public sector, it is worthwhile considering the effect of motivation. This is particularly true for interesting and complex tasks in cases where performance levels are difficult or impossible to assess, which require sustained effort, as autonomous or intrinsic types of motivation are critical to this type of performance (Gagné and Deci, 2005; Weibel et al., 2010). This observation is also acknowledged in current strategic HRM literature, which considers motivation to be a crucial variable for individual performance and ultimately organizational performance (Boselie et al., 2005; Delery and Shaw, 2001).

As stated earlier, the withdrawal behavior could serve as an indicator to signal possible problems with employee motivation. Nevertheless, the main challenge is to translate the knowledge we have on motivation into readily applicable insights that address these motivational problems. Paarlberg et al. (2008) have developed an interesting framework to address issues of motivation and translate these into practical applicable tactics. The framework distinguishes between five levels on which motivation can be addressed. The first level is that of the individual HR-processes, the second refers to the level of the job and tasks at hand, the third to the work environment, the fourth to the mission and the fifth to the societal level. Although this framework was intended to address PSM issues, it can be broadened to address public sector motivation in general. In this chapter, we will only address the first four levels, as these are targeted towards the organization and its constituting elements.

Regarding the level of HR-processes, common HR-processes are recruitment and selection, development and evaluation, all clustered around performance (Tichy et al., 1982). In each of these processes, motivation can be addressed. For recruitment and selection – given that one would like to select autonomously motivated employees into the organization – it makes little sense for controlled motivations to be called upon. Therefore, rather than mainly drawing on monetary or other benefits, employers should try to create anticipatory person-organization fit through employer branding processes. Evidently, controlled motives should not be ignored, but addressing the right mix of autonomous and controlled motives as a foundation for fit will avoid attracting people who do not like the work or are not sufficiently motivated to perform and will eventually turn into 'dead wood'. PSM can play an important role in creating this PE-fit in the public sector, additionally providing a competitive advantage over non-public organizations. Development processes should not only address issues that make employees feel more competent, thus fulfilling their psychological need for competence, but they can also address socialization of PSM (for example, by means of mentoring programs or formal socialization tactics that explicitly aim at PSM). Appraisal and reward processes should avoid crowding-out existing autonomous task motivation and should aim at crowding-in controlled task motivation through careful evaluation of the rewards mix (avoid pay-for-performance) and the nature in which feedback is being provided (in a supportive rather than a controlled way).

At the job level various motivational perspectives intersect and as this level focuses on the core-task, there is a straight and direct link with job performance. The fit between the individual and the job is very important and various insights can provide input into how to design motivation jobs. Varied skills, 'whole' and meaningful tasks create more autonomous motivation and the job level provides ample opportunities to satisfy the needs of autonomy and competence, whereas for relatedness there is less room; however, relatedness is less important in this respect (Gagné and Deci, 2005; Hackman and Oldham, 1980). Emphasizing the social significance of the job (Grant, 2007) and setting clear goals with regard to public service and other types of performance – derived from broad goals and missions and interpreted by manager and supervisors – will also enable the creation of performance gains through enhanced PSM. This demonstrates the need to consciously design or redesign jobs.

At the level of the work organization, work motivation can be increased by: addressing basic psychological needs by having people participate in the design of empowering work structures, removing excessive control systems and creating other forms of staff participation, and developing cooperative interpersonal relationships between co-workers (Paarlberg et al., 2008). Not only does autonomous motivation becomes stronger, but also socialization processes of public values that form the basis of PSM are nurtured in this way. Another element of the work organization is the incentive structure, as it influences other work organization features. As previously stated, incentives may crowd out motivation and pay-for-performance is unlikely to be successful. It is also important to align incentive structures with other elements of the work organization. Wide salary dispersion may conflict with autonomous in general and PSM in particular, negating extra-role behavior (Deckop et al., 1999) and thus cross-cutting the development of interpersonal relationships or employees going the extra mile to participate in the development of the work organization rather than free-riding.

The final level concerns the organizational mission and associated strategy. Most organizations – in both the public as the private sectors – have mission statements nowadays. However, only a limited number apply it as a tool to enhance work motivation. When a mission is based on or formulated in terms of employees' aspirations, person-organization fit increases and value-based motivation (for example, PSM) increases likewise. However, this will only happen to the extent that this falls within the 'employees' zone of existing values' (Paarlberg and Perry, 2007: 396). By using stories and myths, but also symbols and logos, motivation can be enhanced. Leadership also plays an important role in translating the mission into motivation. Transformational leadership or other types of value-based leadership do not only enhance PSM or value-based motivation but they can also foster other types of motivation (Paarlberg and Perry, 2007; Dvir et al., 2002; Vandenabeele, forthcoming) by addressing basic psychological needs and creating a fit between the individual and the environment.

CONCLUSION

Motivation and the related concepts of job satisfaction and retention constitute a set of variables that is crucial to the practice of human resource management in the public sector. Whereas the latter two mainly serve as an indicator – the canary in the coal mine of the organization – of organizational processes influencing the individual employee in a positive or negative way, motivation can be considered to be a linchpin between the individual and their attitudes and behavior within the organization. Several motivational theories provide insights into the dynamics of motivation. Whereas the job characteristics model, goal-setting theory, person-environment fit theory and self-determination theory maintain a general perspective, but have demonstrated their usefulness within a public sector environment, PSM theory holds a clear idiosyncratic public sector perspective. In addition, both the advantages and disadvantages of the use of job satisfaction and retention or the opposed withdrawal behaviors as an indicator have been discussed. Finally, the link with modern human resources perspectives has been addressed and the theoretical insights have been translated into a number of suggestions regarding how to enhance motivation in day-to-day practice.

Despite the encompassing view this chapter tried to take, the field of motivation of employees is evidently much more elaborate than this brief overview would suggest. Some important theoretical venues – such as expectancy theory or social-cognitive theory – have not been discussed and a number of determinants of job satisfaction and withdrawal behavior have remained underdeveloped. Nevertheless, it is the author's firm belief that this account provides useful handles for address issues of motivation in a public sector environment and consequently will contribute to public performance.

REFERENCES

Andersen, L.B. (2009), 'What determines the behaviour and performance of health professionals? Public service motivation, professional norms and/or economic incentives', *International Review of Administrative Sciences*, **75** (1), 79–97.

Aucoin, P. (1990), 'Administrative reform in public management: paradigms, principles, paradoxes and pendulums', *Governance*, **3** (2), 115–137.

Backhaus, K. and S. Tikoo (2004), 'Conceptualizing and researching employer branding', *Career Development International*, **9** (5), 501–517.

Blau, G. and K. Boal (1989), 'Using job involvement and organizational commitment interactively to predict turnover', *Journal of Management*, **15** (1), 115–127.

Boselie, P., G. Dietz and C. Boon (2005), 'Commonalities and contradictions in HRM and performance research', *Human Resource Management Journal*, **15** (3), 67–94.

Boyne, G., M. Poole and G. Jenkins (1999), 'Human resource management in the public and private sectors: an empirical comparison', *Public Administration*, **77** (2), 407–420.

Brewer, G.A. and S.C. Selden (1998), 'Whistle blowers in the federal civil service: new evidence of the public service ethic', *Journal of Public Administration Research and Theory*, **8** (3), 413–439.

Brewer, G.A. and S.C. Selden (2000), 'Why elephants gallop: assessing and predicting organizational performance in federal agencies', *Journal of Public Administration Research and Theory*, **10** (2), 685–711.

Bright, L.A. (2008), 'Does public service motivation really make a difference on job satisfaction and turnover intentions of public employees', *American Review of Public Administration*, **38** (2), 149–166.

Buelens, M. and H. Van den Broeck (2007), 'An analysis of differences in work motivation between public and private sector organizations', *Public Administration Review*, **67** (1), 65–74.

Choi, D.L. (2004), 'Public service motivation and ethical conduct', *International Review of Public Administration*, **8** (2), 99–106.

Christensen R.K. and B.E. Wright (2011), 'The effects of public service motivation on job choice decisions: disentangling the contributions of person-organization fit and person-job fit', *Journal of Public Administration Research and Theory*, **21** (4), 723–743.

Coursey, D. and S. Pandey (2007), 'Public service motivation measurement: testing an abridged version of Perry's proposed measurement scale', *Administration and Society*, **39** (5), 547–568.

Coursey, D., J.L. Perry, J.L. Brudney and L. Littlepage (2008), 'Psychometric verification of Perry's public service motivation instrument: results for volunteer exemplars', *Review of Public Personnel Administration*, **28** (1), 79–90.

Crewson, P.E. (1997), 'Public-service motivation: building empirical evidence of incidence', *Journal of Public Administration Research and Theory*, **7** (4), 499–518.

Deci, E.L. (1971), 'Intrinsic motivation, extrinsic reinforcement, and inequity', *Journal of Personality and Social Psychology*, **22** (1), 113–120.

Deci, E.L. (1975), *Intrinsic Motivation*, New York: Plenum.

Deci, E.L. and R.M. Ryan (2004), *Handbook of Self-determination*, Suffolk: The University of Rochester Press.

Deckop, J.R., R. Mangel and C. Cirka (1999), 'Getting more than you pay for:

organizational citizenship behavior and pay-for-performance plans', *Academy of Management Journal*, **42** (4), 420–428.

Delery, J.E. and J.D. Shaw (2001), 'The strategic management of people in work organizations: review, synthesis and extension', *Research in Personnel and Human Resources Management*, **20**, 165–197.

Dvir, T., D. Eden, B.J. Avolio and B. Shamir (2002), 'Impact of transformational leadership on follower development and performance: a field experiment', *Academy of Management Journal*, **45** (4), 735–744.

Elling, R. and L. Thompson (2008), 'Dissin the deadwood or coddling the incompetents? Patterns and issues in employee discipline and dismissal in the States', *International Journal of Public Administration*, **31** (5), 552–573.

Farnham, D. and S. Horton (1996), *Managing People in the Public Services*, London: MacMillan.

Fields, D.L. (2002), *Taking the Measure of Work: A Guide to Validated Scales for Organizational Research*, Thousand Oaks: Sage.

Frey, B.S. (1997), *Not Just for the Money – An Economic Theory of Personal Motivation*, Cheltenham: Edward Elgar.

Frey, B.S. and R. Regen (2001), 'Motivation crowding theory', *Journal of Economic Surveys*, **15** (5), 589–611.

Fried, Y. (1991), 'Meta-analytic comparison of the job diagnostic survey and job characteristics inventory as correlates of work satisfaction and performance', *Journal of Applied Psychology*, **95** (5), 690–697.

Fried, Y. and Ferris, G.R. (1987), 'The validity of the job characteristics model: a review and meta-analysis', *Personnel Psychology*, **40** (20), 287–322.

Jacobsen, C.B. and L.B. Andersen (forthcoming), 'Performance management for academic researchers: how publication command systems affect individual behavior', *Review of Public Personnel Administration*.

Gabris, G.T. and G. Simo (1995), 'Public sector motivation as an independent variable affecting career decisions', *Public Personnel Management*, **24** (1), 33–51.

Gagné, M. and E.L. Deci (2005), 'Self-determination theory and work motivation', *Journal of Organizational Behavior*, **26** (4), 331–362.

Gagné, M., J. Forest, M.-H. Gilbert, C. Aubé, E. Morin and A. Malorni (2010), 'The motivation at work scale: validation evidence in two languages', *Educational and Psychological Measurement*, **70** (4), 628–646.

Grant, A. (2007), 'Relational job design and the motivation to make a prosocial difference', *Academy of Management Review*, **32** (2), 393–417.

Grant, R. (2002), *Contemporary Strategy Analysis: Concepts, Techniques, Applications*, Malden, MA, USA: Blackwell.

Griffeth, R.W., P.W. Hom and S. Gaertner (2000), 'A meta-analysis of antecedents and correlates of employee turnover: update, moderator tests, and research implications for the next millennium', *Journal of Management*, **26** (3), 463–488.

Gruneberg, M.M. (1979), *Understanding Job Satisfaction*, London: Macmillan.

Hackman, J.R. and G.R. Oldham (1980), *Work Redesign*, Reading: Addison-Wesley.

Hanisch, K.A. and C.L. Hulin (1991), 'General attitudes and organizational withdrawal: an evaluation of a causal model', *Journal of Vocational Behavior*, **39** (1), 110–128.

Herzberg, F., B. Mausner and B.B.F. Snyderman (1959), *Job Attitudes: Review of Research and Opinion*, Pittsburgh: Psychological service of Pittsburgh.

Hood, C. (1991), 'A public management for all seasons', *Public Administration*, **69** (1), 3–19.

Horton, S. (2008), 'History and persistence of an idea and an ideal', in: J.L. Perry and A. Hondeghem (eds), *Motivation in Public Management: The Call of Public Service*, Oxford: Oxford university press, pp. 17–32.

Houston, D.J. (2000), 'Public service motivation: a multivariate test', *Journal of Public Administration Research and Theory*, **10** (4), 713–727.

Jacobsen, C.B. and L.B. Andersen (forthcoming), 'Performance management for academic researchers: how publication command systems affect individual behavior', *Review of Public Personnel Administration*.

Jorgensen, T.B. and B. Bozeman (2007), 'Public values: an inventory', *Administration and Society*, **39** (3), 354–381.

Judge, T.A., C.J. Thoresen, J.E. Bono and G.K. Patton (2001), 'The job-satisfaction performance relationship: a qualitative and quantitative review', *Psychological Bulletin*, **127** (3), 376–407.

Kim, S. (2005), 'Individual-level factors and organizational performance in government organizations', *Journal of Public Administration Research and Theory*, **15** (2), 245–261.

Kim, S. (2009), 'Revising Perry's measurement scale of public service motivation', *American Review of Public Administration*, **39** (2), 149–163.

Kim, S. and W. Vandenabeele (2010), 'A strategy for building public service motivation research internationally', *Public Administration Review*, **70** (5), 701–709.

Khojasteh, M. (1993), 'Motivating private vs. public managers', *Public Personnel Management*, **22** (3), 391–401.

Kristof, A.L. (1996), 'Person-organization fit: an integrative review of its conceptualizations, measurement and implications', *Personnel Psychology*, **49** (1), 1–49.

Kristof-Brown, A.L., R.D. Zimmerman and E.C. Johnson (2005), 'Consequences of individuals' fit at work: a meta-analysis of person-job, person-organization, person-group, person-supervisor fit', *Personnel Psychology*, **58** (2), 281–342.

Kuvaas, B. (2008), 'A test of hypotheses derived from self-determination theory among public sector employees', *Employee Relations*, **31** (1), 39–56.

Landy, F.J. (1989), *Psychology of Work Behavior*, Belmont: Thomson Brooks/Cole Publishing.

Latham, G.P. and E.A. Locke (1991), 'Self-regulation through goal setting', *Organizational Behavior and Human Decision Processes*, **50** (2), 212–247.

Latham, G.P. and C.C. Pinder (2005), 'Work motivation and research at the dawn of the twenty-first century', *Annual Review of Psychology*, **56**, 485–516.

Lewis, G.B. and S.A. Frank (2002), 'Who wants to work for government?', *Public Administration Review*, **62** (4), 395–404.

Little, J.S. and R.K. Triest (2001), 'The impact of demographic change on the labor markets', in J.S. Little and R.K. Triest (eds), *Conference Series 46: Seismic Shifts: the Economic Impact of Demographic Change*, Boston: Federal Reserve Bank of Boston, pp. 131–167.

Locke, E.A. and G.P. Latham (1990), *A Theory of Goal Setting and Task Performance*, Englewood Cliffs, NJ: Prentice-Hall.

Locke, E.A. and G.P. Latham (2002), 'Building a practically useful theory of goal setting and task motivation: a 35-year odyssey', *American Psychologist*, **57** (9), 705–717.

Mann, G.A. (2006), 'A motive to serve: public service motivation in human resource management and the role of PSM in the nonprofit sector', *Public Personnel Management*, **35** (1), 33–48.

Mobley, W.H. (1977), 'Intermediate linkages in the relationship between job satisfaction and employee turnover', *Journal of Applied Psychology*, **62** (2), 237–240.

Mobley, W.H., R.W. Griffeth, H.H. Hand and B.M. Meglino (1979), 'Review and conceptual analysis of the employee turnover process', *Psychological Bulletin*, **86** (3), 493–522.

Mollemans, W. and A. Proos (1990), *Arbeidsmarktbeleid: inzicht in de complexiteit arbeidsmarkt*, Deventer: Kluwer.

Moon, M.J. (2000), Organizational commitment revisited in new public management: motivation, organizational culture, sector, and managerial level', *Public Performance and Management Review*, **24** (2), 177–194.

Moynihan, D.P. (2008), 'The normative model in decline: public service motivation in the age of governance', in Perry, J.L. and A. Hondeghem (eds), *Motivation in Public Management: The Call of Public Service*, Oxford: Oxford University Press, pp. 247–267.

Moynihan, D.P. and S.K. Pandey (2008), 'The ties that bind: social networks, value-based commitment, and turnover intention', *Journal of Public Administration Research and Theory*, **18** (2), 205–227.

Muenz, R. (2007), *Aging and Demographic Change in European Societies: Main Trends and Alternative Policy Options*, Washington: World Bank.

Paarlberg, L. and J.L. Perry (2007), 'Values management: aligning employee values and organizational goals', *American Review of Public Administration*, **37** (4), 387–408.

Paarlberg, L.E, J.L. Perry and A. Hondeghem (2008), 'From theory to practice: strategies for applying public service motivation', in: Perry, J.L. and A. Hondeghem (eds), *Motivation in Public Management: The Call of Public Service*, Oxford: Oxford University Press, pp. 268–293.

Pandey, S.K., B.E. Wright and D.P. Moynihan (2008), 'Public service motivation and interpersonal citizenship behavior in public organizations: testing a preliminary model', *International Public Management Journal*, **11** (1), 89–108.

Parker, S.K., T.D. Wall and J.L. Cordery (2001), 'Future work design research and practice: towards an elaborated model of work design', *Journal of Occupational and Organizational Psychology*, **74** (4), 413–440.

Perry, J.L. (1996), 'Measuring public service motivation: an assessment of construct reliability and validity', *Journal of Public Administration Research and Theory*, **6** (1), 5–22.

Perry, J.L. (1997), 'Antecedents of public service motivation', *Journal of Public Administration Research and Theory*, **7** (2), 181–197.

Perry, J.L. (2000), 'Bringing society in: toward a theory of public service motivation', *Journal of Public Administration Research and Theory*, **10** (2), 471–488.

Perry, J.L. and A. Hondeghem (2008), 'Editors' introduction', in J.L. Perry and A. Hondeghem (eds), *Motivation in Public Management: The Call of Public Service*, Oxford: Oxford University Press, pp. 1–14.

Perry, J.L. and L.W. Porter (1982), 'Factors affecting the context for motivation in public organizations', *Academy of Management Review*, **7**, 89–98.

Perry, J.L. and W. Vandenabeele (2008), 'The behavioral dynamics of Public Service Motivation', in J.L. Perry and A. Hondeghem (eds), *Motivation in Public Management: The Call of Public Service*, Oxford: Oxford University Press, pp. 56–79.

Perry, J. and L.R. Wise (1990), 'The motivational bases of public service', *Public Administration Review*, **50** (3), 367–373.

Pinder, C.C. (2008), *Work Motivation in Organizational Behavior*, New York: Psychology Press.

Porter, L.W. and R.M. Steers (1973), 'Organizational, work, and personal factors in employee turnover and absenteeism', *Psychological Bulletin*, **80** (2), 151–176.

Productivity Commission (2005), *Economic Implications of an Ageing Australia: Research Report*, Canberra: Productivity Commission.

Rainey, H.G. (1982), 'Reward preferences among public and private managers: in search of a service ethic', *American Review of Public Administration*, **16** (4), 288–302.

Rainey, H.G. (2003), *Understanding and Managing Public Organizations*, San Francisco: Jossey-Bass.

Rainey, H.G. (2009), *Understanding and Managing Public Organizations*, San Francisco: Jossey-Bass.

Rainey, H.G. and P. Steinbauer (1999), 'Galloping elephants: developing elements of a theory of effective government organizations', *Journal of Public Administration Research and Theory*, **9** (1), 1–32.

Reeve, J. (2009), *Understanding Motivation and Emotion*, Hoboken: Wiley.

Ritz, A. (2009), 'Public service motivation and organizational performance in Swiss federal government', *International Review of Administrative Sciences*, **75** (1), 53–78.

Ritz, A. and C. Waldner (2011), 'Competing for future leaders: a study of attractiveness of public sector organizations to potential job applicants', *Review of Public Personnel Administration*, **31** (3), 291–316.

Rousseau, D.M. (1995), *Psychological Contracts in Organizations: Understanding Written and Unwritten Agreements*, Thousand Oaks: Sage.

Ryan, R.M. and E.L. Deci (2004), 'An overview of self-determination theory: an organismic-dialectic perspective', in Deci, E.L. and R.M. Ryan (eds), *Handbook of Self-determination Research*, Suffolk: University of Rochester Press, pp. 3–33.

Sagie, A. (1998), 'Employee absenteeism, organizational commitment, and job satisfaction: another look', *Journal of Vocational Behavior*, **52** (2), 156–171.

Schneider, B. (1987), 'The people make the place', *Personnel Psychology*, **40**, 437–453.

Scott, P.G. and Pandey S.K. (2005), 'Red tape and public service motivation: findings from a national survey of managers in state health and human services agencies', *Review of Public Personnel Administration*, **25** (2), 155–180.

Spector, P. (1997), *Job Satisfaction: Application, Assessment, Causes and Consequences*, Thousand Oaks: Sage.

Steijn, B. (2008), 'Person-environment fit and public service motivation', *International Public Management Journal*, **11** (1), 13–27.

Tichy, N.M., C.J. Fombrun and A.M. Devanna (1982), 'Strategic human resources management', *Sloan Management Review*, **23** (2), 47–61.

Van den Broeck, A., M. Vansteenkiste, H. De Witte and W. Lens (2008), 'Explaining the relationships between job characteristics, burnout, and engagement: the role of basic psychological need satisfaction', *Work and Stress*, **23** (3), 277–293.

Vandenabeele, W. (2007), 'Toward a theory of public service motivation: an institutional approach', *Public Management Review*, **9** (4), 545–556.

Vandenabeele, W. (2008a), 'Government calling: public service motivation as an element in selecting government as an employer of choice', *Public Administration*, **86** (4), 1089–1105.

Vandenabeele, W. (2008b), 'Development of a public service motivation scale: corroborating and extending Perry's measurement instrument', *International Public Management Journal*, **11** (1), 143–167.

Vandenabeele, W. (2009a), 'The mediating effect of job satisfaction and organizational commitment on self-reported performance: more robust evidence of the PSM-performance relationship', *International Review of Administrative Sciences*, **75** (1), 11–34.

Vandenabeele, W. (2009b), *Management Interventions as Conditions for Motivation Crowding of Motivation in the European Commission: A Mediational Analysis of Basic Needs Satisfaction*, paper presented at the annual EGPA-conference, St. Julians, Malta.

Vandenabeele, W. (2011), 'Who wants to deliver public service? Do institutional antecedents of public service motivation provide an answer? ', *Review of Public Personnel Administration*, **31** (1), 87–107.

Vandenabeele, W. (forthcoming), 'Explaining public service motivation: the role of leadership and basic needs satisfaction', *Review of Public Personnel Administration*.

Vandenabeele, W. and D. Coursey (2010), *Explaining Career Attitudes – Public Service Motivation vs. Public Sector Motivation in Flemish State Government*, paper presented at the International Research Society for Public Management XIV annual conference, Bern, Switzerland.

Vandenabeele, W., A. Hondeghem and T. Steen (2004), 'The civil service as employer of choice in Belgium: how work orientations influence attractiveness of public employment', *Review of Public Personnel Administration*, **24** (4), 319–333.

Vansteenkiste, M., B. Neyrinck, C.P. Niemiec, B. Soenens, H. De Witte and A. Van den Broeck (2007), 'On the relations among work value orientations, psychological need satisfaction and job outcomes: a self-determination theory approach', *Journal of Occupational and Organizational Psychology*, **80** (2), 251–277.

Verquer, M.L., T.A. Beehr, and S.H. Wagner (2003), 'A meta-analysis of relations between person-organization fit and work attitudes', *Journal of Vocational Behavior*, **63**, 473–489.

Vigoda, E. (2000), 'Internal politics in public administration systems: an empirical examination of its relationship with job congruence, organizational citizenship behavior, and in-role performance', *Public Personnel Management*, **29** (2), 185–210.

Vigoda-Gadot, E. and S. Meiri (2007), 'New public management values and person-organization fit: a socio-psychological approach and empirical examination among public sector personnel', *Public Administration*, **86** (1), 111–131.

Weibel, A., K. Rost and M. Osterloh (2010), 'Pay for performance in the public sector – benefits and (hidden) costs', *Journal of Public Administration Research and Theory*, **20** (2), 387–412.

Wittmer, D. (1991), 'Serving the people or serving for pay: reward preferences among government, hybrid sector, and business managers', *Public Productivity and Management Review*, **134** (4), 369–383.

Wright, B.E. (2001), 'Public sector work motivation: review of current literature and a revised conceptual model', *Journal of Public Administration Research and Theory*, **11**, 559–586.

Wright, B.E. (2004), 'The role of work context in work motivation: a public sector application of goal and social cognitive theories', *Journal of Public Administration Research and Theory*, **14** (4), 59–78.

Wright, B.E. (2007), 'Public service and motivation: does mission matter?', *Public Administration Review*, **67** (1), 54–64.

Wright, B.E. and B.S. Davis (2003), 'Job satisfaction in the public sector: the role of work environment', *American Review of Public Administration*, **33** (1), 70–90.

Wright, B.E. and S.K. Pandey (2008), 'Public service motivation and the assumption of person – organization fit: testing the mediating effect of value congruence', *Administration and Society*, **40** (5), 502–521.

Wright, B.E. and S.K. Pandey (2011), 'Public organizations and mission valence: when does mission matter', *Administration and Society*, **43** (1), 22–44.

12. Trade unions and organizational change in the public sector: the new politics of public sector industrial relations

Miguel Martínez Lucio

INTRODUCTION

Changes in the public sector since the 1970s have been pretty dramatic in developed and developing countries, and since the 1990s one could argue many countries are now reforming and changing the structure and content of their public sector and relevant service provision. From a state oriented and collective logic in terms of public services there has been a steady shift toward a market and individualized approach. That this shift has brought countless issues, major social distortions and new forms of conflict is undeniable (see Martínez Lucio, 2007). However, the post-Second World War consensus on public services has been challenged. In terms of the regulation of employment within this sector there have been parallel changes as well. Public sector industrial relations have tended to be more regulated in one form or another, with trade unions being important in various countries within these processes. However, the process of marketization and de-centralization has questioned the role of these more regulated forms. The changes in terms of employment and worker representation have been broad, ranging from the greater use of subcontracting to the development of more intensive performance management schemes. One could argue that there has been greater work intensification within the way public sector workers perform their tasks and a greater sense of uncertainty, insecurity and flexibility.

In light of these facts, this chapter will endeavour to achieve four objectives. Firstly, it will outline in broad terms the way the public sector has been structured and managed in terms of its employment relations. There is a great deal of variety in relation to such traditions across different countries, but the aim will be to try to outline some of the salient features of such systems. Secondly, the changing nature of trade unionism will be discussed in relation to the public sector. It is my contention that we tend to view trade unions in quite a narrow manner, in many cases, yet the past 20 years have seen significant developments and processes of innovation in terms of their structures and strategy in the USA and key parts of the European Union. Thirdly, the chapter will outline the development of specific human resource management strategies (HRM) within the public sector. These have led to changes within employment relations, although how trade unions have in certain instances responded to these is worth noting, as is the fairly inconsistent and often contradictory development of HRM processes themselves within the sector. Finally, the chapter ends with an overall discussion about how unions should be viewed with regard to the public sector in terms of their innovative and new organizational agendas. The chapter ends with an outline of the contribution and necessity of trade unionism as a moral, social and economic player within the public sector.

UNDERSTANDING THE CONTEXT OF PUBLIC SECTOR INDUSTRIAL RELATIONS

It is generally argued that in broad terms the public sector system of employment has a tendency in most countries to be regulated (Bach et al., 1999). The role of the political imperative within the public sector (Ferner, 1987) is such that the role of formal rules and regulations appear to configure various aspects of the employment relation. However, there is a great deal of diversity and variety within this regulated context in terms of the level of regulation, the actors involved and the effectiveness of the processes (for example, efficiency, social rights amongst workers and even levels of corruption).

Firstly, positions within the public sector are normally more detailed and specific – that is not to suggest that this corresponds with any eventual outcomes in terms of worker behaviour. In this sense they are more bureaucratic in nature. In terms of recruitment, promotion and management structures are normally more delineated in one form or another. Employment contracts have, in relative terms, been more stable and linked to stronger internal labour markets and systems such as seniority. This can be seen to be the case in countries such as Japan and Spain, for example. The public sector has historically been, in most countries, separate in terms of its external labour market when compared to the private sector, consisting of a specific public sector identity and ethos. The public sector has been known not solely to have a distinct identity based on a specific ethos linked to 'public service', which, whilst varying in terms of degree of clarity and outcomes across countries, does determine a different set of roles. It also normally has very strong professional identities (see Kirkpatrick, 2006) which are high profile and resonant in comparative terms: for example, public health services, educational services and policing. There is a curious balance within the public sector – which again will vary in terms of the national context according to the point of emphasis – between bureaucratic forms of organizational control over workers on the one hand, and quite high levels of professional autonomy, especially at the higher end of public service employment (for example, academics and medical professionals). This curious mix of bureaucratic determination in terms of areas such as employment entry and exit, for example, run in parallel with quite high levels of autonomy in terms of task execution and decision-making in some areas of the public sector. Hence, the public sector can be driven by strong formal and informal rules within the management and conduct of its workforce.

The second feature, in general terms, is the importance of formal bargaining and/or political negotiation and intervention in relation to the processes of wage setting and the determination of working conditions more generally. The role of national and sectoral structures within the public sector in the European and US context has historically been significant in setting rates of pay, for example. This has emerged across time as a way of delineating the public sector and its social role, as in countries like Spain. In fact, such countries have a curiously different status of employment for civil servants, who are seen as permanent employees with quite unique terms and conditions of employment (with the aim of limiting any patronage and external influences on decision making). In countries such as the UK much has been determined by centralized bargaining although, as outlined later, this has begun to change. In Germany the role of formal bargaining mechanisms has been combined with unilateral regulation by public authorities (Keller, 2011). Hence, the terms and conditions of employment have been centralized (nationally or at sector level) and determined through unilateral regulation or collective bargaining.

Thirdly, whilst trade unionism is indeed varied across countries in terms of their levels of membership, legality and roles, within the public sector it could be argued that they are significant institutional actors in terms of influencing key aspects of work and employment regulation. In Nordic European countries trade unions generally continue to have membership levels well over 70 per cent. Whilst trade unions have suffered a marked decline in the private sector of various countries, the public sector – whilst not changing in this effect – has seen a greater degree of resilience in terms of membership levels. The public sector trade union tradition consists of various forms, ranging from specific occupational and public service sector unions to more general trade union structures. The trade union presence has been a central feature in those contexts with a more liberal democratic tradition of industrial relations in terms of collective bargaining, the establishment of rules for recruitment, progression and retention, and individual and collective worker representation on grievances. Having once been the passive dimension of industrial relations due to relatively stable employment and payment systems, as well as the growth or stability of the public sector in general, during the post-Second World War period, trade unions have, in the public sector, become more assertive and engaged across a range of issues in the past few decades.

Hence, we need to appreciate the nature of the public sector and its legacies before discussing the changes taking place. The public sector environment is a combination of formal rule-making, strong professional identity, organized stakeholders such as trade unions (and increasingly consumers as well) and relatively stable processes. Political contingencies remain an important factor, as Batstone et al. (1984) pointed out in the past. However, these have begun to change and be subjected to various pressures, although how these pressures are mediated provides the public sector with a unique set of features.

TRADE UNIONS AND ORGANIZATIONAL CHANGE

Focusing on trade unions, there is a tendency, amongst various observers of public sector human resource management and industrial relations (other than that covered by the field of sociology) to see trade unions through two sets of lenses. The first views public sector trade unions as being fundamentally part of a previous 'bureaucratic' legacy of the public sector, failing to innovate and come 'on board' the organizational changes driven through by marketization and managerialization. The second, which is closely related, tends to view the trade union movement as experiencing a sharp decline in membership terms, unable to cope with the social, economic and political changes of a more globalized and corporatized environment (see Martínez Lucio, 2006 for a review of these kinds of perspectives). These perspectives, unlike those linked to a more sensitive and grounded study of industrial relations, tend to ignore how trade unions are engaging with such changes, which we will discuss. Secondly, they tend to ignore the fact that trade unions evolve and adapt, and that they were adapting and innovating even before new forms of human resource management become vogue. Consequently, there are two things we need to discuss: the diverse tapestry of trade union roles historically in relation to the public sector, and the manner in which they are evolving strategically. Otherwise we are left with a binary vision of the world which does not understand trade unions.

Firstly, as mentioned above, trade unions have played a variety of roles in the regulation of the public sector in the case of the European Union, the US and countries such as Japan. In key parts of Latin America we have seen public service unions influence the regulation of employment relations through a combination of negotiation and mobilization at specific times. In addition, we can clearly detect a link between professional identity and professional association. This is not always linked to a more 'traditional' type of trade unionism, yet that separation is blurring, especially in the US and the UK. Hence, professional identity has become increasingly regulated through a range of bureaucratic processes, which can on occasion involve and be influenced by trade unions. Wilding (1982) highlights a further link between professional power and state intervention that reinforces the way services are delivered within the public services; and trade unions can facilitate this link.

Secondly, and following on from this point in terms of the radicalization of professionals, we have seen trade unions increasingly organize public sector workers in a more explicit manner. In particular, associations and specific groups such as teachers, nurses, doctors, and others have, since the 1960s in the western sphere of the European Union, engaged with a 'trade union-oriented' approach. There are reasons for this, such as the impact of performance measurement, restrictions in resources and new forms of management – as will be discussed; however, there are other factors. In the US, Germany, the UK, Spain and Japan, one could argue that the new union activist base of the 1960s within the private sector began to be reproduced in the public sector since the initial financial pressures on public services due to the economic crisis of the 1970s, but also due to the social changes in professional classes within education, the university system and social services. The radicalization of the student movement had direct effects on public service employment, especially amongst professionals. In effect, a new form of activist with a new type of political and democratic sensibilities began to emerge. This forms the political and sociological basis of the process of renewal and change within public service unionism. There are extensive discussions as to how this radicalization takes place (Bonnett, 1993) and what the source of that change is (for example, the role of class changes or equality orientations in terms of the teaching professions in the 1990s). However, the transformation of professional identity in the public sector in terms of new forms of radicalism and emancipatory politics is notable in various contexts. Furthermore, the impact of feminist movements 'within' and 'upon' trade unions contributes to a steady reformulation of trade union agendas. Pay differentials, and both direct and indirect discriminatory practices, begin to be challenged by trade unionists within their representative organizations and their employers. The increasing presence of women in the public sector, and, in the case of the UK, France and the US, migrant and minority ethnic workers as well, began to shift the focus of representation in relation to the workforce agenda (for example, working time, family related leave, religious holidays) and the membership composition of public service trade unions. Hence, trade unions began to widen their agenda of interests, and this has, in some cases, led to a new set of negotiating positions and content that began to accelerate in the 1990s around a range of formal political agendas within trade unions. The increasing sensitivity to the equality agenda is greater in the public sector of countries such as Denmark, the Netherlands, and the UK, for example, due to the nature of the employer – the state – which is as a legislator propagating equality in various forms. Hence, the take up of new forms of regulation on questions of equality, and similar initiatives in the European Union such as health and safety rules, has accelerated in the State and its direct employment sector due to these political contingencies, regulatory cultures and changing trade unions 'sociologically'. The 1990s begins to see trade unions, especially public service unions in developed countries, move out of their 'comfort zones' and work in a more diverse set of spaces. Be it UNISON in the UK, VERDI in Germany or the CCOO trade union in Spain – in relation to Europe – there are signs that trade unions have adapted to a new language of inclusion that challenges some of the negative features of earlier bureaucratic and hierarchical forms of management control. This is not generalizable; however, it has been significant in key cases.

The relevance to this discussion is that organizational change within trade unions is a phenomenon which is only partly linked to the changing nature of management. It also indicates that trade unions may read and interpret changes in terms of management, not solely as a threat to their own traditional roles, but also as a threat to the workforce in terms of these new, broader agendas. This means that, for example, developments in performance management systems within the public sector are in fact not solely engaged with or opposed due to their individualizing effect on collective worker identity and work-related processes, but also because they impact on workers in a broader sense in terms of health and equality terms, for example. This requires, therefore, that we comprehend trade unionism in terms of this broader view of what they do, if we are to fully comprehend the complexity of human resource management and change. Responses by trade unions, in the form of negotiations or mobilizations, to management 'change' initiatives may be linked to a broader range of concerns and views about their impact and the way they effect workers in the public sector by virtue of their gender, ethnicity, age, and not solely their professional status.

HRM AND TRADE UNIONS IN THE PUBLIC SECTOR

The question of HRM in relation to industrial relations and the trade union movement is a curious debate. The emergence of a more market-oriented and unitarist form of HRM since the 1980s has been the subject of a wide discussion. HRM now has an extensive literature. It has many dedicated journals and academic conferences. Many academics in the area of organizational and employment studies – especially within the Anglo-Saxon world – work within academic HRM Departments. However, the re-crafting of the language of personnel management and administration in the 1980s to include the term 'human resource management' was not without a critical debate (Keenoy, 1990). The re-labelling of employees or workers as human resources, and the presumed Americanization this entailed in terms of greater managerial prerogative, brought a significant set of responses. The central thrust of the process of re-labelling HRM presumed a more proactive approach on the part of managers, and represented a move away from an environment where outcomes had been negotiated in a more pluralistic organizational culture and process (Keenoy, 1990; Martínez Lucio and Weston, 1992). The main reactions focused on the challenge that this unitarist move presented to the tapestry of internal organizational representation. The debate was often presented by listing the differences between personnel management and HRM in terms of their cultural, strategic and technical features (Storey, 1994). The main concern here was with the consistency of change. HRM arrived as an Anglo-Saxon curiosity – an ideological mission in the US linked to the emergence of a new right (Guest, 1990) – that was also based on a steady undermining of regulatory cultures in the European and other contexts. In fact, HRM can be seen as an attempt to internalize regulation, taking it out of the arena of industrial relations, and locating it within the boundaries of the firm, and located firmly in terms of management prerogative rather than collective bargaining.

However, these developments in management strategy within the public sector may be the outcome of a diverse set of imperatives – technological, consumer power oriented, resource limitations and the impact of market/neo-liberal ideologies – such that they complicate the emphasis and orientation of management strategies (Martínez Lucio, 2007). There may be a shift to what some commonly label a 'hard' form of control-led HRM, but this does not mean that it is consistent or even effective. In a major overview of developments in HRM/new management practices (NMP) in the European, New Zealand and US contexts, Bach and Bordogna (2011) argue that most countries have adopted some type of public sector change in the form of outsourcing, performance management, the partial erosion of the status of public service employees and bargaining decentralization; but beyond the core Anglo-Saxon countries these changes are varied and uneven, suggesting no uniform development where state traditions remain significant, such as in Western Europe. In fact, they suggest this unevenness is also the case in the Anglo-Saxon liberal market economies. Convergence around NMP is questionable.

We can discuss ways in which trade unions have engaged with such issues across various dimensions, using the dimensions in Martínez Lucio and Roper (2011): HRM practices, performance management, communication strategies, the rethinking of collective participation, and the re-structuring of management into 'leadership'. To this we can add the form of the organization itself and the impact of outsourcing. This adds an external HRM dimension which unions have been known to respond to and influence.

Firstly, in terms of practices, HRM is often introduced as a set of practices under the label 'high commitment practices'. These can take many forms, but normally they are introduced in an ad hoc fashion. It can be done in a slightly disconnected manner, which actually exposes management to criticism from trade unions due to their tokenistic nature (Oswick and Grant, 1996). However, secondly, when it comes to questions of performance management, the issues become more challenging for trade unions and the workforce. In the UK and US context, there has been a more systematic use of performance management in terms of consumer surveys, cost-related measurements and new forms of workload management. These have led to trade unions and workers developing a more calculating view that in some cases can lead to a more instrumental outcome and view of work (Grimshaw and Roper, 2007). Be it educational attainment measures or efficiency measures, trade unions have found new spaces to be able to organize and question the validity of management claims as well as their social outcomes. The movement towards measurement opens a whole new dimension within industrial relations as the customer is referenced in terms of their needs, not solely by management vis-à-vis workers, but also by trade unions vis-à-vis management and governments. Thirdly, in terms of communication this has become a new space within which management can redefine the 'collective' traditions of public sector work in terms of representation through individual forms of communication such as team briefings, circulars, and email communications, to name a few. The problem here is that trade unions have increasingly been forced to develop their own forms of communication and engagement of an individual nature. The use of information outlets such as Internet-based websites that address individual issues and concerns is common in countries with strong traditions of collective union engagement, as well. In the UK, the Union Modernization Fund, which was developed by the government between 2003 and 2012, supported the development of a range of trade union websites in terms of their interactive features (Stuart et al., 2009). In addition, trade unions such as the CCOO public services section in Spain have developed a more focused dialogue and set of resources with regard to members. The curious issue here is that not only do trade unions on occasions respond to the substance of management actions; they are also propelled by such developments to reconsider their own internal communications and systems. There is a curious set of outcomes in this respect with regard to how unions 'learn' from management strategies even in the process of engaging against it in terms of the impact on their members. In Spain, trade unions have, in parts, absorbed the language of modernization referenced by management to redefine it as a more open and democratic process. There is evidence of unions seeking to undermine the more closed and bureaucratic features of management by defining organizational change as transparency, fairness and social effectiveness (author's own research in the Aragon Region). Whether this leads to substantive changes is another matter, but the field of communication is being widened and changed as management becomes subject to a range of counter-strategies and interventions. This is partly due to a fourth factor, which is the management use of such communication devices to by-pass collective regulation within the public sector. In this case, management are also seen in various contexts to try and push forward decision making at a faster pace that 'outflanks' trade unions due to their slower procedural processes. However, in the current context of public sector resources being challenged, it is now quite common to see unions revert to a more legal route in terms of their responses to such developments, for example, by referencing the way agreed consultation procedures may be ignored or undermined. A part of these changes, driven by management, are linked to a view of a more decentralized system of bargaining and consultation that allows for a greater degree of localization of public service delivery. However, as Fairbrother (1994) noted in the 1990s, attempts to de-centralize public service delivery and employment relations can have contradictory effects by bringing local management and trade union activists into the discussions and negotiations on a range of issues that had once been the preserve of higher level discussions. It potentially opens the management process concerning elements of the employment relation to a much wider discussion and set of challenges. This leads to a fifth dimension of HRM in the public sector (Martínez Lucio and Roper, 2011) as noted in the case of the UK and the US. Many new forms of management development focus on leadership, but also provide an ideological dimension of a neo-liberal nature, aimed at managing contexts with high levels of autonomous professionals (Lawler, 2009). Yet these developments allow trade unions to challenge the language and motives of governments in trying to 'commercialize' and 'liberalize' management because of the way they break with, or undermine, collective and democratic dialogue. There is increasing evidence of trade unions in various contexts questioning the way management education and training is driven by a private sector view. In the Royal Mail and National Health Services in the UK, the unions have managed to highlight the ideological uses of such developments and how they can undermine a more open and balanced social dialogue due to their more assertive nature.

In addition to these internal organizational features of HRM, there are also external features which have implications for industrial relations. The development of subcontracting in terms of public services has led to the development of a more decentralized and relatively boundary-less structure. The use of other private sector service providers in a range of public services is a dominant trend. Decentralization within the public sector has undermined the discourse of the good employer and had many negative effects on equality initiatives and developments (Conley et al., 2011). However, trade unions have responded to such developments in terms of decentralization in a variety of ways. Firstly, where possible they have opposed such developments through mobilizations and public campaigns, as in the case of the health services in the UK. They have also used sector-level bargaining frameworks and the legal rights of workers to sustain frameworks for maintaining the working conditions of those being transferred from public services to the private sector in terms of their area of work. There have also been attempts to manage subcontracting and regulate it through monitoring and engaging directly with the process, as in the recently privatized Irish telecommunications sector (MacKenzie, 2009).Trade unions have also developed strategies around worker centres and local community strategies in parts of the US as an attempt to engage with migrant workers employed by subcontractors and employment agencies (Fine, 2007); there are a range of research projects on unskilled workers who are employed in the public sector indirectly, and how campaigns around pay and decency at work have developed.

It is likely that in many cases trade unions have not responded strategically and effectively to the development of HRM as either a challenge to their role or as an opportunity for a new type of dialogue with management within public services. However, there are sufficient cases to show that there is no clear displacement effect from HRM strategies, and that it can be responded to in various ways by trade unionists and collective systems of representation. This is due to the broad and uneven nature of HRM itself, and the manner in which it is implemented, and also to the way it can lead to tensions as it exposes organizational relations and hierarchies to the responses of stakeholders who question its assertions. Whilst trying to 'de-politicize', such management-led developments actually 're-politicize' employment relations.

One response has been to try to create a high-trust dialogue on such issues within a framework of partnership working and mutual gain. This has been a significant development in the attempt to fuse HRM and industrial relations by re-constructing dialogue and discussion around broader issues that compel management to engage with social issues, whilst unions are forced to engage with efficiency-related issues. Rubenstein and McCarthy (2010) have studied school reform in the US, and how unions and management have collaborated on economic and social employment issues through on-going meetings and the establishment of a dialogue in a new and broader range of issues. These developments have been established due to the political commitment of those involved, intensive training in joint working, and, very importantly, stability in the respective leaderships of the interested parties. This allows for reciprocal relations to develop. In the UK, the health services have seen examples of such joint working in terms of focused training, on-going dialogue on reform around work and employment processes, and forms of conflict management through the role of the national conciliation body ACAS as a third party. The challenge facing such a dialogue has been maintaining relations and organizational memory on previous transactions at a time when there is a greater turnover in management and union staff, as well as increasing stress levels (Stuart and Martínez Lucio, 2008; Martínez Lucio and Stuart, 2007). As pointed out, there are problems such as instability in public sector management and trade union leadership. There also needs to be a political underpinning in terms of worker rights for such practices to be sustained (see Thörnqvist, 2007, on the Swedish case), a political commitment to trade unions, and a supportive and regulated learning environment within the organization and the labour market. If not, then such forms of dialogue and partnership can be used as a form of legitimation for implementing hard forms of management control and work intensification (Danford et al., 2011).

In effect, it is important that we therefore understand how trade unions develop strategies within, between and beyond workplaces of the public sector. These vary according to national and sector level contexts, yet there are different ways in which trade unions are inscribing themselves within the management and regulation of the public sector employment relations. Within the workplace we have seen how trade unions engage with parallel communications systems and new forms of individual relationships with their membership. These need not undermine their collective context: if anything, collectivism is premised on the representation of the individual. In relation to performance management, we see how measures can be used and referenced by trade unions, when they indicate high levels of productivity and effectiveness and low levels of rewards. Even on questions of absence management and the detailed micro-management of staff, it is not unheard-of for trade unions to establish alternative frameworks for the development of fair absence management and social management regimes (Perrett and Martínez Lucio, 2006). Externally, trade unions can establish social and political alliances around public services with social movements and non-government organizations more generally. The customer can be inscribed into mobilizations – as can their interests – in defence of public services, thus inverting the idea that the customer and their interests are opposed to collective representation and professional worker autonomy in the public sector. The moral space, which is the public sector and the services it provides, is subject to the intervention of a range of stakeholders, challenging the belief that management is the sole articulator of 'what customers want'. They are becoming an important feature of public service industrial relations in various developed and democratic contexts. These diverse strategies can underpin and enhance trade union interventions in the form of mobilizations *and* negotiations with regard to the public sector. The 'game' of public service industrial relations has more players and issues on the agenda and therefore more 'politics' (an irony, given the neo-liberal and managerial emphasis on markets and marketization as a de-politicizing process).

CONCLUSION: THE CONTRIBUTION OF UNIONS IN A CHANGING ENVIRONMENT AND THE ESTABLISHMENT OF NEW AGENDAS AND POLITICS

This chapter covers much ground, and representing the diversity of different national systems is not an easy task. However, hopefully what has been achieved is a view of public sector trade unions and industrial relations that considers them to be embedded in the politics, management and practices of the sector. In an age when management and business studies is replete with stereotypes and caricatures in terms of 'traditional ways of working', the negative role of 'bureaucracy' and the 'reactive' nature of 'trade unionism' in an 'individualized' world, it is essential that we are cautious and better informed about the realities of organizations and their contexts. Trade unions remain a significant part of the public sector and have been clearly innovating and developing new roles for the past 20 to 30 years. Research within a range of academic disciplines has confirmed the novel ways in which trade unions have attempted to shape public sector employment and service delivery in general. There are new and old roles combined, which have developed a new set of agendas within public services.

Firstly, and probably more obviously, there is a stronger bureaucratic feature to the determination of employment conditions within the public sector. Given the heavy reliance on performance measures and transparency, there is a new public bureaucracy and organizational process that has invited social and political engagement – partly by default, as some would argue the objective has been to intensify the work of public sector servants and workers. This has meant the once closed public realm has been opened, ironically, to new actors and discussions. It has also led to trade unions developing new individually and collectively focusing voice mechanisms in countries such as the UK, Spain, the Netherlands and the US. How effective these are remains to be seen, but they now form part of the tapestry of this sector.

Secondly, we have seen trade unions begin to articulate stronger commitments to equality – especially gender equality – in many OECD countries and their public services. Public sector trade unions have become spaces within which questions of gender, racial and sexual equality have found greater tolerance and engagement. This has major ramifications on management, as these issues are much higher on the organizational agenda in cases such as the US and the UK (not always known for strong systems of industrial relations generally); they bring to public sector management a greater challenge in terms of management processes. Issues of fairness and good employment best practices are a terrain that allows for trade union-led mobilizations, but also potential spaces for joint working between governments, management and trade unions.

Thirdly, the quality of the working environment remains important, especially as trade unions have faced up to work intensification and new concerns with issues such as bullying and workplace stress, by referencing the importance of the public servant and their positive predisposition in relation to those cared for in education, health and social services, for example. There is an increasing link made between the quality of working life and the quality of service. In a context of recession and public sector expenditure cuts, this has come to the fore throughout much of the European context. There is also a greater attention to issues such as mediation and conflict resolution within public services, given the public's sensitivity to the sector and any collective conflicts within it.

Finally, many of these developments are being discussed in what is a more co-ordinated set of international trade union structures within the public sector. This new feature will begin to resonate within public sector management as a greater degree of dialogue on the above is structured and used for the development of national strategies. Trade unions in the public services are thus becoming more strategic and more innovative as they systematically fuse consumption issues with production/service delivery issues. The emergence of an international set of public service trade union structures will contribute to this as experiences and innovation within trade unions are shared. It varies by place, but there is enough evidence to suggest that we are witnessing a new trade unionism that will challenge managerial approaches and market-leaning politics through informed dialogue and social action.

REFERENCES

Bach, S. and L. Bordogna (2011), 'Varieties of new public management or alternative models? The reform of public service employment relations in industrialized democracies', *International Journal of Human Resource Management*, **22** (10–12), 2086–2110.

Bach, S., L. Bordogna, G. Della Rocca, and D. Winchester (eds) (1999), *Public Service Employment Relations in Europe: Transformation, Modernisation or Inertia?*, London: Routledge.

Batstone, E., A. Ferner and M. Terry (1984), *Consent and Efficiency*, Oxford: Blackwell.

Bonnett, A. (1993), 'The formation of public professional radical consciousness', *Sociology*, **27** (2), 281–297.

Conley, H., D. Kerfoot and C. Thornley (2011), 'Gender equality and modernization of public sector employment', *Gender, Work and Organisation*, **18** (5), 439–442.

Danford, A., B. Carter, D. Howcroft, H. Richardson, A. Smith, P. Taylor (2011), '"All they lack is a chain": lean and the new performance management in the British civil service', *New Technology, Work and Employment*, pp. 83–97.

Fairbrother, P. (1994), *Politics and the State as Employer*, London: Mansell.

Ferner, A. (1987), 'Industrial relations and the meso-politics of the public enterprise: the transmission of state objectives in the Spanish national railways', *British Journal of Industrial Relations*, **25** (1), 49–75.

Fine, J. (2007), 'A marriage made in heaven? Mismatches and misunderstandings between worker centres and unions', *British Journal of Industrial Relations*, **45** (2), 335–360.

Grimshaw, D. and I. Roper (2007), 'Partnership: transforming the employment relationship in public service delivery', in P. Dibben, P. James, I. Roper and G. Wood (eds), *Modernising Work in Public Services: Redefining Roles and Relationships in Britain's Changing Workplace*, Basingstoke: Palgrave.

Guest, D. (1990), 'Human resource management and the American dream', *Journal of Management Studies*, **27** (4), 377–397.

Keenoy, T. (1990), 'A wolf in sheep's clothing', *Personnel Review*, **19** (2), 3–9.

Keller, B. (2011), 'After the end of stability: recent trends in the public sector of Germany', *International Journal of Human Resource Management*, **22** (10–12), 2167–2184.

Kirkpatrick, I. (2006), 'Post Fordism and organisational change within the state administration', in L.E. Alonso and M. Martínez Lucio (eds), *Employment Relations in a Changing Society*, London: Palgrave Macmillan.

Lawler, J. (2009), 'Individualisation and public sector leadership', *Public Administration*, **86** (1), 21–34.

MacKenzie, R. (2009), 'Union responses to restructuring and the growth of contingent labour in the Irish telecommunications sector', *Economic and Industrial Democracy*, **30** (4), 539–563.

Martínez Lucio, M. (2006), 'Trade unionism and the realities of change', in L.E. Alonso and M. Martínez Lucio (eds), *Employment Relations in a Changing Society*, London: Palgrave Macmillan.

Martínez Lucio, M. (2007), 'Trade unions and employment relations in the context of public sector change: the public sector, "old welfare states" and the politics of managerialism', *International Journal of Public Service Management*, **20** (1), 5–15.

Martínez Lucio, M. and I. Roper (2011), 'HRM in public services', in I. Roper, R. Prouska and U. Chatrakul Na Ayudhya, *Critical Issues in Human Resource Management*, London: CIPD.

Martínez Lucio, M. and M. Stuart (2007), 'Sustaining new industrial relations in the public sector: the politics of trust and co-operation in the context of organisational dementia and disarticulation', in P. Dibben, P. James, I. Roper and G. Wood (eds), *Modernising Work in Public Services*, Basingstoke: Palgrave.

Martínez Lucio, M. and S. Weston (1992), 'Trade union responses to human resource management: bringing the politics of the workplace back into the debate', in P. Blyton and P. Turnbull (eds), *Reassessing Human Resource Management*, London: Sage.

Oswick, C. and D. Grant (1996), 'Personnel management in the public sector: power, roles and relationships', *Personnel Review*, **25** (2), 4–18.

Perrett, R. and M. Martínez Lucio (2006), *A Bitter Pill to Swallow?*, London: UNISON.

Rubenstein, S.A. and J.E. McCarthy (2010), *Collaborating on School Reform*, working paper Rutgers School of Management and Labor Relations, USA.

Storey, J. (1994), *Developments in the Management of HRM*, Oxford: OUP.

Stuart, M. and M. Martínez Lucio (2008), 'The new benchmarking and advisory state: the role of the British advisory, conciliation and arbitration service in facilitating labour – management consultation in public sector transformation', *Journal of Industrial Relations*, **50**, 736–751.

Stuart, M., M. Martínez Lucio and A. Charlwood (2009), *The Union Modernisation Fund – Round One: Final Evaluation Report*, BIS Employment Relations

Research Series, no. 104, London: Dept for Business, Innovation and Skills, p. 180.

Thörnqvist, C. (2007), 'Changing industrial relations in the Swedish public sector', *International Journal of Public Services Management*, **20** (1), 16–33.

Wilding, P. (1982), *Professional Power and Social Welfare*, RKP: London.

PART IV

Human resource management practices and public sector performance

13. High performance work systems, performance management and employee participation in the public sector

Pauline Stanton and Karen Manning

INTRODUCTION

The changing nature of public sector management is a global phenomena that has led to both opportunities and challenges for the management of public sector employees. New public management (NPM) initiatives such as corporatization, privatization and outsourcing of services have focused on achieving greater accountability and transparency and improved efficiency and effectiveness. In theory, such developments lead to improved organizational and service performance and better 'value for money' for cost conscious governments.

In theory, a move away from rigid bureaucracy and highly centralized pay and conditions regimes should give employers more strategic choice over their human resource policies and enable them to create the conditions for more flexible work practices that can lead to high performing employees and hence improved organizational performance (Kessler and Purcell, 1996). However, empirical evidence suggests that public sector reform can also lead to job loss, work intensification and lack of job security which in turn has led to skill shortages and high labour turnover in a range of services and professions (Brunetto et al., 2011; Willis et al., 2005). A key question is, has public sector management reform led to work practices that involve employees in decision making and focus on employee participation and development or has it led to practices that focus on employee monitoring and control. In other words, has public sector reform led to conditions that create or undermine the creation of a 'high trust' climate that is necessary for high performance work systems (HPWS)?

In this chapter we explore this question by focusing on high performing work systems and their application in the public sector. First, we outline the key features of HPWS and identify some of the criticisms in their application. Second, we define some characteristics of the public sector, and explore some of the research in this area in public sector organizations. Third, we explore two key, but sometimes contradictory elements of HPWS, namely performance management and employee involvement and participation. We argue that these two elements often lead to different types of practices and lead to different behaviours influencing a truly high performing environment. Finally we suggest some strategies for future research and development.

UNDERSTANDING HIGH PERFORMANCE WORK SYSTEMS

HPWS can be defined as a broad set of human resource management (HRM) practices that work together to play a key role in the achievement of organizational goals and improved organizational effectiveness and in turn make organizations more competitive (Becker and Huselid, 2006; Kalleberg et al., 2006, Boxall and Macky, 2007, Bartram et al., 2007). While there is no agreed set of HPWS practices they include both traditional HR practices such as selective recruitment, job security, performance appraisal and training and development, as well as more general approaches to the organization of work such as team work, information sharing, high quality work, employee participation in decision making and even transformational leadership (Zacharatos et al., 2005; Kalleberg et al., 2006; Boxall and Macky, 2007; Macky and Boxall, 2007). HPWS research focuses on 'bundles' of practices that influence and align employees' attitudes and behaviours with the strategic goals of the organization: increasing employee commitment and individual performance (Bonias et al., 2010). While HPWS is a relatively new term, similar concepts such as high involvement or high commitment work practices have been around for a number of years (Guest, 2011). A key feature in each of these approaches is the belief that increased participation in decision making empowers employees and generates increased employee productivity (Zacharatos et al., 2005; O'Donoghue et al., 2011).

Criticisms of HPWS are similar to those of strategic HRM, first do they actually work – do they lead to better performance and if so, exactly how do they do that (Bosalie et al., 2005; Guest, 2011); and second, whose interest are they in – they might lead to higher productivity but do they also lead to work intensification for employees (Godard, 2004; Mackey and Boxall, 2007). Finally much of the early research into HPWS took place in the manufacturing sector (Appelbaum et al., 2000; McDuffie, 1995) where it can be argued the nature of work and the links to output are often more measureable than in the people orientated services that are typical of the public sector.

As Guest (2011) argues the answer to the first question still eludes researchers and is still highly contentious. We do not explore this issue further here. Instead we note that despite criticism there is evidence that HPWS are being applied in a range of public sector organizations internationally and here we explore some of these findings.

WHAT IS THE PUBLIC SECTOR?

As Data et al. (2005) argue, industry context is important for understanding people management practices. The industry determines not only the kinds of employees and the nature of the work, but also influences the key goals of organizations within the industry or sector and identifies what is valued in the industry. In this respect, the public sector is very broad and hence we include in our definition all persons employed by the various tiers of the civil branches of a government, for instance, the national, state and local governments. The public sector plays a pivotal role in OECD countries providing for the management of urban centres, infrastructure, healthcare, social and education services, amongst other things. Governments in OECD countries are generally composed of a number of layers with the number of layers, as well as the formal relationship between the layers, varying from country to country (Charbit and Michalun, 2009).

Despite the complexity of the sector we suggest that the public sector has three key features that impact on the management of its employees. First, it is heavily influenced by contextual factors in particular by public policy (Willis et al., 2006). Second, the diverse nature of the work and the workforce is a challenge, public sector organizations are diverse in size, type of work performed and history (Kalleberg et al., 2006), parts of the public sector for example the healthcare sector are highly feminized (Stanton, 2006) and the public sector in Western nations is highly unionized compared to the private sector (Lucio, 2007; Bennett, 2010; Bach and Kolins Givan, 2011). Third, the scope of the public sector can also be viewed according to the employment status of its employees. It is in this respect, and through the 'civil service' model, that traditionally key distinctions between public and private employment conditions and the associated expected behaviours of the employee occurred. The 'civil service' model of public service was based on public rather than private employment law, comprising key differences: employment was generally for life, with recruitment typically starting at the beginning of a career and with promotion reserved for insiders. Remuneration was based on seniority, rather than performance. There was a great emphasis on 'objectivity', loyalty and due process and an emphasis on formal certificates and diplomas. Special retirement schemes were also part of this employment arrangement (Charbit and Michalun, 2009).

THE CHANGING NATURE OF THE PUBLIC SECTOR – IMPACT OF NEW PUBLIC MANAGEMENT PRINCIPLES

In the last 30 years the public sector reform agenda in many OECD countries has been driven by NPM principles focusing on introducing more private sector characteristics into a sector that was increasingly seen to be inefficient, ineffective and costly. The main goals of the reform agenda can be summarized: such as reducing and/or eliminating differences between the public and private sector and shifting accountability towards results rather than processes. Bach and Bordogna (2011) summarize the NPM policy components under four headings:

- Structural reorganization towards market-type governance mechanisms result in a breakup of public services into smaller units.
- Attempting to increase efficiency by privatization and outsourcing.
- Use of managerial techniques such as leadership skills and performance management and emphasis on consumers and service quality to strengthen the power and responsibilities of public managers.
- Altering the traditional employment relationships by reducing the influence of unions and life-time employment.

There is no doubt that the introduction of these policies has dramatically changed the traditional method of employment in the public sector internationally in the last few decades. As an example the experience in the Australian Public Service (APS) readily illustrates the change in character of public service delivery throughout the OECD. The self-described characteristics of the APS in the 21st century are flexibility, efficiency and accountability of outcomes, a more diverse workforce, increased contract employment, greater scope for public servants to be dismissed, government advisory work shared with consultants, greater similarity with the private sector in organization and service delivery, greater control over bureaucracy by the political arm of government and greater access to information by citizens (Verspaandonk et al., 2010). The reform agendas of European governments also revolve around the devolution of previously centralized structures and an increase of managerial discretion, a focus on performance and quality assessment systems and increased reliance on non-governmental and commercial service provision (Hurley et al., 2010).

Such developments however are not just the preserve of OECD countries and developed nations. Even transitional economies such as China and Vietnam have seen rapid changes in the nature of their government sectors in particular their State Owned Enterprises as they struggle to compete with the influx of foreign owned private companies and as they move into joint venture partnerships (Thang and Quang, 2005; Zhu et al., 2008; Lamond and Zheng, 2010). Hence public sector reform is a worldwide phenomena that has a marked effect on the management of employees (Hurley et al., 2010).

HIGH PERFORMANCE WORK SYSTEMS IN THE PUBLIC SECTOR

NPM reforms and the focus on accountability and decentralization have arguably led to new opportunities for public sector managers to have greater strategic choice in the management of their staff (Kessler and Purcell, 1996; Bach, 2000). An increased focus on performance and quality assurance and greater managerial discretion impacts directly on the way employees are managed. In recent years HPWS, SHRM and the impact on employee relations have been explored to a much greater extent in the public sector (Kalleberg et al., 2006; Bartram et al., 2007; Bach and Kolins-Given, 2011). Clearly there are some differences in how reform is enacted in different countries: for example, Bach and Kolins-Givan (2011) analyze developments in public service employment relations in the UK and the US over the last two decades that relate to NPM style reforms. As they note, 'Although there are some similarities in the reform agenda, there are marked variations in the interpretation and implementation of NPM reforms, which reflect differing administrative traditions and the malleability of NPM reforms'.

Kalleberg et al. (2006), also in the USA, suggest that there are also differences within the public sector as to the implementation of HPWS. Based on evidence from their survey of public sector organizations in the US, they argue that 'establishments seem to use different high-performance work practices depending on the work that they perform and the environment in which they perform it'. Brunetto et al. (2011) also see differences in the way reform impacts on the work of different professional groups in different parts of the public sector. They found that even within the same government jurisdiction and within the same institutional framework there can be differences between the ways professionals experience workplace change. For example, they found great differences in perceptions around the same government policies between nurses and the police in Queensland, Australia. Similarly many European countries have introduced variable or performance-related pay for their public servants. For instance Denmark first introduced performance related pay for their municipal employees in 1997, and by 2005 had expanded the scheme to 80 per cent of employees. The effect of these schemes is however at best mixed – showing good results for teachers and civil servants, but less so for healthcare workers (Prentice et al., 2007; as cited by Hurley et al., 2010).

We can even see some differences within sectors, for example, Kessler and Purcell (1996) suggested that the health sector reforms in UK in the early 1990s allowed managers a degree of strategic choice in employee relations. Since that time, there has been a great deal of literature that focuses on SHRM in general and HPWS in particular in hospitals, in a range of western countries, which would suggest that is the case (Aitkin et al., 2000; West et al., 2002; 2006; Bartam et al., 2007; Bonias et al., 2010). Stanton et al. (2010), investigating HR practices in three case study hospitals in Victoria Australia, found that despite working within a centralized Industrial Relations (IR) framework, and centralized health policy frameworks and accreditation processes each hospital had an enormous amount of control over their own HR structures, systems and practices with quite different outcomes. These outcomes related to the commitment of the CEO and ownership of HRM by the senior leadership team.

Whilst we can see evidence of a great deal of divergence in the public sector in relation to the impact of government reform and the implementation of a range of HRM practices, we can also see some similarities between the public and private sectors. For example Wood and de Menezes (2011) undertook a study of the effect of wellbeing on four dimensions of HPWS using Britain's workplace employment relations survey of 2004. This included both private and public sector employees while some differences were evident, they note 'In general the public sector was consistent with the whole sample' (Wood and de Menezes, 2011: 1600).

Similarly Wang et al. (2011) examined the impact of HPWS techniques on workers' attitudes and behaviours in China. This study included both private enterprises and state owned enterprises. The results show '. . . that the HPWS enhanced their organizational commitment, and reduced work withdrawal behaviours and turnover intentions' (Wang et al., 2011: 2419). However, there were different pathways to these outcomes between SOEs and private firms, for example, training rated highly in both samples whereas empowerment was not so strong in the SOE sample.

Overall the evidence suggests that there are many new developments in people management in the public sector internationally, mostly related to the improvements in employee performance. Many of these developments are clearly linked to the opportunities afforded to managers by public sector reform. They are not just pertinent to Western nations, as even in transitional and developing nations there is evidence that moving from state owned enterprises to a more corporate business model can lead to more flexibility and local control over HRM policies. State owned enterprises need to adopt new performance based practices not only to compete with the private sector but also to keep their high performing and talented employees who otherwise might be attracted to the higher salaries and better opportunities in foreign owned enterprises (Hahn and Stanton, 2011). However, the question remains – what is the impact of such practices on employees and employee performance in the public sector?

ARE HPWS WORKING AND FOR WHO?

There is evidence that clearly demonstrates a link between people management practices and organizational performance in healthcare (Aitkin et al., 2000; West et al., 2002; 2006; Bartam et al., 2007; Bonias et al., 2011). However, there is no agreement as to what creates that link, as Harris et al. (2007: 452) argue 'there is insufficient evidence to suggest that any one element of HRM may be superior to another in terms of its impact on performance' suggesting 'a confusing picture in the HR performance literature regarding which practices, policies and or systems are linked to performance'. At the organizational level, recent research suggests a number of factors influencing the adoption and successful application of HPW practices. These include the overall strength of the HRM system in relation to distinctiveness, consistency and consensus of HRM policies and practices (Bowen and Ostroff, 2004; Stanton et al., 2010), the role and commitment of the senior management team (Bartram et al., 2007) and the role of the line manager (Purcell and Hutchinson, 2007). In addition empirical research has demonstrated the centrality of employee attitudes mediating the relationship between HPWS and individual performance (Boxall and Purcell, 2008; Mackay and Boxall, 2007). From the employees perspective it is often their relationship with their individual supervisor and their experience in the work group that influences their attitude to their work and their work effort. However, two key elements of HPWS that are examined here include how the performance of employees is managed and how much opportunity do employees have to participate in decision making.

PARTICIPATION AND PERFORMANCE

Employee involvement and participation can be defined in a number of ways ranging from general concepts, such as '. . . any workplace process that allows employees to exert some influence over their work and the conditions under which they work' (Markey and Hodgkinson, 2003: 112), to more structural features of company and employee voice mechanisms such as joint consultative committees (Dundon et al., 2004; Cregan and Brown, 2010). Employee participation can be enacted through 'indirect' mechanisms such as statutory representative arrangements, union bargaining structures, joint consultative committees and company councils (Benson, 2000; Lavell et al., 2010) or 'direct' mechanisms such as quality circles, team meetings and meetings between employers and employees (Dundon et al., 2004).

Employee participation can be expressed collectively through trade union mechanisms or individually through grievance processes (Dundon et al., 2004). Employee participation can be also be analyzed through other forms of communication and information sharing processes that are present at the workplace, such as newsletters, suggestion schemes and intranet or more participatory decision making forums such as team meetings (Marchington and Wilkinson, 2005). O'Donoghue et al. (2011), studying employee participation in the Australian healthcare sector identified eight preconditions from the literature for successful employee participation. These were strong management support, trade union support, perceived benefit, supportive policy, job security, workplace trust, organizational size and participatory ethos. From a study of three hospitals they found that despite both management and unions believing that employee participation was beneficial and government policy in place that encouraged employee participation, in practice employee participation was limited. This was largely due to the fact that hospital managers were constantly under pressure to achieve government performance targets and limited by budgetary constraints, which both undermined trust and focused trade unions on collective bargaining and defending existing agreements. Employee participation did not feature very highly in either union or management agendas. On the other hand, Bennett (2010) exploring employee voice initiatives in the UK public sector found a range of both direct and indirect mechanisms in place. He argued that 'the high levels of indirect voice mechanisms identified suggest that unions continue to play a key role in the public sector in terms of consultation and negotiation and there is little evidence that they are being supplemented by more direct modes of staff involvement' (Bennett, 2010: 453).

Employee empowerment is closely linked to employee participation, in that it can be seen as 'management practices and behaviours aimed at sharing power, information and rewards with employees to improve results' (Fernandez and Moldogaziev, 2010). Fernandez and Moldogaziev (2010) drawing on the 2006 federal human capital survey in the US found that 'providing employees with job-related knowledge and skills and granting them greater discretion, positively influence employee perceptions of performance'; whereas those practices relating to reward or provision of information regarding organizational goals did not influence employee perceptions of performance. They suggest that 'effective use of employee empowerment hinges, therefore, on the manager's knowledge of the array of empowerment practices available to them and the impact of these different practices on performance' (Fernandez and Moldogaziev, 2010).

Spreitzer (1995) also introduces the concept of psychological empowerment which includes meaning, competence, self-determination and impact, as key elements. Within healthcare, studies have found psychological empowerment to be an important antecedent of employee performance outcomes (Laschinger et al., 2004), with perceptions of psychological empowerment among healthcare professionals showing a positive relationship with their perceptions of quality of patient care (Harmon et al., 2003; Scotti et al., 2007). Bonias et al. (2010) examining HPWS in one large tertiary hospital in Australia found that elements of psychological empowerment namely autonomy, competence and meaning positively influenced the relationship between HPWS and perceptions of the quality of patient care. Unfortunately Leggat et al. (2011), reviewing empirical evidence in the Australian healthcare sector found 'little evidence of the implementation and maintenance of the necessary components of HPWS'. Instead they found outdated models of work organization, linked to a combative style of industrial relations and defensive trade union practices underpinned by a gap between government policy and organization practice. In other words, the policy context has a direct impact on organizational practice.

This brings us to the tricky issue of the management of employee performance. Individual employee performance outcomes are usually focused on performance appraisal, measurement, review and development activities. Ideally they can be perceived as an integrative umbrella term which includes job design; staffing; learning and development; rewards and remuneration; employee counselling, discipline, and even termination (Nankervis and Crompton, 2006; Nankervis and Stanton, 2011). Employee performance management in theory should be linked to the strategic directions of the organization and cascade down through the organization encouraging desirable employee behaviours (Nankervis and Stanton, 2010; Hahn and Stanton, 2011). There are also quite different approaches to employee performance management – one which focuses on employee development and involvement and the other on employee monitoring and control (Morris et al., 2011). Here in is the problem, while much of the performance management literature (Nankervis and Stanton, 2011) exalts the benefits of a developmental approach to employee performance management, it is Brunetto et al.'s (2011) contention that public sector reforms have led to more monitoring and control, which in turn has led to increased pressure on staff and hence, in their study, more nurses leaving the health sector. For example, Brunetto et al. (2011) argue that government policies in Australia have led to an increased focus on auditing and paperwork, worsening workloads and an increased pace of work that impacts on attitudes to supervision practices. In turn, supervision practices driven by the external environment contribute to increased labour turnover leading to shortages of skilled labour in nursing.

This view is supported by Morris et al. (2011), who studied the introduction of performance appraisal for university academics in Australia. They argued that despite the developmental rhetoric, in the context of government reforms that have been based on gaining greater efficiencies in the sector and increased accountability of academics, performance management practices have focused on control and monitoring. Such practices have led to cynicism from academics and have failed to motivate or develop the academic workforce.

Additionally, as Brown et al. (2010) argue the quality of the performance appraisal process is also important – a poor performance appraisal, particularly one that focuses on monitoring and control, leads to lower job satisfaction and organizational commitment and greater intention to quit.

There is even more evidence of this to be found in qualitative case studies, which highlight work intensification, often when workers are confronted with greater responsibilities as a result of decentralization and performance management techniques as witnessed in the public sector (Delbridge, 2007). One of the key processes adopted by the public sector to implement NPM reform is that of outsourcing services, otherwise known as 'contracting out'. This has more normally been associated with competitive tendering type arrangements where specific programs, services or at least discrete fragments are contracted to private providers. Stinson et al. (2005), when reviewing the impact of contracting out on the health industry identify the decline in quality of work life as a likely outcome. In a study of contracting out health services in Canada, they reveal a number of pressures on workers arising from contracting out including downward pressure on pay and benefits and heavier workloads, poor training and reduced job security. Hall (2000) in his work confirms these findings; and a study by Boardman and Hewitt (2004), conducted in a Western Australian hospital produces results suggesting that there are unintended consequences of outsourcing in areas of cost, quality and externalities.

CONCLUSIONS

At the beginning of this chapter we argued that HPWS has two contradictory elements, namely performance management and employee involvement and participation, which we explored through the lens of public sector implementation of HPWS. We argue that these two elements often lead to different types of practices and different behaviours influencing a truly high performing environment.

We identified three key features of the public sector impacting on the management of employees: the contextual factors particular of public policy making, the diverse nature of the work and the workforce and finally the scope of the public sector in relation to the employment status of its employees.

The academic literature appears divided: on one hand, survey evidence indicates that HPWS improve employee autonomy and increase financial rewards, which in turn increase job satisfaction; on the other hand, qualitative studies point to the danger of work intensification. However it is possible that the different research approaches simply look at different sides of the same coin, employees may experience increased job satisfaction, while at the same time experiencing the downside of work intensification. Finally, we suggest some strategies for future research and development.

While the literature assists us in identifying the public policy context in which HPWS operate, and thus which workers would benefit in moving to HPWS, customization of practices to local conditions is essential. A further corollary to this is the need to ensure that external conditions align and support HPWS practices rather than undermine them. O'Donogue et al.'s (2011) study of employee participation in the Australian healthcare sector provided a pertinent example in this respect.

A possible research direction is to explore how the link between management intentions and management practices at the level closest to the employee interact, either supporting or hindering each other; and how this influences employee responses to organizational outcomes. In turn this will help to improve HRMs contribution to organizational performance.

Finally, there is a need to understand how HPWS can be customized to specific sectors and occupational levels within the public sector. We need to better understand the complexity and difference within the public sector and within different occupational groups, especially given the changes the public sector has undergone in the last 20 years.

REFERENCES

Aitken, L.H., D.S. Havens and D.M. Sloane (2000), 'The magnet nursing services recognition program: A comparison of two groups of magnet hospitals', *The American Journal of Nursing*, **100** (3), 26–36.

Appelbaum, E., T. Baily, P. Berg and A.L. Kalleberg (2000), *Manufacturing Advantage: Why High Performance Work Systems Pay off*, Ithaca, NY: ILR Press.

Bach, S. (2000), 'Health sector reform and human resource management: Britain in comparative perspective', *International Journal of Human Resource Management*, **11** (5), 925–942.

Bach, S. and L. Bordogna (2011), 'Varieties of new public management or alternative models. The reform of public service employment relations in industrialized democracies', *The International Journal of Human Resource Management*, **22** (11), 2281–2294.

Bach, S. and R. Kolins Givan (2011), 'Varieties of new public management? The reform of public service employment relations in the UK and USA', *The International Journal of Human Resource Management*, **22** (11), 2349–2366.

Bartram, T., P. Stanton, S. Leggat, G. Casimir and Fraser, B. (2007), 'Lost in translation: exploring the link between HRM and performance in healthcare', *Human Resource Management Journal*, **17** (1), 21–41.

Becker, B.E. and M.A. Hueslid (2006), 'Strategic human resources management: where do we go from here?', *Journal of Management*, **32** (6), 898–925.

Bennett, T. (2010), 'Employee voice initiatives in the public sector: views from the workplace', *International journal of Public Sector management*, **23** (5), 444–455.

Benson, J. (2000), 'Employee voice in union and non-union Australian workplaces', *British Journal of Industrial Relations*, **38** (3), 453–459.

Boardman, A.E. and E.S. Hewitt (2004), 'Problems with contracting out government services: lessons from orderly services at SCGH', *Industrial and Corporate Change*, **13** (6), 917–929.

Bonias, D., T. Bartram, G. Casimir and P. Stanton (2010), 'Does psychological empowerment mediate the relationship between high performance work systems and the quality of patient care', *Asia Pacific Journal of Human Resources*, **48** (3), 319–337.

Bosalie, P., G. Dietz and C. Boon (2005), 'Commonalities and contradictions in HRM and performance research', *Human Resource Management Journal*, **15**, 67–94.

Bowen, D. and C. Ostroff (2004), 'Understanding HRM-firm performance linkages: the role of the "strength" of the HRM system', *Academy of Management Review*, **29** (2), 203–221.

Boxall, P. and K. Macky (2007), 'High-performance work systems and organisational performance: Bridging theory and practice', *Asia Pacific Journal of Human Resources*, **45** (3), 261–270.

Boxall, P. and J. Purcell (2008), '*Strategy and Human Resource Management*', Basingstoke and New York: Palgrave Macmillan.

Brown, M., D. Hyatt and J. Benson (2010), 'Consequences of the performance appraisal experience', *Personnel Review*, **39** (3), 375–396.

Brunetto, Y., R. Farr-Wharton and K. Shacklock (2011), 'Using the Harvard HRM model to conceptualise the impact of changes to supervision upon HRM outcomes for different types of Australian public sector employees', *International Journal of Human Resource Management*, **22** (3), 553–573.

Charbit, C. and M. Michalun (2009), 'Mind the gaps: managing mutual dependence in relations among levels of government', OECD Working Papers on Public Governance, no. 14, OECD Publishing.

Cregan, C. and M. Brown (2010), 'The influence of union membership status on worker's willingness to participate in joint consultation', *Human Relations*, **63** (3), 331–348.

Data, D.K., J.P. Guthrie and P.M. Wright (2005), 'Human resource management and labour productivity: does industry matter', *Academy of Management Journal*, **48** (1), 135–145.

Delbridge, R. (2007), 'HRM and contemporary manufacturing', in P. Boxall, J. Purcell and P. Wright (eds), *The Oxford handbook of human resource management*, Oxford: Oxford University Press, pp. 405–427.

Dundon, T., A. Wilkinson, M. Marchington and P. Ackers (2004), 'The meaning and purpose of employee voice', *International Journal of Human Resource Management*, **15** (6), 1149–1170.

Fernandez, S. and T. Moldogaziev (2010), 'Empowering public sector employees to improve performance: does it work?', *The American Review of Public Administration*, **41** (1), 23–47.

Godard, J. (2004), 'A critical assessment of the high-performance paradigm', *British Journal of Industrial Relations*, **42** (2), 340–378.

Guest, D. (2011), 'Human resource management and performance: still searching for some answers', *Human Resource Management Journal*, **21** (1), 3–13.

Hall, R. (2000), 'Outsourcing, contracting-out and labour hire: implications for human resource development in Australian organizations', *Asia Pacific Journal of Human Resources*, **38** (2), 23–41.

Hahn, P. and P. Stanton (2011), 'Managing employee performance in Vietnam', *Asia Pacific Business Review.*

Harmon, J., D.J. Scotti, B. Behson, G. Farias et al. (2003), 'Effects of high-involvement work systems on employee satisfaction and service costs in veterans' healthcare', *Journal of Healthcare Management*, **48** (6), 393–406.

Harris, C., P. Cortvriend and P. Hyde (2007), 'Human resource management and performance in healthcare organisations', *Journal of Health Organisation and Management*, **21** (4/5), 448–459.

Hurley, J., S. Craig, M. Bober, S. Schulze-Marmeling and S. Riso (2010), 'Current restructuring developments in local government', background paper, European Foundation for the Improvement of Living and Working Conditions, March.

Kalleberg, A., P. Marsden, J. Reynolds and D. Knoke (2006), 'Beyond profit? Sectoral differences in high performance work practices', *Work and Occupations*, **33** (3), 271–302.

Kessler, I. and J. Purcell (1996), 'Strategic choice and new forms of employment relations in the public service sector: developing an analytical framework', *The International Journal of Human Resource Management*, **7** (1), 206–229.

Laschinger, H.K.S., J. Finegan, J. Shamian and P. Wilk (2004), 'A longitudinal analysis of the impact of workplace empowerment on work satisfaction', *Journal of Organisational Behaviour*, **25** (4), 527–545.

Lamond, D. and C. Zheng (2010), 'HRM research in China: looking back and looking forward', *International Journal of Human Resource Management*, **1**, 6–16.

Lavelle, J., P. Gunnigle and A. McDonnell (2010), 'Patterning employee voice in multinational companies', *Human Relations*, **63** (3), 395–418.

Leggat, S., T. Bartram and P. Stanton (2011), 'High performance work systems: the gap between policy and practice in health care reform', *Journal of Health Organisation and Management*, **25** (3), 282–297.

Lucio, M. (2007), 'Trade unions and employment relations in the context of public sector change', *International Journal of Public Sector Management*, **20** (1), 5–15.

Macky, K. and P. Boxall (2007), 'The relationship between "high performance work practices" and employee attitudes: an investigation of additive and interaction effects', *International Journal of Human Resource Management*, **18** (4), 537–567.

Marchington, M. and A. Wilkinson (2005), *Direct Participation and Involvement in Managing Human Resources: Personnel Management in Transition*, Oxford: Blackwell Publishing Ltd.

Markey, R. and A. Hodgkinson (2003), 'How employment status genders access to employee participation in Australian workplaces', *International Employment Relations Review*, **9** (2), 111–127.

McDuffie, J.P. (1995), 'Human resource bundles and manufacturing performance: flexible productions systems in the world auto industry', *Industrial and Labor Relations Review*, **48** (2), 197–221.

Morris, L., P. Stanton and J. Mustard (2011), 'Performance management; the academic experience', *25th Association of Industrial Relations Academics of Australia and New Zealand (AIRAANZ)*, Auckland, New Zealand, 2–4 February.

Nankervis, A. and R. Compton (2006), 'Performance management: theory in practice?', *Asia Pacific Journal of Human Resources*, **44** (1), 83–101.

Nankervis, A. and P. Stanton (2011), 'Linking strategic HRM, performance management and organizational effectiveness: perceptions of managers in Singapore', *Asia Pacific Business Review*, **17** (1), 67–84.

O'Donoghue, P., P. Stanton and T. Bartram (2011), 'Employee participation in the healthcare industry: the experience of three case studies', *Asia Pacific Journal of Human Resources*, **49** (2), 193–212.

Purcell, J. and S. Hutchinson (2007), 'Front-line managers as agents in the HRM-performance causal chain: theory, analysis and evidence', *Human Resource Management Journal*, **17** (1), 3–20.

Scotti, D.J., J. Harmon, S.J. Behson and D.J. Messina (2007), 'Links among high performance work environment, service quality and customer satisfaction: an extension to the healthcare sector', *Journal of Healthcare Management*, **52** (2), 109–124.

Spretizer, G. (1995), 'Psychological empowerment in the workplace: dimensions, measurement and validation', *Academy of Management Journal*, **38**, 1442–1465.

Stanton, P. (2006), 'Industrial relations in the public hospital sector', in M. Bray and P. Waring (eds), *Evolving Industrial Relations*, North Ryde: McGraw Hill.

Stanton, P., T. Bartram, S. Young and S. Leggat (2010), 'Singing the same song: translating HRM messages across managerial hierarchies in Australian hospitals', *International Journal of Human Resource Management*, **21** (4), 567–581.

Stinson, J., N. Pollak and M. Cohen (2005), *The Pains of Privatization Canadian*, Canada: Centre for Policy Alternatives.

Thang, L.C. and T. Quang (2005), 'Human resource management practices in a transitional economy: a comparative study of enterprise ownership forms in Vietnam', *Asia Pacific Business Review*, **11** (1), 25–47.

Verspaandonk, R., I. Holland, N. Horne (2010), 'Chronology of Changes in the Australian Public Service 1975–2010', Parliamentary Library Background Note, Australia.

Wang, S., X. Yi, J. Lawler and M. Zhang (2011), 'Efficacy of high performance work practices in Chinese companies', *The International Journal of Human Resource Management*, **22** (11), 2419–2441.

West, M., C. Borril, J. Dawson, J. Scully, M. Carter, S. Anelay, M. Patterson and J. Waring (2002), 'The link between the management of employees and patient mortality in acute hospitals', *International Journal of Human Resource Management*, **13** (8), 1299–1310.

West, M.A., J.P. Guthrie, J.F. Dawson, C.S. Borrill and M. Carter (2006), 'Reducing patient mortality in hospitals: the role of human resource management', *Journal of Organisational Behaviour*, **27**, 983–1002.

Willis, E., S. Young and P. Stanton (2005), 'Health sector reform and industrial reform in Australia', in P. Stanton, E. Willis and S. Young (eds), *Workplace Reform in the Healthcare Industry: the Australian Experience*, Basingstoke: Palgrave Macmillan.

Wood, S. and L.M. de Menezes (2011), 'High involvement management, high-performance work systems and well-being', *The International Journal of Human Resource Management*, **22** (7), 1586–1610.

Zacharatos, A., J. Barling and R. Iverson (2005), 'High-performance work systems and occupational safety', *Journal of Applied Psychology*, **90** (1), 77–93.

Zhu, Y., N. Collins, M. Webber and J. Benson (2008), 'New forms of ownership and human resource practices in Vietnam', *Human Resource Management*, **47** (1), 157–75.

14. Human resource management and public organizational performance: educational outcomes in the Netherlands

Laurence J. O'Toole (Jr), René Torenvlied, Agnes Akkerman and Kenneth J. Meier

SUMMARY

In recent years researchers have focused systematically on whether public management matters for the performance of public organizations. Management of organizations' human resources (HR) is one such managerial function, and a growing literature argues for its importance in delivering results. In this chapter the focus is on the link between human resource management (HRM) and organizational performance on behalf of students' educational attainment in schools. It is often asserted, but much less often demonstrated, that good HRM can improve public organizational outputs and outcomes. We test for the relationship using nationwide data from schools providing primary education in the Netherlands, along with results from a survey administered to all primary school principals in the country. Controlling for a range of other variables, we find that school managers' deliberations with their educational team contributes positively, and some HR-related red tape influences negatively, schools' educational outcomes. The findings validate arguments in the literature on the importance for performance of public organizations' management of their human resources.

A focus on the performance of public organizations is prominent in both management practice and research (see, for instance, Boyne et al., 2006; Frederickson and Frederickson, 2006; Ingraham and Lynn, 2004; Lynn, Heinrich and Hill, 2001; Walker, Boyne and Brewer, 2010). Particularly provocative has been the scholarly agenda directed at the determinants of performance (Boyne, 2003).

Among the possible determinants, public management has now clearly been shown to matter for the outputs and outcomes of public services (for instance, Andrews, Boyne and Walker, 2006; Meier et al., 2007; O'Toole and Meier, 1999). Of course, 'management' encompasses many functions. Earlier research shows that a number of these are essentially uncorrelated (see O'Toole and Meier, 2011), so the various possible contributions of public management to performance are best examined in careful and distinct fashions.

An aspect of public management that certainly should matter for performance is the management of an organization's human resources. The literature certainly suggests as much, and many public managers would insist on the key role of human resource management (HRM) in influencing results. However, while virtually everyone is convinced of the importance of HRM to organizational performance, the systematic evidence is far from overwhelming.

One strategy for making progress is to identify some important aspects of HRM that are amenable to measurement and then estimate their effects on organizational outputs and outcomes. That is the approach taken in this chapter. We focus here on a core positive aspect of HRM – management's regular involvement of internal stakeholders in the deliberations needed to make decisions about the management of the organization; and also one potential barrier to HRM's efficacy – the red tape that can impede rewarding productive employees for their contributions to the organization's objectives. As the discussion below indicates, there are reasons to expect the former to assist organizational performance and the latter to hinder it.

The next section of this chapter sketches the theoretical logic underpinning this analysis and indicates the relevant research that precedes the current analysis. We then undertake a systematic empirical study of the subject by testing for the hypothesized relationships in the empirical setting of government-funded primary school education in the Netherlands. In this coverage, we first summarize the context, the data, and the measures employed in the research. We then estimate the effect of these positive and negative aspects of HRM across hundreds of primary school organizations from all parts of the Netherlands. The design employed here isolates the HRM influences by controlling for a broad range of other variables that might constitute potential influences on educational performance. The chapter then discusses the results and their implications.

HRM AND PERFORMANCE: THEORETICAL EXPECTATIONS

Public management encompasses many functions. Some have to do with managing sets of relationships between the core organization and its environment – tapping opportunities available in the organization's setting or protecting the core organization from potentially perturbing outside forces. These functions have to do with external management.

Most attention from researchers, however, has been directed toward the myriad of internal-managerial responsibilities that public managers face. Internal management has to do with the coordination of people and resources in a structured setting to accomplish public objectives. Accordingly, the content of this function involves the management of finances and capital resources (buildings, infrastructure, equipment, etc.), the alignment of information technology in support of goals, the stabilization and fine-tuning of organizational structure to ease coordination and overcome cognitive and other limitations on decision making (Simon, 1997), and the management of the organization's people – its human resources.

Ultimately, research on management and performance should explore all these facets of internal management, but doing so in a single study is not feasible. Here we deliberately under-specify and focus on the last-mentioned coordinative element listed above: the management of human resources. We do so for several reasons. One is the labor-intensive nature of the empirical settings studied here, education, where the talent, training, motivation, and effort of many professionals is clearly crucial to performance. Indeed, such educational organizations, 'coping' organizations, in the parlance of Wilson (1989), have had their production functions extensively studied; it is clear that the ability to recruit and motivate highly trained educational professionals in a competitive labor market is positively related to educational outcomes. Doing so, in turn, requires dedicated and talented management. If human resource management (HRM) should matter anywhere, in short, it should matter in education. Another reason to focus on HRM is that extensive literature emphasizes its importance generally in the public sector (for reviews and analyses of some of this literature see Nigro, Nigro and Kellough, 2006; Shafritz et al., 2001). A high-visibility study of 'management capacity' – the government performance project – theorized that human resource management is one of four key management 'subsystems' linked via leadership and driven toward higher performance by a system of managing for results (Ingraham, 2007; especially Selden and Jacobson, 2007; Ingraham, Joyce, and Donahue, 2003). Furthermore, a study based in part on formal theory concludes that the personnel function in government is the most critical one for those concerned about results that comport with the 'core governmental values – judgment, balance, rationality and accountability' (Bertelli and Lynn, 2006: 131, 103–31). A modest amount of conceptual and empirical literature on business organizations is also supportive of the notion that human resource management generally, including employee development efforts, can be important contributors to organizational performance (for literature reviews and conceptual contributions, see Jacobs and Washington, 2003; Wood, 1999; for empirical findings supportive of this theme, see Koch and McGrath, 1996; Li, 2000). Indeed, some economic analyses have emphasized the importance of human resources (see Ellingsen and Johannesson, 2007; Lazear and Shaw, 2007; Pfeffer, 2007), and some empirical work has been conducted on public education. For instance, economists have explored teacher labor markets and sorting (Boyd et al., 2003; Lankford, Loeb and Wyckoff, 2002), as well as the impact of teacher quality on student achievement (Rivkin, Hanushek and Kain, 2005). These studies, however, do not explore the impact of management on the performance of school organizations.

For all these reasons, it seems reasonable to expect the component of internal management that has to do with human resource management to be related to performance. Of course, even this narrowing of the subject distills a rather large set of managerial practices and responsibilities. Earlier work began to delve into the subject by estimating the influence of managing human capital on public organizational performance (O'Toole et al., 2009) and also the boost to performance associated with training and development efforts (Andrews et al., Unpublished). For the purposes of our empirical analysis, we focus here on what we regard as a key aspect of HRM that can be expected to be related to organizational performance: the regular involvement of and consultation with an organization's staff regarding a broad range of managerial responsibilities and considerations.

There are a number of reasons to expect that the consultative aspects of human resource management might have organizational performance effects. Top management regularly involving others in discussions regarding a whole range of organizationally relevant matters can increase the amount of information brought to bear on decisions, stimulate new ideas, incorporate the preferences held by members of the organization, and also motivate people to contribute to the cause. Coordination across specialties and levels may also be enhanced. While the research literature on employee participation sometimes shows no direct causal link between participation itself and individual productivity (Miner, 2005: 208–216; Schermerhorn et al., 2010: 218–20), it is likely that real discussion with organizational employees about matters of practical interest – whether directly about achieving the organization's core tasks or how to analyze and improve organizational processes, or finding ways to address practical issues as they arise – can enhance outcomes, especially when such discussions are regularly planned and implemented in situations which require goal consensus among employees. It is this aspect of HRM that we examine in this chapter.

The first hypothesis to explore, therefore, is this: The more that public managers involve their team in discussions about the broad set of issues facing the organizations – not merely the matters under people's immediate jurisdiction and specialization – the higher the performance of the organization.

Also relevant is the extent to which managers have the flexibility to reward (or sanction) organizational personnel who perform well (or poorly). This subject, of course, is a longstanding theme in public HRM. While regulations associated with civil service systems have been shown to prevent politicization and abuse, in many cases they are alleged to make motivating employees more difficult. While we expect regular discussions among the organizational staff to contribute to performance, we expect personnel-related 'red tape' to impede performance (Pandey and Kingsley 2000; Pandey and Scott 2002; Rainey 1979; 1983; Rainey, Pandey and Bozeman, 1995).

The second hypothesis examined here, is: the more that managers see rules and regulations as restricting their ability to reward high-performing employees, the lower the organization's performance.

The first hypothesis, therefore, refers to a behavioral pattern within the organization, and one that is typically under the discretion of top managers. The second references the rules, or institutionalized features of organizational life. While it might be supposed that in the case of schools in the Netherlands, the empirical context for this study, there would be substantial variation across schools on the former practice but much uniformity for the latter, there is actually substantial variation in both.

To isolate the possible effects of these HRM-related features, it is also important to control for a range of variables that could be expected to influence organizational performance as well. In general terms, these are variables related to task difficulty, resources available for achieving organizational goals, and governance structure in which the organizations operate.

In formal terms, our hypothesized expectations can be represented as follows:

$$O_t = \beta_1(HRM_t) + \beta_2(HRRULES_t) + \beta_3(X_t) + \varepsilon_t$$

where O_t refers to organizational outcomes at time t, HRM_t refers regular deliberations at time t by top managers on a range of tasks with those in the organization, and $HRRULES_t$ represents regulations that restrict managers' ability to reward high performance among employees, X_t is a vector of control variables, ε_t is an error term and the βs are estimable parameters. The result is a relatively simple linear model that will permit us to assess the impact of a portion of the internal management of human resources, along with its regulation, on organizational performance while controlling for the other influences on performance. We expect the sign of the coefficient for HRM to be positive and that for HRRULES to be negative.

SAMPLE AND MEASURES

The context of the present study is formed by the Dutch system of primary education. In the Netherlands, 6864 primary schools are responsible for the education of more than 1.5 million school pupils in the ages between four and 12. Dutch primary schools have two main responsibilities: (a) to qualify pupils by promoting their cognitive skills in language and arithmetic, and (b) to socialize pupils by promoting their social and moral development in citizenship behavior (Dutch Education Council, 2009). School principals must translate these broad responsibilities into the educational program of their school. In addition, they coach teachers; develop plans for pedagogical quality, student care and quality control; and monitor pupil performance. School principals also have considerable administrative duties associated with the day-to-day management of the school. They are responsible for the planning of activities, human resource management, and the development and maintenance of buildings. School principals are the main representative of the school in external contacts and therefore maintain relationships with organizations and actors in the school environment, for example: the parent committee, the school board, local government, public libraries, youth care, the Inspectorate of Education or test suppliers.

Primary schools vary with respect to their educational philosophy or denomination: almost 70 per cent of all primary schools in the Netherlands are denominational schools. All Dutch primary schools are governed by a school board. Although 30 per cent of all 1069 school boards in the Netherlands are responsible for a single school, most school boards govern more than one school (sometimes even more than 60 schools). School boards often delegate much authority to the school principal. Nevertheless, the school board is formally accountable for the internal organization, the personnel and employment policies, and the financial management of the school – and ultimately for the school's performance (Turkenburg, 2008). All schools are assessed on the same final attainment levels (among others a standardized test for all pupils), which has driven the standardization of educational programs offered by primary schools. Certified test suppliers provide the standardized tests. The standardized attainment levels make it possible to compare – and monitor – performance for all primary schools.

To test the hypotheses we use a pooled dataset of Dutch primary schools. The first component of this pooled dataset is from the Dutch Inspectorate for Education, which provides precise information about performance of individual schools, as well as a wide range of control variables. The second component of the pooled dataset is information from a survey among principals of Dutch primary schools. In the framework of the 'Dutch School Networks & Learning (DSNL) project' we held a nation-wide survey among principals of Dutch primary schools. The survey data were collected in early 2010, using an internet survey. Principals of all Dutch primary schools were invited by mail and email to participate in the survey. The invitation included a personal link to the project website. A reminder was sent after two weeks. After six weeks, the response rate was 19.55 per cent (n = 1348). This rate is comparable to response rates reported by other studies of Dutch school principals, and is substantial given the work pressure on school principals, the size of the questionnaire, and the prevalence of survey research in this sector. A non-response analysis shows that schools in the sample do not differ with respect to a large number of relevant characteristics. The two datasets were matched by using the unique 'BRIN' number, assigned by the Dutch ministry of Education, Culture and Science. This number is a four digit code which allows the ministry to identify primary schools as separate educational units.

The dependent variable in the present study is the school's average score of pupils on a standardized test which is taken in the second half of the eighth and final grade of primary education. Roughly 75 per cent of all primary schools participate on voluntary basis in this 'CITO' test – which is named after the independent institute which develops, supplies, and administers the scores. The CITO test score is based on three sub-tests: language (100 questions), arithmetic (60 questions), and study competences (40 questions). Pupils' scores on these 200 questions are transformed on a scale between 501 and 550. Schools are allowed to exempt specific, well-defined categories of pupils from the test: pupils with severe language problems who have lived in the Netherlands for a shorter period than four years, pupils with an indication for special education, or pupils with an indication for vocational secondary education. Despite this room for discretion, the CITO test-score is considered to be authoritative by the Dutch Inspectorate for Education, as well as by most teachers and parents. Pupils' referrals to specific levels of secondary education are based to a large extent on their CITO test scores. We use the 2010 test scores because the questions in our questionnaire pertain to the school year 2009–10.

The first independent variable 'managerial activity in team involvement' was measured using 10 items that each covers a specific aspect of the daily functioning of the school. These aspects were derived on the basis of in-depth interviews with school principals, board members, and representatives from the inspectorate of education. The items are: (1) identity and external communication, (2) school housing and maintenance, (3) financial matters, (4) personnel and employment policy, (5) quality of education, (6) pupil results and performance monitoring, (7) pupil care; (8) educational quality, (9) external relations, (10) scheduling and other practicalities. Involvement was measured using a six-point Likert scale, with daily, weekly, monthly, quarterly, yearly and never as categories. We used a factor score as the measure of HRM involvement.[1]

The second independent variable, 'rule restrictions', taps rules and regulations that are viewed as restricting managers' ability to reward high-performing employees. This variable was measured using the item 'the formal pay structures and rules make it hard to reward a good teacher' from the standard measurement of personnel red tape (Rainey 1979; 1983; Rainey, Pandey and Bozeman 1995). School principals were asked to indicate their level of agreement with this statement on a four-point Likert scale, which is the HRRULES scale.

We included several other variables that pertain to the school principals' management of the schools daily operations and routines. Firstly, we constructed an indicator for the (self-reported) quality of the school's personnel. We asked the school principal to grade the school team, as a rough indicator for perceived quality, on a scale between '1' and '10' (O'Toole and Meier, 2009). Secondly, we took the management ratio – the full time equivalents of managerial appointments as a proportion of the full time equivalents of the total school personnel – as an indicator for the centralization of the school organization. Thirdly, we took the mobility ratio of school personnel – the full time equivalents of changes in personnel as a proportion of the full time equivalents of the total school personnel – as an indicator for the stability in the school organization. Data on both ratios were supplied by the Dutch Inspectorate for Education.

To measure managerial networking activity towards external actors and organizations, a detailed list was composed of organizations with which school principals could maintain relations. This list was determined on the basis of interviews with key informants in the education domain, school principals, and members of school boards. The procedure resulted in a list of 41 different external organizations and relevant actors. Managerial networking variables were measured by asking each school principal, for each of these organizations, 'how frequently do you interact with this type of organization?' (O'Toole and Meier 1999; 2011). This frequency of interaction was measured using a five-point scale, with categories ranging from 'never' (0), 'yearly' (1), 'several times per year' (2), 'monthly' (3), and 'daily' (4). An unrotated factor analysis reveals the existence of one factor with an eigenvalue larger than one on which all items load positively. We saved this factor as an indicator for the general networking activity of school principals.

Finally, we added a number of control variables to the analysis that may confound the relation between HRM practices and performance. We first control for institutional characteristics of the school and school board. Past evidence shows that school performance is sometimes associated with these institutional characteristics. Data was provided by the Dutch Inspectorate for Education. As primary schools are organized in different 'school denominations' we include dummies for 'Roman Catholic', 'Protestant' and 'Other' (with non-denominational schools as reference group). Some primary schools are governed in a single school board arrangement, while other schools are part of a multi-school arrangement, which allows them to share management tasks. Additionally, we incorporate variables that capture other important differences between primary schools that may affect school performance. One important variable is school size, measured as the number of pupils, teachers and teacher assistants. A gender-specific characteristic that relates to HRM practices is the percentage of female teachers. Schools with a high percentage of disadvantaged pupils are often involved in specific education programs, which require substantial administrative processing by the school. The percentage of disadvantaged pupils obviously has a strong expected impact on school performance. Finally, we control for characteristics of the principals themselves: their gender, years of experience as a school principal, and how many hours they spend weekly on the job as a school principal.

Table 14.1 presents descriptive statistics for the main variables and their correlations. In the ultimate analyses, 491 cases have valid scores on all available variables. The dependent variable, average school CITO score, varies between 515 and 545 (this range of school scores is slightly smaller than the range between 505 and 550 defined for individual pupils). The other variables show ample variation, although team quality and HRRULES are slightly skewed towards the left. Correlations are

Table 14.1 Descriptive statistics of and correlations between main variables in the analysis (n = 491)

Variable	Mean	S.d.	Min	Max	1	2	3	4	5	6
1. Cito score 2010	535.28	4.15	515	545	1.00					
2. Team involvement (HRM)	-0.01	0.91	-2.32	3.07	0.09	1.00				
3. Team quality	7.62	0.76	5	10	0.01	0.06	1.00			
4. Management ratio	6.69	5.35	0	27	-0.04	0.02	0.02	1.00		
5. Mobility ratio	0.73	2.35	0	23	-0.01	-0.01	-0.02	0.10	1.00	
6. Rule restrictions (HRRULES)	3.24	0.82	1	4	-0.08	0.08	-0.04	-0.05	-0.01	1.00
7. Networking activity	0.08	0.82	-1.94	2.89	-0.16	0.35	0.03	-0.05	-0.06	0.11

Note: S.d. is standard deviation.

generally quite low (Pearson's rho is between 0.10 and 0.35). Still, this correlation is well below the commonly accepted boundary of 0.70 for multicollinearity. Thus, the correlation matrix replicates the phenomenon, commonly reported by studies of (public) management, that the different management (and HRM) variables tap quite different aspects of the public management production function (O'Toole and Meier, 2011).

RESULTS

To test our hypotheses we performed a series of nested OLS regression analyses. Table 14.2 presents the results. The first model simultaneously tests effects of all variables that represent aspects of HRM in the school organization: the school principal's activity in involving his or her staff regarding a broad range of managerial responsibilities and considerations (HRM), the extent to which rules restrict the school principal to reward high-performing employees (HRRULES), the index for team quality, and the two ratios: for management and staff mobility. The results of the test of model 1 show that HRM has a strong significant effect on school performance in the expected direction. Hence, hypothesis 1 is corroborated by the school data (positive predicted effect of HRM on performance). HRRULES has a significant negative effect on performance ($p < 0.05$ in a one-tailed test). Hence, hypothesis 2 is also corroborated by the data (negative predicted effect of HRRULES on performance). Yet although the effects are significant, the explained variance of the regression of average school performance is close to only two per cent.

In model 2 we add the effect of managerial networking activity. The effect is highly significant but negative – which is in the opposite direction to what is normally found (O'Toole and Meier, 2011). Including managerial networking activity as a variable renders the effect of HRRULES non-significant. The explained variance increases to six per cent. In model 3 we add all other control variables that pertain to characteristics of the principal, the school, and the school team. The effect of HRM remains highly significant and positive, and the effect of HRRULES remains negative and turns significant again. Institutional characteristics and indicators for school size are significantly associated with school performance: larger schools perform better, those requiring more teacher assistants perform worse, and non-denominational schools perform significantly worse than schools that are based on a specific denomination. Together, these variables account for 16 per cent in the variation of primary schools' average scores on the CITO tests.

Finally, in model 4 we add the percentage of disadvantaged pupils as

Table 14.2 OLS regression of schools' average standardized test scores (CITO scores) of pupils 2010 (n = 491)

	M1	M2	M3	M4
Team involvement (HRM)	0.467**	0.811***	0.747***	0.409**
Rule restrictions (HRRULES)	−0.443*	−0.355	−0.425*	−0.421**
Team quality	−0.036	−0.023	0.084	0.136
Management ratio	−0.039	−0.047	−0.010	0.029
Mobility ratio	0.003	−0.017	−0.003	−0.025
Managerial networking activity		−1.124***	−0.858***	−0.296
Gender principal = female			0.082	0.675*
Age principal			0.010	0.008
Experience principal			0.016	0.003
Hours spent on job by principal			0.005	0.015
Number of pupils			0.007**	−0.000
Number of teachers			−0.043	0.049
Number of teacher assistants			−0.089***	−0.003
Percentage female teachers			−0.012	−0.061***
Average age personnel			0.057*	0.082***
Single school board = 1			0.872	0.012
Denomination Catholic[†]			2.125***	1.146***
Denomination Protestant[†]			1.326**	0.618
Denomination other[†]			2.103**	1.636**
Percentage disadvantaged pupils				−0.134***
Constant	537.248***	537.021***	532.348***	535.356***
R^2	0.018	0.061	0.157	0.417

Note: [†] Non-denominational schools are the reference group; * $p < 0.10$; ** $p < 0.05$; *** $p < 0.01$ (all two-tailed).

a control variable. This appears to be a crucial control variable, since it is highly correlated with the average CITO test score ($r = -0.597$), and because it might possibly explain away effects of the HRM variables of our interest. Schools with a high percentage of disadvantaged pupils may require many more HRM-related activities. Moreover, these schools may also be subject to stricter rules and regulations regarding the school's HRM policies – due to special regimes for these schools. The results, presented in the last column of Table 14.2, reveal that the expected effects of HRM and HRRULES firmly hold when controlling for the percentage of disadvantaged pupils and become more significant in this more fully specified model. The negative effect of managerial networking activity becomes insignificant, suggesting that this type of managerial behavior is – at least partly – sparked by the special needs of schools with a population characterized by a high proportion of disadvantaged pupils. However, such a dampening effect does not exist for the HRM-related management variables. The explained variance increases to 42 per cent, thus suggesting that this is a key control variable. The finding is also consistent with the idea that to examine the performance of public organizations one needs to control for task difficulty – in this case, the needs of the pupils.

CONCLUSION

The management of human resources is a central function of all public managers. Substantial literature and extensive investment in training are devoted to the notion that public managers can improve the performance of individuals who work in the organization. Using Dutch schools as the empirical test case, this study examined two aspects of human resource management and their impact on organizational performance – employee participation in management decision making and perceived limits to rewarding employees. These two aspects of human resource management seek to tap into the motivations of employees, that is, are they motivated by the commitments to the organization that are generated by participation in its processes, or is motivation more reflective of financial incentives? The short answer is that both appear to be operating in Dutch schools.

The size of impacts for these two elements of human resource management is not massive, but it is worth noting. Over the full range of the data in a well-specified model, participation might generate differences as large as 2.4 points, while the limits on financial incentives have an effective size of approximately 1.2 points. Since the two measures are virtually uncorrelated (with $r = .08$), the combined maximum effect size is close to 3.6 CITO points, more than one-tenth of the full range of the school scores. Much of the variation in student outcomes is the result of the mix of students and their degree of disadvantage, factors that are not under the direct control of management.

The present study is hardly the final word on the role of human resource management in public organizations, and its impact on organizational performance. Our measure of management participation assessed the frequency of that participation but not its quality. A more refined measure that can distinguish these aspects is well worth pursuing. Similarly, the measure of financial restrictions is only one aspect of red tape that might limit the actions of a manager. Red tape also affects other processes such as procurement, personnel hiring and termination, and in this case, how employees, that is teachers, interact with students and students' parents. Finally, the study examines only the overall impact of human resource management on performance. Management is also about the selection of key problems that need attention, and human resource management is no exception. It is quite possible that human resource management is more likely to affect disadvantaged children more than advantaged children if that is where management has set its priorities. In sum, while some progress has been made in unpacking the HRM-performance relationship, much remains to be done.

NOTE

1. An unrotated factor analysis reveals the existence of one factor, on which all items load positively and strongly with an eigenvalue of 3.62.

REFERENCES

Andrews, R., G.A. Boyne, K.J. Meier, L.J. O'Toole (Jr) and R.M. Walker, 'Investing in people: Training, turnover and organizational performance', Unpublished paper.

Andrews, R., G.A. Boyne and R.M. Walker (2006), 'Strategy content and organizational performance: an empirical analysis', *Public Administration Review*, **66** (1), 52–63.

Bertelli, A.M. and L.E. Lynn (Jr) (2006), *Madison's Managers: Public Administration and the Constitution*, Baltimore: Johns Hopkins University Press.

Boyd, D., H. Lankford, S. Loeb and J.H. Wyckoff (2003), 'Analyzing the determinants of the matching of public school teachers to jobs: estimating compensating differentials in imperfect labor markets', NBER Working Paper, no. W9878, accessed at http://ssrn.com/abstract=430592.

Boyne, G.A. (2003), 'Sources of public service improvement: a critical review and research agenda,' *Journal of Public Administration Research and Theory*, **13**, 367–94.

Boyne, G.A., K.J. Meier, L.J. O'Toole (Jr) and R.M. Walker (eds) (2006), *Public Services Performance: Perspectives on measurement and Management*, Cambridge: Cambridge University Press.

Dutch Education Council (2009), *The State of Affairs in Dutch Education 2009*, The Hague: Dutch Education Council.

Ellingsen, T. and M. Johannesson (2007), 'Paying respect', *Journal of Economic Perspectives*, **21** (4), 135–49.

Frederickson, D.G. and H.G. Frederickson (2006), *Measuring the Performance of the Hollow State*, Washington DC: Georgetown University Press.

Ingraham, P.W. (ed.) (2007), *In Pursuit of Performance: Management Systems in State and Local Government*, Baltimore: Johns Hopkins University Press.

Ingraham, P.W., P.G. Joyce and A.K. Donahue (2003), *Government Performance: Why Management Matters*, Baltimore: Johns Hopkins University Press.

Ingraham, P.W. and L.E. Lynn (Jr) (2004), *The Art of Governance: Analyzing Management and Administration*, Washington, DC: Georgetown University Press.

Jacobs, R.L. and C. Washington (2003), 'Employee development and organizational performance: a review of literature and directions for future research', *Human Resource Development International*, **6** (3), 343–54.

Koch, M.J. and R.G. McGrath (1996), 'Improving labor productivity: human resource management policies do matter', *Strategic Management Journal*, **17**, 335–54.

Lankford, H., S. Loeb and J. Wyckoff (2002), 'Teacher sorting and the plight of urban schools: a descriptive analysis', *Educational Evaluation and Policy Analysis*, **24** (1), 37–62.

Lazear, E.P. and K.L. Shaw (2007), 'Personnel economics: the economist's view of human resources', *Journal of Economic Perspectives*, **21** (4), 91–114.

Li, L.X. (2000), 'An analysis of sources of competitiveness and performance of Chinese manufacturers', *International Journal of Operations and Production Management*, **28** (3), 375–92.

Lynn, L.E. (Jr), C.J. Heinrich and C.J. Hill (2001), *Improving Governance: A New Logic for Empirical Research*, Washington, DC: Georgetown University Press.

Meier, K.J., L.J. O'Toole (Jr), G.A. Boyne and R.M. Walker (2007), 'Strategic management and the performance of public organizations: testing venerable ideas against recent theories', *Journal of Public Administration Research and Theory*, **17** (3), 357–77.

Miner, J.B. (2005), *Organizational Behavior 1: Essential Theories of Motivation and Leadership*, Armonk, NY: M.E. Sharpe.

Nigro, L., F. Nigro and J.E. Kellough (2006), *The New Public Personnel Administration* (6th Edition), Belmont, CA: Thomson Wadsworth.

O'Toole (Jr), L.J. and K.J. Meier (1999), 'Modeling the impact of public management: implications of structural context', *Journal of Public Administration Research and Theory*, **9** (4), 505–26.

O'Toole (Jr), L.J. and K.J. Meier (2009), 'The human side of public organizations: contributions to organizational performance', *American Review of Public Administration*, **39** (5), 499–518.

O'Toole (Jr), L.J. and K.J. Meier (2011), *Public Management: Organizations, Governance and Performance*, Cambridge: Cambridge University Press.

O'Toole (Jr), L.J., K.J. Meier and S. Nicholson-Crotty (2009), 'The human side of public organizations: contributions to organizational performance', *American Review of Public Administration*, **39** (5), 499–518.

Pandey, S. and G.A. Kingsley (2000), 'Examining red tape in public and private organizations: alternative explanations from a social psychological model', *Journal of Public Administration Research and Theory*, **10** (4), 779–99.

Pandey, S. and P.G. Scott (2002), 'Red tape: a review and assessment of concepts and measures', *Journal of Public Administration Research and Theory*, **12** (4), 553–80.

Pfeffer, J. (2007), 'Human resources from an organizational behavior perspective: some paradoxes', *Journal of Economic Perspectives*, **21** (4), 115–34.

Rainey, H. (1979), 'Perceptions of incentives in business and government: implications for civil service reform', *Public Administration Review*, **39**, 440–48.

Rainey, H. (1983), 'Public agencies and private firms: incentive structures, goals and individual roles', *Administration & Society*, **15**, 207–42.

Rainey, H., S. Pandey and B. Bozeman (1995), 'Research note – public and private managers perceptions of red tape', *Public Administration Review*, **55**, 567–74.

Rivkin, S.G., E.A. Hanushek and J.F. Kain (2005), 'Teachers, schools, and academic achievement', *Econometrica*, **73** (2), 417–58.

Schermerhorn (Jr), J.R., J.G. Hunt, R.N. Osborn and M. Uhl-Bien (2010), *Organizational Behavior* (11th Edition), New York: John Wiley & Sons.

Selden, S.C. and W. Jacobson (2007), 'Government's largest investment: Human resource management in states, counties, and cities', in P.W. Ingraham (ed.), *In Pursuit of Performance: Management Systems in State and Local Government*, Baltimore: Johns Hopkins University Press, pp. 82–116.

Shafritz, J.M., D.H., Rosenbloom, N.M. Riccucci, K.C. Naff and A.C. Hyde (2001), *Personnel Management in Government: Politics and Process* (5th Edition), New York: Marcel Dekker, Inc.

Simon, H.A. (1997), *Administrative Behavior* (4th Edition), New York: Free Press.

Turkenburg, M. (2008), *De school bestuurd. Schoolbesturen over goed bestuur en de maatschappelijke opdracht van de school* (Governance of schools: School boards on good governance and the social mission of the school), The Hague: The Netherlands Institute for Social Research.

Walker, R.M., G.A. Boyne and G.A. Brewer (2010), *Public Management and Performance: Research Directions*, Cambridge: Cambridge University Press.

Wilson, J.Q. (1989), *Bureaucracy: What Government Agencies Do and Why They Do It*, New York: Basic Books.

Wood, S. (1999), 'Human resource management and performance', *International Journal of Management Reviews*, **1** (4), 367–414.

15. Case study of 'peak performing' public sector units and successful change efforts

Michela Arnaboldi and Giovanni Azzone

INTRODUCTION

Since the mid-1980s, government reforms have been characterized by a managerial shift, addressed as new public management (NPM) (Hood, 1991; 1995; Lapsley, 2008), in which organizations have been challenged to move away from centralized, homogenous, bureaucratic models to new configurations characterized by autonomy and flexibility (Pollitt, 2009). This increased autonomy has created higher heterogeneity of performances among public administration, which still raises the questions (Lapsley, 2009; Arnaboldi and Azzone, 2010; Pipan and Czarniawska, 2010; Arnaboldi and Palermo, 2011) of how these differences emerged within the same legislative context, and how some organizations – here addressed as peak performers – have been able to better seize the opportunities offered by autonomy. More specifically, in this contribution, we analyze how and on which factors peak performers have leveraged to enact a process of change, which is now visible in markedly better performances.

To unfold these arguments, empirically, the authors draw on their 20 years of research in various areas of the public sector (university, central government, local authorities) in two different countries (Italy and UK). In all cases significant differences are recognized among administrations performances, which may sometime reach 200 per cent, although they act within the same legislative framework. These outcomes emerged to be linked to the diverse patterns adopted during the process of change, in which the capabilities of leaders, but more widely of all human resources, had been central.

In particular the longitudinal inter-sector observation highlighted common 'internal drivers' which have been deployed by peak performers to face the change; these drivers are here articulated around four categories:

Pervasive commitment: which is the capability to ensure the interest in the process of change of firstly top management and governing bodies, but more generally of all human resources, pervasively, across the organization.

Bridging competence: which is intended as the capability to identify missing competences and then implementing mechanisms appropriate to bridge the gap.

Flexible coordination: which is the capability to flexibly coordinate all the initiatives that are incrementally and, sometime, not linearly enacted during the process of change.

Operational consolidation: which is the capability to integrate the results achieved by innovations into institutionalized processes, avoiding that 'old' practices undermine the operational integration of 'new' configurations.

To develop our argument this contribution articulates as follows: the second section illustrates new public management and the specific context of the research; the third section presents the framework; the fourth section shows the results followed by some concluding remarks.

CONTEXT: NEW PUBLIC MANAGEMENT, AUTONOMY AND PERFORMANCES

The 2000s financial events and the most recent Eurozone crisis have accentuated the modernization pressure on public services, which has been for years a continuous priority in the agenda of many governments. The inception of this mounting pressure goes back to the early 1980. Its first practitioners emerged in the UK under Prime Minister Margaret Thatcher and in the municipal governments in the US that suffered most heavily from the economic recession and tax revolts. Next, the government of New Zealand and Australia joined the movement (Gruening, 2001). Their successes put administrative reforms on the agendas of most OECD countries and other nations as well (OECD, 1995; Hope, 2001) and this trend has become known as new public management (NPM) (Hood, 1991; 1995; Lapsley, 2008), as a term that characterizes the general shift of public sector organizations towards approaches closer to business methods. The term NPM was coined because some generic label seemed to be needed for a general, shift in public management styles. The term was intended to cut across the particular language of individual projects or countries.

This international movement is characterized by seven key dimensions: (1) the disaggregation of public organizations into separately managed 'corporatized' units for each public sector 'product'; (2) greater competition both between public sector organizations and between public sector organizations and the private sector; (3) greater use within the public sector of management practices drawn from the private sector; (4) stress on discipline and parsimony in resource use; (5) active control of public organizations by visible top managers wielding discretionary power; (6) more explicit and measurable (or at least checkable) standards of performance for public sector organizations; (7) attempts to control public organizations in a more 'homeostatic' style according to pre-set output measures (Hood, 1995).

Recently there has been a debate on the outcome of NPM, the appropriateness of its principles nowadays and its future (for example, Osborne, 2006; Lapsley, 2009; Levy, 2010). The discussion of these contributions is beyond the scope of this work; however there are two common issues which are noteworthy: first the emphasis, yet again, on the need for government of urgent actions; second the awareness that the increased autonomy from NPM reforms has created higher heterogeneity of performances among public administrations (Lapsley, 2009; Arnaboldi and Azzone, 2010; Pipan and Czarniawska, 2010; Arnaboldi and Palermo, 2011). This variety and the presence of peak performers are present in all the countries which undertook NPM reforms, suggesting the importance of organizational leverages beyond the specific context in which these institutions are situated.

To empirically investigate how and on which factors peak performers have leverage to enact a process of change, the results draw on 20 years of research in various areas of the public sector – university, central government, local authorities – in two countries, Italy and the UK. Notwithstanding our focus is organizational leverages and understanding of the specific country setting is provided.

The UK has always been regarded as one of the earliest countries in which NPM principles have been applied; in their comparative work on public management Pollitt and Bouckaert (2000) defined the UK as a 'high reformer' together with New Zealand. Some scholars, like Gruening (2001), attribute the origin of the NPM movement in the British context at the time of Prime Minister Thatcher's conservative government in the late 1970s. The advent of this government marked a breakthrough in the UK, opening the way to a holistic reform which implied a tight fiscal policy, the control of inflation and the reduction of public spending. While the initial struggles were directed towards civil service cuts, at the beginning of the 1980s the government focused on improving financial and general management and increasing efficiency. Following Prime Minister Thatcher's victory in the 1987 election, the administration launched a number of restructurings: market-type mechanisms were introduced on a large scale (healthcare, community care and education): the 'purchaser/provider split' was imposed by central government; performance measurement systems were intensified; electricity (1990–93) and railways (1994) were privatized; more than 140 executive agencies were created (Zifcak, 1994). The main tendency of the 1990s is represented by two major trends: a huge emphasis on 'customer services' and the concern to maintain and intensify the contracting out and marketization. The New Labour government of 1997 retained some of what had gone before. They intensified the 'league table' system still further, rebranded the Citizen's Charter Programme and launched a 'service first' initiative. More recently, the UK government has tightened its action on public expenditure in the face on the Eurozone crisis, going back to the initial policy of reduction of public spending and tight control of the debt.

Italy is instead considered a follower of the NPM movement (Pollitt and Bouckaert, 2000), starting its major reforms in the mid-1990s. Italy devoted the 1990s to 'catching up' with the leading OECD countries in economic and governance reforms, but the scope of reforms by multiple governments (state, regions and local authorities) was considered remarkable (OECD, 2001). As in many OECD countries, structural reforms in Italy began within a programme of macroeconomic stabilization. In the run-up to qualify for membership of the European Monetary Union, the Maastricht criteria gave the Italian government strong incentives to reassess its economic policies. A political consensus developed that an ambitious programme of stabilization was needed, not only for the European Union, but also to create the longer-term foundations for sustainable growth.

The initial struggles of central government were directed toward the State–citizen relationship. The first law, of this revitalizing process, appeared in 1990 (law n.142/1990) affecting many aspects of the public management, but it was in 1997 that the central government set a comprehensive legislative reform plan. The 1997 reforms aimed to re-balance powers between the centre and sub-national governments, and re-launch the administrative simplification policy based on processes of continuing accountability and an aggressive reorganization of government to improve coherency and efficiency in policy processes. Four basic principles were incorporated in the reforms: decentralization; simplification and liberalization; managerial orientation in managing human resources; separation between political and administrative issues, tasks and responsibilities. Subsequently the articulation of the Italian reform has been conducted via the enactment of a number of sectorial laws, mainly concerned with the definition of new governance structures or more advanced systems of accounting and auditing. With the recent Eurozone crisis, Italy has set out an urgent plan for recovery in which public sector downsizing and a tighter fiscal policy are central.

Summarizing Italy and UK, despite differences in time and approach, they have both undertook several reforms in the light of NPM principles, providing autonomy to organizations in all sectors of the public administration. Within each respective setting, organizations were not equally able to seize the opportunity provided by the increased autonomy originating differences in performances which are, sometimes, noticeable. The following section illustrates this heterogeneity, and then presents how peak performers were able to take advantage of new institutional conditions to improve.

FRAMEWORK: ANALYZING PERFORMANCES IN THE PUBLIC SECTOR

As discussed previously, this chapter aims to identify the 'internal drivers' explaining why some administrations reached peak performances in NPM reforms. Hence, we compared the results of groups of 'similar' (for instance, providing the same services in a single country) administrations, to understand:

1. If there are significant differences in the performance within each group (that must be due to internal drivers).
2. If the factors that characterize peak performing administration are the same in each group (hence, they are not country-specific or industry-specific).

The research approach is articulated in three stages:

1. Define a set of indicators that can be used to compare the results of administrations in a same group.
2. Design a benchmarking system, that can be used to compare different administrations.
3. Define a framework to understand, through case studies, the internal factors that are specific to a peak performer.

Designing the Set of Indicators

In general, the performance of an organization can be defined by comparing inputs and outputs (Figure 15.1). In private companies, we can measure both inputs and outputs in monetary terms; hence we can have a

Figure 15.1   The input/output approach

synthetic performance indicator, either as an absolute measure (like cash flow, profit or residual income) or a as a ratio (as return on investment).

In public administration, we cannot follow such a simple approach, as:

- We are unable to measure inputs and outputs in monetary terms. In many cases, there is no market for public services, and, even when such a market exists, the 'value' of the service cannot be completely understood measuring costs and revenues. We must also take into account 'equity' that can lead an administration to provide the service to all citizens, even if in some cases it will turn in an economic loss.
- There is an important time lag between inputs and outputs. On one hand, some actions of public administrations are aimed at preparing for the future (like investments in new technologies, personnel training, maintenance of buildings and infrastructures); on the other hand, we will be able to measure the value of the output of an administration only in the future: the result of a hospital will be measured by the long term survival of a patient; the results of an university by the employability of its graduates.

Hence, we decided not to use a single indicator, but a set of measures that, together, provide a complete view of the performance of the administration (Figure 15.2).

A first performance is the ratio between the quantity of outputs produced (products, services, procedures) and the available resources (efficiency).

Efficiency is a critical performance when the output of the service is standardized. However, usually in public administrations the 'quality' of output is as important as its quantity. Hence, we must also measure the 'effectiveness' of the administration, which is the capacity to produce an output with features (quality, time, etc.) consistent with customers' needs.

As we noticed above, public administrations also must guarantee 'equity' in services, for instance, the possibility for all citizens to access public services, a third critical performance.

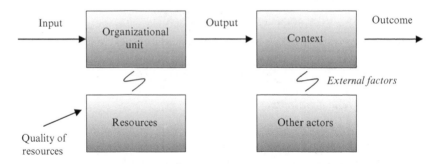

Figure 15.2   A summary of the indicators typology

The framework 'efficiency, effectiveness, equity' provides a complete picture of an administration only in the short term. To ensure a long term attitude, we must consider two other indicators, concerning output and input respectively. For the output, we must monitor the long term effect of PA activities (outcome), using indicators like the employability for universities and the long term survivals for patients, even if it is very hard to understand which share of such indicators is under the direct responsibility of each administration. Finally, to avoid a short-term bias, reducing long-term investment to improve efficiency, we must also measure the quality of the available resources.

Hence, as we illustrate further in this contribution, to identify peak performer administration, we must consider different type of performances:

- efficiency;
- effectiveness;
- equity;
- outcome;
- quality of resources.

Benchmarking Performances and Identifying Peak Performer Administrations

The comparison of the performance of different administrations, even when doing a similar job, must consider another problem. In general, we are unable to summarize in a single indicator the set of services an administration provides, somehow weighting their importance. Public administrations are in charge of completely different services: how can we compare the value of primary schools and of the 'safety' that local police provides? Besides, such services involve different users and that makes it more difficult to weight the importance of each service. Hence, we com-

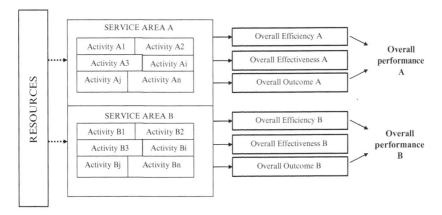

Figure 15.3   The activity based model

pared different administrations measuring their specific performance in each service.

We must also consider that the internal organization of each administration can differ, leading to possible bias when trying to compare organizational units involved in a same service in different administrations. In the research, to overcome such problem, we decided to follow an activity based approach (Kaplan, 1983; Johnson and Kaplan, 1987; Bhimani and Brimson, 1989; Mitchell, 1994; 1996; Arena et al., 2009). Figure 15.3 shows a representation of the model.

The model is firstly based on the identification of the 'map of activities' for each service. This activity map offers a measurement system to compare the performances of administrations on a common basis; one of the main criticism of the use of benchmarking in the public sector is the lack of homogenous data, hence the poor reliability of comparative analysis: the use of activity model allowed the homogenous data to overcome the problems of intra-organizational divisions. In addition to a common activity map, administrations need to identify a common 'pool of resources' they want to allocate; this is particularly important for the comparison of efficiency indicators. For these latter, finally, we need to define a 'driver'; for instance, the output upon which homogenous costs are divided.

To identify the peak performers, as we are unable to define a set of common weights to synthesize the different performances and the different services, we decided, in the end, to use the data envelope analysis. This method determines empirically an optimal frontier, identifying the best practices among a group of organizations (Zhu, 2003), without requiring the definition of weights. This analysis defines a frontier, in which different mixes of performances are allowed. Figure 15.4 and 15.6 show examples of frontiers, considering efficiency and effectiveness.

RESULTS: HETEROGENEITY IN PRACTICE

This section presents the results in two sections. The first part shows the heterogeneity of performance in some sectors of the two countries; the second part instead focused on peak performers and the leverages of their achievements.

Heterogeneity of Performance

The definition of measures and common protocols in benchmarking had been far from being straightforward; however the 20-year empirical evidence of our studies highlighted enormous improvements, leading to consolidated and shared frameworks (Arnaboldi and Azzone, 2010). Specifically this contribution refers to four experiences (two in Italy and two in the UK) to point out the heterogeneity of performance across organizations belonging to same sub-sector, before discussing the endogenous factors affecting performance diversity.

Concerning the UK, the first picture is provided by local authorities in Scotland. As more generally in the UK, here the pressure from the central government to define measurement frameworks was higher than in Italy, guiding administrations to a continuous confrontation for defining performance indicators (Arnaboldi and Laspley, 2003; 2008; 2009). This bilateral confrontation has led to the definition of two types of comparative performance frameworks: (1) centrally ruled by Audit Scotland and (2) voluntary benchmarking initiatives. In both cases administration are compared over a rich set of indicators: effectiveness, equity, efficiency, outcome and the quality of resources. These comparisons show the heterogeneity of organizations' performances within similar administrations, as shown in Figure 15.4.

Figure 15.4 illustrates the performance of Scottish local authorities in one service, waste management. Specifically administrations are positioned in the graph according to two indicators included in the Audit Scotland reports (2011): net cost of refuse collection per premise, overall cleanliness index (ranging from 60 to 100). LAa, LAb, and LAc form the 'optimal frontier': these organizations have the highest performances in waste management (though with different mixes of efficiency and effectiveness) against other local authorities.

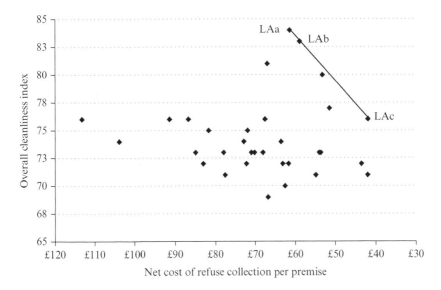

Source: adapted from Audit Scotland (2011).

*Figure 15.4   Waste management performances for Scottish local
authorities*

Focusing on efficiency, a clear example of differences is provided by the comparison of the total expenses per pupil of English secondary schools, here (Figure 15.5) aggregated by local authorities (median value). The graph shows the variance of the median spend per pupil, with difference of more than 200 per cent. Analyzing the detail of each secondary school, variance becomes even greater.

Regarding Italy, the benchmarking among homogenous authorities is less driven by the central government; however several administrations have voluntary developed frameworks to compare their performance. We focus in this contribution on two experiences, in which the authors participated as action researchers (Arnaboldi and Azzone, 2010; Arena et al., 2009; 2010). The first research is the construction of a performance framework to benchmark universities' support services. As for UK administrations, the heterogeneity of performance is marked. Figure 15.6 shows the positioning of 17 major universities in terms of efficiency (cost per student) and effectiveness (overall students' satisfaction) in student support services.

UNI a and UNI b form the 'optimal frontier' showing the highest mix of efficiency and effectiveness performance in students' support services.

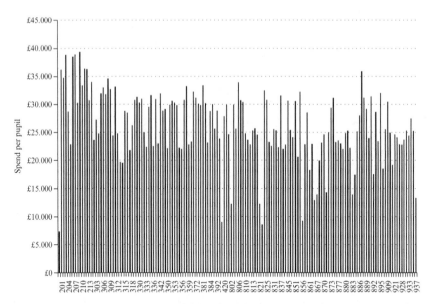

Source: adapted from Department of Education (2010).

Figure 15.5   Spend per pupil – secondary schools in England aggregated by local authorities

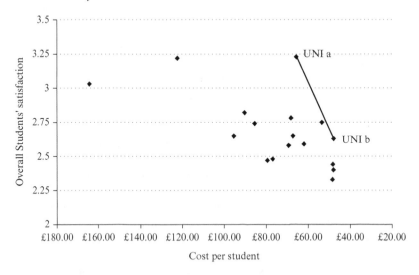

Source: adapted from Arena et al. (2009).

Figure 15.6   Italian universities – efficiency and effectiveness in student support services

Table 15.1   *Italian municipalities – efficiency and effectiveness within*
                kindergarten services

Municipality	Effectiveness (% of satisfied requests)	Efficiency (cost per available place)
A	59%	7208
B	85%	5838
C	59%	9369
D	67%	11 000
E	92%	6491
F	88%	4707
G	67%	8337
H	56%	6451
I	99%	7335
L	64%	11 805
M	42%	9617
N	19%	11 703
O	61%	5701
P	64%	10 680
Q	41%	9497
R	69%	9654
S	88%	10 420
T	65%	11 167
U	80%	9751

Source: Based on data collected directly from Italian municipalities.

A final illustration of heterogeneity is provided by municipalities in Italy;
Table 15.1 shows the performances of kindergartens, in terms of efficiency
and effectiveness.

Peak Performers' Drivers

Starting from the heterogeneity presented above, this section analyzes how
peak performers in various sectors and services have been able to better
seize the opportunity provided by NPM reforms both in the UK and in
Italy. In particular four 'internal drivers' were evidenced as central during
our longitudinal observation: pervasive commitment, bridging competence, flexible coordination and operational consolidation.

Pervasive commitment
The importance of commitment in leading organization to improve their
performances is indeed not a novelty; however what it is less frequently

discussed is the need to create a 'pervasive' commitment across the administration, ranging from politicians, top managers to employees. This moves away from the idea of a single 'hero' (Greener, 2004) guiding the whole organization, introducing the importance of propagating an initial idea and progressively convincing other actors of the importance of change. A positive example is provided by a Scottish local authority (Arnaboldi and Lapsley, 2010), labelled here LAScot. LAScot started in 2004 a major project for revisiting the management of city assets, including school, roads, building and cultural heritage. The central actor of this intervention was the asset manager, who however immediately recognized the importance of building a network of actors across the authority. The asset manager initially involved line managers in charge of different categories of assets, forming a team, and building a solid picture of assets' performances. With the evidence stemmed from numbers, the assets' team was able to convince even politicians, who were regarded as being reluctant to base decisions on rational schemes. Finally the commitment was transmitted at the lowest level of the hierarchy through the first line team, but also outside, to citizens, in order to communicate and motivate critical decisions (for example, cutting funds for schools' refurbishing).

Bridging competence

In all the successful cases, regardless the sector or the country, the achievement of better performances is based on solid competences in key areas for the administrations. The longitudinal experience in UK and Italian administrations evidenced however that, in the long-run, what is central is not the actual presence of competences, but the capability of leaders and managers to dynamically and constantly identify gaps in competences and finding sustainable ways to bridge these gaps.

An interesting example is provided by an Italian university (UNI Ita), which started, at the beginning of the 2000s, a progressive renewal of its managerial competences (Arnaboldi and Azzone, 2004; 2005; 2010). The initial commitment came from the governing bodies, who identified the need to better control the use of resources. To face the lack of internal competences different strategies were carried out, such as: the acquisition of external human resources, by enrolling managers from the private sector or other universities; the involvement of managers in projects supported by external consultants. The initial effort has been maintained over the years, adapting the competence needs to the changing environment; more recently, for example, this university enforced its communication capabilities, with a specific focus on the potentiality of social networks, in order to engage more widely and in a timely manner with prospective, students, alumni and even citizens.

Flexible coordination

The examples presented in the two previous sections, highlight the importance to rapidly adapt organizations to external changes. This flexibility needs, on one hand, the capability to seize 'windows of opportunities' and enact new initiatives; but on the other hand these discrete innovations need to be coordinated, to avoid duplication and inconsistencies; this capability is addressed here as flexible coordination. An interesting example of this capability is provided by a major Italian Court House, which has undertaken in 2008 an overall project of reorganization to improve its performances (Agostino et al., 2012). Although strategic goals and a project plan were delivered, since the beginning it was evident that it would have been impossible to predict all the necessary initiatives, given the complexity and turbulence of the organizational and institutional context.

Initially the innovation department head was put in charge of the internal coordination, with the role of supporting external consultants and coordinating internal actors. Despite his unquestionable technical competences, he was revealed to be unable to follow the dynamic evolution of interventions, and to relate interventions going on in different parts of the court house. During the intervention, it became evident that another manager (the accounting head) had this capability, and she was progressively charged with coordinating responsibilities. She was able to capture the connections, and sometime inconsistencies, of different interventions; furthermore she was able to communicate with a wide range of actors (officers, judges, managers, consultants), adapting her language to the specific situation.

Operational consolidation

While the first three leverages emphasize innovative and adaptive capabilities, the latter dimension points to the consolidation of the results achieved in institutionalized processes. This need has been proven by institutional research several times (for example, Meyer and Rowan, 1997; Burn and Scapens, 2000; Lounsbury, 2008), reporting how innovative practices are undermined by old institutionalized routines. To avoid a 'return to the past' the operational consolidation of new practices is central, as exemplified by the case of a healthcare organization in the UK, here generically referred to as Health UK (Arnaboldi and Lapsley, 2004; 2005). This organization addressed the introduction of modern costing technology – activity based costing (ABC) – upon the advocacy of a member of the senior management team. Despite an earlier attempt to introduce ABC failing, this second effort was successful, largely by clearly analyzing, and then substituting, operational processes and costing methods previously used in different parts of the organizations. This change required several years, during which the project team constantly monitored actual practices and the performances of ABC in providing more precise and useful information to managers. An important contribution to the consolidation was the implementation, after a pilot case, of an ad hoc information system, which eased the shift from the experimentation to the wider adoption across Health UK.

CONCLUSION

This contribution recounted the experience of several public administrations in the UK and Italy to analyze how peak performers have been able to seize the opportunities initiated by NPM reforms. Four internal drivers have been presented through the illustration of case studies; these drivers are: pervasive commitment, bridging competence, flexible coordination and operational consolidation.

In conclusion we provide some transversal remarks. Firstly, these results highlighted the importance of a wider participation in innovation across the organization; this situation favours the implementation of planned intervention, but also the origination of new ideas and competences. Secondly, performance numbers proved to be central during all the phases of change interventions: to motivate the change; to measure achievements; to continuously monitor the coherence between 'solutions' and the external environment. Thirdly, all the cases proved the importance of action-learning to involve employees and to form internal capabilities, raising the issue of the type of training usually provided in the public sector. Finally, a background element of peak performers in adopting the four leverages was their endurance in time, usually several years, and effort, in term both of financial and human resources.

REFERENCES

Agostino, D., M. Arena, M. Arnaboldi (2012), 'Leading change in public organizations: the role of mediators', *Leadership & Organization Development Journal*, forthcoming.

Arena, M., M. Arnabold and G. Azzone (2010), 'Student perception and central administrative services: the case of higher education in Italy', *Studies in Higher Education*, **35** (8), 941–59.

Arena, M., M. Arnaboldi, G. Azzone and P. Carlucci (2009), 'Developing a performance measurement system for the central administrative services of the universities', *Higher Education Quarterly*, **63** (3), 237–63.

Arnaboldi, M. and G. Azzone (2004), 'Benchmarking university Activities: an Italian case study', *Financial Accountability and Management*, **20** (2), 205–20.

Arnaboldi, M. and G. Azzone (2005), 'Incrementalism and strategic change: a university's experience', *International Journal of Educational Management*, **19** (7), 552–63.

Arnaboldi, M. and G. Azzone (2010), 'Constructing performance measurement in the public Sector', *Critical Perspective on Accounting*, **21** (4), 266–82.

Arnaboldi, M. and I. Lapsley (2003), 'Activity based costing, modernity and the transformation of local government: a field study', *Public Management Review*, **5** (3), 345–75.

Arnaboldi, M. and I. Lapsley (2004), 'Modern costing innovations and legitimation: a health care study', *Abacus*, **40** (1), 1–19.

Arnaboldi, M. and I. Lapsley (2005), 'Activity based costing in health care: a UK case study', *Research in Health Care Financial Management*, **10** (1), 59–73.

Arnaboldi, M. and I. Lapsley (2008), 'Making management auditable: the implementation of best value in local government', *Abacus*, **44** (1), 22–47.

Arnaboldi, M. and I. Lapsley (2009), 'On the implementation of accrual accounting: a study of conflict and ambiguity', *European Accounting Review*, **18** (4), 809–36.

Arnaboldi, M. and I. Lapsley (2010), 'Asset management in cities: polyphony in action?', *Accounting, Auditing and Accountability Journal*, **23** (3), 392–419.

Arnaboldi, M. and T. Palermo (2011), 'Translating ambiguous reforms: doing better next time?', *Management Accounting Research*, **22** (1), 6–15.

Audit Scotland (2011), *Compendium 2011/10 – Performance Information*, accessed at http://www.audit-scotland.gov.uk.

Bhimani, A. and J. Brimson (1989), 'Advanced manufacturing technology and strategic perspectives in management accounting', *European Accounting News*, January.

Burns, J. and R.W. Scapens (2000), 'Conceptualising management accounting change: an institutional framework', *Management Accounting Research*, **11** (1), 3–25.

Department of Education (2010), *Performance Table 2010*, accessed at http://www.education.gov.uk.

Greener, I. (2004), 'Talking to health managers about change: heroes, villains and simplification', *Journal of Health Organization and Management*, **18** (5), 321–55.

Gruening, G. (2001), 'Origin and theoretical basis of new public management' *International Public Management Journal*, **4**, 1–25.

Hood, C. (1991), 'A public management for all seasons?', *Public Administration*, **69** (1), 3–19.

Hood, C. (1995), 'The 'new public management' in the 1980s: variations on a theme', *Accounting, Organizations and Society*, **20** (2/3), 93–109.

Hope, K.R. (2001), 'The new public management: context and practice in Africa', *International Public Management Journal*, **4**, 119–34.

Johnson, H. and R.S. Kaplan (1987), *Relevance Lost: The Rise and Fall of Management Accounting*, Boston, MA: Harvard Business School Press.

Kaplan, R.S. (1983), 'Measuring manufacturing performance: a new challenge for managerial accounting research', *Accounting Review*, **58** (4), 686–705.

Lapsley, I. (2008), 'The NPM agenda: back to the future', *Financial Accountability and Management*, **24**, 77–95.

Lapsley, I. (2009), 'New public management: the cruelest invention of the human spirit?', *Abacus*, **45**, 1–21.

Levy, R. (2010), 'New public management end of an era?', *Public Policy and Administration*, **25** (2), 234–40.

Lounsbury, M. (2008), 'Institutional rationality and practice variation: new directions in the institutional analysis of practice', *Accounting Organizations and Society*, **33** (4/5), 349–61.

Meyer, J.W. and B. Rowan (1977), 'Institutionalized organizations: formal structure as myth and ceremony', *The American Journal of Sociology*, **83** (2), 340–63.

Mitchell, F. (1994), 'A commentary on the applications of activity-based costing', *Management Accounting Research*, **5**, 261–77.

Mitchell, M. (1996), 'Activity-based costing in UK universities', *Public Money and Management*, January–March, 51–7.

OECD (1995), *Governance in Transition: Public Management Reforms in OECD Countries*, Paris: OECD.

Osborne, S. (2006), 'The new public governance?', *Public Management Review*, **8** (3), 377–87.

Pipan, T. and B. Czarniawska (2010), 'How to construct an actor-network: management accounting from idea to practice', *Critical Perspective on Accounting*, **21**, 243–51.

Pollitt, C. (2009), 'Bureaucracies remember, post-bureaucratic organizations forget?', *Public Administration*, **87** (2), 198–218.

Pollitt, C. and G. Bouckaert (2000), *Public Management Reform, a Competitive Analysis*, Oxford: Oxford University Press.

Zhu, J. (2003), *Quantitative Models for Performance Evaluation and Benchmarking*, Boston, MA: Kluwer Academic Publisher.

Zifcak, S. (1994), 'New managerialism: administrative reform in Whitehall and Canberra', Buckingham: Open University Press.

16. Public sector human resource management education in the United States: contemporary challenges and opportunities for performance improvement

Jared J. Llorens

INTRODUCTION

While public sector employment in the US has experienced a number of transformational periods since the nation's founding, from the merit-based reforms of the late 19th century to management centered new public management (NPM) practices of the 1990s, the rapid pace of technological change and the global economic turmoil of the past five years have served as catalysts for a renewed push to transform public sector employment. From Europe to the US, public sector employers and employees are in the process of redefining the traditional norms of public sector employment in areas such as recruitment, compensation, collective bargaining and job security. As a result, the task of effectively and efficiently managing public sector human resources has also been transformed. Within the US, this transformational push has manifested itself with the growing use of technology in core human resource management (HRM) functions, efforts at the state and local levels of government to reduce public employee rights and benefits, and efforts at the federal level of government to substantially limit employee compensation in light of growing budget deficits (O'Keefe et al., 2010; Maher and Nicas, 2011).

As Llorens and Battaglio (2010) point out, these transformational forces currently impacting public sector employment will ultimately necessitate a reevaluation of how public managers and HRM specialists are educated to effectively develop and manage the workforce of the future. While the traditional paradigm of HRM education has presumed the presence of a stable civil service employment base managed through highly rule-bound and standardized personnel systems, public managers and HRM specialists will increasingly be tasked with hiring and retaining employees using flexible compensation strategies, adapting to the unique needs of a younger generation of employees and leveraging rapidly evolving technological applications. While this transformation will inevitably impact all facets of educating future public managers, its impact upon HRM education will be truly transformative. This chapter seeks to shed further light upon this topic by specifically addressing the current educational framework for educating public managers and specialists in the US, outlining a select group of challenges facing the field, and last, discussing opportunities and strategies for more effective approaches to HRM education.

HUMAN RESOURCE MANAGEMENT EDUCATION FOR PUBLIC SECTOR PROFESSIONALS

Given the contemporary challenges to effective public sector HRM, it is quite logical to inquire about the current capacity of educational programs to equip and prepare public managers and HRM specialists with the necessary skills to effectively manage the workforce of the future. Within the US context, the educational framework for future and current public managers and HRM specialists is quite varied, which makes comprehensive assessments of the state-of-the-art quite difficult. Unlike legal and medical professions, there are no requisite degree programs or centralized credentialing processes, and in many public organizations, the educational background for managers and HRM specialists can consist of a complex mix (see Table 16.1) of traditional graduate degree programs in public administration and policy, on-the-job training, formal institutional training, formal education in related degree fields such as business management, or certification programs offered by HRM associations.

Given its focus on HRM education within the public sector context, this chapter will first focus on traditional graduate degree programs.

While, in general, public administration graduate degree programs vary considerably by subject area focus (for instance, policy, public finance, etc.) and targeted sector of student placement (for instance, local, state or federal government), most mainstream programs in the US belong to the National Association of Schools of Public Affairs and Administration (NASPAA).[1] NASPAA serves as the primary accrediting body for the field and, as such, establishes standards for membership that outline specific areas that all accredited programs must address in their curriculum. In order to become accredited members of NASPAA, degree programs are evaluated by representatives from accredited peer institutions with regards

Table 16.1   *Framework of human resource management education in the US*

Educational format	Target audience	Examples
University-based graduate programs in public administration	Pre-service and in-service professionals	NASPAA accredited programs
Formal institutional training	In-service professionals	US Government's Graduate School USA
Association-based certification programs	HRM Specialists	International Public Management Association for Human Resources – Certified Professional Program
Graduate programs in related disciplines	Pre-service and in-service professionals	Business administration degree programs offering coursework in HRM
On-the-job training	In-service professionals	Agency development/mentorship programs

to their adherence to NASPAA's program standards. Accreditation standards cover a wide range of subject areas, from faculty qualifications to student recruitment, and while past accreditation standards outlined specific curriculum subject areas that were to be covered by all accredited programs, NASPAA's current standards have adopted a competency-based approach. This approach is much broader than past standards and provides programs with the ability to tailor their curriculums to their specific missions and labor market needs. To provide a measure of consistency across program areas, NASPAA identifies universally required competencies for all program participants, which hold that all graduates of accredited programs are competent in the ability to:

- lead and manage in public governance;
- participate in and contribute to the policy process;
- analyze, synthesize, think critically, solve problems and make decisions;
- articulate and apply a public service perspective;
- communicate and interact productively with a diverse and changing workforce and citizenry (NASPAA, 2009).

Given the open interpretation inherent in the competency-based approach, there are no standards specifically related to competencies in HRM for either managers or public HRM specialists beyond the general competency to 'lead and mange in public governance'. As such, skills in this area are covered to varying extents at the programmatic level. Some programs might choose to incorporate core HRM competencies as part of broader public administration/management coursework (for instance, a targeted lectured in a public management course) and other programs might offer dedicated courses in areas such as public personnel policy or employee labor relations. Evidence of variation in program coverage of HRM was found in Koven, Goetzke and Brennan's (2008) study of top public administration programs. They found that of the top 37 programs that received NASPAA accreditation, less than 40 per cent required at least one course in HRM, and Llorens and Battaglio (2010) later found that of those top programs that were not accredited by NASPAA, less than 25 per cent required at least one HRM course.[2]

While such limited coverage of HRM may be somewhat disconcerting given the importance of the HRM function in many organizations, the task of educating HRM specialists and managers may take place in a number of venues beyond traditional university-based educational programs. In addition to traditional graduate level instruction, public managers or HRM professionals seeking targeted instruction on core HRM competencies can also take advantage of certification programs offered through professional associations.[3] For example, the International Public Management Association for Human Resources (IPMA-HR) is one such organization that provides three separate certifications programs, one for human resources professionals seeking general instruction, one for those seeking specialized instruction in a specific competency and one for senior level executives seeking instruction on managing HRM departments (IPMA-HR, 2011). The Society for Human resource management (SHRM) is another association that offers broader HRM certification programs targeted for both private and public sector HRM professionals. Offering separate certification programs for professionals, senior professionals and global professionals, SHRM certification programs address competencies in such areas as health care benefits, compensation and diversity management (SHRM, 2011).

Additionally, larger public organizations may seek to develop their own programs to educate managers and specialists on key HRM issues. The US federal government's HRM training programs provide a great example of this type of approach. With a workforce of approximately 2 million, not including contract employees, it would be virtually impossible for the federal government to rely solely upon university-based educational programs and associations to address its HRM educational needs, and it would also be quite difficult to do so through one centralized agency. Given the scope of its educational needs, the federal government maintains a multi-faceted approach that relies on the expertise of both its lead HRM agency, the US Office of Personnel Management (OPM), and individual agencies. For example, OPM operates a centralized management training program that provides federal managers with the ability to take formal coursework in relevant HRM areas such as 'conflict resolution' and 'coaching and mentoring' (US Office of Personnel Management, 2011). Additionally, the federal government has benefited from the presence of Graduate School USA, a federal training center formerly housed in the US Department of Agriculture. Operating on a reimbursable basis in regional centers across the US, the School educates thousands of federal, state and local government employees annually, and offers HRM courses in such topics as compensation, recruitment and human capital management (Graduate School USA, 2011).

Finally, public managers and HRM specialists may also obtain critical HRM skills through related educational programs or on-the-job training. For example, like public administration programs, many business administration programs offer coursework in HRM and there are also a number of universities which offer graduate level education specifically in HRM. While generally focused on private sector employment, much of the coursework in these types of programs is readily transferable to public sector environments.[4] While often not as formal as traditional training programs, on-the-job training programs can provide a wealth of developmental experiences in HRM for mangers and specialists alike. For example, there are number of public employers that provide new and existing employees with the opportunity to be mentored by senior specialists either formally or informally.

CONTEMPORARY CHALLENGES TO EFFECTIVE PUBLIC HRM PRACTICE IN THE US

As stated earlier, the current transformational environment for public sector employment presents a number of critical challenges for effective HRM. In many respects, the underlying forces driving these challenges, see Figure 16.1, are the result of NPM personnel reforms of the past 20 years, and more recent challenges which have directly resulted from broader changes related to advancements in technology, the shifting expectations of younger generations of employees and most recently, the global economic downturn affecting government tax revenues and expenditures. When combined, these forces portend major challenges for rank and file public managers at all levels of government, as well as HRM specialists.[5]

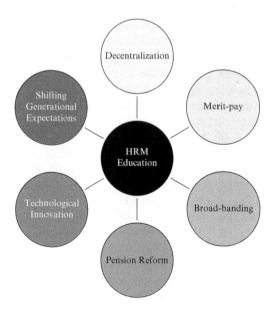

Figure 16.1   Challenges facing human resource management education

Key Reform Driven Challenges

Since the passage of the Pendleton Act of 1883, public sector employment and accompanying civil service systems in the US have been characterized by a tripartite focus on merit-based selection processes, security of tenure for rank-and-file public employees and a commitment to political neutrality. However, reforms initiated in the late 1970s and advanced more aggressively in the mid-1990s sought to address many of the inefficiencies inherent in traditional civil service systems that were directly related to the underlying principles of civil service employment. Two reforms, in particular, have presented the most substantial challenge to effectively managing public sector human resources: the decentralization of personnel authority and performance-based compensation (Llorens and Battaglio, 2010).

Decentralization
One of the major components of the new public management (NPM) reforms of the 1990s was the decentralization of core HRM processes from centralized personnel centers to agency managers. In many traditional civil service systems, centralization and standardization was viewed as essential in order to maintain a commitment to merit. However, for many public employers, the centralization and standardization of processes such

as recruitment and compensation had come to be characterized as slow, inefficient and inadequate as a means of adapting to the specific needs of 'street level' administrations. The common hypothetical scenario used to critique the system was of a manager who successfully recruited a talented candidate, but was only able to hire that candidate if they were able to navigate lengthy mazes of civil service tests and personnel boards. As many reformers anecdotally pointed out, it was virtually impossible to maintain a high performing workforce under such circumstances. As a result, many public employers took decisive steps to decentralize these processes and provide managers with the opportunity to carry out many of the tasks that had once been the sole province of HRM specialists working in a central personnel office (see, for example, Hays and Sowa, 2006).

While it is difficult to argue against the benefits of added flexibility and responsiveness in managing an organization's human resources, the reality of such a shift in responsibility is that many newly empowered managers and administrative units may not possess the requisite HRM subject expertise or institutional knowledge required to effectively manage this new responsibility. As a result, decentralization reforms have heightened the need for frontline administrators to develop critical HRM competencies to compensate for the weakened role and influence of HRM specialists operating out of centralized personnel offices.

Compensation
In addition to decentralization, there are two related NPM reforms, broad-banding and merit-pay, that have significantly altered public sector compensation systems in reformed environments. Traditionally, public sector compensation has prioritized position-based, internal pay equity where positions of equal worth receive equal compensation (Klingner et. al., 2010). Under these traditional systems, there is much less emphasis on the individual performance of employees or variation in the skills that they might bring to a particular position. For managers and HRM specialists operating within these systems, there is also very little discretion in setting annual or hourly pay rates or rewarding exceptional performers, and from the employee's perspective, there are relatively few opportunities to negotiate higher pay rates for individual employees beyond seeking higher level positions within the organization.

In an effort to provide public managers with the ability to strategically use compensation to improve program performance, many public employers have enacted broad-banding and merit-pay plans (see, for example, Kellough and Nigro, 2002; Hays, 2004; Whalen and Guy, 2008). Under broad-banding, pay rates for specific occupations are set at the discretion of a manager within a specified range or band. For example, in a traditional compensation system, the annual pay rate for an entry-level accountant may be set at $45 000 (US), but under a broad-banded plan, the eligible pay rate for a particular candidate for the accountant position may range from $35 000 to $55 000 (US). As a result of this approach, managers may set candidate-specific pay rates that account for differences in education, prior experience or past performance.

Similar in purpose to broad-banding pay plans, merit-pay plans seek to provide managers with the flexibility to link individual employee pay rates to their job performance. In contrast to traditional systems which deemphasize individual employee performance in the pay setting process, merit-pay plans typically base annual pay increases on an individual employee's performance as documented in their annual or quarterly performance appraisal. In theory, linking employee pay increases to the results of employee performance appraisals serves to better motivate employees, as well as increase organizational performance (Kellough and Lu, 1993).

In terms of HRM education, however, transitioning to broad-banded or merit-pay plans requires a much more sophisticated approach to managing compensation than under traditional systems.

First, under traditional systems, managers and HRM specialists alike are allowed to rely upon pay setting policies in setting pay rates, and as a result, both groups can remain relatively unaware of the intricacies of local, regional and national labor markets. However, when setting individual pay rates within a particular range under broad-banding system, it is imperative that both managers and HRM specialists make themselves aware of fluctuations in prevailing rates or the quality of candidates that can be expected in regards to a given pay range. In other words, with the added flexibility of setting pay rates comes the responsibility of properly assessing what those rates should reasonably be. If managed ineffectively, managers could easily find themselves paying too much for particular candidates, thus taking valuable public resources away from other areas of the organization. The additional burden for HRM specialists under such systems is no less substantial. While HRM specialists can simply follow existing classification and compensation guidelines in traditional systems, they must become much more consultative under broad-banded pay systems to ensure that managers are properly determining employee pay rates and are in no way biased in their decisions.

Second, establishing effective performance appraisal instruments is critical for those organizations transitioning to merit-pay plans, but the difficulty in achieving this task is directly related to the complexity of many public sector occupations. While establishing effective appraisal instruments may be somewhat straightforward for for-profit organizations with clear performance indicators (for example, selling durable goods such as cars or electronic equipment), doing so for public sector occupations (for example, an accountant in a large bureaucratic organization) with multiple or long-term goals can be much more of a challenge. In these instances, effectively distinguishing employee performance levels is often fraught with disagreement and dissension. In such cases, it is absolutely necessary for both managers and HRM specialists to maintain accurate, up-to-date position descriptions, and adopt appraisal instruments that capture the full complexity of public sector occupations, not simply a one-size-fits-all approach.

Technological Advancement, Millennial Employees and Market-Driven Pension Reform

Technological advancement and millennial employees

Overall, the pace of technological advancement over the past 20 years has been nothing short of revolutionary, and one would be hard pressed to find a facet of the modern, white-collar workplace that has not been impacted in some form by the advent of new technologies. From the beginnings of web-based information sharing to more recent developments related to mobile computing devices such as smartphones, technology has both improved information sharing processes in the modern workplace and created the need for a more technologically savvy workforce.

For the public sector, the impact of technological advancements has been widespread, but, arguably, the human resource management function has been one of the areas most affected by these advancements. Overall, technological advancements have impacted a vast array of HRM functions, from workforce development to records management, but its impact upon the recruitment arena has been the substantial. In just the last 20 years, the public sector recruitment function has transitioned from a largely paper-based, labor intensive process to one that is highly technical and evolving at a very rapid pace (Llorens and Kellough, 2007; Llorens, forthcoming).

Traditionally, public sector employers operated recruitment systems that relied upon local or regionally based job announcements, as well as the efforts of a limited number of recruitment staff. For example, if a vacant position were open with the US federal government in Dallas, Texas circa 1980, federal recruiters would have most likely posted a formal vacancy announcement in local federal buildings and may also have sent recruiters to local universities and employment centers (Llorens and Kellough, 2007). Under these traditional recruitment systems, applicant pools were limited to interested candidates from a defined geographic region, and applicants were generally required to submit paper-based applications by mail. Additionally, the relevant vacancy information available to job candidates was limited to the facts that could be contained on a printed job announcement. Given conventional wisdom which suggests that larger applicant pools increase the likelihood of selecting high quality candidates, it is clear to see that these types of recruitment systems fell quite short of soliciting the best and brightest into a candidate pool.

By the mid-1990s, however, advancements in personal computing and internet access had greatly transformed recruitment systems in both the public and private sectors. Simply stated, the ability to both post and exchange large quantities of information through web-based portals allowed employers to advertise vacancy information to a virtually limitless applicant pool and also allowed potential applicants to apply for positions electronically. Turning back to the previous example of filling a vacant position in Dallas, Texas, federal recruiters, using web-based recruitment portals, became capable of advertising local vacancies nation-wide, thus expanding their applicant pool and increasing the likelihood of attracting high quality candidates. The inherent advantage of web-based recruitment methods has been the catalyst for the development of the US federal government's US Jobs website, and, for many public employers at the state and local levels of government, web-based recruitment is now the norm (Cober et al., 2000; Zusman and Landis, 2002; Kim and O'Connor, 2009; Selden and Orenstein; 2011; Llorens, forthcoming).

In recent years, however, web-based recruitment technologies have been greatly influenced by two related movements: the growing presence of Millennial employees and job candidates and the expanding use of web-based social networking tools. Members of the Millennial generation are generally between the ages of 18 and 29 and recent research has highlighted their unique characteristics compared to members of Generation X (30–45), Baby Boomers (46–64) and members of the Silent generation (65 and older) (Pew, 2010a). Having grown up in a time of technological innovation, Millennials are commonly considered 'digital natives' given their familiarity with web-based media and recruiting members of this generation into the workforce will almost certainly entail web-based recruitment methods (Yeaton, 2008). Further, Millennials have also been greatly shaped by the growth of more recently developed social networking tools, and for many, social networking sites such as Facebook and Twitter serve as a primary means of communication and information gathering. In fact, the Pew Research Center recently reported that 75 per cent of Millennials acknowledge having a social networking profile, which is more than double that of Baby Boomers (30 per cent) and substantially greater than that of members of Generation X (50 per cent) (2010).

Given their projected growth in the labor market, many progressive employers have taken significant steps to increase their social media presence in an effort to attract and communicate more effectively with Millennial job candidates. Public employers such as the US State Department and Internal Revenue Service (IRS) have fully adopted such practices and maintain recruitment profiles on such popular social networking sites as Facebook, Twitter, Tumblr and also post related media on sites such as Youtube and Flickr (US Internal Revenue Service, 2011; US State Department, 2011a). Additionally, the IRS has gone one step further in its efforts by seeking to attract those job candidates who have an interest in web-based gaming. The agency actively maintains a presence on the popular virtual game Second Life and also hosts interactive web-based games that allow potential job applicants to test their skills as a financial crimes investigator (2011). Most recently, progressive public employers have begun to leverage mobile computing devices in the search for talented job candidates. For example, the US State Department recently launched a mobile career application (app) for Apple's popular ipad and iphone, Blackberry devices, and mobile computing devices using Google's Android operating system (US State Department, 2011b).

In terms of HRM education, the movement towards more technologically-driven recruitment methods will necessitate the presence of both public managers and HRM professionals who are technologically adept and possess the ability to transform public sector recruitment systems to remain competitive in an environment of oftentimes hyper-technological change. The dynamics of the labor market suggest that those employers who are unable to adapt to a changing recruitment landscape will operate at a competitive disadvantage in the quest for talented candidates, and may potentially experience performance losses as a direct result.

Pension reform
While merit-pay and broad-banding reforms are generally proposed as tools that can allow managers to more effectively manage their human resources, the recent global economic downturn has served as the catalyst for additional compensation reforms aimed at cutting employment costs. In particular, public sector pension reform has arisen as one of the more popular of these reforms, but given the role that pensions have traditionally played in the public sector, such reform efforts will have significant implications for managers and HRM specialists.

For many public employers, especially those in the US, the use of pensions has been a key component in the retention of a qualified workforce. Pensions traditionally operate as defined benefit style retirement plans were participants contribute to their retirement while they are employed and are guaranteed a defined benefit, for life, after their retirement. Since public sector pay rates have traditionally fallen below comparable private sector pay rates, many public employers have provided relatively generous pension plans as a means of rewarding employees when raising pay rates to comparable levels may be deemed unfeasible for political reasons (Cayer, 2010). While pensions are not portable for employees, they are considered beneficial since they guarantee an income stream for life upon retirement and remove the burden of retirement planning from the employee.

Pensions, however, have become increasingly costly to maintain given losses to government pension investments in the equity market and inadequate funding on the part of employers (Pew, 2010b). As a result, many employers are now proposing and adopting the use of defined-contribution style retirement plans that substantially reduce the financial burden upon employers. Defined contribution plans rely upon employee and employer matched contributions to a retirement account that is invested in the market at a risk level determined by the employee. Upon retirement, employees are provided with the accumulated contributions plus accrued interest. Unlike pension plans, defined contribution plans are portable, but retired employees must survive upon their one-time disbursement for the remainder of their lives. Further, the employer's financial commitment to the retiree ends upon retirement. From a HRM perspective, the shift from pensions to defined contribution plans holds the potential to dramatically impact the recruitment and retention of qualified employees to the extent that public sector pay rates are not at sufficiently high levels to offset lower benefit levels. While employees participating in pension plans typically remain with an employer, despite lower pay rates, since their retirement benefits are not portable, employees in defined contribution plans may be more likely to re-enter the labor market in search of higher pay rates if they can take their accumulated retirement contributions with them. For managers and HRM specialists, this shifting employment relationship typically requires an increased focus on effective recruitment, compensation and retention strategies.

OPPORTUNITIES FOR IMPROVEMENT IN PUBLIC SECTOR HRM EDUCATION

Given the myriad challenges facing public managers and the public sector HRM profession in particular, there are a number of substantial opportunities for performance improvements related to curriculum components, academic/practitioner exchanges and developing topics in the field.

First, the academic field of public administration would benefit from a more directed and specified alignment with contemporary HRM professional needs and practices. While there are a number of avenues for receiving training in key HRM subject areas, public administration programs will continue to serve as one of the primary educational bases for many in the field. In terms of existing standards for NASPAA accredited programs in public administration and policy, coverage related to the area of human resource management is overly broad, especially given the key contemporary role of HRM policies in public management. Simply requiring competencies in the 'ability to lead and manage' without outlining key topic areas related to these competencies are of very little benefit to public administration and policy programs with a generalized focus. Further, accreditation standards should also ensure that program curriculums maintain approaches to HRM education that not only train future managers and specialists on operating within traditional civil service systems, but also prepare them to operate within a growing environment of reformed HRM systems. It is of no benefit to these future employees if the academic training that they receive prior to entering public service prepares them for the realities of a traditional civil service environment which, for many public employers, is no longer the norm.

Second, the contemporary challenges facing public managers and HRM specialists highlight the growing need for more robust linkages between the practitioner and academic communities. While academic programs must retain their dual focus on both teaching and research, both areas of focus should remain informed by contemporary and emerging challenges facing the applied field of HRM. This growing need was recently pointed out in a research symposium emanating from the Minnowbrook III conference in 2010.[6] Speaking of public administration (PA) scholarship and practice in general, Bushouse et al. (2011: i101) note that:

> The issue is not that the field lacks good scholarship but rather that PA research, like most academic research, is conducted outside of practice. Research questions are driven by academic discourse rather than the pressing problems of public managers, resulting in a gap between what we research and what practitioners need.

To close this gap between academic research and the realities of applied practice, Bushouse et al.'s recommendations include more engaged scholarship by academics, greater adoption of effective knowledge sharing strategies to disseminate applicable research and more engaged teaching by public administration educators. The latter recommendation is most applicable to the current challenges facing public HRM education. In outlining specific steps for increasing the connection between what students learn in the classroom and the realities of practice, the authors suggest alternative pedagogical approaches that allow students to address 'real world' problems facing public managers. For example, instead of simply describing common recruitment methods employed in the public sector, an HRM instructor might have students consult with a local public employer on ways in which they might improve their existing approach to recruitment through the use of new social media technologies.

Finally, and most challenging, it would benefit the current field of public HRM education to develop more systematic linkages between university-based programs, institutional HRM education programs, and association-based certification programs. As previously discussed, the current educational framework is characterized by a wide range of educational opportunities ranging from formal coursework in public administration to agency training programs. While this current approach may reach a broad population in need of HRM education, it can also result in operational inefficiencies where subject areas are duplicated or not fully addressed. One can envision tangible benefits to a more efficient system of HRM education where academic programs provide students with a firm theoretical and applied grounding in topics such as recruitment and compensation that were informed by an understanding of what topics and practices might be covered through institutional training or certification programs. For example, if an academic program in public administration found that the majority of its students found employment in local and federal agencies, that program could then tailor its HRM curriculum to the educational opportunities that would be available to their students post-graduation. Additionally, the development of formal linkages between university-based programs and institutional development programs might potentially result in increased job opportunities for program graduates.

CONCLUDING THOUGHTS

While it can be argued that the field of public sector HRM has consistently been defined by its ability to adapt to the changing needs and demands placed upon public sector employment, it would appear that the forces impacting the field over the past 20 years have been truly transformative. To adequately prepare public managers and HRM specialists to adapt to these transformative forces, it is imperative that the field of public sector HRM education also adapts to meet the contemporary needs of applied practice. In sum, this chapter has sought to provide an overview of how the current HRM educational framework in the US is structured to meet this task, discuss the major challenges affecting the HRM profession and HRM education, and finally, provide suggestions for program improvements. While the discussed topics are by no means intended to be exhaustive of all of the issues facing the field of HRM education, it is hoped that this chapter can serve as a foundation for further efforts to address the growing importance of the field.

NOTES

1. The vast majority of public administration programs in the US offer degrees at the Post-Baccalaureate, Master's degree level. While there are a number of programs that also offer Baccalaureate and Doctoral degrees, these offerings are generally considered supplemental to the traditional Master's in Public Administration (MPA) degree.
2. NASPAA accreditation is voluntary for universities offering degrees in public administration.
3. Common core competencies in HRM include those related to the workforce planning process, the acquisition and retention of qualified employees, the development of new and existing employees, and the disciplinary process (Klingner et. al., 2010).
4. For an overview of the both public administration and HRM graduate degree programs, see Llorens and Battaglio (2010).
5. There are also a number of additional challenges to contemporary HRM practices not discussed in this section. These include the growth of at-will employment and challenges related to privatization. For further discussion, see Llorens and Battaglio (2010).
6. The Minnowbrook III conference was held in 2008. Participants included leading junior scholars in the field of public administration and public management, and the aim of the conference was to discuss critical issues facing the field. Prior conferences were held in 1968 and 1988.

REFERENCES

Bushouse, B., W. Jacobson, K. Lambright, J. Llorens, R. Morse and O. Poocharoen (2011), 'Crossing the divide: building bridges between public administration practitioners and scholars', *Journal of Public Administration Research and Theory*, **21** (1), i99–i112.

Cayer, N.J. (2010), 'Managing employee benefits', in S.E. Condrey (ed.), *Handbook of Human Resource Management in Government*, San Francisco: Jossey-Bass.

Cober, R.T., D. Brown, A. Blumental, D. Doverspike and P. Levy (2000), 'The quest for the qualified job surfer: it's time the public sector catches the wave', *Public Personnel Management*, **29**, 479–95.

Graduate School USA (2011), *Subject Areas*, accessed 14 November 2011 at http://graduateschool.edu/index.php?option=com_content&task=view&id=163&Itemid=266.

Hays, S.W. (2004), 'Trends and best practices in state and local human resource management: lessons to be learned?', *Review of Public Personnel Administration*, **24**, 256–275.

Hays, S.W. and J.E. Sowa (2006), 'A broader look at the "accountability" movement: some grim realities', *Review of Public Personnel Administration*, **26**, 102–17.

International Public Management Association for Human Resources (IPMA-HR) (2011), *Certification*, accessed 26 October 2011 at http://www.ipma-hr.org/professional-development/certification.

Kellough, E.J. and H. Lu (1993), 'The paradox of merit pay in the public sector: persistence of a problematic procedure', *Review of Public Personnel Administration*, **13**, 45–64.

Kellough, J.E. and L.G. Nigro (2002), 'Pay for performance in Georgia state government: employee perspectives on GeorgiaGain after 5 years', *Review of Public Personnel Administration*, **22**, 146–66.

Kim, S. and J.G. O'Connor (2009), 'Assessing electronic recruitment implementation in state governments: issues and challenges', *Public Personnel Management*, **38**, 47–66.

Klingner, D.E., J. Nalbandian and J. Llorens (2010), *Public Personnel Management: Contexts and Strategies* (6th Edition), Upper Saddle River, NJ: Prentice Hall.

Koven, S.G., F. Goetzke and M. Brennan (2008), 'Profiling public affairs programs', *Administration and Society*, **40**, 691–710.

Llorens, J. (Forthcoming), 'A model of public sector e-recruitment adoption in a time of hyper technological change', *Review of Public Personnel Administration*.

Llorens, J. and R.P. Battaglio (2010), 'Human resources management in a changing world: reassessing public human resources management education', *Review of Public Personnel Administration*, **30**, 112–32.

Llorens, J., and E.J. Kellough (2007), 'A revolution in public personnel administration: the growth of web-based recruitment and selection processes in the federal service', *Public Personnel Management*, **36**, 207–22.

Maher, K. and J. Nicas (2011), 'Ohio voters reject public-union limits', *Wall Street Journal*, 9 November, accessed 15 November 2011 at http://online.wsj.com/article/SB10001424052970204190704577026360072268418.html.

National Association of Schools of Public Affairs and Administration (NASPAA) (2009), *NASPAA Standards 2009: Commission on Peer Review and Accreditation*, accessed 26 October 2011 at: http://www.naspaa.org/accreditation/NS/naspaa standards.asp.

O'Keefe, E., P. Bacon and J. Davidson (2010), 'Obama announces 2-year pay freeze for federal workers', *New York Times*, 29 November, accessed 15 November 2011 at http://voices.washingtonpost.com/federal-eye/2010/11/obama_announces_pay_freeze_for.html.

Pew Research Center for the People and the Press (Pew) (2010a), *Millennials a Portrait of Generation Next: Confident, Connected, Open to Change*, accessed 7 October 2011 at http://pewsocialtrends.org/files/2010/10/millennials-confident-connected-open-to-change.pdf.

Pew Center on the States (2010b), *The Trillion Dollar Gap. Underfunded State Retirement Systems and the Roads to Reform*, accessed 5 June 2011 at http://downloads.pewcenteronthestates.org/The_Trillion_Dollar_Gap_final.pdf.

Selden, S., and J. Orenstein (2011), 'Content, usability, and innovation: an evaluative methodology for government recruiting websites, *Review of Public Personnel Administration*, **31**, 209–23.

Society for Human Resources Management (SHRM) (2011), *SHRM Education*, accessed 26 October 2011 at http://www.shrm.org/Education/Pages/default.aspx.

US Internal Revenue Service (IRS) (2011), *Explore Your Future: Follow the Money*, accessed 7 October 2011 at http://www.icwgames.com/followthemoney/index.html.

US Office of Personnel Management (2011), *Leadership Development & Training*, accessed 14 November 2011 at https://www.leadership.opm.gov/.

US State Department (2011a), *Careers*, accessed 14 November 2011 at http://www.state.gov/careers/.

US State Department (2011b), *US Department of State Careers: Mobile Web*, accessed 15 November 2011 at http://apps.usa.gov/u-s-department-of-state-careers/.

Whalen, C., and M.E. Guy (2008), 'Broadbanding trends in the states', *Review of Public Personnel Administration*, **28**, 349–66.

Yeaton, K. (2008), 'Recruiting and managing the "Why?" generation: Gen Y', *The CPA Journal*, **78**, 68–72.

Zusman, R.R. and R.S. Landis (2002), 'Applicant preferences for web-based versus traditional job postings', *Computers in Human Behavior*, **18**, 285–96.

Index